MONSTROUS SERIAL KILLERS ENCYCLOPEDIA

TITLES BY BEN OAKLEY

FICTION

HARRISON LAKE INVESTIGATIONS

The Camden Killer

The Limehouse Hotel

Monster of the Algarve

HONEYSUCKLE GOODWILLIES

The Mystery of Grimlow Forest

The Mystery of Crowstones Island

SUBNET SF TRILOGY

Unknown Origin

Alien Network

Final Contact

NONFICTION

TRUE CRIME

Bizarre True Crime Series

Orrible British True Crime Series

The Monstrous Book of Serial Killers

True Crime 365 series

Year of the Serial Killer

OTHER NONFICTION

The Immortal Hour: The True Story of Netta Fornario

Suicide Prevention Handbook

MONSTROUS SERIAL KILLERS ENCYCLOPEDIA

MEGA THIRD EDITION

BEN OAKLEY

WELVETREES
CAMDEN

First published in 2019 and 2020 by Twelvetrees Publishing.

This edition 2022 by Twelvetrees Camden.

Visit the author's website at www.benoakley.co.uk

ISBN: 978-1-7397149-5-6

Cover design by Ben Oakley.

For information about special discounts available for bulk purchases, sales promotions, book signings, trade shows, and distribution, contact sales@twelvetreescamden.com

Twelvetrees Camden Ltd
71-75 Shelton Street, Covent Garden
London, WC2H 9JQ

www.twelvetreescamden.com

SECTION LIST

Introduction (Mega Third Edition)

This MEGA third edition, released in 2022, is far superior and has been re-edited, reformatted and redesigned to make it even more accessible to true crime fans and readers of the macabre. Read through what's new, what's been updated, and why the Monstrous Serial Killers Encyclopedia Volume One is a must-have for true crime fans and explorers of the macabre.

The Latest Updates

Each of the 250 serial killers listed in this book have been meticulously re-researched to maintain correct information as of 2022. This includes updates to statuses, where some have been executed, died of natural causes, or been released from their sentences.

Each entry has been triple-checked to ensure any new information relating to trials, histories, or victim counts are updated in line with currently available information, which is accessed from prison databases, investigations, or academic articles, all of which are cited in the bibliography.

There is no other serial killer encyclopedia on the market that provides the most up to date information and statistics on the 250 serial killers listed here. There's no need to read old information when you can keep up to date with everything going on, in just one jam-packed book.

Why Serial Killers Kill

This new 80-page section is a fascinating collection of exclusive research articles about the reasons why serial killers kill. It's a new study exploring the cultural, environmental, and societal reasons behind serial killings and violence.

Always wanted to know WHY serial killers kill? Then you've found the right section for you. There will never be just one reason why a serial killer kills. But a combination of some of the reasons listed here might play a major part in the creation of a serial killer.

Some of the reasons are psychological, such as the impact of war, child abuse, and cultural attitudes. Other reasons are environmental and societal, such as the introduction of highways, urbanisation, victim selection, and pornography. They contribute to the ever-increasing opportunities afforded to those of a violent mind-set and enable them to act out on desires that may have remained dormant.

The study covers facts and statistics from the United States and United Kingdom, with a focus on the 20th and 21st Centuries. Parts of the book are hypothetically related to time periods beyond 2022, using 20th Century studies to predict a rise in serial killing from 2028. They are added in this section for context and additional information. See the full bibliography at the end of this book for all studies cited.

60 Extended Case Files

This book remains the culmination of many years of research and data gathering. The aim has always been to put together an ultimate book of serial killers that was more than just a book about serial killers – with multiple volumes going forward. The listings range in length from one to ten pages, with the longest going into more depth about each case. These protracted sections make up the 60 extended case files found throughout these pages.

Over 200 Photos and Images

Whereas the previous edition contained around 80 images, this new MEGA edition is home to over 200 photos and images, making this one of the most complete and accessible serial killer encyclopedia's out there. This includes photo collages at various intervals throughout and images dropped in on various articles and entries.

All photos and images have their correct copyright and usage licenses, which are all listed under the image attribution section of the appendices. Under or nearby each photo is an attribution number written for example as: (Attrib 1.) which links to the same attribution number in the appendices for correct citation. Extra care has been taken to ensure the photos are suitable for all age groups and can be used for publication in this book.

Over 100 Quotes

You'll find over 100 quotes dotted throughout the articles and entries direct from serial killers, investigators, and experts in the field of criminology. Citations for the quotes can be found in the bibliography.

The inclusion of these quotes can help to give you more understanding of the killer in question and the investigation surrounding their case. It also provides an eye-opening look into what goes on in the mind of a serial killer.

Responsible Mental Health Language

There has been a move to more responsible language and reporting when it comes to mental health issues, particular when it comes to self-harm or suicide. Using the mental health media charter, this book is committed to talking about mental health in a responsible manner that considers the vulnerability of sufferers.

You will not find the term 'commit suicide' anywhere in this book, as the term 'commit' suggests blame and criminality. The terms 'died by suicide' or 'took their own life' are included as replacements. There are no images in this book that may trigger those suffering from eating disorders, or that may trigger people to self-harm.

Extra care has been taken to ensure the images and content in this book are responsible with the reader in mind. The book does not go into detail relating to suicide and maintains a balance of the responsibility of reporting the facts with ensuring relevant information is passed across to the reader, without inspiring imitational behaviour.

Responsible Sex Worker Language

Sex workers are adults who receive money or goods in exchange for consensual sexual services or erotic performances. The term recognises that sex work is work. Prostitution, on the other hand, has connotations of criminality and immorality.

In recent years, many sex workers and campaign groups have fought to replace prostitute and prostitution with sex worker. The earliest use of the word prostitute was recorded in 1530 as a word used to sexually dishonour oneself and has been used ever since as someone who sells sex.

The new campaign to use the term sex worker, is also to help bring the varying services related to sex work under one all-encompassing banner. Many people who sell sexual services now prefer the term sex worker and find prostitute demeaning and stigmatising. The term 'sex worker' is used in this book in place of prostitute.

Explanation of Monikers

It might be surprising to learn that almost all of the monikers given to serial killers come from the press and media. The police and investigatory services don't often use monikers unless to encompass a range of victims.

A moniker is a nickname given to a serial killer such as Doctor Death for Harold Shipman, or The Milwaukee Cannibal for Jeffrey Dahmer. They are included in the entries where relevant and where they have been used in the media to name a serial killer, before or after their capture.

The Book contains 250 Serial Killers

Since records began, there have been over 5,000 serial killers that have stained the world with their actions, with over 3,000 in the United States alone. There are 250 of them listed here from all over the world including Russia, the United Kingdom, France, India and of course, the United States.

All laid out in an easy-to-read format with bullet-point statistics at the end of each one containing all the vital information you need. Some you would have heard of, others you might not have done. Due to this new edition being over 600 pages in length, we had to trim down the size of some of the cases. To make space for the kind of case files you want to read, the decision was taken not to list all of the victim names.

For example, if we look at Harold Shipman then we have 215 victims; the highest confirmed and convicted victim count in known history. Simply put, to list the names of all 215 victims and the hundreds of others taken by the killers listed here, would have eaten up the space needed for facts and data.

Fully Researched and Referenced

The Monstrous Serial Killers Encyclopedia is fully researched and referenced, complete with appendices and a bibliography of all studies and data cited within these pages. The book is written in British English, with American English only used in the description of American locations, names, or sayings.

The names of the killers are laid out in alphabetical order by their surname. The book is intended as an encyclopaedic database and does not contain lengthy diatribes on all killers, save for the 60 extended case files. If you wish to read more in-depth true crime stories then seek out the Bizarre True Crime or Orrible True Crime series, also from Ben Oakley and Twelvetrees Camden.

There are no curse words in the book, however some descriptions do include content that may be unsuitable for children. This isn't a sugar-coated book on the creation of fluffy toys, this is a book about humans killing other humans and why they do it. Thus a certain level of justifiable content has been included to fully round out the case files.

In the digital edition of the book you can jump to any section you wish by clicking on the relevant chapter heading. All facts and citations are correct as of May 2022.

I fully hope that you enjoy this book as much as I have had putting it together.

Notes on Why Serial Killers Kill section

When working on a thesis known as 1978: Year of the Serial Killer, I was tasked with researching the cultural and environmental reasons behind why some people choose to kill. The 1970s and 1980s saw serial killing become an epidemic, especially in larger populated countries and there had to be reasons why those decades saw vast amounts of multiple murderers. Turns out, there was.

The intricacies of the human mind are incredibly individual so there will always be unique reasons why serial killers kill. The reasons provided in the Why Serial Killers Kill section reflect cultural, environmental, social and economic factors in the decades before and during the 1970s. Now that we had reasons leading to the year of the serial killer in 1978, two theoretical questions were put forward.

What if 50 years after 1978 there was another rise in serial killing?

Would the 12 reasons be similar in any way?

Then began the 2028: Rise of the Serial Killer project, set 50 years after the year of the serial killer and only a few years out from this edition of the book. The reasons for 2028 were researched in exactly the same manner, trying to find comparable reasons leading up to 2028 that might cause another rise in serial killing.

One could argue that by the mid-1990s, DNA technology had improved so much that serial killers were being caught on their first murder, stopping them before they got going. Yet, in various other cases, there are those that haven't stopped killing and have simply adapted to the ever-changing landscape of technology and surveillance equipment.

Every article from 2028: Rise of the Serial Killer is here in this section, side by side with the original 12 reasons. The hypothetical articles were first published as a thesis on www.benoakley.co.uk and provide similar modern factors to show that we might be moving towards a new wave of serial killing. The 2028 research articles directly follow their counterparts.

For example; The Lure of Celebrity Status article talks about the rise of the celebrity during the 1960s and 1970s and how so many people sought fame and recognition. Whilst some pursued fame through legal and ethical avenues, others had already given up on all things moral. The article describes those serial killers who sought nothing more than infamy.

Jump forward 40 years and fame has become so much easier to take hold of. Thus, the hypothetical 2028 version of the article is The Lure of Social Media Fame, which becomes the companion piece to The Lure of Celebrity Status. In addition, there are further individual research articles to be found within these pages.

What Makes True Crime So Popular and Fascinating?

For some, true crime is putting on those hundred-dollar headphones, kicking back with a drink and listening to their favourite podcaster. For others, it's taking a bit of time out to read a real-life story filled with mystery or intrigue. Where Netflix has garnered attention for its true crime shows, others like Sky and Peacock are commissioning their own at a rampant rate. So what makes true crime so popular? Is there really a culture built around real-life tales of murder?

Let me take you back to the early Nineties, where, as a teenager I would consume books that had titles like 'Mysteries of the Unexplained', 'Cold Case Investigations', 'True Crime Tales', or 'Strange Deaths'. I did this not out of any macabre notion but because the stories within their pages fascinated me.

It is that fascination with true crime and real-life stories that continued to intrigue through my adult years. Because let's face it, most 'fictional' stories, especially mysteries and thrillers, have some basis in reality. As an author, I know I certainly draw on true crime for my works of fiction.

And yet if you're a 'fan' of true crime, you can be looked at weirdly and as someone who is probably up to no good. Tell someone you're a fan of horror movies, death metal, dark fantasy, gore films, or vampire stories then you're less likely to be frowned upon.

Why are fictional horror stories created from the darkest parts of our imagination less frowned upon than real life horror? The answer it seems is simple, it's because true crime is something that is tangible and real while fiction is deemed to be unreal and safe.

True crime teaches and prepares us.

Readers, podcast listeners, and streaming audiences, love true crime for many different reasons but ask them why and you'll probably get one of the following answers. True crime fascinates us, teaches us, and prepares us to avoid falling into the same trap as those we read about.

We think it will never happen to us and hopefully it won't but if we recognise some of the signs from what we've read in true crime books, then it gives us hope that we can protect ourselves, pre-empting the bad around the corner.

We avoid the dark alleyways at night, the email scams, the stranger looking at us weirdly. We walk under cover of light, knowing that the shadows are where evil lies. We walk home in pairs, protected by numbers, safe in the knowledge that most people are alone when they become victims.

True crime – good true crime – teaches us what to look out for, it trains us to know the signs, appreciate them, and change tact to avoid the stigma of becoming a victim. We are more aware of the reasons and motives behind crime, and hope that we never fall into the same trap, empowered by our knowledge of how the world works.

Out of this fascination with true crime, a sub-culture grew, hidden away from mainstream eyes until streaming services brought true crime to the masses, though some could argue that programs like Motorway Cops and other real-life documentary series were giving us true crime long before the internet.

The fundamental element of true crime is that it is a crime that has taken place in the real world and is thus seen as true – obvious I know. But by using that same basis, the very earliest true crime dates back centuries when crime was reported in newspapers and later on radio.

True crime has been with us for centuries.

Stories of murder and robbery and other crimes, though grim and morally questionable, have always intrigued us. Before the days of the internet, when we were told of a murder happening somewhere in the country, we'd turn the radio on, get the signal working on the TV and eagerly await that on-the-hour bong signalling the incoming news report.

There, the newscaster would tell us as much as we were allowed to know about a crime and we ate it up, it made us feel alive, connected us to others who were talking about it, and made us feel part of something.

But does true crime come at the expense of a victim? The victims are certainly the focus in many true crime stories but at the end of the day to have a victim, you need a perpetrator, and it is why or how the perpetrator created a victim that intrigues us further.

Perhaps we want to know if we could ourselves create a victim in such horrific circumstances, perhaps in the case of a robbery, we are curious to know how they done it, why they did it, and what if any process led to them being caught.

Really though, we are fascinated with death as it is our final journey, our ultimate destination, and facing it head on is one way we are able to come to understand our own mortality. We flitter through life on the corridors of time so quickly that we want to know if death really is the end, or the beginning of a new journey.

True crime asks questions of us, begging us to look deeper into ourselves, to understand who we are, why we are, and how we fit into the grand scheme of things. True crime is an avenue in which we can experience the worst the world has to offer from the safety of our own homes.

Understanding that true crime consumption is a safe experience is one way to understand why so many people incorporate it into their daily lives.

True crime is not going away anytime soon.

Watching, reading, or listening to true crime is no different than watching a news report about a murder or other type of crime. Sure, you might not be a 'fan' of the news but you can be a 'fan' of true crime in such a way that you get your fix from an author you're familiar with or a podcaster you like.

Many people go back to the same horror authors, the same death metal bands, the same dark fantasy artist, whose works contain no less horrific aspects than true crime itself. If you can be a fan of dark horror then you can be a fan of true crime.

Though, it is a little strange and immoral to suggest that you have a 'favourite' killer and is in total disregard of the victims. Good true crime gives you an unbiased approach of both the victim and perpetrator of the crime.

The truth is that many people won't buy a book about a victim but they will buy one of the killer. As long as the book or show does not glorify the killer then there is nothing wrong with it. They say sex sales, and the same can be said about murder.

The darkest parts of the human soul will always intrigue and fascinate those who live in the light, the good ones, the morally secure. The ones who consume true crime from a different perspective, one of darkness and evil, are not part of the true crime family and never will be.

We consume true crime to help us understand, learn, and prevent crime. True crime offers a unique view on the world in a way that only true crime can, allowing us to open our eyes to the society around us.

True crime is popular because it always has been, from the early days of news reporting to the present day of streaming, podcasting, and digital books. True crime will never go away and will continue to adapt to the new world it finds itself in.

Ready to dive in?

Encyclopedia of 250 Serial Killers

Alcala, Rodney: The Dating Game Killer

EXTENDED CASE FILE

On September 13th 1978, Rodney Alcala, AKA: The Dating Game Killer, appeared on the national television show; The Dating Game. It marked a surreal and defining moment in the history of serial killers. His total number of victims is unknown but it is suggested to be close to 100. He would generally pose as a fashion photographer to get close to his victims and win their confidence. He would strangle them until they lost consciousness then bring them back around and repeat the process many times before ultimately killing them.

Alcala had been compared to Ted Bundy numerous times, not least because of his charming appearance on The Dating Game TV show. He had a collection of over 1000 photographs of women and young boys, many in sexually explicit poses. It is speculated that some of them could have been other victims as many were not or have not yet been identified.

After a childhood where his father would abandon him and his mother would move them around, he joined the U.S. Army in 1960 at the age of 17. A few years later he went AWOL and was subsequently diagnosed with borderline personality disorder. He has never spoken of his time in the military.

In 1968, Alcala stalked eight-year-old Tali Shapiro as she was walking to school in Hollywood. He told her that he was a friend of her parents and she went with him to his apartment. At the same time, a witness reported the suspicious incident. When police arrived, Alcala escaped out the back door but not before he had abused, raped, and tortured Shapiro. He had beaten her to within an inch of her life with a steel bar. She survived to give a statement but her parents wouldn't allow her to testify against Alcala.

Had they let her do so, she may have stopped a killing spree that some claim could have reached 130 victims. He served only 34 months in prison for the brutal rape. After his release he moved to the East Coast where he went under a new name, and studied film and photography under Roman Polanski, of all people. He would then approach women and young boys claiming he was a fashion photographer and luring them into posing for him.

One victim he lured in such a manner was 23-year-old air hostess Cornelia Crilley. In 1971, her body was discovered in her own Manhattan apartment. She had been raped and strangled and was connected to Alcala 40 years after her death. Between 1971 and 1979 he had tricked up to 1,000 young men, girls and women into believing that he was a professional photographer. A large majority of the photos were of people in the nude or in sexually explicit poses, including pages and pages of naked girls and boys. On September 13th 1978, Alcala made his infamous appearance as a contestant on The Dating Game.

"A successful photographer who got his start when his father found him in the darkroom at the age of 13, fully developed! Between takes you might find him skydiving or motorcycling." – Jim Lange, The Dating Game host, introducing Alcala.

In an even more extraordinary twist, he went on to win the show and won a date with the woman looking for love. Alcala had the bizarre tenacity to appear on the show in public to the country after having killed potentially dozens of victims. After his appearance, he would go on to kill at least another three people.

He was arrested in 1979 and throughout various trials, has been convicted of seven murders. He has been sentenced to death a number of times, some of which were commuted to life. It wasn't until March 10th 2010, that the Huntington Beach Police and New York City Police departments officially released 120 of his photographs in order to seek the public's help in identifying them.

There are another 900 photos in Alcala's portfolio that cannot be released due to their sexual content. Some of the 120 have since been recognised by family members as loved ones who had disappeared without a trace and may have been further victims of The Dating Game Killer. Alcala died of unspecified natural causes in California on July 24th 2021, at the age of 77.

THE FACTS

Born: August 23rd 1943 | Active: 1971-1979

Arrested: July 27th 1979 | Country: USA (California)

Victims: 7-100+ | AKA: The Dating Game Killer / John Berger

Sentence: Death penalty | Status: Died in prison, July 24th 2021

Allen, Howard Arthur

American serial killer of elderly women, active between 1974 to 1987. The murder of 73-year-old Ernestine Griffin on July 14th 1987 was particularly brutal and resulted in his capture. The day before her murder, Griffin had contacted her next door neighbour, a dentist named Dr. Seaman. She told him a man had stopped by her house enquiring about a car that Dr. Seaman was selling, and that the man had left a note with his name and phone number on.

The next morning, the dentist discovered Griffin dead in her home. She had a butcher's knife sticking out of her chest and her face had been smashed in with a toaster. A handwriting expert linked the note to Allen which linked him to the murder. He was quickly arrested and charged.

Allen had previously been sentenced for manslaughter after beating to death 85-year-old Opal Cooper in August of 1974 during a robbery. He was released in January 1985 and committed various robberies until his second murder on May 20th 1985, when he attacked 87-year-old Laverne Hale, who would die from her injuries nine days later. Allen was sentenced to death for all three of his victims but it was later commuted to 60 years due to mental incapacity at the time of the murders.

THE FACTS

Born: August 4th 1949 | Active: 1974-1987

Arrested: February 10th 1987 | Country: USA (Indiana)

Victims: 3 | Sentence: Death penalty, later commuted to life

Status: Died of natural causes in prison on June 5th 2020, aged 71

Angelo, Richard

On November 15th 1987, American medical serial killer Richard Angelo was arrested and taken into custody after assaulting a 73-year-old patient of his. By the time of his arrest, Angelo was only 25-years-old and had killed at least eight people. Sometimes referred to as the Angel of Death, Angelo was a nurse at the Good Samaritan Hospital in the Suffolk County area of New York.

He used poison to kill and was linked with at least ten deaths and the poisoning of at least 25 others. He poisoned his victims to bring on a cardiac arrest so that he could try and resuscitate them in front of other workers at the hospital, in order to be seen as a hero.

Angelo was convicted in December of 1989 of two of the murders, one manslaughter, and one criminally negligent homicide. In four other deaths he was convicted of associated assault. It is suspected that he killed at least ten. Angelo was sentenced to at least 50 years in prison and remains incarcerated at the Great Meadow Correctional Facility in Washington County.

THE FACTS

Born: April 29th 1962 | Active: 1987

Arrested: October 12th 1987 | Country: USA (New York)

Victims: 8-26 | Sentence: 61 years to life in prison

Status: Incarcerated

IMAGE ATTRIBUTIONS
(ATTRIB A1) (ATTRIB 48 TO 53)

PHOTOS ABOVE WERE PUBLICALLY RELEASED FROM ALCALA'S COLLECTION OF PHOTOS. SOME HAVE BEEN IDENTIFIED WHILE OTHERS REMAIN UNIDENTIFIED.

RODNEY ALCALA

Amos, Lowell Edwin: Black Widower

American serial killer, Lowell Edwin Amos, is a convicted murderer whose family members died under suspicious circumstances. The deaths of his mother and all three of his wives led him to gain the moniker of the Black Widower, and a film was later made for the Lifetime Network under the same title.

In 1996, he was convicted of the murder of his third wife, Roberta Mowery Amos. All the murders looked like accidents. He was convicted of premeditated murder and murder using a toxic substance. One of his wives died after a hair-dryer landed in her bath water as she was in it. Another died of a cocaine overdose after he injected a large amount of the drug into her vagina.

After the death of his mother by apparent natural causes, he inherited over $1million USD. No autopsy was carried out due to her age but it is suspected he used sedatives to drug and kill her. He died in 2022 while serving life without parole at the Muskegon Correctional Facility in Michigan.

THE FACTS

Born: January 4th 1943 | Active: 1979-1994

Arrested: November 8th 1996 | Country: United States (Michigan)

Victims: 1-4 | AKA: Black Widower

Sentence: Life imprisonment | Status: Died on January 5th 2022

Acevedo, Francisco

New York serial killer, Francisco Acevedo, killed three women over the course of a seven year period. He would only be caught when DNA submitted from a drink-driving charge in 2010 linked him to the three unsolved murders. Acevedo had never once been a suspect in the murders until his arrest despite his DNA being on the database.

His defence team claimed that Acevedo did have sex with the women but did not rape and murder them. He killed 26-year-old sex worker Maria Ramos in February of 1989, then 28-year-old sex worker Tawana Hodges in 1991. His third and final victim came on May 4th 1996, when he killed 30-year-old Kimberly Moore. She was not known to have been involved in the sex industry.

Moore's body was discovered by a motel clerk in Room 45 of the Trade Winds Motor Court, which is a pay-by-the-hour motel in the Yonkers area. The clerk, Carlos Gonzalez, entered the room to inform the guest that it was past checkout time. After she didn't respond, he pulled the sheets off the bed and saw blood on Moore's forehead

Acevedo murdered his victims by tying them up, raping them and then strangling them to death, and escaped justice for 20 years. Gonzalez became a witness at the trial after being the only person to see Acevedo with one of his victims. In 2012, he was found guilty of all three murders and sentenced to 75 years to life in prison.

THE FACTS

Born: 1968 | Active: 1989-1996

Arrested: April 2010 | Country: USA (New York)

Victims: 3 | Sentence: 75 years to life in prison

Status: Incarcerated

Baekuni: Babe

One-named criminal, Baekuni, AKA: Babe, is an Indonesian serial killer who raped and tortured to death 14 young boys. When he was only a youngster, Baekuni, the son of a farmer, ran away from his home in Java and fled to Jakarta where he became homeless. One night, he was raped on the streets by a gang member in front of a group of people, something which inevitably set him on a darker path.

In 1993, when he was 32-years-old, he began attacking homeless children. He claimed he did this in retaliation for not being able to fight back against his attacker when he was younger. His victims ranged from the age of four to 13 and were mostly runaways or homeless children. Because of this, he was able to get away with killing for so long, undetected under cover of anonymity.

Indonesia is home to very few serial killers and Baekuni's case was considered extremely way, but of course maybe that's because others have been getting away with it unseen. Baekuni was caught in 2010 when he kidnapped a nine-year-old boy, raped him and dismembered his body with a rough-edged knife. The boy's body parts were found on January 8th 2010, and his head was found the day after.

The discovery of the body led to Baekuni's arrest. During his trial, evidence came to light that he had killed at least 14 young boys and attacked another four. Later in 2010, he was sentenced to life imprisonment in a Jakarta prison for the murders of the 14.

THE FACTS

Born: 1961 | Active: 1993-2010

Arrested: January 8th 2010 | Country: Indonesia (Jakarta)

Victims: 14 | AKA: Babe.

Sentence: Life imprisonment | Status: Incarcerated.

Barber, Danny

An American serial killer who murdered four women between 1978 and 1980. He was arrested in 1980 for the murder of 50-year-old Janice Ingram a year earlier. Janice's mother, Ruth Clowers, found her daughter's naked body, she had been beaten to death with a section of metal pipe, in a frenzied attack during a burglary.

Barber later claimed that it was simply a robbery gone wrong, and when Janice had started screaming he hit her to keep her quiet. It was upon his arrest that he confessed to three more killings. Barber killed one unnamed victim on June 18th 1978, then 48-year-old Mercedes Mendez on January 17th 1979, and finally Mary Caperton on April 21st 1980.

At the trial, details were shared that proved Barber had sex with two of his victim's corpses, and that he sexually abused them long after their deaths. He was given a life sentence for each of the three aforementioned murders. For the murder of Janice Ingram, he was sentenced to death, and executed via lethal injection in February of 1999. While he was on death row he created cross-stitch crafts that he sold through a web page. Unsurprisingly, he didn't sell very many, but those he did now change hands on internet marketplaces for hundreds of dollars.

THE FACTS

Born: May 8th 1955 | Active: 1978-1980.

Arrested: May 6th 1980 | Country: USA (Texas).

Victims: 4 | Sentence: Death penalty and three life sentences.

Status: Executed by lethal injection in February 1999.

Barbosa, Daniel Camargo: The Sadist of Chanquito

A Columbian serial killer who raped and murdered up to 150 young girls, one of the largest death counts in serial killer history. He was first suspected of raping and killing 72 young girls and was jailed in 1977. Astonishingly, he had escaped in 1984 to Ecuador where he continued his rampage of killing and claimed another 54 lives.

Barbosa was raised in Bogota but his mother died when he was one. His father married another woman, who was known to have abused, humiliated, and beaten Barbosa as she was unable to have children herself. She would often dress him as a girl and send him to school like it, where he was belittled and bullied. After years of petty crime, Barbosa moved to hunting helpless girls to rape and kill, preferring virgins. He would approach them and pretend to be a foreigner in order to gain their trust.

IMAGE ATTRIB. 2

BAEKUNI

DANNY LEE BARBER

IMAGE ATTRIB. 72

IMAGE ATTRIB. 73

VELMA BARFIELD

Despite being linked to 72 murders, he was originally convicted of the rape and murder of one nine-year-old girl and sentenced to 25 years in prison in Columbia in 1977. For his 1984 prison break, he studied the ocean currents, and escaped in a primitive prison boat, barely making it to shore. Prison authorities at the time claimed that he had died at sea, with the media bizarrely claiming he had been eaten by sharks.

Neither were true, just two weeks after eloping to Ecuador, he abducted and killed a nine-year-old girl, then the next day a 10-year-old. He went on to rape and kill another 52 girls over a two-year period until 1986. Police at the time believed that the murders were a work of a gang, as they couldn't comprehend that only one man was responsible for such mayhem.

After raping his victims, he hacked and dismembered the bodies with a machete and disposed of their remains in forests. Barbosa later stated that he liked young girls because he preferred to attack virgins, stating there was no other reason, though he claimed it gave him pleasure to see the girls cry when he raped them. He was captured in Ecuador in February 1986 and sentenced to only 16 years, which was the maximum available sentence in Ecuador at the time. He once served time alongside fellow Colombian child serial killer Pedro Lopez and was known as the Sadist of Chanquito.

THE FACTS

Born: January 22nd 1930 | Active: 1974-1977 and 1984-1986

Arrested: February 26th 1986 | Country: Colombia/Ecuador

Victims: 72-150+ | AKA: The Sadist of Chanquito

Sentence: 16 years in prison | Status: Killed by another inmate on November 13th 1994

Barfield, Velma: Death Row Granny

On February 3rd 1978, Velma Barfield killed Rowland Stuart Taylor by mixing arsenic-based rat poison into Rowland's beer and tea. Velma was an American female serial killer who took the lives of six people but was only convicted for the murder of Taylor. Raised in 1930s rural South Carolina to a poor family, she was allegedly abused by her father, enabled by a mother who stood by and failed to intervene.

She would steal money from her father to buy things at school that better-off children had. When she stole $80 from a neighbour, her father found out and beat her. Velma later claimed she loved her father because after the beatings he would buy her nice things which would cheer her up.

But Velma escaped her grim situation by marrying herself to schoolfriend Thomas Burke in 1949, when she was 17. They gave birth to two children, but as her new husband began to drink in the way her father used to, Velma decided she'd had enough. Burke's alcoholism came shortly after Velma had a medically forced hysterectomy and she began to feel insecure as a female. When Burke was passed out one night, Barfield took the children out of the house and burned it to the ground, leaving Burke dead inside.

Then she married Jennings Barfield, whose name she kept, and who quickly died of a heart attack in 1971. Shortly after, Velma's mother died of arsenic poisoning but it wasn't discovered until later. Velma realised she could get away with killing people she didn't want in her life and would take pleasure in poisoning people under her care then nursing them back to life. An elderly man she was caring for also died under suspicious circumstances.

When Taylor died the same way as the others, Velma's sister told police she had killed a lot of people the same way. After her arrest in 1978, his body was exhumed as evidence of her crime, leading to a conviction, resulting in a death sentence. While on death row, she confessed to killing six people, including her own mother.

She was executed in November of 1984, aged 52, the first woman to be executed in the United States since 1962. It wasn't until 1998 that the next female would be executed, a double killer named Karla Faye Tucker who was convicted of killing two people with a pickaxe.

THE FACTS

Born: October 23rd 1932 | Active: 1969-1978

Arrested: May 13th 1978 | Country: USA (North Carolina)

Victims: 6 | AKA: Death Row Granny

Sentence: Death penalty | Status: Executed November 1994

Baumeister, Herb: The Haunting of Fox Hollow Farm

EXTENDED CASE FILE

It began with a serial killer and ended up with terrifying hauntings at the place where he buried his victims. American serial killer Herbert Richard Baumeister, AKA: The I-70 Strangler, killed at least 12 young men from 1980 to 1996 and buried their remains at his property on Fox Hollow Farm.

Born in 1947, just after World War Two, he was raised in a relatively normal household with three younger siblings. When he reached puberty, something had changed within him. He became antisocial and withdrew from being with friends and family. Some people who knew him as a teenager, claimed that he played with the bodies of dead animals, and was once caught urinating on a teacher's desk.

One former friend said that something wasn't right with Baumeister and recalled a story about a dead crow. One morning on the way to school, Baumeister had picked up a dead crow and shoved it into his pocket. When he got to school, he left it on the teacher's desk in full view of the class. While a teenager, he was diagnosed by a doctor as having schizophrenia but due to the difference in mental health access we have nowadays compared to then, he was not given any psychiatric treatment for it.

Baumeister was able to cover up the evil from those around him. He married when he was 24-years-old, in 1971, and had three children by his wife, Julie Baumeister. By 1988, he had founded and opened the Sav-a-Lot chain shops in Indiana and became a respected member of the business community and local community. By 1991, after creating a successful business, Baumeister and his family moved to a Tudor-style home and estate in the fashionable Westfield district. The property had a swimming pool, stables and almost 20 acres of land where the family could grow and live in luxury.

Inside the house, however, a tension and a fear was rising, Julie began to believe everything her husband was telling her. Julie split from him multiple times but always returned to him, in a fashion that some would describe as Baumeister having control over his wife. When colleagues and friends visited the house, they saw messy rooms, unclean surfaces and a complete lack of order. The grounds of the property had been left to overgrow and their land was becoming unusable.

In 1994, their son was playing in the grounds when he found a full human skeleton. They waited for Herb Baumeister to return and he explained it away as being one of his father's fake medical skeletons. He claimed to have found it in the garage one day and decided to bury it. Julie believed her husband - but the skeleton belonged to one of his victims.

A year earlier, in 1993, connections in the cases of missing gay men were already being made. A private investigator named Vergil Vandagriff, joined forces with an investigator from the Indianapolis Police Department, named Mary Wilson. They both believed that the missing men might have been connected in some way and began an investigation to connect the evidence. As the investigation gained media attention, they were approached by a gay man who claimed he knew who killed a friend of his.

He gave them a name but the name didn't show up on any searches. The man mysteriously disappeared for a couple of years until 1995 when he phoned the investigation and gave them the number plate of the man who he suspected to have killed his friend. It is unclear whether he had carried out his own private investigation in order to get the license plate, or whether he had been holding on to it until the right time came around.

The license plate linked to Herb Baumeister, and so Wilson approached Fox Hollow Farm to speak to him. She asked to search the house but he refused. Julie Baumeister also refused police to search the house. As the only link was a license plate, the investigation couldn't gain a warrant for the house. By June 1996, Julie Baumeister had finally ended her marriage to Herb, as she had become scared of him. His violent mood swings and weird behaviour had become too much for her to handle.

While Herb Baumeister was on a supposed business vacation, Julie called the investigators and allowed them to search the house and the grounds. The remains of 11 men were unearthed, with only four of them ever being identified. Herb

Baumeister found out about the search of the house and eloped over the Canadian border to Ontario. He wrote a suicide note in which he spoke about his failing marriage and dwindling business but didn't mention the murders at all.

Shortly after, he shot himself dead in Pinery Provincial Park. Julie Baumeister went on to tell the investigation that her ex-husband had made over 100 trips to Ohio on apparent business trips. It was then that the investigation linked Baumeister with the murders of nine more men, whose bodies had been discovered along the main highway between Indiana and Ohio; the Interstate 70. Baumeister's body was discovered eight days after he had killed himself.

The Fox Hollow Farm and house were stripped of everything after the bodies had been discovered, and it stood abandoned for many years. Until it was sold cheaply to Rob and Vicky Graves from Indiana. Everything seemed to be going fine until one day Vicky was cleaning the house and the hoover kept coming unplugged at the wall socket for no apparent reason. It scared her and she began to suspect something was wrong with the house. Then more things began happening.

One day, Vicky came home from work to see Rob painting, and took a good look at his work. She then looked beyond the painting and saw a man outside the window, standing in the grounds of the house. The man turned from her but he had no legs, then he disappeared completely. The family then installed security cameras.

Shortly after, one of Rob's work colleagues named Joe, moved into the spare apartment in the property, with his dog. One night while washing the dishes, there was a knock at the door but no one was there. Then the dog began acting as if someone was in the apartment but no one was there. A few nights later, Joe was walking his dog in the grounds when he saw a man watching them from the woods. The dog gave chase and Joe followed, to see the man even closer, before running back to the house. After speaking to the Graves, it appeared they had seen the same man.

Another night came and another encounter happened. This time the dog was growling at someone who was trying to open the front door. Joe stood up and the door swung open to a strong wind. He went to the door and looked outside but no one was there. Upon turning to head back into the apartment, a man was running towards him from inside the apartment, screaming for his life.

They then began to research Baumeister's victims and Joe watched some old news footage and was certain he had seen the man in the victim list. On another occasion,

Joe's dog uncovered a human bone in the grounds of the estate, in the exact location that he had first seen the man in the woods.

Rob Graves then contacted Mary Wilson, the lead investigator on the case. She came out to the estate and showed them where the bodies had been uncovered. They appeared to be in the same vicinity as the locations of the unexplained phenomena. Suddenly, news of the hauntings grew and an army of paranormal investigators and demonologists descended on the estate.

On one occasion, Joe was in the pool with some others, cleaning the bottom of it, when cold fingers grabbed his neck and pulled him under the water. He escaped and charged out of the pool, screaming at the others to get out before the demon got them to. Another night brought another haunting. Joe was at the computer working when he heard a knife scratching against the wall, and sure enough he saw a knife on the floor. Using the new experience he had gained from the paranormal investigators, he unplugged all the electrics and used his cell phone to record any unheard noises.

Afterwards, he replayed the recording on the cell phone and a voice crackled through the audio; 'I am the married one.' Because all his victims had been gay men, it was suddenly believed that Herb Baumeister himself had returned to Fox Hollow Farm to haunt those who ventured there.

The Graves no longer live at the property. Instead, week in and week out, there are paranormal investigators on site, believing that the property and grounds are amongst the most haunted in Indiana. On one occasion, a large team of investigators arrived at the estate and stayed for six months. The team included a physics expert, a demonologist, EVP and visual specialist, and an army of psychics.

It appeared to them, at least, that evil never dies.

THE FACTS

Born: April 7th 1947 | Active: 1980-1996

Country: USA (Indiana) | Victims: 12+

AKA: The I-70 Strangler/Herb | Sentence: Killed himself before sentencing

Status: Suicide by shooting on July 3rd 1996

Berdella, Robert Andrew: The Kansas City Butcher

EXTENDED CASE FILE

On June 23rd 1987, Kansas based serial killer Robert Andrew Berdella Jr. dragged a sedated 20-year-old Larry Wayne Pearson into his basement. He would then violently torture Pearson for the next six weeks before beheading and dissecting his remains in August of 1987. Pearson was one of six victims to fall foul of one of the evilest killers in the modern era.

Berdella was the eldest son of a deeply religious family, his father was of Italian descent. Raised in Ohio, he was sent on religious education courses and attended the local church for mass. During his childhood he was afflicted with various impediments that saw him bullied in school and beaten by his father.

When he was young, his father rarely allowed him to socialise outside of religious sermons and family chores. As such, Berdella became a loner and was known to have been socially awkward. When he was five-years-old, he was diagnosed with near-sightedness and had to wear thick-rimmed glasses. Combined with a speech-impediment, he withdrew from society at an early age.

In doing so, Berdella didn't follow in his younger brother's footsteps and take up sport, instead becoming lethargic and gaining weight. Because of this lethargy, his father would often compare him to his younger brother, belittling him for not being like his other son.

Although Berdella's father abused his children he would pay particular attention to his eldest son. He emotionally and physically abused them, sometimes beating them with a leather belt. As he reached his teenage years, Berdella became confused about his sexuality, which he kept to himself. He finally came out as gay in his late teens. On Christmas Day 1965, when Berdella was 16-years-old, his 39-year-old father died of a heart attack while at home.

Berdella turned to religion in the hope that faith would somehow see him through what he described as a difficult time, regardless of his father's abuse towards him. When he didn't find what he needed, he began reading up on other religions and soon started to lose faith in what he had been taught as a youngster.

At around the same time, he had turned his withdrawal into a mask of exaggerated confidence. He became difficult to be around due to his new rudeness and attitude towards others. Then he saw a 1965 film called The Collector. In the case of Berdella, it was one of the first known instances of a movie directly impacting the thought processes of someone who had the potential to kill and would go on to kill.

The plot of The Collector is about a man who abducts women and holds them captive in his basement. It is a direct correlation to the exact process used by Berdella in his future murders. Except that he chose men instead of women.

Two years later in 1967, Berdella moved to Kansas and went to the Kansas City Art Institute where he was known to have become a promising student, but things quickly took a turn for the worst. After falling in with the drug crowd, he started to abuse drugs and alcohol, and even began dealing to other students.

Some serial killers torture small animals in their childhood years, due to being able to overpower small animals where they can't overpower human abusers or carers. Berdella started late and used art as an excuse for torturing animals. As part of his art, he used sedatives on a dog to see the effects, then tortured and cooked a duck in front of other students – for art. After that he left the institute after widespread condemnation.

He was arrested a few months later in possession of Marijuana and LSD. It is unclear whether the LSD was the type known as Orange Sunshine Acid which is the type that Charles Manson and other known criminals went on to use.

He stayed in Kansas and moved into the now infamous 4315 Charlotte Street, in the Hyde Park area of Kansas City. He enjoyed using male sex workers and spent a lot of time in gay bars in the city, openly taking part in casual sexual encounters with other men. He would spend time with drug addicts and homeless people and gain their trust by plying them with drugs.

Ever since his teens, he took pleasure in and saw the benefits of becoming pen-pals with people. He then wrote letters to people all over the world including to Vietnam and Burma, two countries that were very much off-limits to the Western world at the time. In return he would receive photos of ancient sites and small items from those countries, and so his collection began to grow.

In disregarding mainstream religion he had developed a belief and understanding in alternative religions and occult magic. This would lead him to opening a rather unique shop in 1982. He opened a booth at the Westport Flea Market called Bob's Bazaar Bizarre, which was an antique and curiosity shop. It sold things like primitive art, Asian artefacts and jewellery. He subsidised his earnings by stealing items for his booth and then started taking lodgers at his home.

He became friends with the son of one of his fellow booth operators, Jerry Howell. When Jerry was 19-years-old, on July 5th 1984, he became Berdella's first victim. Berdella promised to give him a lift to a dance contest but instead drugged him with heavy sedatives, took him home and tied him to his bed. Over the next 24 hours, Berdella raped, tortured and beat Jerry. He died after the drugs stopped his heart and he gagged on his own vomit.

Berdella then dragged the body to the basement to try and resuscitate him but instead he suspended the body from the feet. As Jerry's body was hanging upside down, Berdella cut his throat and other arterial veins in order to drain the blood from the corpse. A day later he returned to his basement and used a chainsaw and knives to dismember the body. He wrapped them in newspapers and put them in several trash bags, which were collected shortly after and taken to the landfill.

We know all this in such great detail because Berdella had been keeping extremely elaborate notes and photographs of his victims and other assaults. His notes detailed each individual act of torture and abuse and outlined the intense physical and mental satisfaction that he took from carrying out the murders in such a way.

He killed another four young men after Howell and his final victim was on June 23rd 1987. Larry Wayne Pearson was initially one of Berdella's lodgers and Berdella hadn't planned on killing him. After he bailed Pearson out of jail, he made a crude remark about gay men, and Berdella saw red. Berdella drugged him and dragged him into the basement – where the horror began.

For the following six weeks until August 5th, when he finally killed him, Pearson was tortured and abused in the most horrific of fashions. He would be injected with drain cleaner and had piano wire tightened around his wrists to cause nerve damage. Berdella broke one of Pearson's hands with an iron bar and electrocuted him with an electric transformer.

He kept Pearson in various states of sedation and moved him around the house, including the second bedroom where he would rape and abuse him further. Towards the end, Pearson summoned the energy to bite Berdella's penis during a session of forced fellatio. Berdella then beat him to death and later dismembered him in the basement. He stored Pearson's head in the freezer before burying it in the backyard.

Although Pearson was his last murder, another victim escaped his clutches in 1988. 22-year-old Christopher Bryson managed to escape from the house. He jumped from a second floor window and was wearing nothing except a dog collar around his neck. He broke his foot when he jumped but managed to call out for help. Someone heard him and called the police, and Berdella was subsequently arrested.

334 Polaroid images and 34 snapshot prints were found in the apartment when it was searched. There was a possible link with a total of 20 murders but only six could be verified using his notes and confession. Berdella was sentenced to life in prison without parole. He died of a heart failure on October 8th 1992, while incarcerated at Missouri State Penitentiary.

THE FACTS

Born: January 31st 1949 | Active: 1984-1988

Arrested: April 2nd 1988 | Country: USA. (Missouri)

Victims: 6 | AKA: The Kansas City Butcher

Sentence: Life in prison | Status: Died in prison in 1992

Bergamo, Marco: The Monster of Bolzano

Italian serial killer Marco Bergamo, AKA: The Monster of Bolzano, murdered five women between 1985 and 1992 in Bolzano, Italy. During his childhood he suffered from a stutter and skin disease that saw him be bullied by family and other school pupils. In his teenage years he collected knives and always had a knife on his person.

At the age of 26-years-old, in 1992, he had surgery to remove one of his testicles. This combined with his isolation and social awkwardness was one of the reasons why he went on to kill. Before he claimed his first victim, he tried his hand at becoming a welder and carpenter but couldn't find work that would bring in decent money.

15-year-old Marcella Casagrande was his first victim in 1985. She had been butchered by Bergamo in her own home and had been stabbed multiple times. Six months later, he murdered 41-year-old teacher, Anna Maria Cipolletti, who was known to have been involved in prostitution to subsidise her teaching wage. She had been stabbed 19 times by Bergamo but no sexual abuse had taken place.

The murders stopped until 1992, when Bergamo killed three women in less than eight months. On January 7th, the body of 24-year-old Renate Rauch's was found in a deserted parking lot.

Bizarrely, Bergamo left a note on her grave stating how sorry he was, even signing it with the initial of his first name. On March 21st he picked up 19-year-old Renate Troger who was hitchhiking from Milan. Her mutilated body was found a few days later.

On August 6th, he stabbed 20-year-old Marika Zorzi 28 times before leaving her body on the side of the road. On the same night, police were carrying out checks of vehicles in the region due to the murders.

Bergamo was pulled over and police found bloodstains on his passenger seat and documents of the last victim in the trunk. He was ultimately convicted of five murders and sentenced to life in prison. He died of a lung infection on October 17th 2017.

THE FACTS

Born: August 6th 1966 | Active: 1985-1992

Arrested: 1992 | Country: Italy (Bolzano)

Victims: 5 | AKA: The Monster of Bolzano

Sentence: Life imprisonment | Status: Died in prison in October 2017

PHOTO OF THE REAR OF FOX HOLLOW FARM

THE BUILDING AND GROUNDS ARE NOW CONSIDERED HAUNTED

IMAGE ATTRIBUTIONS (ATTRIB A54) (ATTRIB A55) (ATTRIB A56)

HERB BAUMEISTER

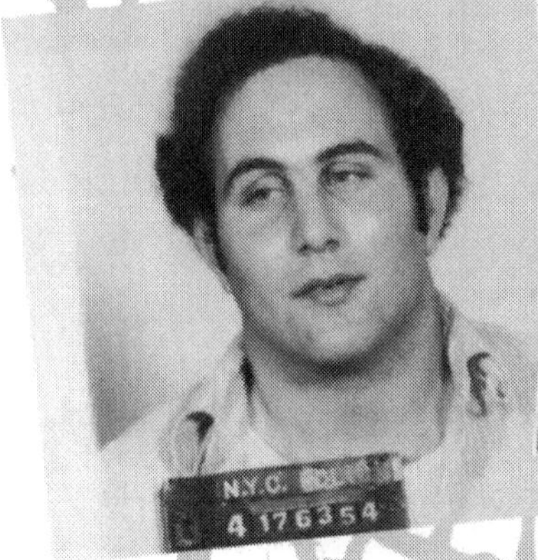

BERKOWITZ IN 2003

IMAGE ATTRIBUTIONS (ATTRIB A58) (ATTRIB A59)

DAVID BERKOWITZ

Berkowitz, David: The Son of Sam

EXTENDED CASE FILE

Berkowitz's campaign of terror brought 1977 to its knees and set the horrific standard for the year to follow. He killed six people between 1976 and 1977 but his trial in 1978 caught the public's interest. He was born Richard David Falco in 1953 Brooklyn, New York, to a poor Jewish family. His mother was a waitress who struggled to provide for him and he was adopted by Pearl and Nathan Berkowitz, whose name he took.

Berkowitz's first victims came in a double stabbing on Christmas Eve 1975. He stabbed two women in Co-op city using a hunting knife, both of whom went on to survive but wouldn't be associated with Berkowitz until his arrest. One of the women was discovered to be 15-year-old Michelle Forman, the other was never identified. In July 1976, he walked up to a car window and fired three shots into the car then calmly walked away, killing 18-year-old Donna Lauria and injuring 19-year-old Jody Valenti.

In October 1976, he used the same pattern and shot at a couple in a car but they managed to speed away with severe injuries. A month later, he fired at two students on the porch of one of their homes, both survived the shooting. In January 1977, he shot a couple sitting in their car, killing the female, Christine Freund. On March 8th, 19-year-old student Virginia Voskerichian was killed as she walked home from University.

In April, he shot another couple dead in their car, and then wrote a letter to police referring to himself as the Son of Sam. He attacked two more people in June, who survived, and killed his last victim in July. He was arrested in August 1977 when officers searched his car and found a gun on the back seat, along with maps of the crime scenes.

Berkowitz holds a unique place in the history of serial killers in that his crimes were not focused on sexual or personal predication. He used a gun and never stayed around to mutilate or damage the bodies further. Although not all serial killers mutilate victims or are driven by sexual perversity, it is a common trait. Berkowitz didn't portray these traits and the way he would just walk away from his crimes showed a man who didn't seem to have a care in the world. In fact, Berkowitz would later claim that he was lashing out in anger against a world he felt had abandoned him.

When his apartment was searched, officers found satanic symbols on the walls and doors. Berkowitz claimed he joined a satanic cult in 1975 – which were not hard to find in the mid-1970s. He went on to say that other members of the cult would also kill people and would sometimes act as a lookout for his own murders.

Although the existence of the cult could never be proven, the investigation and indeed some of the survivors still maintained that Berkowitz was not acting alone. This tied into the witness reports of different people at the scene, different cars, and different shapes in the shadows.

There was even a bizarre claim that Berkowitz's former neighbour, Sam Carr, had a dog possessed by a demon that told him to kill people. Berkowitz himself claimed that his nickname was based on Sam the dog, whether it was possessed or not depends on how far you're willing to go to believe that theory.

Immediately after his conviction, the Son of Sam Law was passed as a pre-emptive legal statute by New York State Legislature. The huge interest in Berkowitz's case and trial led publishers and producers stepping over each other to buy his story. The public curiosity and media presence in the case led many to believe that he would sell his story as quick as he could get it out. Many didn't want a serial killer to make money from his or her crimes.

It was the first legal restriction of its kind in the United States. The legislation would then be invoked eleven times from 1977 until 1990. It was even invoked in the case of Mark David Chapman, who had killed John Lennon. The law was changed constantly in the years that followed but similar laws are now in place in 44 States. In June 1978, Berkowitz was convicted of six murders and given six life sentences.

THE FACTS

Born: June 1st 1953 | Active: 1976-1977

Arrested: August 10th 1977 | Country: USA (New York)

Victims: 6 (+9 wounded)| AKA: Son of Sam/The .44 Calibre Killer

Sentence: Six life sentences | Status: Incarcerated

Bible Belt Strangler

Also known as 'The Redhead Murders', the killings are a series of murders linked to an unidentified serial killer. The first suspected victim was in 1983, and the killings may have continued until 1992. Many of the victims remain unidentified but most of them had red hair, hence the moniker.

The killings linked to the Bible Belt Strangler, so called because of the locations of the bodies, took place in numerous states, including Tennessee, Arkansas, Kentucky, Mississippi, Pennsylvania, and West Virginia. The bodies were abandoned along major highway and interstate routes. It has long been suspected that the victims were either hitchhiking or involved in prostitution.

In February 1983, the body of a white female with auburn hair was discovered in West Virginia, by an elderly couple who thought they had found a mannequin. Two years later, she was linked to the first identified victim, 28-year-old Lisa Nichols, whose body was found in September 1984 in West Memphis, but not identified until a year later. She had been strangled to death and was identified through fingerprints.

On New Year's Day 1985, the body of a young woman with curly red hair was found on an embankment in Campbell County, Tennessee. She had been strangled to death three days earlier. Her identity remained a mystery until September 2018, when she was identified as 21-year-old Tina Marie McKenney Farmer of Indiana, who was last seen hitchhiking before getting into a truck.

In 2019, DNA evidence proved that her killer was convicted kidnapper, Jerry Leon Johns, who had died in prison four years earlier. He had been convicted of kidnapping and partially strangling another young woman with red hair at around the same time as Tina was killed.

Johns has never been linked to the other victims of the so-called Bible Belt Strangler. Another three unidentified victims and one who was identified in 2018, were positively linked to the spate of murders, though apart from Johns, the identity of the killer or killer remain a mystery. There is believed to be a total of six to 11 victims that have been attributed to one unidentified serial killer.

THE FACTS

Active: 1983-1992 | Country: USA

Victims: 6-11 | AKA: The Redhead Murders | Status: Unsolved

Biegenwald, Richard: The Thrill Killer

An American serial killer and arsonist sometimes called 'The Thrill Killer' murdered at least six people over a 25-year period in Monmouth County, New Jersey. He is suspected of two other murders in the same time frame and would mostly shoot his victims but some were stabbed.

Biegenwald had a rough upbringing and was physically abused by his alcoholic father. When he was just five-years-old, Biegenwald set fire to the family home and was sent away for psychiatric observation. He was drinking and gambling by the time he was eight-years-old, then bizarrely set himself on fire when he was 11.

The first murder took place in 1958, when Biegenwald was only 18. He had stolen a car to rob a shop, where he gunned down the shop worker, Steven Sladowski. He was arrested two days later and convicted of murder, then served 16 years of a life sentence until his release for good behaviour in 1974.

In June 1978, he shot and killed police informant John P. Petrone at an abandoned airport. Then three years later, he shot dead Maria Ciallellam, before dismembering her body and burying her remains at his own mother's house. He then stabbed to death Deborah Osbourne on April 8th 1982 and buried her body on top of Maria Ciallellam's remains.

In August 1982, he shot dead Anna Olesiewicz after luring her off the streets and disposed of her body behind a Burger King restaurant. His final victim was a drug dealer named William Ward, who he shot dead at his home. Biegenwald was arrested in 1983 and sentenced to death before having it commuted to life on appeal. He was known as The Thrill Killer simply because his only motive was that he got a kick out of murder.

THE FACTS

Born: August 24th 1940 | Active: 1958-1983

Arrested: January 22nd 1983 | Country: USA (New Jersey)

Victims: 6-8 | AKA: The Thrill Killer

Sentence: Death penalty, commuted to life | Status: Died in 2008

Bishop, Arthur Gary

On October 14th 1979, in Utah, serial killer and sex offender Arthur Gary Bishop claimed his first victim. Four-year-old Alonzo Daniels was lured from the grounds of his family's apartment complex and drowned in Bishop's bathtub. Bishop later buried the body in the desert.

Not content with one murder, in November 1980, Bishop lured 11-year-old Claude Peterson from an ice-rink under the pretence of purchasing some roller-skates. Peterson was then beaten to death and his body buried near to Daniels in the desert. Despite being questioned, Bishop was not considered a suspect at the time, though in hindsight, the evidence was already there.

In October 1981, Bishop lured four-year-old Danny Davis from a supermarket and took him to his home. Again, despite numerous witnesses, Bishop was not a suspect in the disappearance. Davis was raped and beaten to death before being buried near the locations of the first two. Investigators put numerous shoppers and shop workers through hypnosis in the hope they could find out any more information on the suspect but it proved unsuccessful.

It was another two years before Bishop killed again, he lured a young boy named Troy Ward to his home where he drowned him in the bathtub, assaulted him and beat him to death. His fifth and final victim was 13-year-old Graeme Cunningham, who vanished in July of 1983, he too was brutally murdered.

Police finally linked Bishop to the abductions and arrested him, where he confessed to all five murders. He then led police to the burial sites of every one of his victims, which if he hadn't done then there was the suggestion he may have got away with it. He was found guilty of five murders in March 1984 and sentenced to death for all of them. Bishop was executed by lethal injection on June 10th 1988.

THE FACTS

Born: 1951 | Active: 1979-1983

Arrested: January 1980 | Country: USA (Utah)

Victims: 5 | AKA: Roger Downs (alias)

Status: Executed by lethal injection

Black, Robert: Smelly Bob

EXTENDED CASE FILE

There have been many British serial killers but perhaps none more disturbed and horrific than the story of rapist and murderer Robert Black. Black was a paedophile and killer who operated from 1969 to 1987. He was a truck driver who made regular work trips to mainland Europe where it is suspected he murdered dozens more, and as time has moved on, the links have become more certain.

He was also prime suspect in the infamous 1978 disappearance and murder of 13-year-old Genette Tate, who had vanished on her newspaper delivery round in Devon, on England's Southern Coast. Her murder remains unsolved but linked to Black.

Black was born in Grangemouth, Scotland, in 1947. As his mother didn't know who Robert's father was, she had him adopted soon after and he was taken in by a couple who lived in Kinlochleven, in the Scottish Highlands.

Black went through life with the surname of Tulip, which he took from his adopted parents. He was called 'Smelly Bobby Tulip' by school friends due to his poor hygiene – and the name stuck. When he was growing up, he became an outcast and was prone to outbursts of anger and aggression.

From an early age, Black believed he should have been born a girl, and at five-years-old was caught comparing his genitalia with a girl of the same age. From the age of eight, he would insert objects into his anus and was known to have carried on with the unusual practice into his adulthood.

Black was knowing to wet the bed on regular occasions, which has been linked as one of the many pre-cursors to violence in later life. Every time he did so, he was beaten by his foster mother and couldn't fight back, resulting in numerous marks and regular bruising on his body.

When he was 11, both his foster parents died from apparent natural causes, and he was adopted by another couple in the small village. In the same year, he dragged a younger girl into a public toilet and attempted to rape her.

Concerned by his violent and abusive behaviour, his new foster parents had him removed from their care to a mixed-sex children's care home near Falkirk on the central belt of Scotland. Straight away, Black tried to abuse some of the girls there and sent to a stricter care home for boys only.

While there, and for the next three years, he was abused himself by a male carer and would regularly be forced to perform oral sex on him. He was also bullied physical and sexually by the other boys despite requiring to be constantly isolated due to his behaviour.

In 1963, when he was 16, he left the care home on his own accord and more into a small flat. He became a delivery boy for a local butcher and manipulated the deliveries so that he could deliver to houses with young girls who were alone. He later claimed to have touched or attacked at least 30 young girls on his deliveries.

In the same year, he lured a seven-year-old girl to an abandoned air-raid shelter then throttled her until she passed out, before masturbating over her body. He was arrested but a psychiatrist's report claimed it was only a one-off and he was let go without punishment.

Black was only 16 at the time and had attempted rape multiple times, been raped himself, and sexually attacked over 30 girls. It should have been clear to psychiatrist's then that Black was an immense danger to society. As it was, he was left to evolve from an abuser to a killer.

In 1968, when he was 21, Black moved to London after being released from a borstal on another offence of child abuse. He moved to a bedsit near King's Cross Station where young children were in plentiful supply.

He had multiple jobs, including a life-guard position that he was fired from for sexually touching a young girl – which comes as no surprise in hindsight. He started collecting child pornography through a contact at an illegal book shop in King's Cross.

He later managed to get hold of VHS tapes depicting child abuse. He also covertly took photos of children at swimming pools and in shops and kept the images in locked suitcases, due to the amount of material he had amassed.

He then moved into the attic of a Scottish couple in the area and got himself a long-distance driving job. In his truck he kept various disguises including different types of glasses. He also alternated between having a long beard and no beard at all.

His first confirmed murder victim came when he was 34, in August of 1981. He abducted nine-year-old Jennifer Cardy in Northern Ireland, while on a long-haul journey. She had been riding her bike near to a main road when she vanished.

Hundreds of volunteers joined the search for the girl, and her body was found in a large lake, six days later by two fishermen. Black had brutally raped and drowned the girl. The police suspected the killer might have been a truck driver due to the location of the lake to the trunk road.

Even though it would have been someone who was familiar with the roads around it, no connection was made to Black and his past convictions. It seemed that Black was able to get away with abuse and murder so easily that he ended up incorporating it into his truck routes.

His second confirmed murder victim was 11-year-old Susan Claire Maxwell, from Cornhill-on-Tweed, close to the Scottish border. Maxwell had been playing sports with friends and walked home alone, before being kidnapped by Black.

300 officers and hundreds more volunteers were involved in the search and an investigation was made of every property in the area, along with a huge amount of open land. A month later, in August of the same year, her decomposed body was found by a lorry driver in a shallow grave at the side of the road. She had been tied up and gagged, with her underwear carefully positioned under her head.

Another three confirmed victims turned up from 1983 to 1987. There were also multiple disappearances and murders that were later linked to Black. In the United Kingdom alone, six more disappearances and murders were attributed to him.

There were also disappearances and murders across Ireland, the Netherlands and Germany. All of the victims vanished or were killed at the same time as Black would have been in the areas on his long-haul European journeys.

A full victim list and linked victim list can be found after the bibliography at the back of this book.

The nationwide manhunt for Robert Black was one of the most expensive and most resource-heavy UK murder investigations of the 20th century. But he was caught when a member of the public witnessed one of his abductions.

On 14th July 1990, 53-year-old retiree David Herkes was cutting his grass when he saw a blue van slow down on the other side of the road. Herkes started to clean the blades of his lawnmower and happened to look up to see the feet of a small girl lifted from the pavement and into the van.

He watched as Black pushed the girl into the passenger seat before quickly getting in and driving away. Already, Herkes believed he had witnessed an abduction and wrote down the registration number. He realised it might have been the six-year-old daughter of his neighbour and ran to her house where they called the police immediately.

Within minutes the area was covered in police vehicles. A short while passed and Herkes continued to describe what had happened to officers. Suddenly, Black had decided to drive back through the town on his way northwards and Herkes recognised the van instantly.

He shouted to officers who jumped in front of the van and pulled Black from his seat. The father of the missing girl charged into the van and found his daughter tied up in a sleeping bag. She had already been sexually abused but had survived and would go on to make a full recovery. It was the last child that Black would ever touch.

In 1994, Black was convicted of the rape and murder of three girls, along with kidnapping and sexual assault. He received a sentence of life imprisonment with a minimum of 35 years. The case caused outrage in the United Kingdom and saw protests calling for the death penalty to be reinstated in the country.

Up until his death, he was charged with another murder from 1981 and was about to be charged with more when he died of a heart attack in January 2016. He was already a prime suspect in most of his suspected victims.

Robert Black remains one of the worst serial killers to walk the streets of the United Kingdom and Europe. Not only was his brutality unheard of in the British Isles at the time, but the huge number of lives he affected was never forgotten.

The unusual aspect of the Robert Black case is that many unsolved murders and disappearances of young girls across the United Kingdom and Europe in the 1980s and 1990s, continue to be linked to him.

Many feel that Black has become a catch-all name for many local police forces to use for 'solving' unsolved cases. Not unlike Henry Lee Lucas in the United States, when at one point in time, over 3,000 murders were attributed him, clearing the unsolved slate of many local law enforcement agencies.

Due to his extensive travelling and number of disappearance on his truck routes, it is possible that Black was one of the most prolific serial killers ever to walk the British Isles and Europe. But with his passing, Smell Bobby Tulip has taken his numerous secrets to the grave.

THE FACTS

Born: April 21st 1947 | Active: 1969-1990

Arrested: July 14th 1990 | Country: United Kingdom/Europe

Victims: 4-21+ | AKA: Smelly Bob

Sentence: Life imprisonment with a minimum of 35 years

Status: Died of a heart attack in prison in January 2016

Bonin, William: The Freeway Killer

EXTENDED CASE FILE

In California, American serial killer William George Bonin, AKA: The Freeway Killer, murdered at least 21 boys and young men over a 13-month period between 1979 and 1980 in Southern California. He used regular accomplices to help him kidnap and kill young men. Most of the bodies were recovered near roadsides and highways, leading to the Freeway Killer moniker.

Bonin was born in 1947 in Connecticut, to alcoholic parents, but his mother placed him in a Catholic convent after domestic violence in the household had escalated. Unfortunately, the convent was known for its harsh discipline, and Bonin was beaten and punished most of the time he was there. After a brief stint with the U.S. Air Force, Bonin turned to petty crime, and from 1968 began abusing young men and boys before escalating to murder, some of which are listed below.

On August 5th 1979, in Newport Beach, California, 17-year-old German tourist Marcus Grabs was raped and brutally murdered. Grabs was backpacking the United States when he was approached by Bonin and accomplice Vernon Butts. Grabs was raped, beaten and stabbed 77 times. His bound and nude body was discovered the next day beside a road in Malibu.

On September 12th 1979, in Los Angeles, the nude body of 17-year-old David Murillo was discovered near a highway. He had disappeared three days earlier while cycling to the movies. His head had been crushed with a tire iron and he had been raped and strangled. Bonin was later convicted of the murder.

On February 3rd 1980, in West Hollywood, 15-year-old Charles Miranda was picked up by Bonin and accomplice Gregory Matthew Miley. Charles was raped, beaten, and strangled to death with his own shirt because Miley was not able to get sexually aroused. His restrained and nude body was discovered the next morning beside an alley in Malibu.

On the same evening, after dumping Charles's body, the pair of murderers sought another victim. They picked up 12-year-old James McCabe who was on his way to Disneyland with family. Bonin raped McCabe in the back of the van and they both later beat and strangled him to death. McCabe's body was found in a dumpster three days later. Miley, who helped Bonin kill some of his victims, was sentenced to 25 years to life in prison.

On March 14th 1980, in Van Nuys, California, 19-year-old Ronald Gatlin was hitchhiking when he was picked up by Bonin. Gatlin's body was found the next day in Duarte, he had been raped, beaten, and strangled to death.

On March 20th 1980, in Hollywood, 14-year-old Harry Todd Turner was picked up by Bonin and accomplice William Ray Pugh. Turner's nude body was found the next day in an alley in downtown Los Angeles. He had been raped, beaten, and strangled to death by Bonin. Pugh, who was present during the murder of Turner, was sentenced to six years for voluntary manslaughter.

On April 10th 1980, in Los Angeles, 16-year-old Steven Wood was going about his business in the early afternoon when he was picked up by Bonin. Wood's nude body was discovered the next morning in an alley on an industrial estate. He had been raped, brutally beaten, and strangled to death with a ligature.

On April 29th 1980, in the parking lot of a supermarket in Stanton, California, 19-year-old Darin Lee Kendrick was abducted by Bonin and accomplice Vernon Butts. Kendrick had been collecting shopping carts and was lured into Bonin's van by the offer of free drugs. During the night, he was raped, tortured, and strangled to death.

He had been forced to ingest an acid which left him with internal burns and had an ice pick inserted into his ear that severed his upper spinal cord. His nude body was found the next day in an industrial park. Butts, who helped Bonin kill some of his victims, took his own life in 1981 while awaiting trial.

On June 13th 1980, in California, after extensive surveillance, Bonin was captured and initially convicted of 10 murders then another four in a separate trial. Although convicted of 14 murders in total, he was known to have killed at least 21, with some investigators suspecting it may have been closer to 44. In 1986, after a lengthy trial, he was sentenced to death and executed by lethal injection in California on February 23rd 1996.

THE FACTS

Born: in 1947 | Active: 1972-1980

Arrested: June 1980 | Country: USA (California)

Victims: 21-44 | AKA: The Freeway Killer

Status: Executed by lethal injection in 1996

WILLIAM BONIN AS A YOUNGSTER IN 1963

THE VAN HE USED TO ABDUCT HIS VICTIMS

IMAGE ATTRIBUTIONS (ATTRIB A91) (ATTRIB A92) (ATTRIB A93)

WILLIAM BONIN

(ATTRIB A94)

ROBERT EUGENE BRASHERS

Brandt, Charlie

Brandt killed himself in 2004 after stabbing his wife to death then decapitating and heavily mutilating his niece, even going as far as removing her heart. He had shot his mother dead in 1971 and injured his father with his own gun. His mother was pregnant at the time and her baby was also killed. Unbelievably, Brandt was only 13-years-old. After his mother's death, he spent only one year in a psychiatric hospital before being released.

On September 20th 1978, 12-year-old Carol Sullivan was abducted from a school bus stop in Volusia County. Two weeks later, her skull was found inside a paint can by a man exploring the shoreline of a lake. Brandt was living in the area at the time but could not be conclusively tied to the murder. Other suspects include Vincenzo Alestra and Henry Lee Lucas but the murder remains unsolved.

Brandt moved to Florida shortly after the Sullivan murder. On September 15th 2004, after not hearing from her friend for a while, Debbie Knight went to Brandt's niece's house. When she couldn't get in through the front door, she entered the property through the garage, and walked into a scene from a horror movie where she found the decomposing body of Brandt hanging from the rafters. He had used bedsheets to hang himself.

When the police arrived, they broke into the main part of the house and found Brandt's wife, Teri, laying on the couch, she had been stabbed seven times in the chest and her innards were on display. Michelle Jones, Brandt's niece, had been decapitated and gutted, with her heart and organs removed. Her head had been left next to her body.

Brandt's suicide in 2004, after the murder of his wife and niece, meant that no investigation was undertaken but it didn't stop investigators linking him to other murders in Florida and neighbouring states from 1973. Though he conclusively killed four people including the unborn child, he has been positively linked to another four.

THE FACTS

Born: 1957 | Active: 1971-1985

Country: USA (Florida) | Victims: 4-8

Status: Died of suicide in 2004

Brashers, Robert Eugene

One of a few serial killers in history to have been identified after their death. Robert Eugene Brashers was identified in 2018 through the use of genetic genealogy, and positively linked to the 1990 murder of Genevieve Zitricki, in South Carolina. He had previously been convicted of a 1985 assault and shooting in Florida.

The Zitricki murder had remained unsolved for 28 years. As part of a Greenville cold case investigation in 2018, her body was exhumed in order to retrieve a full DNA sample. They linked Brashers to the murder instantly as they already had his profile on record. Brashers had broken into Genevieve's apartment, raped and beat her before strangling her to death, leaving her body to be discovered in the bathtub.

Brashers was then conclusively linked to the 1997 rape of a 14-year-old girl in Tennessee, and the 1998 double murder of a mother and daughter, Sherri and Megan Scherer, in Missouri. It is claimed that each of his victims had a striking similarity to his wife at the time and may have been the motive for the rapes and murders.

In 1999, when police approached him about a different incident, he escaped justice forever by shooting himself dead, leaving the families of the dead and injured wondering why he had committed the crimes.

THE FACTS

Born: March 13th 1958 | Active: 1985-1999

Country: USA | Victims: 3

AKA: Mr. Maroon (alias) | Status: Died of suicide in 1999

Briley Brothers, The

The three Briley brothers killed at least 12 people between them during their reign of chaos. The brothers were raised in a happy home with caring parents but their behaviour was considered unusual. They were big fans of collecting dangerous animals including tarantulas and piranhas.

Their father later claimed his son's eyes would light up with glee when they fed small mice to their pets. It unnerved him so much that he padlocked his door at night in case they came into his room.

The first murder was committed by Linwood Briley in 1971 when he was 16-years-old. He pointed a rifle out of his bedroom window and shot his elderly neighbour dead. When a police investigation led back to the Briley brothers, Linwood stated that he thought the neighbour had heart problems so she was going to die soon anyway. It was his only motive for the murder. Linwood served only one year in a rehabilitation home.

From 1979, Linwood, Anthony and James Briley, committed a series of rapes, robberies and random murders over an eight-month period, killing at least 11 people and suspected of up to 20. The brutality and callousness of the murder spree had the city of Richmond, Virginia, in fear during their campaign.

They were all arrested in October 1979, after police heard gunfire in a residential house. Both Linwood and James were sentenced to death for their part in the murders and executed in the electric chair in 1984 and 1985 respectively. Anthony, being the younger of the three was sentenced to life in prison plus 119 years, where he resides to this day.

THE FACTS

Born: 1954 (Linwood)/1956 (James)/1958 (Anthony)

Active: 1971-1979 | Arrested: October 1979

Country: USA (Virginia) | Victims: 12-21

Sentence: Death penalty (Linwood and James)/Life in prison (Anthony)

Status: Linwood (executed 1984)/James (executed 1985)/Anthony (Incarcerated)

Brown, Vernon

On August 25th 1980, in Indiana, the body of nine-year-old Kimberly Campbell was found in a vacant house. She had been tied up, beaten, raped and strangled to death by Vernon Brown, a drifter who spent time in at least 22 states across a 10 year period. Despite the vacant house belonging to Brown's grandmother and the fact he was seen with Campbell the evening before, there was not enough physical evidence to charge him.

Brown had already spent time in prison during the 1970s for sexually abusing a 12-year-old girl and other crimes against minors. An arrest warrant was issued in 1981 for his involvement in Campbell's murder and six counts of child molestation, but he had skipped states and moved to Missouri. In March 1985, while Brown was working under an alias in an apartment complex in St. Louis, he stabbed and strangled to death 19-year-old Synetta Ford.

In a bizarre twist, Brown's homeless wife told police that Brown had admitted to the murder but he wasn't able to be charged because Missouri law at the time had a ban on testimony by a spouse – and so he got away it, for a while. A year-and-a-half later, Brown loaded up on PCP then raped and strangled nine-year-old Janet Perkins, whose body was found close to Brown's home.

He was arrested in Missouri on October 27th 1986 and sentenced to death for the murders of Ford and Perkins. Though he was positively linked to Campbell's murder, sending him to trial in Indiana proved fruitless as he was already under two death sentences in Missouri. Brown was executed by lethal injection on May 17th 2005.

THE FACTS

Born: 1953 | Active: 1980-1986

Arrested: October 1986 | Country: USA (Indiana/Missouri)

Victims: 3 | Status: Executed in 2005

Browne, Robert Charles

An American career criminal who confessed to killing 48 people, mostly women, between 1970 and 1995 but was convicted of two murders. On September 17th 1991 in Colorado, Browne killed his neighbour, 13-year-old Heather Dawn Church, who he had stabbed with a screwdriver multiple times. Her remains were found two years later and Browne was arrested in 1995, convicted and sentenced to life in prison.

He claimed that he killed women in South Korea and Vietnam when he was serving in the U.S. Army and was subsequently discharged for drug abuse. He was also married six times before his conviction. In 2006, he confessed to the murder of 15-year-old Rocio Delpilar Sperry, whose body was never found. Browne stated that he dismembered the body in her own apartment, popped out the joints and carried her remains out in various bags before burying them in a shallow grave. The remains have never been found.

Browne then confessed to 48 murders in total, and though many researchers believe them to be false, investigators have subsequently linked him to seven additional murders using his confessions and story. On March 20th 2000, while serving life for the murder of Church, he sent a cryptic letter to the district attorney's office.

"The score is, you one, the other team 48. Seven sacred virgins entombed side by side, those less worthy are scattered wide." – Robert Browne.

Two years later a cold-case team decided to investigate the details of the letter and wrote letters back to him. Browne eventually provided enough information to substantiate the killings of the seven people that the investigatory team had already linked him to. They claimed that there was information Browne knew that only the dead would have known.

Browne claimed he would kill women because he was disgusted with them and that they had low moral character traits. He was an opportunistic killer who would go for long road trips and hoped to find a victim along the way. He used a variety of different methods to kill including strangling his victims, stabbing, shooting and using chemicals, before dismembering them and placing their body parts in garbage bags. He disposed of the remains in lakes, rivers, ditches and over cliff faces.

In his confession of 48 victims he claimed that bodies could be found in nine states. They included; Colorado, New Mexico, Washington, California, Louisiana, Mississippi, Oklahoma, Texas and Arkansas. Investigations into his crimes and claims slowed down when no bodies were recovered.

THE FACTS

Born: October 31st 1952. | Active: 1971-1985

Arrested: March 28th 1995 | Country: USA

Victims: 2-48 | Sentence: Life imprisonment

Status: Incarcerated

Bunday, Thomas Richard

On August 29th 1979 in Fairbanks, Alaska, 19-year-old Glinda Sodemann went missing. Two months later, her decomposed body was found in a shallow grave near a highway in the city. She had been murdered by serial killer Thomas Richard Bunday who killed at least five young women from 1979 to 1981 in Alaska.

Born in 1948, Bunday was raised in Tennessee, the youngest of a family of four. His father was a veteran of the Second World War and developed PTSD because of it. Though he attempted to keep his illness under control, he ended up being aggressive towards his wife and children. Bunday joined the U.S. Air Force in 1967 and married a high school sweetheart, who had a child with another man while Bunday was on tour in Southeast Asia.

He was serving in the Air Force at the time of the Sodemann murder at the Eielson Air Force Base near Fairbanks, where his wife had joined him. A year after the Sodemann murder on June 13th 1980, he lured 11-year-old Doris Oehring into his car then attacked and strangled her to death. Her brother witnessed the abduction and claimed the suspect was wearing an Air Force uniform.

In 1981, Bunday killed three more young women, 20-year-old Marlene Peters, 16-year-old Wendy Wilson, and 19-year-old Lori King. King's decomposed body was found a few weeks later close to Eielson A

d shortly before her disappearance, Marlene Peters' partially decomposed body was found. In October 1981, not far from Wilson's body, the decomposed body of King was found near to the Eielson Air Force Base. Bunday made the list of top three suspects but he had been transferred to a base in Texas.

Bunday was arrested on March 7th 1983 in Texas and confessed to all five murders in lurid detail. Incredibly, despite the confession to being a serial killer, the police let him go as there was no warrant for his arrest. One week later, on March 15th, Bunday killed himself by driving his motorcycle directly into an oncoming truck at high speed. The elusive arrest warrant had been issued just days prior to his death. Bunday remains one of Alaska's few known serial killers.

THE FACTS

Born: September 28th 1948 | Active: 1979-1981

Arrested: March 7th 1983 | Country: USA (Alaska)

Victims: 5 | Status: Died by suicide before arrest

Bundy, Ted

EXTENDED CASE FILE

On January 15th 1978, serial killer Ted Bundy paid a visit to the Chi Omega sorority house of the Florida State University. He beat and strangled to death two female victims and bludgeoned another three who went on to survive the attack. He had intended to kill five people in one day, and this attack alone had displayed the level of intensity that Ted Bundy had inflicted on the United States from 1974.

Unsolved murders that were thought to have been carried out by Bundy but not proven date back to 1966. He would go on to admit to 30 murders but had been linked to many more and so the final death-toll could have been a little or a lot higher. Since he was executed in 1989, there is no way to know for sure how many he had killed.

Ted Bundy would come to hold a special place in the annals of serial killer history and would become the face of the so-called epidemic and the infamous poster boy for the psychopathic few. His story would culminate in 1979 with a trial that was televised to the world and threw the spotlight on serial killers like no other before him.

Some would argue that Jack The Ripper has more stories, books, and articles written about him, and while that might have been true in Victorian England, books on Bundy outnumber Jack by ten to one. And Bundy was different in that he had actually been caught, while Jack remains officially unidentified.

There are many piles of information regarding Bundy out there, including a Netflix documentary series, a 2019 film starring Zac Efron, and from my own research, at least 310 books and regurgitated pamphlets. Which is why this case file doesn't go into depth as there is so much data out there already. One of the most popular Bundy books is 'The Stranger Beside Me' by Ann Rule.

Bundy's capture by police officer, David Lee, is worthy of note here. Lee had stopped Bundy's car when it showed up as being stolen but wasn't aware who was inside. After approaching the car, Bundy jumped out and attacked Lee, which caused him to fire off two warning shots. He gave chase and fought Bundy to the ground, overpowering him in a violent struggle, before bundling him into the back of the car. Lee was unaware he had just caught a man who was on the FBI's Ten Most Wanted Fugitives list.

"I wish you had killed me," Bundy had said to Lee, in an extraordinary revelation.

It appears it could be one of the most interesting things that Bundy was ever recorded saying. It always seemed to many researchers that he thought himself beyond the law and would never be caught. If he wished Lee had killed him, then he did not want to face any trial for his crimes.

In psychology, there is a difference between wanting to die and wanting to be killed. Wanting to die is usually a consequence of having a mental illness and usually involves active or passive suicidal ideation. Wishing to be killed is a consequence of someone not willing to take their own life but wanting that responsibility to be placed on another. It is an attempt to hide away from one's sins and to not face the fear of judgement.

It was unusual then that Bundy moved to represent himself in the courts. He oversaw the trials himself, regardless of the defence team he had amassed. The decision to represent himself in court was based on a rampant display of control and delusion. We know that delusion is strongly associated with mental health disorders, but in the 1970s it wasn't as closely linked as it is now.

It's not untoward to say that Bundy saw himself as a higher class of human being, regardless of his own sins. Being able to speak about himself and his crimes in the third person narrative would have elevated his belief that he was more important than others. He had a controlling, possessive personality that became even more evident while he was on death row.

"The ultimate possession was, in fact, the taking of life." – Bundy to a fellow inmate.

He was also studied by and conversed with the FBI Behavioural Analysis Unit during his decade on death row. The reports and findings that arose from understanding Bundy would go on to assist investigators all over the world. They uncovered a new understanding of the serial killer phenomenon and it was mostly Bundy that had paved the way for this knowledge.

Every serial killer has their own individual intricacies that make them who they are and allows them to do what they do but profiling them became a little easier after the Bundy trial. However, he had already kicked off a wave of crime in which other serial killers would aim to better his death-toll.

Although he confessed to 30 murders, it has been suggested he killed more than that. His sexual desires were sometimes sated on a return to his own crime scenes where he would perform sexual acts with the corpses. He also had removed the heads of 12 of his victims, keeping some of them as mementos.

Alongside Jack The Ripper, Ted Bundy is the most written about serial killer in history and is still firmly in the public spotlight. But as we delve deeper into this book, we'll see that there were far worst serial killers active at the same time.

THE FACTS

Born: November 24th 1946 | Active: 1974-1978

Arrested: February 15th 1978 | Country: USA

Victims: 30+ | AKA: Ted

Sentence: Death penalty | Status: Executed in 1989

Bianchi, Kenneth & Buono, Angelo: The Hillside Stranglers

EXTENDED CASE FILE

On February 16th 1978, The Hillside Stranglers claimed their tenth and final victim in California. 20-year-old Cindy Lee Hudspeth was raped and strangled to death, her body was put into the trunk of a car which was pushed off a cliff to cover up the crime. At the time, the crimes were suspected to be of one serial killer and so the moniker of The Hillside Strangler was used. It was only upon their capture that two serial killing cousins came to be known as the stranglers.

Kenneth Bianchi and his cousin, Angelo Buono, were convicted in early 1979 for the kidnapping, rape, torture, and murder of ten females aged from 12 to 28-years-old over a five month period from October 1977 to February 1978. They became known as The Hillside Stranglers as they dumped their victim's bodies in the hills surrounding the greater Los Angeles area.

PITKIN COUNTY COURTHOUSE IN ASPEN THAT BUNDY ESCAPED FROM

DR. RICHARD SOUVIRON PRESENTS DENTAL EVIDENCE AT THE TRIAL OF TED BUNDY FOR THE CHI OMEGA MURDERS

IMAGE ATTRIBUTIONS (ATTRIB A7) (ATTRIB A8) (ATTRIB A12) (ATTRIB A13) (ATTRIB A14)

TED BUNDY

Bianchi was born to an alcoholic sex worker in 1951, who disowned him shortly afterwards. His adoptive mother would come to call him a compulsive liar from the moment he could talk and was diagnosed at the age of five-years-old, with petit mal seizures, which are triggered by abnormal electrical activity in the brain. It causes a brief trance-like state where the sufferer falls in and out of consciousness. Absence seizures, as they are otherwise known, usually have a genetic reason for someone suffering from them.

Due to his seizures, he was in and out of the doctors where it was discovered that he had involuntary urinating problems. This led to him feeling and suffering from a great deal of humiliation. From then he developed anger-led behavioural problems and was diagnosed at the age of 10 with passive aggressive personality disorder.

When his adoptive father died in 1964, Bianchi showed no signs of emotional attachment nor responded with grief in any way. He had become devoid of emotion at the event and it was something that would break down the moral barrier further before taking his first victim. It wasn't until 1977 when he began spending time with his cousin that he would begin to kill.

Buono had been raised separate from Bianchi but they would both develop into the killers they became. Born in 1934, Buono was 17 years older than Bianchi, and turned into a career criminal with records for grand theft auto, assault, and rape. He had also developed a controlling attitude towards women and used sex workers regularly, even imprisoning two in his home at one point. It wasn't long before both cousins began working as pimps. Their passion for control and power escalated, and by late 1977 they had begun killing.

The murders began with three sex workers – always deemed an easy victim choice by violent individuals – in October and November 1977. Their bodies were discovered strangled and naked in the hills. It was only when the cousins kidnapped girls from middle-class areas that the media and law enforcement picked up their investigation of the killers.

In the child abuse research article found in this book, we learn that if child victims were from working class or impoverished backgrounds then their cases were not deemed as important. Bianchi and Buono would sexually abuse and torture their victims before disposing of their bodies. They were known to have experimented with different methods of murder. Among them were lethal injections of chemicals, electric shocks and carbon monoxide poisoning.

Bianchi would ultimately be the downfall of the duo's reign. Their killings came to an end in February 1978 when they realised that the police were closing in on them. In January of the following year, Bianchi's desire for death consumed him. He was working as a security guard when he lured two females into a house. Karen Mandic and Diane Wilder were pushed down the stairs and then strangled to death.

Because Bianchi had previously killed with Buono and not alone, he ended up leaving too many clues. A routine check linked him to the addresses of two of the Hillside Strangler's victims, and both cousins were arrested shortly after. Their trial would go on to become one of the most expensive trials in the history of the California legal system at the time, and Bianchi would later testify against Buono.

The Hillside Stranglers would infect the national psyche as much as any other serial killer of the time. That their combined trial was one of the longest in history and was pounced upon by the media is a damning incitement of the way that serial killers were portrayed at the time, with sensationalism overriding factual content. Both men were convicted of 10 murders between them, and an additional two for Bianchi.

THE FACTS

Born: May 22nd 1951 (Bianchi)/October 5th 1934 (Buono)

Active: 1977-1978 | Country: USA

Arrested: January 13th 1979 (Bianchi)/October 22nd 1979 (Buono)

Victims: 10/12 | AKA: The Hillside Stranglers

Sentence: Life imprisonment for both

Status: Buono died on September 21st 2002/Bianchi remains incarcerated

Burtsev, Roman: The Kamensky Chikatilo

Russian serial killer and paedophile, Roman Burtsev, AKA; The Kamensky Chikatilo, raped and killed six children over a three year period. All of his victims were murdered in his hometown of Kamensk-Shakhtinsky, in Rostov Oblast. He was born in 1971 and raised by alcoholic parents before committing his first murder when he was 22-years-old.

On September 5th 1993, he spotted 12-year-old Yevgeny Churilov and his 7-year-old sister Olesya Churilova playing near a junk yard. He decided that he wanted to take the girl's virginity as he took a liking to her but didn't want to leave any witnesses. So he killed the boy by punching him and then hitting him over the head with a large piece of junk metal, then raped the girl and strangled her to death, before disposing of both their corpses in one of the garbage sites nearby.

He hid their corpses so well that they wouldn't be discovered until after his arrest. He then killed four more times, in 1994, 1995 and then two in 1996. On July 1st 1996, he abducted nine-year-old Ira Ternovskaya from a riverbank where she was playing. He then raped her and killed her before burying her in a shallow grave nearby.

Two weeks later on July 16th, he raped and murdered 12-year-old Natasha Kirbabina, then went to a nearby house and asked the elderly owner if he could borrow a spade. He then went back to where he left her body and buried her in a shallow grave, before throwing the spade away. The elderly lady contacted police after he didn't return the spade and described him to police.

A day later, on July 17th, Burtsev was arrested, and confessed to six murders. His motive for the murder was the pleasure he got in taking young girls' virginities and the passion for hiding his victims, in which he took great care. It was only when he led police to the burial grounds, that the bodies were found. He was convicted in the same year and sentenced to death, which was later commuted to life in prison, where he remains to this day.

THE FACTS

Born: April 13th 1970 | Active: 1993-1996

Arrested: July 17th 1996 | Country: Russia (Rostov Oblast)

Victims: 6 | AKA: The Kamensky Chikatilo

Sentence: Death penalty commuted to life | Status: Incarcerated

Butcher of Mons, The

EXTENDED CASE FILE

In Belgium, at least five murders were committed by an unidentified serial killer named The Butcher of Mons, in one of the country's most infamous unsolved crimes. All of the victims had been dismembered and their body parts placed in plastic bags on the side of public roads and other public areas for all to see.

The first murder took place in January 1996 and the last in July 1997. Because of the Marc Dutroux case that had gripped the Belgian press at the time, the Butcher of Mons murders were put front and centre with him.

Dutroux had been jailed in 1996, in the longest and most infamous trial in the country's history, and the case was still fresh on people's minds. As the investigators looked closer at the bodies in the bags, they realised that there was no evidence pointing to Dutroux as the killer, as the press suggested. Not least because Dutroux was a murderer and rapist of children, and the Butcher of Mons killed adults.

It wasn't until March 1997 that the bags started to be discovered. A police officer named Olivier Motte found eight bags beneath the Rue Emile Vandervelde in Cuesmes, with various limbs and body parts originating from three different victims. A further bag was found on the same street just one day after, along with another near to the Path of Worry.

On April 12th 1997, two more bags were found near the Hainre River, in Havré, containing feet, a head, and other body parts. All the remains were discovered in the Mons region and were dumped along streets and rivers with poetic names, including the aforementioned Path of Worry, the River Haine (Hate) and the Chemin de Bethlehem. All the victims were known to have passed through Mons Railway Station and were considered poor or having troubles in their lives.

When the investigation found more bags spread throughout Mons, theories began to abound about who or what the killer was. The way in which the bodies had been dissected and mutilated had been carried out with a precision that only a medical professional would have had, so the culprit was suspected of having had medical training. The local police reached out to the FBI for help, who came up with their own profile to assist the investigation. They concluded the killer would have had a stable job with a relatively normal life, as all the victims were killed on the weekends. As soon as the European media got hold of the story, they began alleging involvement of religious sects and occult groups as a possible reason for the bodies in the bags. The media disagreed that the killer was a surgeon, instead leaning on the more newsworthy cult connection.

The first known victim was on January 4th 1996, when 42-year-old Carmelina Russo was reported missing. She had last been seen at her home in Mons and was known to have frequented the Mons Railway Station. Three weeks later, in the Nord region of France, her pelvis was discovered.

On July 21st 1996, 43-year-old Martine Bohn was reported missing. Martine was a French transsexual and sex worker who was known to have frequented various underground bars in Belgium and France. She had left her family many years before and had no social life outside of drinking and prostitution. She was the only victim that appeared to have been killed out of a sexual motivation. A few days later, her torso was pulled out of the River Haine by a fisherman. Both breasts had been sliced off, and no other body parts were found at the time.

On December 22nd 1996, 33-year-old Jacqueline Leclercq went missing. Some reports put her last-seen date in January of 1997, but newspaper clippings at the time show she went missing in December and had a reported missing date in January. Leclercq was a young mother of three who had split from her husband and had been denied custody of her children. She had become transient and began hanging around the Mons Railway Station for unknown reasons. Her remains were discovered as part of the first eight bags beneath the Rue de Emile Vandervelde.

In March 1997, 21-year-old Nathalie Godart vanished. She was a single mother whose child had been taken into care because of problems in her own life. Godart lived in a rundown Mons bedsit and was a regular at various bars and gathering points in the city. People knew her as being extremely promiscuous with men but she had never charged for sex. Some of her body parts would later be found in the River Haine.

The last confirmed victim of the Butcher was 37-year-old Begonia Valencia, who vanished in July 1997 from her home in the area of Frameries. Her bones and skull were found half a year later in Hyon, just outside of Mons. Valencia was known to have taken a local bus, like clockwork every evening, and it is claimed that the Butcher could have picked her up at a station in Mons.

Ten years after Valencia's disappearance, one of her neighbours gave an interview to reporters investigating the case. It was from this interview that the bus and station connection came about, and the neighbour told a story of a mysterious person who came back to the town once a year.

This unidentified person would drop a wreath into the local river, on the anniversary of Valencia's disappearance, in order to keep her memory alive. No one has ever come forward to claim responsibility for the wreath, leading cold case investigators to believe there was a slim possibility it could have been the Butcher himself.

One of the prime suspects in the case was a Montenegro native named Smail Tulja (Smajo Džurlić). He changed his name to Tulja after fleeing New York were a murder took place that matched the victims in France. In September of 1990, in New York City, Tulja's wife, Mary Beal, went missing. Her remains were discovered three weeks later in two garbage bags left on the side of the street. She had been beheaded and had been dismembered into smaller parts. The similarities between the New York murder and the Belgium murders were overwhelming.

Tulja fled to Mons and then to Albania in the early 2000s. In 2006, two female victims were found in bags in Albania. They too had been dismembered and dissected. A year later, in 2007, Tulja was arrested in his home country of Montenegro. At the request of Albanian police, the FBI were brought in who made immediate connections between all the murders and the arrest of Tulja.

Montenegro had become an independent nation in 2006 and did not have an extradition treaty with the United States. But the Montenegro court still managed to convict him in 2010 of the murder of Mary Beal, and he was sentenced to 12 years. Unfortunately for the continuing investigation, Tulja died in prison in 2012, making his connection to the other murders more difficult.

The FBI and NYPD suggested that Tulja had killed eight people, seven across Europe and one in New York. The Belgian and Albanian investigators failed to make any conclusive connections to Tulja and the murders in their countries. This meant that since 2012, more suspects have been put forward as the Butcher of Mons.

In 2010, 62-year-old French doctor, Jacques Antoine, was arrested for assaulting a woman at her apartment. The investigators then discovered two letters that had been sent to them a few months earlier by Antoine's son, and in the letters he said that his father was the Butcher.

The letter claimed that Antoine had frequented the Mons region multiple times from the mid-1980s to 1997, with various garbage bags in his vehicle. There was also mention of a predilection towards firearms, and further stories of him carrying trash bags around. No evidence was found linking Antoine to the murders but he remains a tentative suspect to this day.

Another suspect is British murderer and suspected serial killer, John Sweeney, AKA: The Canal Murderer, who claimed his first victim; 33-year-old American model Melissa Halstead, in Amsterdam in 1990. He dismembered her body and put her remains in two holdalls, which were later fished out of the Amstel River.

In 2000, Sweeney murdered 31-year-old Paula Fields in London. Fields was a crack cocaine addict and sex worker from Liverpool who lived in North London. Her remains were found in 2001, when six holdalls were fished out of the Regent's Canal at the King's Cross section. Ten of Field's body parts were discovered in them, but her head, hands, and feet were missing. Sweeney was sentenced to life in prison for her murder in 2011.

It was suspected that Sweeney may have lived in Belgium at the time of the Butcher murders but no solid link has ever been made. The murder and disposal of his victims demonstrated a great deal of planning and premeditation. He was also a carpenter who would have had access to specialist cutting tools.

The identity of the Butcher of Mons remains unknown to this day, and various cold case investigations are ongoing, in the hope that one day, the Butcher will finally be identified.

THE FACTS

Active: 1996-1997 | Country: Belgium

Victims: 5 | Status: Unsolved

Catlin, Steven David

Catlin was convicted of the murders of his mother and two wives and sentenced to death in California. He was adopted as a toddler and was unruly growing up, never managing to settle with his new family. He dropped out of high school early and started a life petty crime which led to him being arrested on forgery charges when he was 19.

His first marriage was said to have been marred by domestic violence, abuse and his own drug addiction but he married again without divorcing his original wife after using a fake name on a marriage license. He then went on to marry another two times with most relationships ending because of his abuse and aggression.

Catlin killed his mother and two of his wives by poisoning them with a toxic herbicide called paraquat, which proved fatal when ingested. Traces of the herbicide were found in the forensic material taken from all three bodies. His motive was initially to kill for financial gain but he was known to talk about the control and power it gave him, a motive seen among many serial killers.

He was convicted in 1986 for the 1984 murder of his fifth wife, Glenna Kaye Catlin and was sentenced to life in prison. In June 1990, he was sentenced to death for the murders of his fourth wife, Joyce Catlin, in 1976, and his mother, Martha Catlin, in 1984. He remains on death row at San Quentin State Prison in California.

THE FACTS

Born: 1944 | Active: 1976-1984

Arrested: 1986 | Country: USA (California)

Victims: 3 | Sentence: Death penalty

Status: Incarcerated on death row

Chagas, Francisco Das: The Mechanic

Brazilian serial killer and former mechanic, Francisco das Chagas Rodrigues de Brito, raped and killed at least 30 children in the regions of Maranhão and Pará from 1989 to 2003. He was suspected of killing at least 42 but the additional 12 have never been confirmed.

Chagas claimed that he was exacting revenge because he was abused as a child and wanted others to feel his pain but didn't remember the details of his murders. He claimed to have known that he was killing children but had no memory of the intricacies of the murders and couldn't even explain where he had been.

He would rape and then castrate his victims, before burying them in shallow graves. He was arrested in 2004 and initially charged with the murders of two young boys who were found buried beneath the floor of his shack, in a shanty town just off from Sao Jose do Ribamar.

> *"Something was guiding me, directing me. It was like a voice in my head. And it was that thing - the voice - that determined what happened. Sometimes I'm revolted by what I did, but you must understand that something was using me to do this. Good people will understand that." – Chagas, in a 2004 interview with the BBC.*

The trial of Chagas was held in the auditorium of a local club in Sao Jose de Ribamar, because the courtroom wasn't big enough to hold the hundreds of victims' relatives. Even though violence is common in Brazil, serial killing is rare and Chagas is assumed to be the country's worst serial killer. He was known as The Mechanic due to his work with cars and also in the mechanical way he would castrate his victims.

THE FACTS

Born: 1965 | Active: 1989-2003

Arrested: December 2003 | Country: Brazil

Victims: 30-42 | AKA: The Mechanic

Sentence: Life imprisonment| Status: Incarcerated

Chanal, Pierre

French serial killing soldier Pierre Chanal murdered at least eight people between 1980 and 1988, although it is suspected he could have killed 17. The area where he murdered his victims became known as the Triangle of Death.

On August 8th 1987, the body of Irishman Trevor O'Keeffe was discovered in a shallow grave in France. He had been hitchhiking through the country when he was strangled to death by Chanal. In 1988, Chanal was stopped by police, and when they opened his van doors, they discovered a Hungarian hitchhiker who had been tied and gagged.

The van was full of sex toys and a camera where he had been taking various images of men he had picked up. Astonishingly, Chanal was a Chief Warrant Officer in the 4th Dragoon Regiment in France and had previously earned a United Nations medal for his service as a UN peacekeeper in Lebanon.

Chanal was convicted with the kidnapping and rape of the Hungarian hitchhiker and sentenced to 10 years in prison in 1990, with police unable to link him to the murders at the time. He was released in 1995 but police kept a close eye on him and brought him in for questioning multiple times. By 2003, they had linked him to eight of the 17 murders, and arrested him pending charges. Chanal ended the investigation by taking his own life in 2003 while awaiting trial.

THE FACTS

Born: November 18th 1946 | Active: 1980-1988

Arrested: August 9th 1988 | Country: France (Mourmelon)

Victims: 8-17 | AKA: The Triangle of Death Murders

Status: Died by suicide in 2003

IMAGE ATTRIB. A57

ROBERT ANDREW BERDELLA

ROBERT BLACK

IMAGE ATTRIB. A60

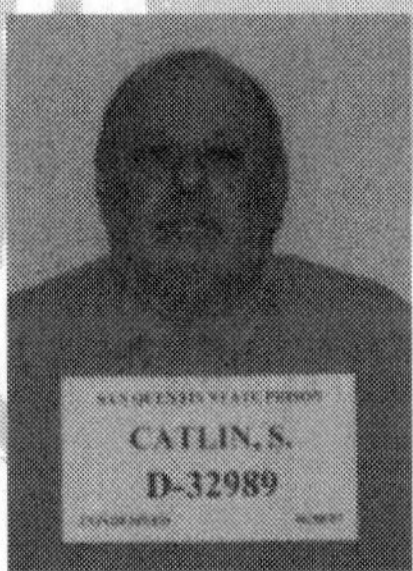

IMAGE ATTRIB. A15

STEVEN DAVID CATLIN

RICHARD TRENTON CHASE

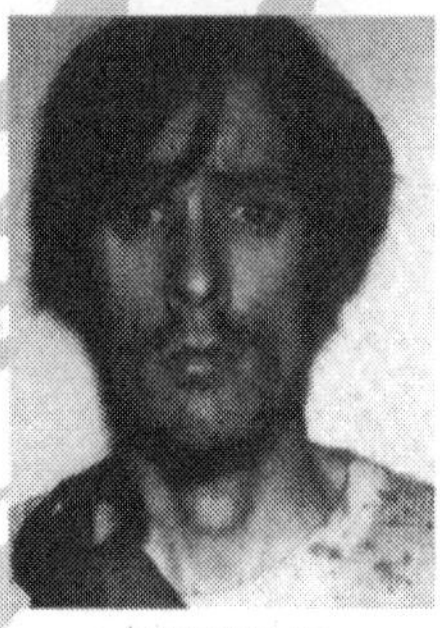

IMAGE ATTRIB. A61

Chase, Richard Trenton: The Vampire of Sacramento

EXTENDED CASE FILE

Richard Chase was the poster boy for bizarre serial killers whose tale included Nazi UFOs, necrophilia, cannibalism, drinking blood, and the belief he was turning to powder. Chase killed six people over a one month period from 29th December 1977 to 27th January 1978. He became known as the Vampire of Sacramento because he drank the blood of his victims, engaged in necrophilia, and ate some of their remains.

He was born in Sacramento in 1950 and was sexually abused by his mother over the first ten years of his life, then developed a fascination with hurting small animals, like cats and small dogs. It was this feeling of ultimate power over another's life that would eventually drive him to kill a human. He enjoyed torturing and killing small animals, and at the age of 10, Chase killed a cat he found on the street and left its body in the open.

Hurting small animals is one way a child can take out their anger and hatred. They are too small to hurt their abusers and hurt smaller animals until such time when they are big enough to hurt other humans.

During his teen years, he was able to hide his mental issues under a veil of alcohol and marijuana which was easily accessible at the time. He constantly got into trouble at school and at home because of it, but he saw it as an escape from the banalities of life and the troubles that plagued him.

Chase was unable to perform sexually as he couldn't maintain an erection and this made him feel humiliated and unable to connect with other people. When he was 18, he voluntarily went to see a psychiatrist about his erection problem. It was under the counselling of his psychiatrist where he learned it was sometimes caused by the repression of anger.

After leaving his mother's house on the belief that she was trying to poison him, he rented an apartment with some friends. During his time in the apartment, it was said that Chase enjoyed walking around in the nude and was constantly high on multiple types of drugs including LSD.

During his time in the apartment he would go through many flatmates, all of which would complain to him and to the authorities about his bizarre behaviour and heavy drug use. One time he nailed the closet door shut in his bedroom because he thought that people were coming out from the darkness and invading his private space.

He began to develop severe paranoia and started to become a fully-fledged hypochondriac, believing that everything was going wrong with his body. At one point, he entered a hospital looking for the person who had stolen his pulmonary artery. He complained that his bones were coming out through the back of his head causing his skull to split and maintained a belief that his stomach was back to front. He also claimed his heart would stop beating and then start up again after a short amount of time.

Chase would wallow in a pit of paranoid delusions and far-fetched hypochondria, brought on by child abuse and a massive consumption of drugs. When he refused to leave the apartment, his flatmates moved out instead. His newfound isolation afforded him the possibility of acting on darker desires. He started to trap then kill more small animals. He would disembowel them and eat the raw meat. He then moved onto purchasing small pets with the intention of killing them.

Chase was under the delusion that his heart was shrinking. The consumption of raw flesh and the drinking of animal blood could stop his heart disappearing from his body altogether. He believed this to such an extent that he once injected rabbit blood directly into his veins – which didn't go to well, and he was rushed to hospital, where he got the nickname of Dracula.

When he was 25-years-old, he was committed as a paranoid schizophrenic to Beverly Manor Institute for the mentally insane. It is reported that anti-psychotic medicines failed to work on him. This could have meant that his schizophrenia and psychosis may have been caused by the drugs that he had previously consumed.

One day, nurses found him with blood around his mouth, they discovered two dead and mutilated birds outside his window that he had lured for capture. It's quite clear that Chase suffered from a mental disorder early on in his life, brought on by physical abuse and humiliation. He may also have been suffering from Renfield Syndrome, a form of clinical Vampirism. After two stints inside the psychiatric hospitals, he was released in late 1976 after being deemed no longer a risk to society. How wrong they were.

He was able to move into another apartment in the city and restarted trapping cats and dogs to kill and consume. In his trial, his mother claimed that Chase appeared on her doorstep one day with a dead cat. He smiled, threw the cat to the ground and ripped it open with his bare hands. Then he smeared the animal's blood all over his neck and face. In an even more bizarre chain of events, his mother failed to contact anyone over the incident.

This was only a few years before he would kill his human victims and drink their blood in a misconstrued belief that he was keeping himself alive. It was because he believed Nazi's had carried out invasive experiments on him causing him to physically need the blood.

Chase was to become synonymous with the term of serial killer. His monstrous crimes are still talked about, discussed, and used as a basis for television shows to this very day. When some people think of serial killers, they might think of schizophrenic individuals who as a child had a tendency for killing small animals and acting bizarrely. Chase fitted every profile available at the time.

On 29th December 1977, Chase killed Ambrose Griffin, a 51-year-old engineer in the city. After a shopping trip, Griffin returned to his car to get the last of the items. When his wife stepped back outside, she saw her husband on the ground next to the grocery bags. Chase had shot him twice. In hindsight, it was a trial run for darker killings.

One month later, on the evening of 23rd January 1978, Chase attempted to break into a house at 2909 Burnece Street. When a neighbour approached him, he stopped, lit a cigarette, stared at her and casually walked away. That same night, he broke into a house along the street but was interrupted by the owners and he ran off, but not before smearing his excrement on some of their belongings.

He moved down the street to 2360 Tioga Way and casually walked into the home of the Wallin family. He bumped into Teresa Wallin as she was taking out the garbage. Chase shot her three times and dragged her corpse to the bedroom leaving a blood trail through the house. He raped her corpse whilst stabbing her multiple times with a kitchen knife.

Chase then proceeded to carve off her left nipple and cut her torso open below the sternum. He removed her spleen and intestines, cut out her kidneys and sliced her pancreas in half. He then placed the kidneys back inside the body as if they were one organ.

He used a yogurt pot to scoop up the blood from inside her body and drink it. He would then rub her blood over his face and neck. Before he left the house, Chase had gone into the garden, picked up some dog excrement and pushed it into her throat and mouth.

The extreme brutality of the Walling murder was to shock not just California, but the whole of the United States. The media got wind of the story and as the killer seemed to have a fascination with drinking blood, Chase earned the dubious title of 'Vampire of Sacramento'.

Four days later, and just one mile from the Wallin house, the Miroth family would suffer a similar, if not worse fate. Chase entered the Miroth residence and shot dead a family friend named Danny Meredith. He stole his wallet and car keys before rampaging through the home.

He shot and killed 38-year-old Evelyn Miroth, her six-year-old son, Jason Miroth, and her 22-month-old nephew, David Ferreira. He raped Evelyn's corpse, cut her open and took some of her organs out before drinking her blood direct from the body. His desire for cannibalism and necrophilia had left nothing to the imagination.

The investigation moved forward very quickly. Chase hadn't tried to hide what he had done. Evidence was easy to come by and when they searched his apartment they found everything they needed to charge, but it wasn't as if they needed to look that hard.

Everything in the kitchen was blood stained, from the fridge to the drinking glasses. One container had pieces of brain fragments and others had small pieces of bone within them. The electric blender had never been cleaned and contained a mixture of blood from numerous animals.

Before his trial, it was claimed Chase virtually turned into an animal when they tried to extract blood from him for a sample. He was subsequently charged with six counts of murder in the first degree, it was a trial that was to last four months during the course of 1978. On 8th May 1979, after only a few hours, the jury returned the obvious verdict of guilty of six counts of murder in the first degree. He was given the death penalty by gas chamber at San Quentin Prison.

Chase gave a series of bizarre interviews in which he spoke of his fear of Nazis and UFOs. He believed he had been secretly killed by a combination of both, reanimated, and forced to kill others in order to keep himself alive. He asked the interviewer, FBI Agent Robert Ressler, for a radar gun, so that he could capture the Nazi UFOs and bring them to justice for the murders.

Chase's delusions also led him to believe that his blood was turning to powder and that he needed blood from other creatures to replenish it, as his heart was shrinking. He was to begin an appeal on the basis that he was only killing to preserve his own life.

Needless to say that Chase would go onto become the poster boy for a paranoid schizophrenic serial killer and the type of killer your parents would warn you about before you went to sleep. He was also feared by other prisoners due to the extremely violent nature of his crimes.

On Boxing Day 1980, a guard found him dead in his cell. He had committed suicide with an overdose of antidepressants that he had collected and saved. When Chase's body was autopsied, it was found that his heart was in a perfectly healthy condition.

THE FACTS

Born: May 23rd 1950 | Active: 1977-1978

Arrested: January 1978 | Country: USA (California)

Victims: 6 |AKA: Vampire of Sacramento/Dracula

Sentence: Death penalty | Status: Died by suicide in 1980

Chikatilo, Andrei: The Red Ripper

EXTENDED CASE FILE

On December 22nd 1978, Andrei Chikatilo lured nine-year-old Yelena Zakotnova into a secretly purchased house where he attempted to rape her. He failed to maintain an erection and because of her moaning and struggling, he strangled and stabbed her to death. In an interview after his arrest, he stated that in the process of stabbing the child he found himself ejaculating.

1978 was the beginning of the reign of Russia's most evil serial killer. Almost all of his victims suffered sexual assault and mutilation resulting in the murders of 52 children and women. He did however confess to 56 murders. Andrei Chikatilo was one of the most revered killers to have ever tarnished the Russian motherland.

He would share a bed with his mother, in fear of the war. But because of his constant bed-wetting, she would berate and beat him for it. He saw the direct results of Nazi occupation and was recorded as saying that he literally saw bodies being blown up into the air to fall down in a crumpled bloody mess to the dangerous streets below.

The sight of this both scared him and excited him. From this obvious and saturated exposure to things that no human should have seen, he started to develop images of torture in his head. His brother also befell a horrific fate.

'They caught my brother, who was only ten, they ate him, and sold some of his flesh for food.' - Andrei Chikatilo, speaking of a group of Ukrainian men.

Chikatilo's first sexual experience was when he was 17-years-old, with a ten-year-old friend of his sister's. It was the first time he was able to ejaculate, and claimed he was only able to do it with images of torture in his mind. He was normally shy around girls but had wrestled his sister's friend to the ground and forced himself upon her.

Because he couldn't physically rape her, he violently sexually assaulted her instead, a pre-cursor of things to come. After a series of embarrassments when girls his age started to question his impotence, he tried to hang himself in his mother's home but his mother and some neighbours helped to lift the noose off. With the feeling of nothing left in his life and the embarrassment of his failures, he moved away to a small town near Rostov-on-don.

Chikatilo went directly into the army but it didn't last long. When he returned home he tried many times to find a girlfriend but he was still unable to perform sexually, and rumours spread about his sexual inadequacies. He felt humiliated and dreamed about torturing the girls who were cruel to him.

He then went on to become a schoolteacher and did finally get married in a somewhat arranged marriage by his sister. Yet, it was not too long before his wife criticised everything he did, including his actions in the bedroom and inadequacies as a man. It is said that he could only attempt conception by ejaculating onto his hands and then pushing it inside his wife. He felt at that time that his life was a disaster and thus his torture fantasies increased.

When his mother died in 1973, he began abusing some of the girls in his school. It started with gentle touching and stroking but then his lust got the better of him and he began to grope and forcefully touch the girls. He said this made him feel powerful and he enjoyed the feeling it gave him.

Most of the time, the school covered it up with denial and lies instead of prosecution, allowing Chikatilo to get away with it. Some would say that with hindsight, it allowed a pervert to become a killer.

It was December 22nd 1978 and the killing of Yelena Zakotnova that would become the catalyst of further killings. Chikatilo later confirmed that he was only able to achieve orgasm through the stabbing of children and women and that the urge to relive the experience of Zakotnova was too overwhelming.

He claimed he didn't have to go looking for victims, and he didn't have to seek them out, as they were always right there and were usually willing to follow him anywhere. It was however, another three years before he killed his second victim, 17-year-old Larisa Tkachenko, who he lured to a forest to drink vodka where he beat and strangled her to death

Her body was found the next day with mud packed into her mouth. The body had been mutilated with a stick and Andrei's own teeth, and he had completely bitten off one of her nipples. 13-year-old Lyubov Biryuk was his third victim when he dragged her into the bushes from a secluded path. Her body was found with 22 knife wounds to the head, neck and pelvic region.

From then on, Chikatilo no longer attempted to resist the dark urges that were coming to him more often than he could control. He was free of any control and even the fear of being caught was lost on him. He had become a killer and nothing was going to stop him living out his fantasies.

He established a pattern, a plan of luring and killing children and young women in secluded areas. Most of the victims were runaways, sex workers and homeless girls, as they were easy to manipulate and gullible enough to do anything for a good drink.

For the next five victims and those that followed, each had evidence of mutilation to the eye sockets caused by a knife. In some cases, their eyes had been entirely gorged out and either allegedly eaten or disposed of somewhere else.

In 1982, he carried out a particularly horrific murder. Ten-year-old Olga Stalmachenok was lured to a cornfield on the outskirts of her town before she was brutally murdered. Her body was found a few days later, and she had been stabbed 50 times in the head and body, her chest had been ripped open and her lower bowel and uterus had been cut out.

After having already brutally killed 15 children and young women, Chikatilo was arrested on suspicion of some of the murders, at least the ones that could be linked with the eye gorging signature. He had been spotted luring young girls away from bus stops and had a knife and rope in his bag when first arrested.

In 1984, Chikatilo was one of 25,000 suspects, and details of the specifics of the crimes were sent to every police station in Russia. But the crimes were difficult to stomach, later victims appeared beheaded and so badly mutilated that one was even thought to have been caught in a harvesting machine.

The prime suspect became Yuri Kalenik, a 19-year-old who had lived in a home for mentally disabled children. He would return to the home to play games with the younger boys and it had aroused suspicion. The head nurse found him and another boy playing on the trolleys and accosted them. She then asked if they knew anything about the murders and the other boy said that Yuri was the killer.

Amazingly, because of this soft accusation, the authorities believed they had broken the case and found the real killer. For the first few days after his arrest, Yuri was beaten violently by investigators looking for a confession. Knowing that the only way to stop the beatings was to confess, Yuri gave a false confession.

Detective Viktor Burakov took over the investigation and changed direction with the case. Yuri's confession would one day be used as a basis for psychological false confession cases. Yuri even managed to lead them to where the bodies were found, he did this by trying to understand what the police wanted of him, and even followed their direction when at one of the crime scenes. Burakov started to disbelieve Yuri's account but he remained in custody until it could be fully disproven.

Because Chikatilo had a strain of two blood types, he would constantly be discounted from the crimes and would continue to get away with it. Before the Autumn of 1984, the investigation had attributed 24 victims to the then unnamed murderer. Semen found at each of the bodies matched up to blood type AB, yet every suspect who had that blood type was either found having an alibi or the incorrect personality match. The investigation was going out of control, and the police and detectives knew nothing more than when they first started.

Chikatilo the killed one victim every two weeks and the investigation could not work out how he was choosing his victims and why the evidence didn't seem to match up. The main issue was in the blood type against the original suspects list. It was the removal of that complete list that was causing the investigation to hit a dead end at every turn.

In August 1985, another body appeared near a small airport outside Moscow, the young girl's body had been mutilated and exposed. Investigator Burakov went to the Capital to examine the victim and was in no doubt that it was the same killer. Moscow detectives linked the killing of three young boys where one had been raped and one had been decapitated. At the same time, Burakov was called back to Shakhty where an 18-year-old girl was found dead with leaves stuffed into her mouth. If any of this sounds slightly familiar, then you might have seen the film, *Child 44*, with Gary Oldman and Tom Hardy. The film is very loosely based on the Chikatilo murders.

On the girl's body they found the same blood type AB, red and blue thread under her fingernails, and a single strand of grey hair. It was the most physical evidence found so far on any of the victims, so the investigation brought in serial killer specialist, Chief Investigator Issa Kostoyev. Issa believed they had already come across the killer during their investigation but did not know it at the time, which was a low-blow to Burakov's investigation. Issa began profiling the killer and used American profiling books that detailed cases of dismemberment and disfiguring of a killer's victims.

'Some killers were driven merely by arrogance and the idea that their victims were objects that belonged to them to do with as they pleased.' – Issa Kostoyev

Issa discovered that Burakov's investigation had resulted in five false confessions, including that of Yuri Kalenik, who was still remanded in custody. Issa was furious and ordered all the information on all crime scenes to be compiled into one report and sent to everyone within the flawed investigation. Then, having finally got hold of all the crime scene reports and known data, a Dr. Bukhanovsky spent months compiling a 65-page report on the suspect. He labelled the suspect; Killer X.

He referred to Killer X as a necro-sadist; someone who needed to watch people die in order to achieve sexual gratification. He believed the multiple stabbing was a way to enter the victims sexually where the killer could not physically do so. The deepest cuts were representative of the height of his sexual pleasure. He even went as far as stating that Killer X mutilated or removed the eyes because he believed in the superstition that his image would be left on them.

Suddenly the investigation began picking up pace, and with the report, the profiling and the evidence, they looked close to catching their killer. Then, just as suddenly as moral picked up again, the murders stopped and the investigation dried up. It would remain static for another six years.

Chikatilo had become wary and followed the investigation down to the most intimate detail. He held onto his urges somewhat and tried to change his methods of murder. He moved his killings away from Rostov-on-don to the Ukraine and further afield Ural towns in Russia, many of them were not ever linked to him at the time until after his confession.

It was six years later, in 1990, after the discovery of even more bodies linked to the same killer, that a massive police operation got under way. Saturation of nearby bus stops, train stations and public gardens were evident by the amount of police acting as a deterrent. It was the biggest police investigation in Russia's history at the time. It seemed as though everyone had been involved at some point along the way.

On November 6th 1990, Chikatilo killed his last victim, ending a serial killer's reign that began 12 years earlier. He was arrested coming out of a cafe after being watched actively seeking out young females to talk to and attempt to lure. Police arrested Chikatilo and placed him in a cell with a gifted informant but he was not willing to admit or say anything against himself.

The next day, Kostoyev chose to handle the interrogation himself. It was a meeting of a serial killer and detective that some would fill their books with, such was the information that eventually came out of it. Chikatilo confessed to being a sexual deviant but for days never actually confessed to having anything to do with the murders.

A medical examination showed that Andrei Chikatilo's blood type was 'A' which was different to the blood type found in his other bodily fluids. Chikatilo's semen had a very weak type 'B' antibody making him an exceedingly rare case. But it would not have been enough to stand up in court if the entire investigation were to rely on his rare blood type.

They needed a real confession and it would be down to Dr. Bukhanovsky to finally get the confession from him, who agreed to question him but only out of a professional interest and not from a legal standpoint. Chikatilo would later say that he gave up everything to Dr. Bukhanovsky because he seemed to be the only person who ever really understood him. Finally, he broke down and admitted that he had done everything and more.

It was immediately apparent that the initial number of 36 victims was going to be a long way off the final number. Chikatilo remembered the details of each of his murders and would go through them in turn, one by one. He would never stick to a pattern, some murders were planned, others were opportunistic killings. He would also squat beside the bodies and cut them so as not to get blood on his clothes. Chikatilo would sometimes go as far as putting his semen inside a uterus that he had removed from a victim, then, as he walked along a path, he would chew on it.

'The cries, the blood and the agony gave me relaxation and a certain pleasure.' - Chikatilo.

He claimed the reason for mutilating or cutting out his victim's eyes was because he had initially believed an old urban legend that the image of a murderer is left imprinted on the eyes of the victim. It confirmed the same fact that had been written in Dr. Bukhanovsky's report.

He enjoyed playing with the blood of his victims and confessed to tearing at the victim's genitalia, nipples, tongues and lips with his teeth. He chewed upon the uterus of his female victims and the testicles of his few male victims. But he still maintained that he never ate them, he simply chewed and discarded. He was ultimately found guilty of 52 murders and sentenced to death for each and every one.

In 1992, another Russian serial killer, Alexander Pichushkin, came to the fore. Upon his arrest in 2006, he talked about Andrei Chikatilo in his own confessions. He claimed that he wanted to kill more than Chikatilo and some say he might have succeeded. For it is a dark part of human nature that when one serial killer is captured, there will always be another in the shadows, awaiting his or her time in the spotlight.

THE FACTS

Born: October 16th 1936 | Active: 1978-1990

Arrested: November 20th 1990 | Country: Soviet Union

Victims: 52-56 | AKA: The Red Ripper/The Butcher of Rostov

Sentence: Death penalty |Status: Executed by shooting on February 16th 1994

Choon-Jae, Lee: Hwaseong Serial Murders

For 30 years, the infamous Hwaseong Serial Murders in South Korea remained unsolved until a convict in jail for killing his sister-in-law in 1994, confessed to killing an additional 14 women. Lee Choon-Jae was later confirmed to have killed 10 women from the Hwaseong Serial Murder list by way of DNA evidence.

From 1986 to 1991, at least ten females between the age of 14-years-old to 71-years-old were found tied, raped and strangled with their own clothing. Until 2019, the murders remained unsolved and one of the country's most notorious unsolved crimes.

Serial killing is rare in South Korea, or at the least, not brought into the public eye. This is one of the only cases where a killer using the same modus operandi had been identified in the country. Because of the ridiculous notion of statute of limitations, the killings could not be investigated after 2006 and the murders fell into the graveyard of the unsolved.

Statute of limitations means that there is a maximum time limit placed on crimes for when legal proceedings can be brought to an individual. Many Western countries have a statute of limitations in place. The United Kingdom is the exception in that there is no current time limit in place.

A list of over 21,000 suspects was put together over the years but it wasn't until 2019 when Choon-Jae was revealed as the killer. He was already in prison serving a life sentence for the murder of his sister-in-law but due to the statute of limitations will never be tried for the Hwaseong Serial Murders, despite irrefutable DNA evidence and his own confession. He does, however, remain in a South Korean prison, where he is likely to stay for the rest of his life.

THE FACTS

Born: January 31st 1963 | Active: 1986-1994

Arrested: 1994 | Country: South Korea.

Victims: 11-15 | AKA: Hwaseong Serial Murders

Sentence: Life imprisonment | Status: Incarcerated

Christiansen, Thor Nis

A Danish-American serial killer from California who killed four women with an intention of killing more. He had been obsessed with the idea of shooting women and having sex with their corpses from an early age. After moving to California from Denmark with his family at a young age, Christiansen struggled to fit in. When he reached school-age he began drinking alcohol and smoking copious amounts of marijuana, leading him to putting on a large amount of weight.

In his late teens, he moved out of his parents' house, dropped out of high school, and began working as a gas station attendant. In late 1976, he stole a 0.22 calibre pistol from a friend, as he was overcome with fantasies of shooting women and decided to act on his fantasies.

(ATTRIB A95)

(ATTRIB A96)

HADDEN IRVING CLARK

(ATTRIB A97)

LEE CHOON-JAE

THOR NIS CHRISTIANSEN

(ATTRIB A98)

He would find his victims while they were hitchhiking for a lift, then he would shoot them in the head. The murders became known as the 'Look-alike Murders', due to the similar look of his victims. Once he killed them, he would drag them away from the roadside to engage in necrophiliac acts with their bodies.

In a bizarre twist, a fifth victim, Lydia Preston, was shot in the head in April 1979 but miraculously survived. After her recovery, she spotted Christiansen in another bar and immediately reported him to police, leading to his capture.

Christiansen was killed in prison in 1981, aged 23, after being stabbed in the exercise yard of Folsom State Prison. Psychiatrists had predicted that he might be killed in prison, as he was young with blonde hair, and his last victim was African-American. His own killer has never been found.

THE FACTS

Born: December 28th 1957 | Active: 1976-1979

Arrested: July 7th 1979 | Country: USA

Victims: 4 | AKA: The Look-alike Murders

Sentence: Life imprisonment | Status: Killed in prison in 1981

Ciudad Juarez Rebels, The

The Ciudad Juárez Rebels is the name of a group of Mexican serial killers who claimed their victims between 1995 and 1996, in Ciudad Juarez. The leaders of the group were Sergio Armendáriz Diaz and Juan Contreras Jurado. There were three other members who would also be sentenced in 2005.

A victim of one of their most notorious crimes was discovered on April 7th 1996. The torso of 17-year-old sales assistant Rosario García Leal was found in an abandoned parking lot on the outskirts of the city. She had vanished in December 1995 and had been subjected to sexual assault before being stabbed to death. It was also suggested by the coroner that she had been kept alive for at least a month before the group killed her

Where she had been discovered, further bone fragments were also found belonging to other victims of the group. On April 8th 1996, a member of a different gang was arrested and confessed to taking part in Leal's kidnapping, leading police to the Ciudad Juárez Rebels. 10 members of the gang were arrested, with five confessing to the murders of eight women. They were subsequently convicted of all eight murders and sentenced to life in prison. It has long been suspected they could have killed up to 14 people between them.

THE FACTS

Active: 1995-1996 | Arrested: 1996 (all members)

Country: Mexico | Victims: 8-14

AKA: Sergio Armendáriz Diaz and Juan Contreras Jurado (Group leaders)

Sentence: Life imprisonment (all members) | Status: Incarcerated

Clark, Hadden Irving: The Cross-dressing Cannibal

EXTENDED CASE FILE

There is perhaps nothing scarier than the killer who eats their victims. We are drawn to these grim cases of evil wrongdoings with a macabre fascination for how they played out and the reasons behind them. True crime has a way of drawing us in and gripping hold of us tight.

It's bad enough when one person is convicted of cannibalism but coming from a family of cannibals is something on a whole other level. For Hadden Irving Clark, AKA: The Cross-dressing Cannibal, he was simply following in the footsteps of his brother – who killed and ate his girlfriend.

Hadden was suspected of being a serial killer but it had never been confirmed. He is known to have killed two people, one child and one adult, but it has been suggested he killed more when he confessed to killing dozens since 1974.

Born in Troy, New York, in 1952, his childhood was far from peaceful, at least behind closed doors. His parents promoted the image of a perfect family life, his father was a chemist, whose job was high-earning enough to keep them in good stead. Behind closed doors, it was quite different.

His parents were closet alcoholics and were violent towards each other and their children. When his mother was drunk, she referred to Hadden as Kristen, and made him wear girl's clothing, due to her anger that she was birthed a boy instead of a girl.

This had a long-lasting effect on Hadden, and he would dress in women's clothes for most of his private life, even going as far as believing there was a female entity within him that he couldn't control. He would claim that his female alter-ego was responsible for the crimes he committed.

After his father committed suicide when he was a teenager, Hadden's downward spiral to death and madness began. His mother moved the family to Maryland where Hadden turned to torturing and killing small animals. He also bullied other children and was generally anti-social.

He had two brothers and one sister, one of whom was Bradfield Clark , who was convicted of killing and cannibalising a woman who had spurned his sexual advances in 1984. Bradfield had invited Patricia 'Trish' Mak and her husband to a barbecue but Trish's husband couldn't make it, so she went alone to Bradfield's house.

After a night of heavy drinking, Trish refused to be his girlfriend, and Bradfield responded by slamming her head against a wall, strangling her, and cutting up her body. He sliced off her breasts and cooked them on the barbecue grill. He confessed to his crime and was convicted of the murder. If that was bad enough, what Hadden did was even worse.

Hadden's only sister ran away from home as a teenager and later proclaimed that she didn't have a family, relating to them by name only. Who could blame her? Her brothers ended up eating people, after all.

Hadden already had a reputation for being evil by the time his brother was incarcerated. If anyone crossed him or dared to belittle him then he would kill their pets, sometimes leaving the decapitated bodies on their doorsteps.

He trained as a chef and served in the United States Navy until he was discharged after being diagnosed with paranoid schizophrenia. A doctor's report later divulged that Hadden believed birds and squirrels spoke to him, signs of extreme delusion and psychosis – but it was left untreated.

After being discharged from the Navy, Hadden's condition deteriorated and he moved from job to job without a focus, taking cash-in-hand wherever he could. He drifted across the State of Maryland, virtually homeless, and wallowing in his ever-worsening delusions. Occasionally returning to his mother's home to beat her and leave dead animals on the porch.

While living a drifter lifestyle, he was arrested a number of times for various crimes. On one occasion, he vandalised a landlord's property with a hammer then stole some items from the home. But not before killing the landlord's cats and scattering rotten fish heads throughout the property.

He also dressed as a woman to steal purses from churches and residential homes. He pled guilty on all occasions but was never given jail time.

He later claimed to police that he had been killing since 1974, when he was 22-years-old, but the first confirmed – and soon-to-be convicted – murder, occurred on 31st May 1986. He killed a six-year-old girl named Michelle Dorr, who was a friend of his niece, Eliza Clark.

Michelle had grown bored of playing alone and wandered down the street looking for Eliza, but she wasn't in. Clark then lured her to an upstairs room in his brother's house – the only brother to not be in prison. He followed her upstairs, telling her that Eliza was in her bedroom.

When she stepped into the room, he pushed Michelle to the floor and slashed her with a knife on her back before stabbing her in the throat. He attempted to have sex with her corpse but instead resorted to eating parts of her body and drinking her blood. He then squashed the corpse into a bag, cleaned up most of the blood, and buried the girl in a nearby remote park.

Six years after his first confirmed kill, Hadden claimed his second confirmed kill when he murdered 23-year-old Harvard Graduate, Laura 'Hoho' Houghteling, in Bethesda, Maryland, on 18th October 1992. Since the murder of Michelle, Hadden had taken to dressing as a woman and would do so in public, never truly sure of his sexuality, which had been warped by an abusive mother. Hadden had taken a small job as a gardener for Laura's mother, Penny, when she accused him of stealing tools from the shed. Angry at the accusations, Hadden took his revenge. He entered the family home in women's clothes, then stabbed Laura to death while she was in her bedroom.

He suffocated her with a pillow to ensure she was dead, wrapped her in a blanket, then dragged the body to another remote wooded area and buried her. He later returned to the house, dressed in a wig and women's clothes and walked out the front door, pretending to be his victim, so that people thought Laura was still alive if spotted.

He was caught when a fingerprint on one of Laura's pillows came back as a match for him, due to the records from his previous arrests. He was taken into custody where he confessed, leading police to the body less than a year later.

Realising Hadden's brother was convicted of murder, and linking missing persons cases to his movements, forensic experts descended on the locations he had lived, along with the home where Michelle had been killed. They found traces of Michelle's blood on the wooden floorboards in the upstairs bedroom.

Hadden led them to where he buried Michelle, and then confessed to murdering dozens of women, even claiming to be the killer of the infamous Lady of the Dunes murder. He told police they would find the remains of another victim on his grandparent's property.

When police dug up and searched the grounds of the residence, they didn't find any trace of a body. However, they did find a plastic tub which was full to the brim of over 200 pieces of jewellery, including one of Laura's rings. This meant that Hadden had taken trophies from his victims, along with their flesh.

When questioned about the other pieces of jewellery, Hadden simply said that they had come from his other victims. Despite running checks on the jewellery, investigators were unable to link the pieces to other cases but suspected that at least some of the trinkets did belong to more potential victims.

In 1993, Clark was convicted of the murder of Laura Houghteling and sentenced to 30 years in prison, despite claiming it was his female personality that killed her. In 1999, after another trial, he was convicted of the murder of six-year-old Michelle Dorr and was sentenced to an additional 30 years in prison.

If the jewellery in the tub is anything to go by, then it could stand to reason that the cross-dressing cannibal may indeed have claimed many more victims. He is currently incarcerated at the Eastern Correctional Institution in Westover, Maryland

"I think I have a split personality. I don't like to hurt people but I do things I am not aware of." – Hadden Irving Clark

"We're dealing with a serial killer here. We don't know how many people he killed. The fact is, he was a transient and moved around. How much is truth and how much of it's not? He was a highly active guy for quite a long period of time." – Police Chief Richard Rosenthal – in a press interview for APB news. (2000).

THE FACTS

Born: April 1951 | Active: 1986-1992

Arrested: November 6th 1992 | Country: USA

Victims: 2+ | AKA: The Cross-dressing Cannibal

Sentence: Total of 60 years imprisonment | Status: Incarcerated

Clepper, Gregory

In Chicago, on April 23rd 1996, Gregory Clepper murdered 30-year-old Patricia Scott. He raped and strangled her before pushing her body into a trash bin behind a High School with the help of his own mother and a friend, who were later charged with helping to dispose of the body. Upon his arrest a few days later on May 2nd, Clepper was linked to another 12 murders, under the moniker of the Chicago Southside Strangler.

Clepper was described as a sexual predator, one whose sole motivation was sexual. He was arrested after an acquaintance called the police because Clepper had been bragging about one of his murders. Once the murders were linked, the timeline of his crimes became clear.

It started five years earlier in 1991 when bodies began turning up in garbage bins all over Chicago, almost all of them had been raped or violently sexually abused. At the time, law enforcement wasn't making any connections with the victims and it wasn't until Clepper's arrest that the murders were linked.

To secure a conviction, prosecutors dropped 12 murder charges in exchange for a confession of the murder of Patricia Scott. Clepper was subsequently sentenced to 80 years in prison for the murder without the possibility of parole. As time went on, Clepper was linked to another 15 murders but confessed to killing over 40, which would make him Chicago's most notorious serial killer by body count.

The Chicago Southside Strangler was a moniker given to a serial killer active in Chicago from the 1990s to the 2000s. Over the years, multiple serial killers have been caught and linked with the moniker including Andre Crawford, Hubert Geralds, Kevin Taylor, and of course Clepper. In January 2021, a new investigation began that looked into unsolved murders related to Clepper, which continues to this day.

THE FACTS

Born: 1968 | Active: 1991-1996

Arrested: May 2nd 1996 | Country: USA (Chicago)

Victims: 1-15+ | Sentence: 80 years in prison | Status: Incarcerated

Cole, Carroll

Cole was mostly drunk when he killed his victims but still claimed to have killed 35 women across several states in America, although 15 women and one boy were evidentially linked. Most victims were strangled in parking lots and he would sometimes take their bodies home to sleep with their corpses because they reminded him of his mother.

He claimed he first kill at the age of 10, when he drowned a boy of the same age in a local river. The death of the boy had been listed as an accident until Cole's confession. During his childhood, while his father was fighting in World War Two, Cole was physically abused by his mother, including being whipped, beaten, and forced to watch her adulterous relationships.

Aside from the murder of the boy, which he claimed was opportunistic, he acted out on his dark fantasies when he was 33-years-old. He began picking up women for sex and using sex workers on regular occasions and was known to have been rough with his women. He decided to kill those who were married, simply because they reminded him of his mother, who he had grown to hate.

There have been multiple reports that he ate some of his victims but it has never been proven. It is suggested he falsely claimed he ate his victims to get an insanity charge but at his trial in Texas, in 1981, he was convicted of three murders and sentenced to life with no parole. In February 1984, he was sent to Nevada for a new trial where he was sentenced to death for the murders of two females in 1977 and 1979. A year later on December 6th 1985, Cole was executed by lethal injection, having confessed to 35 murders.

THE FACTS

Born: May 9th 1938 | Active: 1947-1980

Arrested: 1980 | Country: USA (California/Texas/Nevada)

Victims: 5-35 | Sentence: Death penalty

Status: Executed by lethal injection on December 6th 1985

Colonial Parkway Murders, The.

EXTENDED CASE FILE

Between 1986 and 1989, an unidentified serial killer was suspected of killing at least eight people along or nearby the Colonial Parkway of the United States

Commonwealth of Virginia. Three couples were murdered and one couple went missing. It has also been suggested that another two people may have fallen victim to the same killer.

In most countries, the construction of highways or motorways was one of the reasons why serial killing increased through the 1970s and reached a peak in the 1980s. Life was also made extremely difficult for law enforcement because of various state boundaries that existed. It also meant that a serial killer's potential victim might not be recognised as such due to the then disconnected reporting between authorities. The highways provided an opportunity where there wasn't one before.

The four double homicides in the four year period were referred to as The Colonial Parkway Murders. The first recorded murders took place on October 9th 1986, when 21-year-old student Rebecca Ann Dowski and 27-year-old Cathleen Marian Thomas disappeared while out together. It wasn't until October that a jogger spotted a white car alongside the York River. Inside the car, both Thomas and Dowski were found dead, they had been strangled and mutilated.

A coroner's report confirmed they had been tied with rope, strangled and then had their throats slit. Gasoline had been poured on the bodies to hide evidence but the killer or killers had been unable to light it. Their belongings were found in the car meaning that it hadn't been a robbery. Since the murders took place on federal property, the case fell under FBI jurisdiction. Over 150 fingerprints were found in and around the car but did not match any person on the FBI database – and still haven't to this day.

On September 22nd 1987, in Isle of Wight County, Virginia, 20-year-old David Knobling and 14-year-old Robin Edwards were found shot to death. The dating couple were discovered in the Ragged Island Wildlife Refuge, on the south shore of the James River. The two bodies were found by Knobling's father and a search party who were scouring the edges of the river.

According to those who knew them, Robin was an older-looking 14-year-old and had been known for dating older men. However, if the relationship was a sexual one then it would have been illegal under the laws at the time. No shell casings were found and some believe a revolver could have been the murder weapon. Since the Ragged Island Wildlife Refuge was state property, the case was taken over by the state police and not the FBI.

On April 9th 1988, 18-year-old Cassandra Lee Hailey and 20-year-old Richard Keith Call went missing. Richard's abandoned vehicle was found on the Colonial Parkway, only three miles from where the bodies of the two previous victims were discovered. The keys were still in the ignition and the driver's side door was left open.

Their disappearance has never been solved but it has been suggested they may have been murdered, as all the clothes they were wearing when they had gone missing were found inside the car. The case fell under FBI jurisdiction, much to the displeasure of the local police. Richard's family said the car must have been positioned in its resting place on purpose after the alleged killing, because the couple had never used that section of road.

On September 5th 1989, 18-year-old Annamaria Phelps and 21-year-old Daniel Lauer disappeared. At the time of the disappearance, Annamaria had been dating Daniel's brother and was assumed to be having an affair with Daniel. Their bodies were found by deer hunters in the area on October 19th 1989, at a secluded logging road.

The area they were found in was 30 miles away from the I-64 ramp onto Colonial Parkway. The two deer hunters had come across a blanket in the woods, when they lifted it up they found the skeletal remains. Although cause of death could not be determined, knife marks were found on the bones of Annamaria, suggesting a violent demise.

There were two more murders that may have been connected with the Colonial Parkway murders. In 1996, 24-year-old Julie Williams and her girlfriend 26-year-old Lollie Winans, were backpacking through the Shenandoah National Park with their Golden Retriever, where they set up camp just a few feet away from a horse trail. They were last seen by a park ranger who renewed their camping permit and dropped them off at the Stony Man car park.

When they were reported missing, park rangers found their car and the dog, who was freely roaming the area. They then found both bodies nearby. The couple had been bound and gagged with duct tape and were half-naked, their throats had been cut so deeply they were virtually decapitated. It has never been clear whether these two murders were the work of the same killer who was operating in the mid to late 1980s, but it hasn't been ruled out.

In 2010, Detective Steve Spingola released a document regarding the murders and suggested there may have been three separate killers. He also claimed that the

Thomas and Dowski murder might be connected to the Shenandoah murders of Lollie Winans and Julie Williams. He theorized that the two double murders could have been the work of a serial killer targeting lesbian couples.

Some other investigators believe that the killings might have been committed by someone who worked in law enforcement. The windows on the cars were all wound down, leading one investigator to suggest that the only reason to have done so was if they were being pulled over by an officer or ranger.

A deputy who was around at the time, named Fred Atwell, has constantly been mentioned as a person of interest. Most families of the victims stated that his obsession with the murders was unhealthy, and he had worked his way into their lives, too intimately to just be friendly. He was arrested in 2011 for robbing a woman at gunpoint but has never been charged with the murders. There was a fresh appeal in 2021 for new information but the Colonial Parkway Murders remain unsolved.

THE FACTS

Active: 1986-1989 | Country: USA (Virginia)

Victims: 8-10 | Status: Unsolved

Cook, Anthony and Nathaniel

The serial killer brothers raped and murdered white people in Ohio from the 1970s to the 1980s. Both brothers were long-haul truck drivers and claimed a total of nine victims during their campaign of racially motivated violence.

They would generally kill their victims by either shooting them or beating them with a baseball bat, and in some instances; a concrete block. They would take advantage of young lovers parked in isolated locations.

In 1973 they raped and murdered a 12-year-old girl together, which only came out at their trial. From 1980 to 1981, they committed at least nine rapes and murders between them.

IMAGE ATTRIBUTIONS
(ATTRIB A62) TO (ATTRIB A69)

THE EIGHT KNOWN VICTIMS OF THE COLONIAL PARKWAY MURDERS

AS OF 2020, THE IDENTITY OF THE KILLER REMAINS A MYSTERY

COLONIAL PARKWAY MURDERS

The pair were arrested in 1981, with Anthony initially being convicted of murdering a real estate agent. It wasn't until the early 1990s when DNA evidence improved, that the investigation was able to link both brothers to multiple cold case murders.

In 2000, Anthony pleaded guilty to nine counts of murder while Nathaniel pleaded guilty to three murders. Both accepted a plea bargain to avoid the death penalty. Nathaniel was released on parole in 2018 under strict conditions. Anthony remains in prison with the next parole date set for 2025.

THE FACTS

Born: March 9th 1949 (Anthony)/October 25th 1958 (Nathaniel)

Active: 1973-1981 | Arrested: 1981

Country: USA (Ohio) | Victims: 9

Sentence: Nathaniel (15-75 years)/Anthony (15 years to life)

Status: Nathaniel was released on August 8th 2018/Anthony remains in prison

Conahan Jr., Daniel Owen: The Hog Trail Killer

Active in Florida over a two year period in the mid-1990s, Conahan, AKA: The Hog Trail Killer, would be convicted of one murder but positively linked to at least five more. Conahan had come out as gay during his school years, and his parents were not happy with the decision. Thinking it to be an illness, they sent him to a psychiatrist, which forced him to repress his feelings.

He joined the U.S. Navy shortly after school but was discharged in 1978 when he was the cause of a large fight because of his actions towards other men. In 1995, he became a nurse and worked at the Charlotte Regional Medical Center in Punta Gorda but by that point, he had already killed at least two of his victims.

On January 1st 1996, a family living in North Port, Florida, were in for a shock. Their family dog had gone outside and wondered back in with a human skull hanging from its mouth. Police then discovered more bones and pieced together a skeleton. The victim bore resemblance to the body of another skeleton found in 1994, which has never been identified.

On March 7th 1996, the body of John William Melaragno was discovered in North Port. Melaragno had been murdered just ten days prior to his discovery. His body had been mutilated and his genitals had been hacked at but he wouldn't be identified until June 1999. On April 17th, investigators found a man's skull in the woods nearby, and a few hours later they uncovered the rest of the body, who was identified shortly after as Kenneth Lee Smith. A few more hours passed and another man's body was discovered nearby.

The second victim was identified as Richard Allen Montgomery, he had been raped and mutilated and his body dumped in the woods the day prior to the discovery. As soon as the media got wind of two bodies in the woods, talk of a serial killer operating in the area began to do the rounds.

On July 3rd 1996, Conahan was arrested after a number of different witness statements pointed him out as a possible suspect, and his DNA was positively linked to the body of Montgomery. While in custody, further skeletal remains were discovered in the county including one who had been reported missing in 1993.

On August 17th 1999, Conahan was found guilty of the first-degree murder of Montgomery and sentenced to death. But the story of the skeletons didn't end there. On March 23rd 2007, eight different skulls and skeletal remains were discovered in some woods in Fort Myers, Florida. Every single one of them were linked to Conahan and were found only a mile away from the attempted murder site of Stanley Burden who Conahan had tied to a tree and raped in 1994. As of 2022, Conahan remains on death row in Florida.

THE FACTS

Born: May 11th 1954 | Active: 1993-1996

Arrested: July 3rd 1996 | Country: USA (Florida)

Victims: 6+ | AKA: The Hog Trail Killer

Sentence: Death penalty | Status: Death row

Connecticut River Valley Killer, The

EXTENDED CASE FILE

The Connecticut River Valley Killer is a suspected and as yet unidentified serial killer who is linked to at least seven murders on the New Hampshire and Vermont border. The murders took place over a nine-year period from 1978 to 1987.

On October 24th 1978, 27-year-old Cathy Millican was seen photographing birds at the Chandler Brook Wetland Preserve in New London, New Hampshire. The next day, her body was found only a few feet away from where she had been seen. She had been stabbed 29 times in a brutal attack.

On July 25th 1981, 37-year-old student Mary Elizabeth Critchley, disappeared while hitchhiking near Interstate 91 at the Massachusetts and Vermont border. Two weeks later, her body was discovered in a wooded area in New Hampshire. Due to the viciousness of the attack and exposure to the elements, the coroner was unable to give an official cause of death.

On May 30th 1984, another hitchhiker on Route 12 went missing. 17-year-old nurse Bernice Courtemanche vanished in New Hampshire. It wasn't until April 9th 1986, that her remains were found by a fisherman. In that instance, the cause of death was listed as knife wounds to the neck and head.

In New Hampshire on July 20th 1984, another nurse, 27-year-old Ellen Fried, vanished after calling her sister from a pay phone in Claremont. She spoke to her sister about a strange car that was coming and going along the road. Her own car was found abandoned the next day, just a few miles away from the pay phone. Her remains were found over a year later at a wooded area near the banks of the Sugar River. The coroner's report confirmed she had been stabbed to death.

A year later on July 10th 1985, 27-year-old Eva Morse vanished after hitchhiking home from work in Charlestown, New Hampshire. A logger found her remains a year later, reports showed she too had been stabbed in the neck multiple times.

On April 25th 1986, 36-year-old Lynda Moore was working in her yard at her home in Vermont. She was stabbed to death in broad daylight during a violent struggle and was found dead later that day by her husband. Witnesses claimed they saw a suspicious man in the area and a police sketch was subsequently drawn up which led them nowhere.

On January 10th 1987, In Stratton, Vermont, a 38-year-old nurse named Barbara Agnew was stabbed to death in her car during a snowstorm. She had been returning from a skiing trip but never made it home. A snowplough driver found the car at a rest stop and went to see if the driver needed assistance. The window was cracked and blood covered the steering wheel, but there was no one inside. Agnew wouldn't be discovered until March 28th 1987, when her body was found beside an apple tree in Windsor County.

Another possible link to the killings was the April 6th 1988 stabbing of seven-month pregnant Jane Boroski. She had stopped her car to use a vending machine in Winchester, New Hampshire. A man was waiting at her car when she returned and accused her of hurting his own girlfriend. Boroski ran off in fear but the man stabbed her 27 times.

Miraculously, she survived, crawled back to her car and drove to a friend's house two miles away. At one point, she ended up behind the attacker's car but luckily wasn't spotted. Both Boroski and her child survived. Although her daughter grew up to live a relatively normal life, she was diagnosed with minor cerebral palsy due to having suffered brain damage during the attack.

As part of the investigation, Jane Boroski was put under hypnosis. She managed to describe the attack in detail and remembered that the attacker seemed extremely calm and collected. When she stopped struggling with him, he seemed to lose interest and ceased his attack. She also described the car and partial number plate but it has never been traced and the attacker has never been caught. After her attack, the killings stopped.

Many theories regarding the identity of the killer have been put forward in the years that followed. An Idaho police officer concluded that the police sketch was that of a convicted criminal who was in prison shortly after but nothing was confirmed. Another suspect was Michael Nicholaou, a former Army helicopter pilot who served in the Vietnam War.

He was accused of killing civilians in Vietnam and was discharged from the Army because of it. He claimed to have been bitter about the discharge but there are no details as to how he might have killed people in Vietnam. It is also claimed that he was responsible for the murder of his first wife but was never convicted. There is also no DNA evidence linking him to the murders.

Delbert Tallman was another suspect who confessed to killing a woman in 1984. Her murder was similar to most of the Connecticut River murders, but he withdrew his confession and was found not-guilty of her murder. It remains unclear why he withdrew his confession.

Gary Westover was also a suspect who confessed to being involved in the murder of Barbara Agnew; the final 1987 victim. He claimed to have abducted her with three other men and murdered her in the woods. He died shortly after the confession and no further evidence linked him to the crime. As of 2022, the case of the Connecticut River Valley Killer remains unsolved.

THE FACTS

Active: 1978-1987 | Country: USA (Hampshire/Vermont)

Victims: 7+ | Status: Unsolved

Constanzo, Adolfo de Jesús: The Narcosatanist

American serial killer and cult leader Adolfo de Jesús Constanzo was responsible for the deaths of numerous people through ritualistic killings with members of his cult. He was also a drug dealer and ran a cult named The Narcosatanists.

He was nicknamed the Godfather by his disciples and took part in multiple murders within Mexico. By 1987, Constanzo had started to believe that his magic was responsible for the success of the Mexican drug cartels and wished to be a business partner to a crime syndicate known as The Calzadas. When they rejected his wishes, seven members of the Calzadas family were brutally murdered. They were later found with body parts missing. Most of them had their brain removed and one had his entire spine ripped out. The spinal column was never discovered.

In 1988, Constanzo moved the cult to a ranch in the Mexican desert where together they carried out more ritual murders. They started killing drifters and other rival drug dealers. On March 13th 1989, cult members abducted American student Mark Kilroy from a Mexican bar. He was taken back to the ranch where Constanzo killed him in front of his cult.

The American authorities pressured the Mexican police to get answers on Kilroy's disappearance. The investigation ultimately led to Constanzo and the infamous ranch, where fifteen mutilated corpses were unearthed. They also discovered a ritualistic cauldron which contained dead black cats and human brains.

Constanzo died in a firefight with Mexican police when he fled to Mexico City with some of the cult. Police were called to his apartment on an unrelated dispute, and not wanting to go to prison, Constanzo got into a gun fight with them. A total of 14 cult members were subsequently sentenced to 60 years each. Most are still incarcerated to this day.

THE FACTS

Born: November 1st 1962 | Active: 1986-1989

Country: Mexico | Victims: 15+

AKA: Adolfo de Jesús Constanzo/The Narcosatanist/The Godfather

Status: Killed in a shoot-out in 1989

Copeland, Faye and Ray

American serial killing couple Faye Della Wilson Copeland and Ray Copeland killed at least five people at their Missouri farm between 1986 and 1989. They ended up becoming the oldest couple to be sentenced to death, when Faye was 69, and Ray was 76.

Ray was born in Oklahoma in 1914 and began life taking part in petty crime such as stealing livestock for financial gain. He spent a year in prison for his petty crimes and was released in 1940 when he met Faye, whom he married shortly after. It would be 46 years later that they would claim their first victim.

(ATTRIB A99)

FAYE & RAY COPELAND

RICHARD FRANCIS COTTINGHAM

(ATTRIB A100)

(ATTRIB A101)

LOUIS CRAINE

SOMERSET HOSPITAL WHERE CULLEN KILLED 13 OF HIS VICTIMS

(ATTRIB A102) + (ATTRIB A103)

CHARLES CULLEN

Before 1986, Ray had spent decades perfecting illegal money-making methods which involved everything from scamming cattle auctions to not paying farm workers. He began employing drifters on his farm and used them to purchase cattle with bounced checks but when it didn't work the way he wanted it to, he moved up to murder.

In 1989, a previous drifter employee phoned the authorities through a Crimestoppers phone number and claimed he had seen human bones and remains on the farm. He also stated that Ray had assaulted him in a botched murder attempt. Police descended on the farm and the investigation found three male bodies in a barn. Later excavations unearthed further remains.

The Copelands were convicted on five counts of murder. Faye was handed down four death sentences and life without parole. Ray was sentenced to death but he died of natural causes in 1993 whilst on death row. In 1999, Faye's death sentences were commuted to life but following a stroke she was granted medical parole to a nursing home. She too died of natural causes, two days before Christmas Day in 2003. It has been suggested that the couple may have killed up to 12 people on the farm but only five have ever been confirmed.

THE FACTS

Born: December 30th 1914 (Ray)/August 4th 1921 (Faye)

Active: 1986-1989 | Arrested: October 17th 1989

Country: USA (Missouri) | Victims: 5-12

Sentence: Both received death sentences/Faye had hers commuted to life

Status: Ray died of natural causes in 1993/Faye died of natural causes in 2003

Corwin, Daniel Lee

On February 13th 1987, in California, 72-year-old Alice Martin was abducted by American serial killer Daniel Lee Corwin whilst out walking near her home. Her body was found the next day in a field. She had been raped before being strangled and stabbed to death.

Five months later on July 10th 1987, in Texas, 26-year-old Debra Lynn Ewing was abducted at gunpoint by Corwin whilst working at the Vision Center in the city. Her body was discovered two days later in an undeveloped plot of land. She too had been raped before being strangled and stabbed.

On Halloween 1987, Corwin stabbed to death 36-year-old Mary Carrell Risinger at a car wash. He had attempted to abduct her but she fought back and screamed for help. Corwin stabbed her in the neck as her three-year-old daughter looked on from inside the car. Risinger bled to death at the scene.

Corwin killed three people in 1987, but the seeds were laid 12 years earlier. In 1975 when he was just 17, Corwin abducted a classmate from his high school. He bound her in his car, drove her to a remote area and subjected her to a violent sexual assault. Then he dragged her from the car, beat her and stabbed her in the heart. Miraculously, she survived and pulled herself to a road to get help.

Corwin was sentenced to forty years in prison for the rape and attack but was paroled after just nine years of the sentence served. He was released in November of 1985 and went on to kill his three murder victims only 16 months later. He was caught when another victim survived his attack in late 1988. Corwin was subsequently convicted of the three murders, sentenced to death and executed by lethal injection in December of 1998 in Texas.

THE FACTS

Born: September 13th 1958 | Active: 1987

Arrested: 1988 | Country: USA (California/Texas)

Victims: 3 | Sentence: Death penalty

Status: Executed by lethal injection in 1998

Cottingham, Richard Francis: The Times Square Killer

An American serial killer known to have killed six people. He would claim later that he was responsible for up to 100 murders. He is also known as either The New York

Ripper, The Butcher of Times Square, The Times Square Killer, or The Torso Killer. He would generally kill sex workers then dismember his victims and leave their torsos behind.

His first known murder was in October 1967, when he strangled 29-year-old Nancy Schiava Vogel to death. Her nude body was later found under a blanket behind the passenger seat of her car parked in Ridgefield Park, New Jersey. Her murder remained unsolved until Cottingham confessed in August 2010.

In 1979, firemen uncovered two victims in a fire, both had their hands and heads removed and had been set alight. One of them was a Kuwaiti sex worker and the other remains unidentified but both were linked to Cottingham. The missing body parts were never found.

Cottingham was a respected member of the community, which made his arrest and confessions difficult for some to understand. He ran computer systems and networks for a major health insurance firm and was well-liked by colleagues but his personal life was as dark as it came.

Cottingham had become addicted to using sex workers and sex workers and in some instances had become violent with them. In May of 1980, police were called to a motel after people had complained of a screaming girl. When they arrived they caught Cottingham attempting to flee the scene and arrested him.

When police entered the motel room, they found a young sex worker handcuffed to the bed. She had been raped, beaten and stabbed. She also had her nipples partially bitten off. When he was arrested, he was in possession of a pair of handcuffs, a leather gag, two collars, a replica gun and a knife. When police searched his home they found personal items that had been taken from many different murdered sex workers.

Initially receiving a sentence of up to 197 years in prison, he went on to receive further sentences in each successive trial. In early 2020, the 73-year-old Cottingham confessed to three more murders. The deaths most recently connected to him include Jacalyn Harp of Midland Park, Irene Blase of Hackensack and Denise Falasca of Emerson. All three women were strangled in the late 1960s.

In 2021, he confessed to a double murder in 1974, where two girls were raped and drowned to death, and another three murders from 1968 to 1969. Unsurprisingly, his crimes are still being investigated and thus far he has been conclusively linked to 11 murders of young girls in New York and New Jersey. A Netflix documentary about him was released in December 2021 called Crime Scene: The Times Square Killer.

THE FACTS

Born: November 25th 1946 | Active: 1967-1980

Arrested: May 1980 | Country: USA (New York/New Jersey)

Victims: 11+ | AKA: The Times Square Killer/The Torso Killer

Sentence: Multiple life sentences | Status: Incarcerated

Craine, Louis

Craine killed at least four women in South Los Angeles in the mid-1980s. he was one of at least five black serial killers operating in the area at the time, under the collective moniker of The Southside Slayers, though each killer was unknown to the others. Two of Craine's murders were previously attributed to The Southside Slayer.

On May 29th 1987, in Los Angeles, 29-year-old Carolyn Barney was found dead in a vacant lot near a housing project. Her body was found in the same block where Craine's parents lived. Craine was watching the police investigation from afar and was arrested after acting suspiciously at the scene.

He confessed to Barney's murder, and also the murders of 24-year-old Loretta Perry who was found dead in a housing block on January 25th 1987, and Vivian Collins whose body was discovered in an abandoned house in the 1600 block of East Century Boulevard in the neighbourhood of Watts. Both had been raped and strangled to death.

When the investigation picked up after his arrest, Craine was charged with two more murders, that of 30-year-old Sheila Burton who was raped and murdered in November 1984, and 24-year-old Gail Ficklin, who was found dead in August 1985. Both women had been raped and murdered and disposed of in a similar fashion to Craine's other victims.

Craine was sentenced to death in 1989 for the murders of Barney, Perry, Ficklin, and Collins but acquitted on Burton's murder, which has since been attributed to him. Almost all of the victims were young black women who were either sex workers or drug users. The bodies would be dumped in remote parks, in alleys or in vacant buildings.

Within months of being convicted, Craine died from AIDS-related complications. Before his death, he claimed that he had been coerced by police into giving false confessions but it has never been proven.

THE FACTS

Born: 1957 | Active: 1984-1987

Arrested: May 29th 1987 | Country: USA (California)

Victims: 5 | Sentence: Death penalty

Status: Died in November 1989

Crump, Thomas Wayne

On October 4th 1980, in Las Vegas, the body of 25-year-old call-girl Jodie Jameson was discovered in a bathtub at the Sunshine Motel. She had been tied up and strangled with a ligature made of pillowcase fabric before being drowned in the early hours of the morning by serial killer Thomas Wayne Crump who killed at least four people during the early 1980s.

Crump claimed he killed Jamieson because she had robbed him and deserved everything that happened to her. Crump was arrested in a New Mexico prison in 1983 while serving two life sentences for shooting and killing his wife, Rhonda, in Albuquerque. He was also convicted of multiple robberies and later confessed to seven murders. He blamed his cold-bloodedness on the fact he landed behind bars at an early age.

In 1984, For the murder of Jamieson, Crump was sentenced to death and never once showed remorse for his crimes. He was also convicted in the robberies and fatal shootings of a Minnesota man driving through Albuquerque in 1980 and an Albuquerque cab driver in 1982. Despite multiple appeals, he spent 34 years on death row before dying of natural causes in 2018.

THE FACTS

Born: 1940 | Active: 1980-1981

Arrested: 1981 | Country: USA (New Mexico/Nevada)

Victims: 4-7 | Status: Died in June 2018

Cuellar, Cristopher Chávez: The Soulless

In Colombia, Cristopher Chávez Cuellar, AKA: The Soulless, killed at least 15 people over a period of 17 years. He first killed in 1998 when he was 25-year-old. He met a woman at a bar, then kidnapped, raped and stabbed her to death. A warrant went out for his arrest in connection with the crime but he managed to evade police until 2004.

Also in 1998, along with his brother, they murdered a man in cold blood for unknown reasons and were both later arrested and charged with the murder. Cuellar was also charged with the death of the woman in the bar and sentenced to 44 years in prison for the crimes. Amazingly, he was released only a few years later for good behaviour and began racking up his victims.

In 2015, he killed a gas station manager during a robbery and then in February of the same year he committed a crime that shocked Colombia. In an argument over an area of land ownership, Cuellar sought out the children of the couple who wouldn't give him the land.

He lined up their four young sons and executed them where they knelt. A fifth son managed to escape and went with a family member to a military base for protection. After escaping custody, authorities put a 50million Pesos (2.5million USD) reward on his head, and he was captured shortly after.

In November 2015, he was sentenced to 40 years imprisonment for the murders of the four brothers. It has long been suspected that he had killed many more before being caught and has since been conclusively linked to a total of 15. He was nicknamed The Soulless because of the callousness with which he killed the four children.

THE FACTS

Born: 1973 | Active: 1998-2015

Arrested: February 2015 | Country: Colombia

Victims: 15 | AKA: The Soulless

Sentence: 40 years in prison | Status: Incarcerated

Cullen, Charles: The Killer Nurse

EXTENDED CASE FILE

In New Jersey, Charles Cullen, AKA: The Killer Nurse, claimed at least 35 confirmed victims. It has long been suspected he may have killed over 400, making him the world's worst and most prolific serial killer. The claims have long been disputed but at least two investigation teams believe the count to be in the hundreds.

Unlike Harold Shipman, the British medical serial killer who was convicted on 215 counts of murder, Cullen has only ever been convicted of 29, despite 35 being confirmed. Even if Cullen's disturbing count of 400 is ever reached, they would not have been confirmed or convicted and only suspected. However, Cullen's murders had an impact that was felt across the United States.

Born in New Jersey in 1960, he was the youngest of eight children, and his father died in the same year he was born. He would later claim that he was bullied from a young age by his older siblings, their partners and other children at school.

In what became the first of many suicide attempts, when he was nine-years-old, he mixed chemicals together from a science set and then drank them. He survived after having the chemicals flushed through his system. It would be one of at least 20 known suicide attempts, in what was a cry for help that in the 1960s and 1970s went largely ignored.

"You know, maybe if I was nine years old and would have had to die that day, all these lives, including my family, wouldn't be affected in this way." - Charles Cullen.

In 1977, when he was 16-years-old, his mother died in a car crash. He stated it affected him more than he let on at the time and he became aggrieved with the hospital for not releasing the body. Instead, they cremated the body without a funeral.

In 1978, Charles Cullen joined the U.S. Navy and served on a submarine. During his time in the Navy, he was bullied by his fellow comrades and didn't fit in with the team. On one occasion, his comrades found him sat at the missile controls, wearing a doctor's uniform, complete with medical gloves and mask. It was later suggested that it was about the power he had at his fingertips and how it would have made him feel like a god.

He was committed to a Navy psychiatric unit and then discharged in 1984, when it is suspected he claimed his first victim but has never been proven. A couple of years later, he took a medical job at the St. Barnabas Medical Center in Livingston. He married in 1986 and had a daughter. In the same year, Cullen began abusing his dogs and exhibiting strange behaviour.

The first confirmed murder was on June 11th 1988, at St. Barnabas, where he gave a deadly overdose to a patient. He began killing more by contaminating their intravenous medicine bags. He left St. Barnabas in 1992 after an investigation into contaminated bags was opened. The hospital suspected Cullen in at least 20 murders but they couldn't be confirmed.

The killer nurse began working at another hospital in the area while going through a divorce with his wife. In 1993, he moved into a basement apartment by himself where he attempted suicide on multiple occasions. He then began stalking a fellow nurse, Michelle Tomlinson, under the delusion that she was his girlfriend. Cullen would follow her around the hospital and give her unwarranted gifts.

On one night in March of 1993 he broke into her home that she shared with her young son, pretending that they were a couple. He was arrested and received a year's suspended sentence for trespassing. He was then treated for depression in two psychiatric wards. He then got a job at the Hunterdon Medical Center in Flemington, where he murdered five patients in 1996 alone. He moved around between hospitals, taking advantage of a nationwide shortage of nurses.

The eagerness to take on new nurses at any hospital was something that played into Cullen's hands. He was also fired from at least three more hospitals for unknown reasons and spent more time in a psychiatric unit. Every time he murdered a patient, Cullen was suspected of having tampered with the IV bags or having injected the patient directly. No conclusive evidence could be found and even with a history of mental health illnesses, he was still allowed to take nursing work at different hospitals. Even after being fired from most of them!

Charles Cullen was able to continue killing because the hospital managers were more worried about the liability of the hospital, and so criminal investigations were not directed at him. In 2000, he attempted suicide again by lighting a charcoal grill in his bathroom, in an attempt to suffer from the smoke effects and carbon dioxide. He was rescued by neighbours and sent yet again to another psychiatric hospital.

Unbelievably, one hospital, St. Luke's, discovered that he had stolen medicinal drugs that could be used to kill. They offered him a choice; resign and be given a recommendation or be fired. Seven of his co-workers complained to authorities that Cullen might have been killing patients. A small investigation ensued but ended after a few months. They hadn't even looked into Cullen's past.

From September 2002, until his arrest in 2003, the killer nurse worked at the Somerset Medical Center in Somerville, New Jersey. As his depression worsened, he killed at least 13 more people using a combination of easily accessible medicines. However, it was the managers of Somerset Hospital who saw things that others didn't. Cullen had been accessing patient's files who were not assigned to him.

He had been requesting medication that had not been prescribed and cancelled orders of repeat prescriptions. But the hospital delayed in requesting assistance from authorities, allowing Cullen to kill at least five more people. In October 2003, Cullen's final victim died of an insulin overdose. Records showed that Cullen had administered the overdose. Astonishingly, Somerset fired him - under suspicion only. It took a nurse named Amy Loughren to alert the police herself.

Police then began a full investigation and kept Cullen under surveillance. The investigation used Loughren to enter Cullen's house, with an attached recording device. From the talk she had with Cullen, the investigation was able to put together enough evidence to make an arrest. After a lengthy trial in 2006, in which Cullen taunted judges and families of the victims, he was sentenced to 11 life sentences. He was later sentenced to additional life sentences for further murders. He avoided the death penalty by reaching a plea agreement with the prosecution team.

On March 10th 2006, when Cullen appeared in court again, he repeatedly taunted Judge William Platt by ordering him to stand down. He repeated his taunts for half an hour until the judge ordered Cullen to be gagged with a towel and duct tape. It still didn't stop him mumbling his discontent of the court, leading families of the victims to shout back.

'If my grandmother was alive right now, she'd say to you, 'I hope you rot in hell, you sick son of a bitch.' - A family member of one of the victims.

In 2004, New Jersey passed the Patient Safety Act. It allowed hospitals and medical staff access to a confidential reporting system, to be used when someone is suspected or for adverse events. Cullen could move from job to job because each hospital was unwilling to share negative experiences of their own. The new reporting system allowed hospitals to be more open in their reporting of their own staff or colleagues, to an outside authority.

Since then, more than 30 States have passed laws to protect employees or managers who speak up against colleagues or employees. This also came off the back of numerous cases brought against each hospital from the families of the victims.

Did Charles Cullen really kill 400 people? As absurd as it sounds, there is a high probability that Charles Cullen could have murdered close to 400 people. This was due to his moving around between hospitals and the hospital manager's decisions to protect their own liability rather than open criminal investigations.

Cullen later claimed that he enjoyed watching his patient's deterioration over a period of days and that he killed on impulse. It was the power of life and death he held in his hands that drove him to kill over and over again.

He claimed to have not remembered how many he had killed and how he chose his victims, stating that his entire life had been lived under a fog of mental health decline and delusion.

Two later investigations concluded that Cullen may indeed have killed up to 400 patients over a 19-year period. Though, due to some patient records being 'lost' or doctored, we may never know the true scope of Cullen's crimes. As of 2022, Cullen remains incarcerated at a prison in New Jersey and will likely never be released.

THE FACTS

Born: February 22nd 1960 | Active: 1984-2003

Arrested: December 14th 2003 | Country: USA

Victims: 29-400 | AKA: The Killer Nurse

Sentence: Multiple life sentences | Status: Incarcerated

Dahmer, Jeffrey: The Milwaukee Cannibal

EXTENDED CASE FILE

On June 18th 1978, Jeffrey Dahmer, The Milwaukee Cannibal, killed his first victim. He would go on to rape, mutilate, murder and dismember a total of 17 boys and men from 1978 until his arrest in 1991.

'I always had a sense that it was wrong. I don't think anybody can kill somebody and think that it's right.' - Jeffrey Dahmer.

He would go on to become one of the most infamous serial killers in known history. One only has to type his surname into a search engine to be met with tens of thousands of articles about him.

It was the way in which he killed his victims and kept their bodies that would go on to shock the world. He was only 18-years-old when he killed his first victim, a hitchhiker named Steven Hicks. Dahmer's parents were going through a messy divorce and he was left alone in the family house. He picked up Hicks and brought him back to have a night of drinking beer.

Dahmer claimed he saw an opportunity to act on dark thoughts that had been inside of him for quite some time but mostly killed Hick's because he didn't want to stay the night. He slammed a dumbbell weight into Hick's head, then went on to mutilate, dissect and dissolve the body. Dahmer spread the remains throughout the family garden.

Prior to the interstate systems, hitchhiking had never really been heard of or was limited to a certain mindset. The creation of the interstates, as shown in the Highways to Hell section towards the end of this book, gave rise to the hitchhiker. And thus gave rise to a greater pool of potential victims for those who would act on their dark fantasies. Just like Dahmer.

It would be another nine years before he killed again. All his victims were male and all his victims were mutilated, dissected and dissolved. That a killer would be able to hide the murder for nine years is horrific enough. But the longer that Dahmer wasn't punished for his crimes, the more powerful he would have felt.

'I think in some way, I wanted it to end. Even it meant my own destruction.' - Dahmer

From 1987, he would pick up men from gay bars and take them back to a hotel room and later his home. He discovered he was gay while in puberty and sought gay bars and gay bathhouses from an early age. He would drug his victims, rape them and mostly strangle them to death. But it was his fascination with the corpses that would see him become infamous amongst serial killers.

Dahmer engaged multiple times in necrophilia, having sex with the corpses until rigor mortis would set in. He would take photographs of his victims to log each part of the dismemberment and decomposition process, then preserve the skulls and genitals for display in his home and sometimes cannibalise parts of their flesh while he waited. By 1991, he had begun to kill on average one person each week.

> *'The only motive that there ever was, was to completely control a person; a person I found physically attractive. And keep them with me as long as possible, even if it meant just keeping a part of them.' - Dahmer*

He began to believe he could turn his victims into zombies who could be controlled as submissive sex toys. He started drilling holes into their skulls and injected boiling water or hydrochloric acid into their brains to lobotomise them. Astonishingly, one victim managed to escape onto the street and call for help. Dahmer convinced police that it was his extremely drunk boyfriend – and he got away with it.

It was July 22nd 1991, when another one of his victims, Tracy Edwards, escaped and flagged down a police car. When the officers entered Dahmer's home, the true extent of his crimes were displayed for them to see.

They found a severed head in the fridge and three more heads placed around his home. They found the pictures of the dead bodies in various stages of dismemberment and even found a human heart in the freezer. In Dahmer's closet, a bizarre altar was discovered made out of skulls and candles, all adjoined with wax. He confessed straight away to all his crimes.

When Dahmer was a child, he underwent a double hernia operation - not the most common of operations for a child. Before it, he was a happy energetic boy but after the operation, he was known to have changed and become withdrawn into himself. It was also known that his mother was suffering from mental health disorders and was on large doses of anti-psychotic medication throughout her pregnancy with him. Might this have had an effect on Dahmer's own mental health in his formative years?

There are some other potential reasons why he would go on to kill in such a fashion. During school, he was drinking alcohol almost daily; wine, spirits, beer, whatever he could lay his hands on and smuggle in. Alcohol at an early age is known to cause major issues in later life.

From the age of 10, Dahmer was obsessed with the bones of animals. His father, who was a chemist, believed that his son had found his calling and showed him how to clean bones using bleach. This bizarre education formulated his own unique view of the world and led to his passion for murder. He would use exactly the same methods in disposing of his victim's remains by cleaning their skulls using bleach.

'I don't care if I live or die, go ahead and kill me.' - Dahmer

He was ultimately sentenced to 957 years in prison but was killed by another inmate in November of 1994. His killer has never been identified. Dahmer's horrific legacy lives on to this day in books, films, music and pop culture.

THE FACTS

Born: May 21st 1960 | Active: 1978-1991

Arrested: July 22nd 1991 | Country: USA (Milwaukee)

Victims: 17 | AKA: The Milwaukee Cannibal

Sentence: 957 years imprisonment | Status: Killed in 1994.

David, Horst

German serial killer Horst David killed at least seven people from 1975 to 1993. During his marriage from 1963 to 1984, he stayed away from the family as much as possible spending time in the cities of Munich and Hamburg. Due to his addiction with escorts and sex workers, the family had financial difficulties.

The first murder in 1975 was a sex worker named Waltraud Frank, and just two days later, another sex worker, Fatima Grossart, was found dead. David later claimed he had argued with both victims because they had demanded more money than their standard rates for sexual services.

IMAGE ATTRIB. A16

ANDREI CHIKATILO

IMAGE ATTRIB. A4

IMAGE ATTRIB. A70

JEFFREY DAHMER

He divorced in 1984 and moved to Regensburg where he lived on state handouts. It was suspected that towards the late 1980s, he may have murdered more women, but it wasn't until 1993 that he would be linked to another murder, when his neighbour, Mathilde Steindl, was strangled in her home.

His fingerprints were found in Steindl's home but there was no other evidence linking him to the crime. In due course, his profile was sent to a new Automated Fingerprint Identification System (AFIS). It subsequently made a match with the fingerprints on Grossart's body from 1975.

Upon his arrest he confessed to a total of seven murders from 1975 to 1993. Three of the murders had never been investigated as murders because the crime scenes had been set up to look like household accidents. It is suggested that financial gain had been the sole motivation, along with a sexual perversity. In 1995, David was sentenced to life imprisonment for the murders of Grossart, Steindl, and Frank. He confessed to four additional murders. David died of natural causes while in prison aged 81 in November 2020.

THE FACTS

Born: November 22nd 1938 | Active: 1975-1993

Arrested: August 1995 | Country: Germany

Victims: 3-7 | Sentence: Life imprisonment | Status: Died in 2020

DeAngelo, Joseph James: The Golden State Killer

EXTENDED CASE FILE

Not since Ted Bundy has the case of a serial killer been so widely spoken about in media and especially in online forums. His capture brings to end one of the largest serial killing mysteries of the Twentieth Century. It is a complicated case with so many threads of crime coming to a head.

The Golden State Killer was a serial killer, rapist and burglar who killed at least 13 people, committed more than 50 rapes, and over 100 burglaries in California from 1974 to 1986. Each of his known three crime sprees afforded him a new moniker in the media. This was before it became evident that the three monikers were one and the same person.

So, along with the Golden State Killer, he was also the East Area Rapist (EAR) and the Original Night Stalker (ONS). It has also been suggested that there are links to him being the Diamond Knot Killer, The Cordova Cat, The Rippon Court Shooter, and The Visalia Ransacker.

On February 2nd 1978, DeAngelo shot dead Brian Maggiore and Katie Maggiore. DNA has been matched against the two victims and the killer is confirmed to be DeAngelo. It is claimed by one witness that he had already killed 14 people before 1974 and it is an assumption that he killed again in 1978, probably more than once.

He was identified through a DNA match with his fourth cousin on an open data personal genomics website. Subsequently, the investigators built a family tree and zoned in on DeAngelo based on living locations, age at the time of the crimes, and serial killer profiling techniques. They secretly gained access to his DNA from a throw-away item as they were watching him and it came back to be a 100% match.

DeAngelo's father served in World War Two but not much is known about him beyond that. After his parents' divorce, his mother quickly remarried and they moved to California from New York. His childhood and developing years were formed by his father returning from war, divorce and displacement of his home life.

In 1964, he joined the U.S. Navy and was subsequently deployed to Vietnam. In most of the rape cases, the crimes took place too long ago and cannot be tried in a court of law due to the statute of limitations. However, in their place, he is being charged with kidnapping.

In June 1972 he garnered a bachelor's degree in criminal justice at the California State University and subsequently joined the Exeter Police Department in 1973. He was promoted to sergeant and it is suggested that he was using the department as a stepping-stone to becoming an FBI Agent.

Whilst working on the force, he was already operating as the Visalia Ransacker. If witness statements are to be believed, he had already killed many people by that point in time. He then moved from the Exeter Department to the Auburn Police Department in 1976. June 1976 is the first confirmed attack of the East Area Rapist. In 1978, under the same moniker, he moved onto murder. The last known attack of his East Area Rapist name was on July 5th 1979, in Danville, California.

He was then fired from the Auburn Police Department for shoplifting in a Pay & Save store. If we base the assumption that DeAngelo had joined the police in order to use it as a stepping-stone to the FBI, then his dismissal from the Auburn PD would have put to bed any chance he ever had to work with the FBI.

October 1st 1979 is the date of the first attack attributed to the Original Night Stalker (ONS). The more famously known Night Stalker was Richard Ramirez who killed 14 people from 1984 to 1985. On December 30th 1979, Dr. Robert Offerman and Alexandria Manning were killed in their home near Goleta, 100 miles northwest of Los Angeles.

Only three months later, another double murder took place in Ventura. Lyman and Charlene Smith were bound and bludgeoned to death with a fireplace log. Charlene had been sexually assaulted and tied with a curtain cord. Their 12-year-old son found their bodies three days later. DNA collected from the scene was used to identify DeAngelo almost 40 years later.

On August 21st 1980, Keith and Patti Harrington of Laguna Niguel, California, were bludgeoned to death. Keith's father discovered their beaten bodies when he arrived for dinner on the Thursday night. There were more murders in the same area and it wasn't until September of 1981 that the killings stopped - for a while.

In September of that year, DeAngelo's first child was born in Sacramento. As we've discussed with Ted Bundy, some serial killers hold their own family in higher esteem than others. This might seem like a given notion but some serial killers are able to lift up their wives and children as being important to them, they respect and revere their own families. At the same time they focus any hatred they might have garnered towards them on other females or children.

It's important because after DeAngelo's first child, there is an assumed five year gap where no crimes were committed. It wasn't until the May 4th 1986 murder of Janelle Cruz in Irvine, that the investigation would start linking DeAngelo to the new spate of murders and rapes.

His second child was born in 1986 and the third in 1989. Beyond that, there are no crimes committed and some put this down to the fact he now had children of his own and was intent on raising his family. He was arrested in July 2012 for driving under the influence. Little did the officers know they had one of the most notorious killers and rapists in their custody.

It wasn't until March 2018 when he became a suspect due to a DNA match to his fourth cousin on a DNA database and then arrested in April 2018. Which raises the important notion of genetic informants. You didn't really think those ancestry DNA sites were just to find out more about your own family, did you? Mostly they are, of course, but they are being used to a massive extent in the investigation of cold cases and new cases.

There is a theory that DeAngelo was also the Zodiac Killer but there has been no evidence pointing towards it as of 2022, even though some of his killings were similar in style. In June 2020, DeAngelo admitted to 13 murders in a deal with prosecutors, to spare him the death penalty. He also admitted to numerous rapes, burglaries and other crimes at the time. On August 20th 2020, DeAngelo was sentenced to multiple life sentences.

Prosecutors ultimately did not seek the death penalty, due partially to California's moratorium on executions. Judge Bowman said that the sentence he chose was the absolute maximum the court was able to impose under the law.

As such, DeAngelo is now serving a total of 12 consecutive life terms without the possibility of parole, alongside 15 concurrent life sentences and other time for weapons charges. Despite being convicted of 13 murders, most investigations and research suspect there could be at least 87 victims, with many more unidentified and unaccounted for.

THE FACTS

Born: November 8th 1945 | Active: 1974-1986

Arrested: April 24th 2018 | Country: USA | Victims: 13-87

AKA: Golden State Killer/East Area Rapist/Original Night Stalker.

Status: Incarcerated

Dudin, Nikolai Arkadievich: The Grim Maniac

On December 3rd 1987, Russian serial killer Nikolai Arkadievich Dudin, AKA: The Grim Maniac, shot dead his father. He hid the body for a year before an arrest for rape saw him confess to the murder. Dudin was born in 1973 in Mikhalkovo, Ivanovo Oblast, and was beaten by his father as a child. He was only 13-years-old when he killed his father.

Due to his age, he escaped the death sentence and was imprisoned, where he incited riots and was charged with the attempted murder of another inmate. He was released in 2000 but two years later killed at least another 12 people in various incidents across the town of Furmanov. He would use guns, knives and blunt objects to kill his victims.

During May of 2002 alone, he killed nine people in a month of terror. On the first two days of the month, a young female disappeared without a trace, and was later found dead, having been killed by Dudin. On May 8th, Dudin killed an entire family, first by shooting the father dead and then the mother before chasing their 11-year-old daughter and stabbing her repeatedly until she died.

Two days later on May 10th he killed three more people in a triple murder, in a replication of the murders on May 8th. And just a few days afterwards, he killed two more people in a double murder, and if he wasn't caught, he would have continued killing.

In July 2002, he was caught red-handed attempting to kill someone. He was arrested and ultimately sentenced to life imprisonment without parole. Dudin was subsequently sent to a special regime colony; the Supermax White Swan Prison, where he remains to this day.

THE FACTS

Born: December 22nd 1973 | Active: 1987-2002

Arrested: July 17th 2002 | Country: Russia

Victims: 13 | AKA: The Grim Maniac

Sentence: Life imprisonment | Status: Incarcerated

Duncan III, Joseph Edward

Joseph Edward Duncan III is an American serial killer who killed at least seven people from 1996 to 2005. At the age of 15-years-old, in 1980, Duncan was sentenced to 20 years in prison for sexually abusing another young boy. He was released in 1994 after 14 years in prison.

On July 6th 1996, two sisters, 11-year-old Sammiejo White and nine-year-old Carmen Cubias vanished as they were out walking alone. They had left the Crest Motel in Seattle, only to never return. Their decomposed remains were discovered on February 10th 1998, in Washington. They and a 10-year-old boy had been killed by Duncan, but he got away with it until 2005, and although he confessed, he was never charged.

He returned to prison in 1997 for violating his parole on an unrelated charge. He was released from prison again in 2000 when he moved to North Dakota. The prison authorities were unaware they were releasing a serial killer.

On May 16th 2005, multiple bodies of the Groene family were discovered in their home outside the city of Coeur d'Alene, in North Idaho. 40-year-old Brenda Groene and her boyfriend, 37-year-old Mark McKenzie, were found dead along with Brenda's 13-year-old son, Slade Groene. They had all been tied up and bludgeoned to death by Duncan.

Her two other children, nine-year-old Dylan and eight-year-old Shasta were missing from the property and a state-wide AMBER alert was put into action. Seven weeks later, Duncan was spotted in a restaurant holding the hand of Shasta. A waitress and some customers recognised her and subsequently stopped Duncan from leaving the premises. Police turned up to arrest him shortly after.

On July 4th 2005, investigators discovered the remains of Dylan Groene in a remote forest location. He had been shot in the head at close range by a sawn-off shotgun. It took DNA testing to confirm the rest of the remains. In the trial of Dylan Groene, a video was made by Duncan, detailing the torture of the boy, in it he is heard shouting at the top of his voice.

'The devil is here, boy, the devil himself. The devil likes to watch children suffer and cry.' - Joseph E. Duncan – in a video with Dylan Groene.

By 2011, Duncan had been convicted by three courts. Two courts in Idaho for the murders of the Groene family members, and a Californian superior court for the murder of the 10-year-old boy in 1997. In total he received six life sentences and three death sentences. On March 22nd 2019, Duncan lost an appeal to commute the death sentences to life. He died in prison in March 2021 after complications with brain cancer.

THE FACTS

Born: February 25th 1963 | Active: 1996-2005

Arrested: July 2nd 2005 | Country: USA | Victims: 7

Sentence: Three death penalties and six life sentences | Status: Died in 2021

Dutroux, Marc: The Monster of Belgium

EXTENDED CASE FILE

The story of the Monster of Belgium is one of Europe's most infamous and horrific cases, with many bizarre aspects, including underground dungeons, child abuse, government officials, and nationwide protests against the authorities surrounding the incidents.

Belgian-born Marc Paul Alain Dutroux killed at least four young girls and abused many more. His trial would cause such an uproar in Belgium that over 300,000 people would march in memory of the victims.

Through proceeds of crime, Dutroux went on to own seven houses, using three of them for the sole purpose of torturing young girls. At one of his houses in Marcinelle, he built a torture dungeon in the basement and hid it by a concealed concrete door.

When the dungeon was discovered, what was found inside was enough to scar the hearts of even the most hardened investigators. This tale is dark, and involves the horrors inflicted on the innocents, a Europe-wide conspiracy of high-ranking officials involved in people trafficking and paedophiles, and a miscarriage of justice that saw two young girls rot in their chains.

Dutroux was born in 1956 and was the eldest of five children. His parents moved to the Belgian section of the Congo before his first year, as they were teaching French in the region. As the Congo crisis deepened, the family escaped back to Belgium, where the parents divorced in 1971.

Dutroux briefly married when he was 19-years-old, had two children and divorced eight years later in 1983. He met his future second wife, Michelle Martin, while he was still married to his first wife. Together, they would involve themselves in various crimes which would ultimately result in the abduction of five young girls.

At that time, Dutroux was unemployed and survived by carrying out robberies, muggings, and selling drugs. He even stole cars in Belgium and sold them over the border in Czechoslovakia and Hungary, something the police were already keeping tabs on.

Martin helped Dutroux lure their victims into cars where they would take them to their home and rape them. In February 1986, both Dutroux and Martin were arrested for the kidnapping and rape of five girls.

After a lengthy trial in 1989, Dutroux was sentenced to just over 13 years in prison, and Martin received five years for her part in the crimes. Astonishingly, after only three years, Dutroux was released for good behaviour in 1992. If the kidnapping and rape of five girls was bad enough, what happened after 1992 was even worse. The secret dungeon that Dutroux had built was never found and so he decided to put it to full use.

On 24th June 1995, eight-year-old friends Julie Lejeune and Mélissa Russo were kidnapped as they walked home. They were held in Dutroux's dungeon and repeatedly raped, with their ordeals filmed and recorded on VHS.

Around that time, Dutroux had manipulated and secured another accomplice, Michel Lelièvre, who would help him abduct girls. Two months later and the two eight-year-old girls were still being abused and tortured in Dutroux's dungeon.

On 23rd August, Dutroux and Lelièvre kidnapped 17-year-old Ann Marchal and 19-year-old Eefje Lambrecks. They took them to the same house, but because the dungeon was still in use, they chained the two teenagers in one of the bedrooms.

They suffered the same abuse as the girls in the dungeon, but after a couple of weeks, Marchal and Lambrecks were drugged and moved to a Belgian Town called Jumet. There, Dutroux and another accomplice, Bernard Weinstein, murdered the girls and buried them in a shallow grave.

The van used to kidnap the girls had been stolen by Weinstein and another man named Philippe Divers, and they thought they had hidden it well, but it was found by police. Dutroux then suspected that Divers and a friend of his, Pierre Rochow, had betrayed him, so he lured them to Weinstein's home in Jumet.

They then went to search Rochow's home and found his girlfriend, Bénédicte Jadot. They interrogated her but she escaped and called the police. Dutroux decided to cover his own tracks and kill Weinstein, so he kidnapped him and held him in the dungeon, where he tortured him and then buried him alive. During this time, the two eight-year-old girls – now controlled slaves – were still in the house and were allowed to walk around freely while Dutroux was there.

On 6th December, Dutroux was arrested on suspicion of stealing luxury cars. He remained in custody until 20th March 1996. Before he went into custody, he had told his partner, Michelle Martin, to feed the two girls in the house every day without fail.

But Martin was scared of entering the dungeon, expecting to find two emancipated demons tearing at her throat. Fearful of what she would find within, she didn't enter the dungeon and didn't feed the girls. Julie Lejeune and Mélissa Russo died of starvation sometime while Dutroux was in custody.

There had always been questions asked about how Dutroux had so many accomplices. They were all suspected to be members of an underground gang of paedophiles and murderers who made sure that they looked out for and helped each other. This aspect of the Dutroux case gave rise to theories of cover-ups and secrets within the Belgian elite, which we'll look at shortly.

The day Dutroux was released, he went back to the house, removed the bodies from the dungeon and buried them near to Weinstein's body. As much as Martin had disappointed him, Dutroux continued feeding his dark desires.

On 28th May 1996, Dutroux and his former accomplice, Lelièvre, kidnapped 12-year-old schoolgirl Sabine Dardenne. She was taken to the dungeon in the house and repeatedly raped, abused, tortured and starved, over a three month period.

On 9th August, Dutroux and Lelièvre kidnapped 14-year-old schoolgirl Laetitia Delhez, as she was leaving her local swimming pool. There was an eyewitness to the kidnapping, who later described the van and partial license plate to police.

Just four days later, on the 13th, Dutroux, Martin, and Lelièvre, were arrested on suspicion of kidnapping. Police searched Dutroux's properties but didn't find anything and they failed to find the dungeon in the basement, as it had been so well hidden. After intense interrogation, Dutroux and Lelièvre both confessed to the kidnappings. Dutroux led police to the basement where he showed them the secret concrete door to the dungeon. Inside they found Delhez alive and chained to the wall. Astonishingly, 12-year-old Dardenne had survived three months of torture and abuse and she too was rescued from the dungeon.

As the investigation continued and the scale of the crimes were beginning to reveal themselves, Dutroux led them to another of his properties and showed them where he had buried the bodies of the two eight-year-old girls, and Weinstein. On 3rd September, he led police to the remains of Marchal and Lambrecks, in Jumet.

Once news of the murders and rapes were circulated by the media, the public were understandably outraged. Reports were published showing the police could have stopped the situation from getting worse but they had failed on multiple levels.

It then became known that Dutroux had offered money to a police informant to provide him with girls for his dungeon. Dutroux's own mother had written a letter to police, saying that her son scared her, and she was sure he was doing something evil. Her letter was ignored.

On the night that he kidnapped the two teenage girls, he was already under police surveillance. However, the police had only set up the cameras to operate during daylight hours. When police searched his house for the first time in December of 1995, they failed to discover the dungeon

If they had found it, then the two eight-year-old girls might have been rescued before starving to death. While the police were scouring the house, the lead officer heard children's voices but assumed they were coming from outside the property.

The police even collected VHS tapes from the house that showed Dutroux building the door to the dungeon, which would have revealed the secret. But the police never played it because they claimed they didn't have a VCR player at the time.

As the mounting evidence against the incompetence of the police was made public, the anger and frustrations grew within the country. Then came the accusations of cover-ups. Stories began to emerge of a paedophile sex-ring that included members of the police force and politicians within the government itself – something which continues to be talked about and insinuated to this day.

Investigators claimed that much of the evidence gathered against Dutroux was *'flimsy'* and wouldn't stand up in a court of law, and judge Jean-Marc Connerotte agreed with them. Because he agreed the evidence was flimsy, he was dismissed from his position in the judicial system, which understandably enraged the Belgian public yet again. On 20th October 1996, 300,000 people marched on Brussels in support of the families of the victims. The White March, as it became known, was also to protest against the ruling authorities and the police for the failures in their investigation into the missing girls. The demonstrators wanted higher levels of protection for children, along with an independent justice system that could investigate Dutroux without influence from parliament.

When the trial began, the fired judge, Connerotte, was called to the stand as a witness. He testified that he needed bullet-proof vehicles and an armed security team to protect him. When asked who they were protecting him from, he said there were shadowy figures in positions of power who were determined to stop the full truth coming out.

Connerotte testified that some suspects were being protected by people in government and it had hampered the investigation to the point of it being impossible. There were even rumours the Mafia had some influence on the pre-trial hearings. A 17-month pre-trial parliamentary investigation into Dutroux was undertaken, leading to a report in February of 1998. It concluded that Dutroux did not have accomplices in high places. It enraged people further as it was the public's opinion that the government were investigating themselves and clearing their own name.

Dutroux hit the headlines again in April 1998, when he escaped from a courthouse while only one guard was watching him. There were meant to have been two guards but one of them decided to run an errand.

Dutroux fought off the remaining guard, stole a car at gunpoint, and escaped into a dense forest. An estimated 5,000 officers and dozens of helicopters were called in to capture him. The borders of France, Luxembourg and Germany, were put on an '*all-borders-alert*' and effectively temporarily closed.

He was captured in the forest half a day later. The episode resulted in the resignations of a Police Chief, a Minister of Justice, and the Minister of the Interior, affecting many more Government departments and sending public anger sky high once more.

Finally, in 2004, Dutroux's trial began, almost eight years after he had been arrested. Michelle Martin and Lelièvre were tried as accomplices to the crimes. Dutroux was put in a bullet proof glass cage during the trial – for his own protection.

Dutroux testified that he was part of a Europe-wide underground ring of paedophiles that included police officers, top businessmen, medical professionals and high-level government officials.

On 17th June 2004, the jury found Dutroux and Martin guilty of all the charges they had been put up on. Just a few months prior to Dutroux's arrest in early 1996, the death penalty had been abolished in the country. A petition to bring back the death penalty purely for Dutroux was created but fell on deaf ears.

He was given the maximum sentence of life imprisonment without parole. Michelle Martin received 30 years and Lelièvre was sentenced to 25 years. Then another failure by the justice system resulted in yet another uproar among the Belgian public.

After only 13 years of her sentence, Martin was paroled and released into the care of an isolated convent of nuns, known as the Poor Clares of Malonne. When news of her parole had come up, thousands of people protested against it, but again, their protests were ignored.

The convent was sold shortly after which meant that Martin had to find new shelter or return to prison. Bizarrely, a former judge built an apartment onto his farmhouse, purely so that Martin could live there, and she does, to this day.

Lelièvre remains incarcerated despite numerous appeals and parole hearings. Dutroux has also made numerous appeals, on the basis that he is no longer a danger to society, but they have been denied at every turn. He remains incarcerated in solitary confinement at a prison in the Nivelles area of Belgium.

In 2019, when news of Dutroux potentially being released began circulating around Belgium, up to 1,000 people protested in the streets of Brussels, in what they called the Black March, an echo of the White March 23 years earlier.

The case affected Belgium so much that a third of all people in the country with the surname of Dutroux, applied to have it changed. Conspiracy theories abound to this day, not least with the knowledge that over 20 witnesses in the original trial have died under mysterious circumstances.

The Monster of Belgium case is one that has so many threads and people involved, it's no wonder theories and mistrust has grown around it. Rumours of a Europe-wide underground ring of high-ranking paedophiles remain to this day.

The only true certainty in the tale of the monster is that Dutroux – with the help of accomplices – executed unimaginable horrors on young girls across Belgium, and that he will forever be synonymous with one of Europe's most heinous crimes.

In 1996, when she was 12-years-old, Sabine Dardenne was chained to a wall in Dutroux's dungeon for 79 days. She found the strength to testify against Dutroux during his trial. In 2006, 10 years after her abduction, she published a book about the experience called 'J'avais 12 ans, j'ai pris mon vélo et je suis partie à l'école'. It was published in the United Kingdom under the very apt title of 'I Choose to Live'.

THE FACTS

Born: November 6th 1956 | Active: 1986-1996

Arrested: August 13, 1996 | Country: Belgium

Victims: 4+ | AKA: The Monster of Belgium

Sentence: Life imprisonment | Status: Incarcerated

(ATTRIB A104)

(ATTRIB A105)
(ATTRIB A106)

ENTRANCE TO DUTROUX'S SECRET CELLAR

MARC DUTROUX

(ATTRIB A107)

DONALD LEROY EVANS

GARY CHARLES EVANS

(ATTRIB A108)

Eckert, Volker

A German serial killer who confessed to killing six women in various European countries. He was subsequently linked to the murders of nine females in total and has been accused of more murders in different countries throughout his life.

In most of the murders, he would strangle his victims, mutilate them and photograph them. Then he would cut off the hair and pose the corpses in sexual positions, before keeping the hair as trophies of his crimes. Eckert, who was a lorry driver, confessed to killing three sex workers in Spain and two others in France between 1999 and 2006.

Eckert was caught in November 2006 after a Europe-wide arrest warrant was issued by Spanish authorities. He was wanted for killing 22-year-old Bulgarian Miglena Petrova in Spain, by strangling her to death and leaving her body near to a football pitch – with no attempt to cover the crime.

He was caught by a satellite tracking system which was installed in his truck. The investigation were able to retrace the truck's routes which put Eckert at the scene of the Petrova murder. In his truck they found photographs of Petrova's corpse along with other unidentified victims. Because of the photographs of his victims, some investigations into previous unsolved murders were re-opened.

During interviews, Eckert confessed to killing a 14-year-old girl in East Germany in 1974, and then confessed to six murders in total. He has since been positively linked to an additional three. Investigations were closed after Eckert killed himself during proceedings in 2007.

THE FACTS

Born: 1959 |Active: 1974-2006 | Arrested: November 17th 2006

Countries: Germany/France/Spain/Italy/Czech Republic

Victims: 6-9 | Status: Died by suicide in 2007, while awaiting trial

Edwards, Edward Wayne

Born Charles Murray, Edward Wayne Edwards was suspected of murdering at least five people. He was on the 'FBI's Ten Most Wanted Fugitives' list in 1961 for armed robberies at gas stations and has been connected to many more crimes including the Atlanta Murders from 1979 to 1981.

Edwards grew up as an orphan after having witnessed the suicide of his own mother. While in an orphanage he was physically and emotionally abused by the carers. It is suggested that the level of abuse he received, combined with watching his mother take her own life, led to his violent behaviour in later life.

He spent most of his adult life in and out of jail for various offences including robbery but didn't wear a mask as he wanted to be famous. In Ohio, in 1977, Edwards claimed his first two of five known victims. 21-year-old William Lavaco and his girlfriend, 18-year-old Judith Straub were shot dead at point blank range with a shotgun and left in an open field.

Three years later, in Wisconsin, in 1980, Edwards killed young couple Tim Hack and Kelly Drew who were both stabbed and strangled. The double murder became known in the press as 'The Sweetheart Murders'. The fifth confirmed victim was Edwards' foster son, Dannie Law Gloeckner, who was found dead in 1996, having been killed with a shotgun.

In 2009, 32 years after the first murders, Edwards' own daughter, April, tipped off police about her father's possible involvement in them. In 2010, Edwards was sentenced to life for the 1977 murders, and death for the murder of his foster son. In 2011, while awaiting trial for the 1980 murders, he died of natural causes. He was also linked many times as a suspect in the Zodiac Killer investigation and was suspected of having killed more people.

THE FACTS

Born: June 14th 1933 | Active: 1977-1996

Arrested: July 30th 2009 | Country: USA

Sentence: Life imprisonment and death

Victims: 5+ | Status: Died in 2011 while awaiting a third trial

Eijk, Willem Van: The Beast of Harkstede

The Beast of Harkstede was a Dutch serial killer who was convicted of five murders. His victims were all females and he would rape them before strangling them to death. In childhood, he was known for his cruelty to small animals, he would torture dogs, drown cats, and kick ducks until they split open and died.

He was also an outcast who was bullied both physically and emotionally. With no friends, he began collecting dead frogs and insects and refused to study in school. He claimed at the time he would dream about raping and killing older women and turned to petty crime before committing murder.

The first murder came in 1971, when he was 30-years-old. He picked up a 15-year-old hitchhiker named Cora Mantel, who had allegedly missed her bus on the way to visit her boyfriend. Van Eijk then raped and strangled her to death with her own clothing, before dumping her body in a ditch.

In 1974, he killed 43-year-old Aaltje van der Plaat. Her body was found near a road in a field the following day. She had been stabbed multiple times, her stomach was ripped open, and her left nipple had been cut off. Witnesses had seen Van Eijk fleeing the scene, and he was arrested shortly after and sentenced to 18 years in prison for both the Plaat and Mantel murders.

He was released 16-years later in 1990 but had not been rehabilitated, instead, his dark desire for brutal murder had been simmering away. In 1993, the body of 23-year-old sex worker Antoanella Bertholda Fato was discovered. She had been strangled to death while Van Eijk was raping her.

Before Van Eijk was arrested for a second time in 2001, eight sex workers had been murdered in the area where he lived. Although not all could be conclusively linked to him, he was charged with multiple murders and convicted of three. Many more unsolved cases have since been attributed to Van Eijk and although he was ultimately convicted of five murders in total across the years, it is suggested the figure is closer to 10. He died in prison of natural causes in June 2019.

THE FACTS

Born: August 13th 1941 | Active: 1971-2001

Arrested: November 12th 2001 | Country: Netherlands

Victims: 5-10 | AKA: The Beast of Harkstede/Crazy little Willem

Sentence: Life imprisonment | Status: Died in 2019

Escalero, Francisco García: El Mendigo Assesino

Spanish serial killer Francisco García Escalero was convicted for the murders of 11 people over a seven year period from 1987 to 1994. He was a diagnosed schizophrenic who had sex with his victim's corpses and engaged in cannibalism. During childhood, he developed a fascination with death and cemeteries in-between his father's beatings and poor education. Throughout his teens and early adult life, he was committed to various psychiatrist institutions.

He claimed his first murder victim in August of 1987 when he was 39, a sex worker by the name of Paula Martínez. He raped, killed and decapitated Martínez before burning her corpse. He claimed he killed people because the voices in his head told him to, blaming hallucinations caused by schizophrenia that forced him to murder.

In the years that followed he killed lots of homeless people and beggars. Sometimes he stabbed them to death and other times he crushed their skulls with rocks. The burned bodies of some victims were found decapitated. Alongside the murders he would go to local cemeteries and dig up bodies so he could have sex with them, and he was also known to have eaten parts of the corpses.

Escalero was arrested in 1994 after escaping from a psychiatric hospital where he was temporarily being held. He attempted suicide but was stopped in the process when police caught up to him. He confessed to 11 murders and was sent to trial in 1995, where he was declared insane and sentenced to a life term at a high-security psychiatric hospital. He died in 2014 from unknown causes while under psychiatric care.

THE FACTS

Born: May 24th 1948 | Active: 1987-1994

Arrested: April 1994 | Country: Spain | Victims: 11

Sentence: Life term in psychiatric hospital | Status: Died in 2014

Evans, Donald Leroy

American Donald Leroy Evans murdered at least three people from 1985 to 1991 but confessed to over 70 murders stretching back to 1977. He was born in 1957, the seventh of nine children to a violent alcoholic mother who constantly beat her children.

By the time he dropped out of school, Evans was already involved in drug and gang culture. At the age of 16, he attempted to kill himself by mixing a combination of illegal drugs with cockroach poison. In 1986, he was convicted of the rape of a local woman and sentenced to fifteen years in prison but only served five and was released in 1991.

On August 1st 1991, just weeks after his release, Evans kidnapped a 10-year-old girl who he raped and strangled to death. He was arrested only four days later and confessed immediately. It had been suggested that the girl was alive during the rape and died shortly after from her wounds. For that particular crime, he was sentenced to death.

He then confessed to more than 70 murders in 22 different states. At first, the investigation didn't believe him but some of the descriptions of his victims matched up to missing persons and he was convicted of an additional murder.

Evans was stabbed to death in 1999 by a fellow inmate, while in the showers of the Mississippi State Penitentiary. Whatever secrets he had, and the true number of his victims have now gone with him to the grave.

THE FACTS

Born: July 5th 1957 | Active: 1977-1991

Arrested: August 5th 1991 | Country: USA | Victims: 3+

Sentence: Death penalty | Status: Killed by a fellow inmate in 1999

Evans, Gary Charles: The Great Tricep King

American serial killer Gary Charles Evans was a lifetime criminal who terrorised New York until his death in 1998. In October 1991, he spent two weeks on top of a building while he was working out the routine of a coin shop below. He then walked into the shop, asked for a valuation and shot the shop owner in the head.

By 1993, he claimed he had already killed four people and his robbery skills were reaching epidemic levels. He stole almost 1,000 items from an antique departmental store in Vermont and then used an industrial crane to steal a bench from a cemetery.

Curiously, in 1987, Evans managed to befriend David Berkowitz, AKA; The Son of Sam. Berkowitz from then on would refer to Evans as 'The Great Tricep King' on account of his muscular appearance. It is claimed that on one occasion, Berkowitz had become angered by Evans as he had referred to him as 'David Berserk-o-witz.' It remains unclear whether they knew that the other was a serial killer or were simply gym-buddies.

Upon Evans's next arrest in 1998, he confessed to five murders and led police to the resting places of his victims. Almost all of the victims had been dismembered and mutilated. When returning from one of the grave sites, Evans escaped from a prison van, and when police surrounded him, he killed himself by jumping off a high bridge over the Hudson River.

THE FACTS

Born: October 7th 1954 | Active: 1985-1997

Arrested: June 18th 1998 | Country: USA | Victims: 5

Status: Died by suicide in 1998 while awaiting trial.

Evonitz, Richard Marc

American rapist and serial killer, Richard Marc Evonitz, murdered three young girls in Spotsylvania County, Virginia, from 1996 to 1997. He was also convicted of the kidnapping and rape of a 15-year-old girl in South Carolina in 2002, and various rapes in the late 1980s and early 1990s.

While serving in the U.S. Navy in 1987, when he was 23, he exposed himself in front of a teenage girl and masturbated in front of her. When his ship returned to port, he was arrested over the incident and given a three year suspended sentence. He was also suspected of raping two young girls in Virginia, in 1994 and 1995.

His first confirmed murder took place on September 9th 1996. He kidnapped 16-year-old schoolgirl Sofia Silva from her front garden in Spotsylvania County. He raped and strangled her to death, then bizarrely shaved her pubic hair off. Her body was discovered a month later in a wooded area just off from a main highway, she had been found wrapped in a white sheet and had started to decompose.

Half a year later on May 1st 1997, two sisters, 15-year-old Kristin Lisk, and 12-year-old Kati Lisk vanished after leaving their school bus. When their father arrived home and found their bags in the front yard, he raised the alarm, but it was too late. Five days later and 40 miles away, their bodies were discovered on the banks of a river. Like Silva, their pubic hair had been shaved off.

Although DNA from all victims was a match, the investigation struggled to find a suspect. Until June 24th 2002, when Evonitz kidnapped 15-year-old schoolgirl, Kara Robinson, from her friend's yard in South Carolina. He tied her to the bed in his apartment and raped her multiple times. Fortunately, Robinson was able to escape while Evonitz slept.

She went straight to the police but Evonitz escaped to Florida. Police managed to track him down, and on June 27th, when police surrounded him, he put a gun to his head and shot himself dead. Before Evonitz took his own life, he had phoned his sister and confessed to the murders, and more. Since his death, more rapes and murders have been attributed to him.

THE FACTS

Born: July 29th 1963 | Active: 1996-1997

Country: USA | Victims: 3+

Status: Died by suicide in 2002 before he could be arrested

Ferrari, Werner

One of Switzerland's most infamous criminals who killed at least five children in the 1970s. He would lure them away or kidnap them from popular music festivals or carnivals before abusing and strangling them to death. Ferrari was raised by various carers and was known to have been withdrawn from the people around him. It is unclear what might have happened in his childhood to have triggered the violence that he enacted upon others.

He first killed a 10-year-old boy in 1971 before being arrested and serving just eight years for the crime. After his release, between 1980 and 1989, another 11 children were abducted and eight were violently murdered. Three were never found and Ferrari denied any involvement in their disappearances.

Ferrari turned himself in just four days after his last murder in 1989. He called police stating that he had nothing to do with the girl's death. The phone call was tracked which led police to his apartment, where he was arrested and confessed to multiple murders.

In 1995, Ferrari was sentenced to life imprisonment for five murders. In 2004, one of the murder convictions was overturned when it was proven by a new defence team that the DNA evidence had been flawed, but he remains imprisoned for the murders of the four other children and is still suspected of killing at least another three. He remains one of Switzerland's most notorious inmates.

THE FACTS

Born: December 29th 1946 | Active: 1971-1989

Arrested: August 30th 1989 | Country: Switzerland | Victims: 4-7

Sentence: Life imprisonment | Status: Incarcerated

Filho, Pedro Rodriguez: The Pedrinho Matador

A Brazilian serial killer who actively sought to kill other criminals. He killed an astonishing 47 people while inside prison, including another serial killer named Francisco de Assis Pereira. Filho holds the record for the highest number of victims killed behind bars.

Filho has always been a unique serial killer in that he targeted other criminals, leading some to call him the real life Dexter. He was also known as the Criminal Killer or Killer Petey. In addition to his prison murders, he claimed at least another 24 outside of prison, giving him a body count of 71, but up to 100 have been linked to him in total.

Filho said he first felt the need to kill when he was only 13-years-old but held off until he was 14, when he killed the Vice-Mayor of Alfenas in southern Brazil. He killed the Vice-Mayor because he had fired his father after accusing him of stealing, which he hadn't. Still, the murder of a political official at such a young age set the standard for what was to come.

Filho move to São Paulo where he killed a man who was said to have been the real thief that had framed his father. He then continued his route of violence and murdered a drug dealer before meeting a girl named Maria Aparecida Olympia. She lived with him for a short while and they became close until she was brutally murdered by gang members in the city. It is unclear whether it was out of revenge for the murder of the drug dealer.

Filho then went on a rampage, torturing a large number of people and killing others in an attempt to find the person who had killed his girlfriend. By the time he was 18, he had already killed 10 people. Then in a bizarre twist, his father killed his mother with a machete, and so Filho went to the prison and killed his own father, cut out his heart, and ate it.

In 1973, he was sent to prison where he killed 47 other inmates in various institutions. Due to the Brazilian justice system and despite the fact his body count was huge, Filho was released in 2007. Unsurprisingly, he continued to kill other criminals outside of the prison walls, and was arrested again in 2011, on previous charges of inciting riots and further murders.

In 2018, he was released again and has since converted to Christianity after he apologised for his sins upon the world. Filho is also in the process of writing an autobiography. Amazingly, he has a YouTube channel where he gives advice to young people and others thinking of committing crime. As of 2022, he dedicates his life to the prevention of youth crime.

THE FACTS

Born: June 17th 1954 | Active: 1967-2003

Arrested: May 24th 1991 | Country: Brazil | Victims: 70+

AKA: Pedrinho Matador/Killer Petey | Status: Released in 2018

Fokin, Victor: The Grandfather Ripper

Another Russian serial killer, Viktor Viktorovich Fokin, AKA: The Grandfather Ripper, killed at least 10 people over a four year period from 1996 to 2000. He was 60-years-old when he committed his first murder giving him the aforementioned moniker.

In April 1996, a year after his wife died, he lured a 35-year-old homeless woman to his apartment. He plied her with vodka and then hit her on the head with a hammer, killing her instantly. Fokin then dismembered her body and dumped the body pieces into the Yeltsovka River.

Approximately every two months afterwards, the dismembered remains of females were found in different areas, leading to a task force being set up. Fokin was arrested in 2000, much to the shock of the local community, due to his age and previous work within the area.

In 2001, Fokin was sentenced to only 19 years at a corrective prison colony. 10 murders were attributed to him with evidence found in his apartment but the investigators believed he may have murdered many more. He died of natural causes in 2003, aged 68, bringing the investigation to a grinding halt.

THE FACTS

Born: February 19th 1935 | Active: 1996-2000.

Arrested: March 2000 | Country: Russia

Victims: 10+ | AKA: The Grandfather Ripper

Sentence: 19 years in prison | Status: Died in 2003

Fourniret, Michel Paul: The Ogre of the Ardennes

EXTENDED CASE FILE

On December 11th 1987, 17-year-old Isabelle Laville was the first victim to be murdered by the Ogre of the Ardennes. French serial killer Michel Paul Fourniret confessed to killing 11 people in France and Belgium between 1987 and 2001. His wife Monique Pierrette Olivier was complicit in some of the murders and would be sentenced alongside him. It wouldn't be until July 11th 2006, when Laville's remains would be recovered.

Born in 1942, in the middle of World War Two, Michel grew up in a poor household with the threat of war violence hanging over the family's head. Michel stated that in his formative years he had sexual encounters with his mother. The continuing abuse caused him a great deal of trauma and he began to develop an unhealthy view of women as he went through puberty.

He became obsessed with the notion of virginity after he discovered his first wife was not a virgin. This had upset him after learning his wife had been with other men. It was this along with his mother's incestuous abuse that led to him trying to kill mostly virgins, though the true motive behind his crimes has never been found.

His accomplice and future wife, Monique, was already aware of Michel's personality and crimes before they married. While serving time in prison for 15 counts of sexual assault against minors in and around Paris, Michel sought pen pals and placed ads in a religious magazine. Monique answered the ad and many letters were sent between them until his release from jail in 1987.

Through their letters, they developed a pact that would lead to the murders of multiple people upon his release. Michel wrote to her about his fantasy and great desire to kill virgins and young women. Monique then pledged to help Michel abduct young women and girls if he would agree to kill her abusive husband who she had separated from.

Michel never ended up killing her husband but he kept promising he would. However, Monique kept up her side of the pact and helped Michel kidnap, rape and murder multiple victims over many years.

In March 1988, Michel was contacted by 30-year-old Farida Hammiche, who was the wife of a convicted bank robber that Michel had shared a cell with until his release. She claimed there were cash and gold coins buried in a cemetery and she needed help to unearth it. Michel agreed and received a share of half a million French Francs ($87,000 USD).

A month later, Michel and Monique decided to steal the rest of the loot from Hammiche's apartment. They lured her out of her home and drove her to a secluded area where Michel strangled her to death. They then returned to her house to steal the rest of the haul. Hammiche's body was never found. It is unclear how much they managed to steal in total but they purchased an expensive Château in Donchery.

In August 1988, the couple drove to a supermarket and lured 20-year-old Fabienne Leroy to their car. Monique was pregnant with Michel's child and pretended to be ill because of it in order to trap their next victim. They drove Leroy to a forest near a military camp where Michel raped her and shot her in the chest. Her body was found a day later.

In January 1989, Michel took an evening train when he met 21-year-old Jeanne-Marie Desramault, only to learn she was staying at a convent. Once he knew her routine, he met her again at the train station two months later, this time with Monique by his side. They invited Desramault to their home and she accepted as Michel would drive her home after. After finding out she wasn't a virgin, Michel beat her and attempted to rape her. She was gagged and strangled to death, before being buried in the garden of the Château. Her remains were found in 2004.

In July 1989, Michel and Monique finally married and drove to Belgian with their one-year-old son. They caught sight of 12-year-old Elisabeth Brichet and waited for her to leave her friend's house. Michel asked for directions to a doctor's surgery, and she agreed to go with them in the car. The following day, Michel strangled her in their home and buried her in the garden of the Château, close to where Desramault had been buried.

Her disappearance became prime time news and a number of sightings of her were recorded in the years that followed. Many suspects were put forward including Marc Dutroux who was an infamous child killer at the time. After Dutroux's arrest in 1996, the mother of Elisabeth Brichet organised a march in honour of the missing and murdered children of Belgium. Elisabeth's body was found the same day as Desramault on July 3rd 2004.

On November 21st 1990, the couple were convicted of burglary in a court in Nantes. They left the court shortly after and drove to a shopping centre where they lured 13-year-old Natacha Danais, into their vehicle. They drove her to a secluded area near the coast where Michel stabbed her twice in the chest with a screwdriver. He strangled her to death and dumped her body on a beach.

Eight days later, an innocent man named Jean Groix, who was a neighbour of the victim, was arrested after a witness said it was his van at the shopping centre. In a bizarre twist, he was putting up members of the ETA (an armed Basque nationalist and separatist organisation) in his home. It was suspected that Danais had found out about it and Groix silenced her by killing her. A few months later, Groix killed himself in his cell, as he couldn't face being convicted of a child's murder.

Michel later confessed that he killed two more people in France in 2000 and 2001. This came after a 10 year break from killing when the couple had moved to Belgium to buy a small castle. In May of 2000, he abducted 18-year-old student Céline Saison. He drove her back to Belgium where he raped her before strangling her and dumping the body in a wooded area. Her remains were discovered two months later.

In May of 2001, he lured 13-year-old Thai girl Mananya Thumpong. He drove her to a secluded wooded area, raped her and strangled her to death. Some of her bones were found almost a year later, due to wild animals having eaten the flesh of the body.

In 2003, an unnamed 13-year-old girl escaped Michel's clutches and she ran from his van in Belgium. She had been tied by her ankles and wrists and managed to get help.

She was able to identify Michel and he was arrested in June of that year. A year later, Monique confessed that her husband had killed numerous people since 1987. They were both extradited to France for their trials.

They assisted the investigation and led police to the bodies of three of the four missing victims over a two year period. The trial took place in 2008 where Michel was found guilty and sentenced to life for the murders of seven of the victims whose bodies had been discovered. Monique was sentenced to life for being an accomplice in the murders. They were ordered to pay 1.5million Euros in compensation to the families of the victims.

Although convicted of seven murders, he was positively linked to four more, bringing the total to 11 victims. It remains one of France and Belgium's most notorious cases. In May 2021, Michel died of natural causes at the age of 79. In early 2022, various investigations were reopened with the hope that Monique might lead them to undiscovered bodies or a confession of further victims. She remains incarcerated.

THE FACTS

Born: April 4th 1942 | Active: 1987-2001.

Arrested: June 26th 2003 | Country: France/Belgium

Victims: 11+ | AKA: the Ogre of the Ardennes

Sentence: Life imprisonment | Status: Died in 2021.

Fowler, Bobby Jack

American rapist and serial killer Bobby Jack Fowler was suspected of killing 11 people. Advancements in cold case investigation and DNA technology has linked him to a number of murders over a 23 year period from 1973 to 1995.

As part of the Royal Canadian Mounted Police's 'E-Pana Investigations', there is DNA evidence that matches Fowler to the murder of 16-year-old Colleen MacMillen in August 1974 in South Cariboo, British Columbia, whose body was discovered a month later. She was last seen leaving her home to hitchhike to a nearby friend's house.

CHATEAU DU SAUTOU, FORMER HOME OF MICHEL FOURNIRET

POLICE SEARCH AT CHATEAU DU SAUTOU

MONIQUE PIERRETTE OLIVIER

IMAGE ATTRIBUTIONS
(ATTRIB A19) (ATTRIB A20)
(ATTRIB A21A) (ATTRIB A21B)

MICHEL PAUL FOURNIRET

In November 1973, 19-year-old Pamela Darlington vanished from Kamloops, British Columbia, while hitchhiking to a local bar. Her body was found the next day and was suspected to have been a victim of Fowler's. In October 1973, 19-year-old Gale Weys vanished while hitchhiking from Clearwater to Kamloops. Her body was found in a ditch on Highway 5 just south of Clearwater. Her death was also linked to Fowler.

In 2012, investigators used advancements in DNA technology to positively identify Fowler in the murder of MacMillen. The Royal Canadian Mounted Police concluded that Fowler was responsible for at least 10 of the other victims on the list. However, many more murders took place after his arrest in 1995 when he was picked up on a rape charge. Fowler died in prison in 2006 while serving his time for rape, meaning he took many of his secrets to the grave. As of 2022, many of the cold cases remain open investigations.

THE FACTS

Born: June 12th 1939 | Active: 1973-1995

Arrested: June 28th 1995 | Country: USA/Canada | Victims: 1-11

Sentence: 16 years for rape | Status: Died of natural causes in 2006

Francois, Kendall: The Poughkeepsie Killer

EXTENDED CASE FILE

In Poughkeepsie, New York, serial killer Kendall Francois, AKA: The Poughkeepsie Killer, took the lives of at least eight women over a two year period from 1996 to 1998. He took the bodies home and stored them in his house that he shared with his parents.

As a child and into his teen years, Francois had poor hygiene and was bullied because of it. Other children in school called him 'Stinky' and the name stuck, becoming his nickname for years afterwards. He was also mocked for his weight and size, and because of it he became withdrawn from society, not talking much and keeping himself to himself.

The first murders began at the tail end of 1996 when Francois was 25. 30-year-old sex worker Wendy Meyers was murdered on October 24th 1996, she had last been seen at a Valley Rest Motel on the banks of the Hudson River. She had been spotted talking with Francois in his car over prices for her services. He then took her home, and when she wanted to leave quickly, according to his confession, Francois strangled her to death.

He then took her body into one of the bathrooms and washed her corpse clean. Then he put her into a black bin bag and took it to his attic, where the body stayed for almost two years before being discovered. After Meyers death, Francois discovered his blood lust and went on to murder many more in quick succession.

On November 29th 1996, 28-year-old sex worker Gina Barone got into Francois's car and they drove to his garage where they had sex. Francois claimed that after sex, Barone wanted more money and so he strangled her to death in his car, leaving her body in the trunk until the next day. Then he cleaned her body and put in his attic next to the body of Meyers.

Just two days after his second murder, on November 31st Francois killed 31-year-old sex worker Cathy Marsh. He had strangled her so hard that he had broken her hyoid bone, which is a bone in the upper spine just beneath the jawbone. He took the body home, cleaned it and put her in the attic next to the other bodies. Her mother wouldn't report her missing until four months later in March 1997.

In January of 1997, a 47-year-old sex worker named Kathleen Hurley vanished from the street she was working on. She had been brutally murdered by Francois who kept the body in his attic. Shortly after her disappearance, the media started to latch onto the story of sex workers being listed as missing, and the police investigation finally began.

After a local newspaper report asked the question of a serial killer in the county, many sex workers in the area pointed the finger at Francois, among others. They claimed that Francois preferred rough sex and enjoyed choking them. At the time, the police couldn't confirm either way if Francois was the killer so they put him and his home under surveillance.

In the Spring of 1997, the Poughkeepsie police reached out to the FBI for help. On first look, the FBI didn't take the case because there were no bodies and no crime scene. Most times when people were reported missing, there was a simpler reason other than murder. Due to individual circumstances, this could have included people who wished to live off-the-grid, committed a crime themselves, became homeless, family problems, drug issues, and multiple other reasons. A serial killer was the least likely reason.

Francois, aware of the investigation, held his bloodlust at bay, but not for long. On October 9th 1997, 27-year-old sex worker Michelle Eason vanished from the downtown area she was working. She was the first black woman to be killed by Francois, whereas all of the previous and later victims were white and of a smaller build.

One month later, on November 13th, 29-year-old Mary Healy Giaccone was reported missing by her father. Giaccone's mother had just died, and her father went to the police to ask for help in finding her to give her the bad news. When they investigated, it appeared that Giaccone was last seen working the streets back in February of the same year.

Suddenly, the media and area began to fear that a serial killer really was stalking the streets. The Poughkeepsie Journal ran multiple stories on the missing women, and the police kept up the investigation. On January 18th 1998, a police officer followed Francois to his mother's workplace where Francois was giving her a lift. After he dropped her off, police arrested him and asked him to come in for questioning. They gave him a lie-detector test which he passed with flying colours.

Just five days later, he picked up sex worker Lora Gallagher, and took her back to his house. He throttled her during sex, and she passed out, only to awaken later underneath Francois's full body weight. She fought herself free and demanded to be taken back to the streets.

Surprisingly, Francois agreed and took her back downtown, where Gallagher told others about her experience. Sex workers who heard the story then took their concerns to the vice squad. It took an entire month to convince Gallagher to sign an official statement against Francois. But as soon as she did, Francois was arrested, on February 26th 1998. On May 18th, Francois was convicted of the assault on Gallagher. Astonishingly he was only sentenced to 15 days in prison for the assault. Even more astonishingly, he would serve only seven days in prison. It would only be two weeks after his release that he would kill again, on June 12th, when he killed 51-year-old Sandra French, during sex.

He hid her body in the attic after cleaning her body. Due to the smell and the overcrowding of corpses in the attic, he decided to move her body to the crawlspace of his house. On August 12th, 34-year-old Audrey Pugliese was killed by Francois. She suffered the most brutal murder of all the sex workers he killed. Francois claimed that he 'flipped-out' during sex and started punching her in the face, but Pugliese got away and ran into the basement, in an attempt to run out the basement door.

Francois grabbed her and pulled her back to the concrete floor where he continued a barrage of punches to her face. Angry with her, and not content with the punching, Francois started stamping on her. He crushed her ribs, and her stomach, then stamped on her face. Then he strangled her to ensure she was dead, before dumping her body in the crawlspace.

Just two weeks later on August 26th, he killed his final victim; 25-year-old sex worker Catina Newmaster. A day later, he moved her cleaned body to the crawlspace to join the others. The sex worker community was outraged and claimed the police didn't care about them.

'We're low life's, that's what it comes down to. People don't care that we're missing because they think we don't belong on the streets in the first place. It's not just the police, it's the community.' – Interview with a sex worker – Poughkeepsie Journal, July 26th 1998.

Unknown to the community and Francois at the time, there had been an ongoing investigation that involved the local police, state police, and the FBI, who had finally pooled their resources. Yet even though Francois had already been convicted of assault, he still hadn't been caught.

On September 2nd, Francois picked up Diane Franco and took her back to his house where he attacked her during sex. She fought him off and convinced him to take her back to the street. Surprisingly, he agreed, and took her back to where he had picked her up. She reported the attack immediately and police arrested Francois shortly after.

That same evening, a warrant was served on Francois's house, and an army of police and investigators descended on the property. His parents and sister were in the house and were asked to leave so a search could begin. Detectives later stated that the inside of the house had the most overpowering stench of death they had ever encountered.

The house was a complete mess, with clothes and rubbish on the floor, dirty washing, mouldy food strewn about the place, and maggots in the sink. One forensic expert stated the house to be 'completely toxic'. A couple of days later, a total of eight bodies were brought out of the house, as media vans lined the streets. A month later, Francois was charged with eight murders. He pleaded guilty and a trial by jury was not required, thus avoiding the death penalty. He was sentenced to life in prison without the possibility of parole.

Once he was sentenced, more disturbing details of the case were released. One investigator claimed that after spending a few hours in the house that his boots were eroded because of the amount of human 'sludge'. When the bodies decomposed to skeletons, Francois removed their skulls and placed them in a children's paddling pool in the attic.

Back in 1995, he had contracted HIV from a sex worker, and may have been one of the reasons why he decided to kill. His only claimed motive was that he became angry during sex and couldn't control what he was doing. His parents and sister claimed to have no idea what he was doing, despite living in disgusting conditions.

They said that Francois claimed a Raccoon had died somewhere in the house which caused the smell. His neighbours were aware of the smell and the rundown look of the house but didn't complain to authorities or call the police. On September 11th 2014, aged only 43, Francois died in prison of natural causes. The cause of death has never been listed but is assumed to be because of complications related to him being HIV positive.

THE FACTS

Born: July 26th 1971 | Active: 1996-1998

Arrested: September 2nd 1998 | Country: USA (New York)

Victims: 8 | AKA: The Poughkeepsie Killer

Sentence: Life imprisonment | Status: Died in 2014

KENDALL FRANCOIS' FORMER HOME TAKEN THREE MONTHS AFTER POLICE SEARCHED THE HOUSE AND REMOVED THE BODIES

KENDALL FRANCOIS

IMAGE ATTRIBUTIONS
(ATTRIB A22) (ATTRIB A23)

LONNIE DAVID FRANKLIN JR.

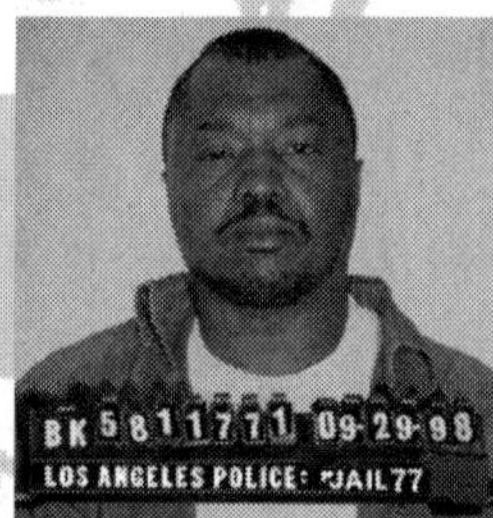

IMAGE ATTRIB. A24

IMAGE ATTRIB. A79

PEDRO RODRIGUEZ FILHO

Frankford Slasher, The

EXTENDED CASE FILE

The Frankford Slasher was a moniker for a serial killer who was active in and around the Frankford region of Philadelphia, in Pennsylvania, from 1985 to 1990. A black man named Leonard Christopher was convicted for one of the nine linked victims. He was convicted on minimal evidence and most witnesses saw the victims with a middle-aged white man before their deaths. All of the victims were sexually assaulted and stabbed to death.

On August 26th, 1985, the body of 52-year-old Helen Patent was found by transit workers at a train yard in Philadelphia. She had been left half-naked and laid out in a provocative manner. She had been stabbed 47 times and her organs had been exposed by the vicious attack.

On January 3rd, 1986, only a few miles from the first victim, the brutalised body of Anna Carroll was found on the floor of her bedroom. She too had been left nude and in a provocative position. She had been stabbed six times and had been gutted, exposing her insides. The kitchen knife used in the attack was left inside of her.

After a third victim was discovered on Christmas Day, 1986, investigators began to make connections. All three victims had been regulars at the Goldie's Bar on Frankford Avenue. The area had been well known for drug users and had a reputation as a big nightlife centre.

On January 8th, 1987, the body of Jeanne Durkin was discovered beneath a storage truck just off Frankford Avenue. She had been stabbed 74 times and was found in a pool of her own blood. She was naked from the waist down and had also been positioned in a provocative position.

Durkin was a homeless woman who was commonly seen sleeping in an entranceway just a few doors down from Goldie's Bar. It was then that investigators realised a serial killer was at large. They informed the media that the crimes were not related, and the killings stopped for an entire year. Until January 1988 when 66-year-old Margaret Vaughan was found murdered in a similar fashion to the previous four victims.

They created a sketch of the murderer who had been seen drinking with her in Goldie's Bar and asked the public for help. Another year passed and another victim was found in January of 1989. 30-year-old Theresa Sciortino was found in her apartment just outside of the Frankford region of the city. She had been stabbed 25 times and was found on the kitchen floor in a pool of her own blood.

Her wounds had been caused by a kitchen knife which was left at the scene. Next to her body was a three-foot section of wood that had been used to sexually violate her with. Investigators discovered that she was also a regular at the Goldie's Bar.

Another year passed and yet another body turned up on April 19th, 1990. The body of Carol Dowd was discovered in an alley near a fish market. She had been raped and stabbed 36 times. Due to the brutality of the attack, her intestines had spilled out of her body. Then a connection was made between Dowd and two of the previous victims; Sciortino and Durkin. They had all been in and out of psychiatric wards in the years prior to their murders.

Upon interviewing some of the fish market employees they met with Leonard Christopher who worked there and lived in the area. He said that he knew one of the victims, Margaret Vaughan. Because he did not have an alibi, he was arrested on May 5th, 1990, and charged with Dowd's murder.

Witness stories were all over the place, some placed him at the scene of the crime, while others said he was of good character and was nowhere near the murder scenes. On June 20th, 1990, Christopher stood trial for the murder of Carol Dowd as the evidence was deemed sufficient.

His description didn't fit the one given by witnesses for the other murders but on December 12th, 1990, Christopher was sentenced to life for the murder of Dowd. The evidence was circumstantial at best, but it didn't matter. Not even when another body was found.

Two months earlier on September 6th, while Christopher was in prison awaiting trial, the body of 30-year-old Michelle Denher was found in her apartment just one block away from Frankford. She had been raped and stabbed 23 times.

Her body had been found in a provocative position and she had a large slash to her stomach which exposed her intestines. Astonishingly, Denher was also a psychiatric patient, who lived just three blocks away from the previous murder and drank in Goldie's Bar. A day before her murder, she had been seen with a middle-aged white man who fitted the original description of The Frankford Slasher. The public were not convinced that Christopher had killed Dowd, and so the story had caught the attention of local media and community groups. One theory even pointed to witchcraft, due to a cult presence in the area that held rituals in a local park.

Investigators have since claimed there is no evidence that pointed to Christopher being The Frankford Slasher. As of 2022, the eight other murders are now part of an active cold case. Leonard Christopher has since died of cancer

THE FACTS

Active: 1985-1990 | Country: USA (Pennsylvania)

Victims: 9 | Status: Unsolved

Franklin, Joseph Paul: The Racist Killer

EXTENDED CASE FILE

In March of 1978, American porn king, Larry Flynt, was shot and paralysed by Joseph Paul Franklin, AKA: The Racist Killer, in Georgia. He ambushed Flynt and his lawyer, in retaliation for an edition of Hustler displaying interracial sex. He would go on to kill between seven and 22 victims.

Born in 1950, he became a white supremacist and killed most of his victims from the late 1970s to the early 1980s. He was born James Clayton Vaughn Jr. to a turbulent family. His father was a World War Two veteran who would physically abuse his children. His mother was considered to be an extremely strict disciplinarian who also physically abused him and his siblings. Franklin would go on to have stunted development in childhood and didn't mature as fast as his peers.

In his school years, he developed an interest in Nazi's, the Ku Klux Klan, and the National Socialist White People's Party. He changed his name to Joseph Paul Franklin to honour Nazi propagandist Paul Joseph Goebbels and former president Benjamin Franklin. He was inspired to kill 'blacks', as he put it, after consuming Hitler's Mein Kampf.

His first notable crime was on July 29th 1977, when he firebombed a Synagogue in Tennessee, completely razing it to the ground. Luckily, there were no deaths as not many worshippers had turned up on the evening he chose. One month later, he shot and killed a young interracial couple who were parked in their car at a parking lot in Wisconsin.

Exactly one year after his first major crime, on July 29th 1978. Franklin shot dead Bryant Tatum outside a Pizza Hut in Tennessee. That same moment, he also shot Tatum's white girlfriend, Nancy Hilton, who would go on to survive the shooting. It has never been made known why he killed exactly one year later but the fact it was the same date suggests more than just coincidence. It's possible Franklin felt the failure of a lack of deaths the year before and sought revenge on the same date in 1978.

'I was looking to cleanse the world of the inferior races.' - Joseph Paul Franklin.

Franklin fitted the drifter killer personality and used the newly constructed highways and interstates to roam up and down the East Coast of the United States. He would look to cleanse the world of mostly black and Jewish people. He paid his way by committing armed robberies at banks and also with blood-bank donations.

Throughout 1980, he attacked and killed at least eight more people, in addition to more murders in the years before. Over the years, he had covered himself in racist tattoos and it wasn't long until the FBI discovered he had been visiting blood-banks. They put out a nationwide alert and a Florida-based blood-bank worker recognised the tattoos and phoned it in. It led to Franklin being caught by the FBI in 1980.

'A government that forbids killing among its citizens should not be in the business of killing people itself.' – Larry Flynt, appealing for Franklin's death sentence to be commuted.

Franklin had attempted to incite a race war and had failed. Throughout various trials up until 1997, he was convicted of eight murders, received six life sentences and two death sentences, though it has been suggested he may have killed at least 20. He was executed by lethal injection on November 20th 2013. He did not make a final written statement or say any last words before his death.

THE FACTS

Born: April 13th 1950 | Active: 1977-1980

Arrested: October 1980 | Country: USA | Victims: 8-20

AKA: The Racist Killer | Sentence: Six life and two death sentences

Status: Executed by lethal injection in 2013

Franklin Jr., Lonnie David: The Grim Sleeper

EXTENDED CASE FILE

On April 15th 1987, the body of 26-year-old Bernita Sparks was discovered in Gramercy Park, Los Angeles. She had died at the hands of LA-based serial killer Lonnie David Franklin Jr. When he was arrested in 2010 he had claimed at least 10 victims but is suspected and linked to a possible 25.

Franklin killed over many decades and is one of the serial killers with the longest time-span of murders. He killed seven destitute black women in South Central Los Angeles from 1985 to 1988 but there was a 14-year gap when there were no killings. He resurfaced in 2002 to begin killing again and claimed at least three more lives. The gap between the killings earned him the notorious moniker of The Grim Sleeper.

Franklin, Jr. was a respected member of the local community and would help people to take their bins out or do some handiwork. So no one would have ever expected him to be a serial killer. In his other life as a killer of women, he would murder sex workers, drug addicts, or homeless runaways. He generally raped them before shooting them in the chest at close range. He then left their bodies in alleyways, in trash cans, or beside industrial bins. He knew the alleys well as he was a sanitation worker at the time.

He kept his victim's underwear and jewellery as a keepsake of his crimes, storing them in boxes at his home. When he was arrested, the investigators found a large collection of pornographic Polaroids. They depicted unconscious women, either dead or alive. There were more photographs than the killings he was convicted of, leading to speculation that he may have killed many more.

Not too much is known about his childhood but he grew up in South Central, an area of Los Angeles known for its violence and high crime rate. Police relations at the time were non-existent, and gang violence became epidemic in the area.

However, in 1974 while in his early twenties, serving in the U.S. Army as a cook, he took part in the gang-rape of a German girl whilst based in Stuttgart. He was discharged a year later due to the incident. In a 1974 trial, the victim, only known as Ingrid W, explained with the help of an interpreter that Franklin and two others jumped out a car and held a knife to her throat. She was gang-raped by the three of them over the course of an entire night.

Franklin testified the encounter was consensual but was convicted in a German court where he served less than a year in prison. During the rape, Franklin was known to have taken photos of the incident, in a dark foreshadowing of the murders to come.

In 1987, he became injured while working as a sanitation worker and spent the following two decades on disability handouts. In 1988, one of his victims, 30-year-old Enietra Washington accepted a ride from him, then he drove her to a quiet alley, raped, beat and shot her. Washington was left for dead near some trash cans but survived. She got away alive and her testimony was instrumental in the recent court case against him.

In 2007, the LAPD created a task force to find The Grim Sleeper and this was partly due to the reporting of an LA Weekly journalist named Christine Pelisek. She had noticed a pattern of murdered black women but with no reports of any arrests, so she wrote a story about it which led to the creation of the task force. It was Pelisk herself who had come up with the Grim Sleeper moniker.

In 2010, Franklin was arrested after the investigation had used familial DNA searching. Franklin's son had previously been arrested for gun and drug offences, and his DNA was on the systems they searched. When they made the match, Franklin was found soon after and charged.

In June of 2016, Franklin was sentenced to death for 10 murders and one attempted murder. It has been suggested that he killed many more. At the time he was killing, there were many more murders happening in the area, which gave rise to the Southside Slayer. The moniker was given to a number of serial killers who were active at the same time, including Louis Craine, and many others. Some of the murders remain unsolved. In March 2020, while awaiting execution on death row, Franklin died of natural causes

THE FACTS

Born: August 30th 1952 | Active: 1985-2007

Arrested: July 7th 2010 | Country: USA (California)

Victims: 10+ | AKA: The Grim Sleeper

Sentence: Death penalty | Status: Died in 2020

Furlan, Marco and Abel, Wolfgang

German-Italian serial killing duo, Wolfgang Abel and Marco Furlan were sentenced to 30 years each on February 10th 1987. They took part in the murders of at least 28 people between them from 1977 to 1984 in Germany, Italy and the Netherlands, and were known collectively as Ludwig.

On December 17th 1978, a gay waiter in Italy was stabbed 30 times with two blades left sticking out of his back. At each crime scene they left a leaflet, written in Italian, it showed a Nazi Eagle and swastika and each of them had a different slogan. 'We are the last of the Nazis' and 'Death comes to those who betray the true god' being two of them.

They burned most of their victims alive, and claimed the highest body counts in two arson attacks. On 14th May 1983, they set fire to a red-light cinema called Eros, in Milan, killing six people and wounding 32 others. On 17th December of the same year they burned down a strip club in Amsterdam, killing 13 people.

They were both caught in 1984 and were sentenced to 30 years each on February 10th 1987. Furlan was subsequently released in 2010. Abel was released to house arrest and then finally released to live amongst us in 2016. As of 2022, their current whereabouts are unknown.

THE FACTS

Born: March 25th 1959 (Abel)/January 16th 1960 (Furlan)

Active: 1977-1984 | Arrested: March 4th 1984

Country: Italy/Germany/Netherlands | Victims: 28

AKA: Ludwig | Sentence: 30 years in prison

Status: Furlan was released in 2010/Abel was released in 2016

Gacy, John Wayne: The Killer Clown

EXTENDED CASE FILE

On December 22nd 1978, the very same day as Andrei Chikatilo's first victim, John Wayne Gacy, The Killer Clown, was arrested, in a bizarre coincidence, referred to as the dark day of 1978.

In February of 1978, Gacy killed a 19-year-old man named William Kindred. William told his girlfriend he was going to a bar for the evening but ended up becoming another of Gacy's 33 victims. It is suggested there could be many more victims attributed to him but William was the last victim to be buried in Gacy's crawl space.

The Killer Clown would rape and kill dozens of young men over a small time period of just a few years in Illinois. 29 of his victim's remains were discovered in the crawlspace and other areas beneath his home. He would kill his victims mostly in the middle of sexual acts of bondage or raping them with various sex toys. He would achieve an orgasmic-like feel by taking their lives in such a manner.

Gacy was one of three children, born in Chicago, in 1942, in the middle of World War Two. His father was a World War One veteran and would physically abuse his wife and his children. He had also become an alcoholic after his return from the war.

In one of this book's research articles, we talk about the legacy of World War Two but not so much about The Great War, 30 years before. It goes without saying that a survivor or veteran of any war is susceptible to various mental disorders or depression. That Gacy's father abused him could have been a direct result of his own traumas experienced in World War One.

Gacy's father would beat him with leather belts and broomsticks and put his sisters in higher esteem than him. It was this sexual belittlement that led to Gacy growing up believing he was a 'sissy' and would grow up 'queer'. Something that would be one of the main elements of his murders in that he only killed boys and men.

When he was seven, Gacy was caught sexually assaulting a young girl. His father then whipped him with a strip of hardened leather as punishment. That same year, Gacy was sexually abused by a family friend in a van but kept the abuse secret at the time through fear of his father's punishments.

Gacy became an extremely complicated person growing up. His sexual confusion was coming to the forefront of his mind and his inability to fit in simply wasn't working for him. He moved to Las Vegas in 1962 and became a mortuary attendant. He would sleep on a bed behind the embalming room and watch the morticians embalm the bodies. Once, when he was alone, he laid in a coffin with a deceased teenage boy, where he embraced and caressed the body.

He moved back to Illinois, married for the first time and became a candidate for the Democrat Party. He then became a KFC franchise manager and was generally respected in the community. His wife gave birth to two children but then started divorce proceedings when he was convicted of male rape.

During his killing campaign and because of his services at fund-raisers, children's parties and parades, he would regularly dress up as Pogo the Clown or Patches the Clown. These monikers led to Gacy being nicknamed The Killer Clown.

Rumours had begun to spread that he was having sexual relationships with other men who worked for him in the KFC restaurants. He was a member of the United States Junior Chamber Organisation known as Jaycees, which was a training organisation for people aged between 18 and 40. The Waterloo Jaycees Club had a dark side where Gacy relished in prostitution, drug addiction and ample amounts of pornography.

In 1968 he lured a man to his home, on the same day his wife was giving birth to his son. He tied him up and raped him but the man went straight to police and Gacy was arrested. Gacy was sentenced to ten years but served less than two years for good behaviour. He was so angered at his wife for the divorce proceedings that he disowned her and his two children, never seeing any of them again.

He then married a second time to an old school friend, never had children and subsequently divorced a few years later. During their marriage he was heavily involved in gay pornography and his wife would find wallets and personal items of other men but never questioned it.

A few months before he married again, Gacy had claimed his first known victim. In January 1972 he picked up a 16-year-old boy name Timothy McCoy. Gacy would claim that McCoy approached him with a knife and he defended himself only to then stab McCoy in the chest multiple times. Gacy buried him in the crawlspace of his house and covered the body with a layer of concrete.

One of Gacy's employees named David Cram, lived with Gacy for a while after his second divorce. Together they dug the trenches under the crawlspace in his house. It is claimed later than Cram could have been helping Gacy with the killings and movement of the bodies.

His second victim in 1974 was a teenage boy of unknown origin. He put the body in his closet but fluid leaked from the boy's mouth and nose and so for subsequent victims, Gacy would push rags or the victim's own underwear into their orifices to stop them leaking.

He killed most of his victims over a two year period from 1976 to 1978. He would generally rape them as part of sex games and then torture, stab or strangle them to death. In 1977, he abducted 19-year-old student Robert Donnelly from a bus stop at gunpoint. Gacy abused, tortured and raped him with various sex toys and tools. He also tortured him with water torture by dunking his head in a bath, raped him constantly, violently assaulted him and beat him. But then Gacy threw him in his car and drove him back to Donnelly's own home.

Donnelly stated in an interview that the pain from the torture had been so bad, he wished Gacy had killed him. Police turned up at Gacy's house but he claimed they had consensual BDSM sex and he was released with no charge. As the net closed in, Gacy would later state he knew he was going to be caught, when he started dumping bodies in the river instead of burying them in the crawlspace of his house.

The investigation into the bodies in the river led back to Gacy, so he quickly flooded the crawlspace under the house to hide the evidence. When an evidence technician named Daniel Genty went down there as part of the investigation, he waited for the water to drain away. He found skeletal remains, decaying flesh and obvious signs of multiple murders. He told the investigation; 'I think this place is full of kids.'

Upon his arrest, Gacy confessed to the murders and claimed that he had lost count of the amount of bodies in the crawlspace. He had thought about covering the crawlspace in concrete completely to hide the evidence but he never got around to it. He killed five people during 1978 alone and they were all dumped in the river. During the investigation, 26 bodies were recovered from the crawlspace and one beneath the concrete floor of his garage. A week later, another body was recovered under the dining room floor.

Gacy was convicted of 33 murders and sentenced to death by lethal injection for 12 of them. He was executed in 1994 but the execution was marred by a botched IV tube. There was a problem with the tube when the drugs solidified and had to be replaced, the execution subsequently took 18 minutes. Following his death, Gacy's brain was removed for medical study.

THE FACTS

Born: March 17th 1942 | Active: 1972-1978

Arrested: December 21st 1978 | Country: USA (Illinois)

Victims: 33 | AKA: The Killer Clown

Sentence: Death penalty | Status: Executed in 1994

WHITE HOUSE PHOTOGRAPH OF FIRST LADY ROSALYNN CARTER WITH DEMOCRATIC PARTY ACTIVIST AND SERIAL KILLER JOHN WAYNE GACY

JOHN WAYNE GACY IN CLOWN SUIT

PAINTING BY GACY

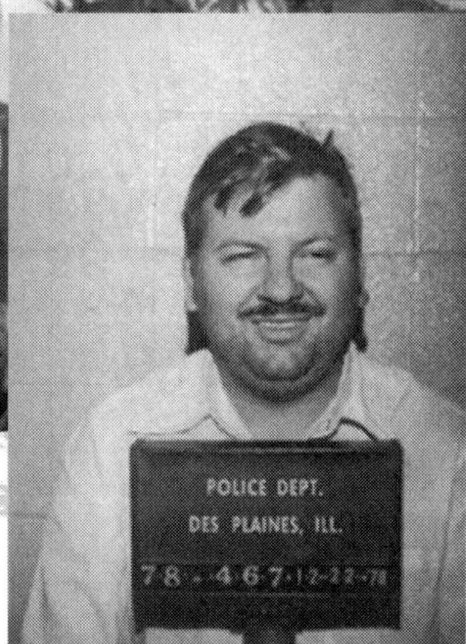

IMAGE ATTRIBUTIONS
(ATTRIB A3) (ATTRIB A25)
(ATTRIB A26) (ATTRIB A71)

JOHN WAYNE GACY

Gallego, Gerald and Charlene: The Love Slave Killers

EXTENDED CASE FILE

Between 1978 and 1980, Gerald Armond Gallego and Charlene Adell Gallego, who became known as The Love Slave Killers, hunted young girls and turned them into sex slaves before brutally murdering them. They would go on to kill ten people in California before their arrest in 1980.

Gerald came from a disruptive childhood, his mother was a sex worker and his father was a violent criminal who killed two policeman and became the first person to be executed in a gas chamber in Mississippi, in 1955. No doubt, not the best role model to have had in life.

His mother and her various boyfriends abused Gerald in his formative years. During her time as a sex worker, she allowed some of her clients to sexually abuse him too. It is said that this level of abuse and neglect led him to sexually abuse a six-year-old girl when he was only 13-years-old. During his teens and early adult life, he was arrested 23 times on various criminal charges including robbery and assault.

When Charlene was young, her mother was badly hurt in a car crash. She would then join her father on his business trips when her mother was home bound. She was said to have been a smart and intelligent young girl. For unexplained reasons, she turned to heavy alcohol and drug use in her early teens and told everyone she was having sex with a black man, to shock her peers, as it was considered immoral within her own family.

She married twice before meeting Gerald, her first husband was a wealthy heroin addict and his addiction increased her own dependency on drugs. Her first husband would later claim that Charlene was a sex addict whose fetishes included lesbian sex and threesomes with sex workers. It is unclear why sex would become overtly important to someone of such a young age. It was never known if she was abused in childhood or not.

Gerald worked as a barman and truck driver. Amazingly, he was married a total of seven times, including two marriages to the same woman. He would leave them mostly because they were running out of money. He would also begin to abuse his daughter on a regular basis. When he married Charlene, he was already married to his previous wife.

Gerald enjoyed rough sex and Charlene was happy to oblige his violent perversity. It is claimed they were more sexually compatible than others had been in their own lives. Charlene said in court that Gerald preferred to sodomise her during most sessions and that it was a painful experience, though she would feign enjoyment to make him happy.

On September 11th 1978, two teens, Rhonsa Scheffler and Kippi Vaught went missing from a mall in Sacramento. It was Charlene who lured them into a van that was parked close by. Gerald used a handgun to threaten the girls before tying them up. They drove all the way to Baxter where he abused and raped the girls before shooting them in the back of the head.

In June of 1979, two more girls were abducted in Nevada. Gerald beat them to a bloody death with a hammer and a shovel. Their bodies remained undiscovered for over two decades. They couple abducted and killed six more people before their final two victims.

In November of 1980, they kidnapped two students at a fraternity party. The young man was shot and found later near a lake, and the girl, Mary Sowers, was taken to the Gallego's apartment. She remained captive as Gerald abused and raped her. Afterwards, he took her to the middle of a field and shot her in the back of the head.

The kidnapping of the two students was witnessed and the police tracked the Gallego's number plate. It seems the Gallego's had been sloppy in their final abduction and were subsequently arrested. Charlene testified against her husband in a plea deal that only saw her receive a 16-year sentence. Charlene claims that it was Gerald who killed every single one of them.

'There were victims who died, and there were victims who lived. It's taken me a hell of a long time to realize that I'm one of the ones who lived.' - Charlene Gallego

Doubt has sometimes been thrown on her responsibility of the crimes but she was released in 1997 under a new identity. She was discovered a few years later living a life in the same neighbourhood where the murders took place and has shown no remorse for her crimes.

She was revealed by a local reporter in a bizarre interview regarding a different matter, which has never been made public. However, the community discovered and have revered her presence ever since.

One resident claimed that Charlene had been a thanksgiving guest of hers the year before. She had been sitting across from the parents of one of her victims and they never knew. Due to potential lawsuits, her new identity will not be revealed here but the community in question is enraged.

'Gallego's audacity at moving back to the area where most of the killings took place pales to her ongoing audacity of hosting fundraising events, and leading a veterans' event, including posing for photographs. She doesn't care.' - Local reporter.

Gerald was sentenced to death in 1983 and spent his last days on death row awaiting execution. He died of cancer in a Nevada prison medical centre, in 2002.

THE FACTS

Born: July 17th 1946 (Gerald), October 10th 1956 (Charlene)

Active from 1978-1980 | Arrested: November 17th 1980

Country: USA (California) | Victims: 10 | AKA: The Love Slave Killers

Sentence: Death penalty (Gerald)/16 years in prison (Charlene)

Status: Gerald died in 2002/Charlene was released in 1997

Garavito, Luis: The Beast

EXTENDED CASE FILE

Luis Garavito, AKA: The Beast, killed children and teenagers in Colombia, from 1992 until 1999. In just a seven year period, his confirmed number of victims totals 138 but is suspected to be around 300. He has since been described as the world's worst serial killer by body count alone.

In terms of number of convicted victims, Harold 'Dr. Death' Shipman, from the United Kingdom, is the world's worst serial killer after being convicted of 215 murders and linked to a total of 250. Another Colombian, Pedro Lopez, was convicted of 110 murders and is sometimes listed as the world's worst serial killer, but The Beast is even worse.

On June 8th 1996, a young boy went missing in the town of Boyaca. He had been lured to his death by The Beast. Five days later, the decapitated body was discovered in a remote area, the boy's penis had been sliced off and stuck inside his mouth.

The boy's mother discovered that Garavito had bought her son sweets before the disappearance and he was arrested on suspicion of the murder. He told police he bought the boy candy but nothing more, he was believed and the police didn't follow up on it. Just four days later, he killed a 13-year-old boy in the nearby town of Pereira.

Born in Genova, Colombia, in 1957, he was the eldest of seven children. Garavito and his brothers were beaten regularly by their father, and he was also emotionally, physically, and sexually abused by his neighbour. And for the crimes inflicted on him, he would take revenge by hurting hundreds of children.

Before he turned to murder, he drifted from job to job, becoming an alcoholic in the process. Because of his alcoholism, he became aggressive and had a temper that he found difficult to control. It is claimed that he attempted suicide at least once and had been in and out of psychiatric care for five years before the killings began.

'We are not facing some sort of criminal genius, we are confronting an individual who had no inhibiting restraints to killing.' - Pablo Gonzalez: state prosecutor

His victims were mainly young boys between the ages of six to 16. He would lure them from the streets of Colombia or over the border in Ecuador. He would then rape, beat, torture and slaughter his victims, burying them in shallow graves in rural locations across both countries.

In Colombia, in the early 1990s, the country was suffering from the effects of a long-running civil war and many children were either abandoned or living below the poverty line. Many were not listed as missing and Garavito's crimes went unnoticed for many years.

As with Pedro Lopez, Garavito would bury his victims in mass graves and once one site was discovered, the authorities finally took notice. Even in 2022, some bodies are still being discovered on the outskirts of rural villages where the victims match Garavito's other victims.

He kept souvenirs of his victims, which sometimes included their passport photos and items of clothing. He also kept a detailed list of when and where most of them died. Most of the remains were found with broken bones, most likely inflicted whilst the boys were still alive.

Garavito admitted to raping or sexually abusing every single one of his victims. He kept some of the victims tied up for two or three days at a time, usually to a tree by a leash. He would play with them and abuse them softly before raping them in a rising crescendo that would end with their deaths. Some victims were found with bite marks on their genitals.

He would usually kill them by cutting their throats and bleeding them dry, then dismember the corpses with a dull knife before burying parts of them in different places. He remembered where he buried every single one of his victims, so much so that he would draw the investigators a map to most of them. He led police to one mass grave at a ravine that consisted of 25 skeletal remains.

In a similar fashion to Pedro Lopez, he would lure boys with the promise of cakes or candy. Occasionally, he would pretend to be a priest in order to gain their trust. A lot of children were addicted to drugs in Colombia at the time, and the promise of drugs was another method that Garavito used to lure them to isolated areas.

He did this in over 54 cities across the two countries, making the links and investigation even more difficult. He would also spend time watching his victims to ensure that a boy was worthy of being his victim. His preference was for lighter-skinned boys with soft skin.

Upon his arrest, Garavito confessed and asked forgiveness from the investigators. He claimed that a demon would possess him and take control of his body during the murders. This combined with the alcohol consumption meant that he was not in control of his body when raping and killing. He even said that upon his release from prison, he wished to begin a political career, with a focus on helping abused children.

In 1998, the bodies of three children were found on the outskirts of Genua, Colombia, and an investigation into a possible serial killer opened. A mother of one of the boys told police about an older man who was seen with her son before he disappeared and gave a solid description to them.

On April 22nd 1999, Garavito was arrested on an attempted rape charge after being stopped by a member of the public. The investigators looking into the rape began to believe they had The Beast in custody. An interrogation led to Garavito confessing to the murders, and it is claimed the descriptions of his murders brought him to tears.

At one of the mass graves, a pair of glasses had been found. The glasses were designed for a rare eye condition that Garavito happened to suffer from. At other graves, empty bottles of alcohol, his shoes or his own underwear were found buried with the victims. The police took DNA from the pillow and bedsheets in his police cell and it matched the DNA found at the mass graves.

He was charged with 172 murders and convicted of 138. The exact location of the prison where he is serving his sentence is unavailable to the public due to the fear that he would be killed immediately. Garavito was sentenced to 1,853 years in prison. Astonishingly, because of good behaviour and the way the Colombian sentencing system works, his sentenced was reduced to 22 years. Even more astonishingly, he is eligible for parole in 2023.

THE FACTS

Born: January 25th 1957 | Active: 1992-1999

Arrested: April 22nd 1999 | Country: Colombia/Ecuador

Victims: 138-300 | AKA: The Beast/El Loco

Sentence: 1,853 years in prison, commuted to 22 | Status: Incarcerated

Gargiulo, Michael Thomas: The Hollywood Ripper

American serial killer, Michael Thomas Gargiulo, AKA: The Hollywood Ripper, killed at least two women but has been linked with at least two more murders. In 2019, he was convicted of two murders, and has been heavily linked to another murder in 1993.

In Illinois, where Gargiulo grew up, he murdered his 18-year-old neighbour, Tricia Pacaccio, by stabbing her to death on her porch. A few years later, Gargiulo moved to Los Angeles in a suspected effort to escape the investigation. While living in Hollywood, he began killing again.

On February 21st 2001, Gargiulo stabbed up-and-coming actress Ashley Ellerin, 47 times, in a frenzied attack at the victim's home. The stabbing was so brutal that her head had nearly been severed. The depth of the blade had passed through her body on numerous occasions. One of the stab wounds to the head entered the skull and had removed a section of bone, as if it were a piece of a puzzle.

On the night she was killed, she had planned to have dinner with Hollywood actor Ashton Kutcher. In May 2019, Kutcher testified at Gargiulo's trial about his planned evening with Ellerin. Kutcher had knocked on Ellerin's door later that night but there was no answer. He then assumed Ellerin had left early because he was a little late and left the property. Ellerin was discovered by her housemate the following day.

In December of 2005, Gargiulo stabbed to death his El Monte neighbour, 32-year-old Mario Bruno, who was stabbed 17 times at her residence, 19 miles from Hollywood. She had been asleep in her bed when the attack began.

In April 2008, Gargiulo went to the Santa Monica home of his new neighbour, Michelle Murphy, and attempted to kill her. Murphy fought back and overpowered him, kicking him away from the bed. Gargiulo had apparently expressed his apologies before he left her home.

Gargiulo was arrested shortly after and charged with the two Hollywood murders, the murder of his 18-year-old neighbour in 1993, and one of attempted murder. Due to multiple delays, the trial didn't begin until 2019. In August of that year, he was convicted of the two Hollywood murders.

In March 2020, a jury handed down the death sentence but sentencing was delayed until July 2021, while the judge considered a defence motion regarding a sheriff who may have been smuggling contraband into the county jail at the time of the trial. Gargiulo was ultimately sentenced to death.

In March 2022, a motion was filed to extradite Gargiulo back to Illinois to face the music for killing his 18-year-old neighbour. A current ongoing investigation has linked his DNA to a total of 10 victims, meaning there may be more trials to come.

THE FACTS

Born: February 15th 1976 | Active: 1993-2005

Arrested: June 6th 2008 | Country: USA (Illinois/California)

Victims: 3-10 | AKA: The Hollywood Ripper

Sentence: Death penalty | Status: Incarcerated

Gary, Carlton: The Stocking Strangler

EXTENDED CASE FILE

African-American, Carlton Michael Gary was convicted of armed robbery and the murders of three elderly women in Columbus, Georgia, from 1977 to 1978. He is suspected of killing four more but was never convicted, bringing his total to seven, but has since been the subject of controversy since his execution in 2018.

Carlton's father abandoned him until a brief reunion when he was 12-years-old. He constantly moved around with his mother and was found to be malnourished most of the time. In the modern era, malnourishment in children is generally the responsibility of the parents and classified as child abuse but in the 1970s it was passed over.

His aunt was a maid for elderly, wealthy women, and it was in his time spent with his aunt that his hatred and fascination with elderly women seeped into his thought processes. His childhood saw him turn to crime pretty quickly. He began to use drugs heavily and was arrested multiple times before he was 18. mostly for robbery, arson, or assault.

When he was 20, two elderly women were killed in the Albany region, and a third was assaulted. Upon his capture by way of fingerprints, he claimed that it was an accomplice who had murdered the women and that he only robbed them. His testimony against John Lee Mitchell, the 'accomplice', had no material evidence except Carlton's own words. Even so, Mitchell was convicted of the murders while Carlton served time on a robbery charge.

On parole in 1975, he moved to New York, where two elderly women were attacked. One was killed and the other survived, who claimed it was a black man similar to Carlton who had attacked her. Carlton wasn't charged at the time, but due to a different parole violation for robbery was sent back to prison. In 1977, he escaped from prison and moved back to Columbus, Georgia.

On September 16th 1977, a 60-year-old woman named Feme Jackson was brutally raped, beaten and subsequently strangled to death with a nylon stocking. Nine days later, he killed 71-year-old Jean Dimenstein in a similar fashion, followed by two killings in October, 89-year-old Florence Scheible and 69-year-old Martha Thurmond. Three days after Christmas, he killed 74-year-old Kathleen Woodruff. At all but Woodruff's crime scene, he had left a stocking that had been used to strangle his victims.

On February 12th 1978, an elderly lady named Ruth Schwob was attacked. Ruth managed to trigger her bedside alarm causing Carlton to flee the scene. Not being able to end the night without killing, he broke into another house only two blocks away and raped and strangled 78-year-old, Mildred Borom, his third convicted victim. His final known victim was Janet Cofer in April of 1978.

Carlton was arrested in December 1978 and charged with seven murders, to be convicted of three. After a brief escape from prison in 1983, he was rearrested in 1984, and sentenced to death in 1986. He spent 22 years on death row before being executed by lethal injection in 2018. Around the time of his execution, a group of supporters and researchers suggested that Carlton's conviction was questionable.

They point to the fact that many fingerprints were only connected to the murders years after they had occurred, his initial interviews had not been recorded, and his confession was handwritten by a police officer a week after he had given it. While on trial, Carlton denied having given the confession, though he was connected by DNA to the previously unsolved murder of Marion Fisher in New York in 1975, which brought his tally to nine in total.

THE FACTS

Born: December 15th 1952 | Active: 1975-1978

Arrested: December 1978 | Country: USA (Georgia/New York)

Victims: 9-11 | AKA: The Stocking Strangler

Sentence: Death penalty | Status: Executed in 2018

Gaskins, Donald Henry: Pee Wee

Nicknamed 'Pee Wee', Gaskins was confirmed to have killed 15 people over a 30-year period from 1953 to 1982 in South Carolina. He claimed that he killed 110 but it has never been proven. There was a suspicion that he just wished to be known as the serial killer with the highest body count.

When he was a child, Gaskins was bullied and mocked for having a smaller stature, which is where his nickname came from. He was neglected as a child, so much so that he only learned his given name of Donald when it was read out in court. At one-year-old, Gaskins drank a bottle of kerosene which caused convulsions that lasted throughout his early years.

As he grew up, he became involved in robberies, assaults and gang rape with some of his acquaintances. He was subsequently charged with the crimes and sent to a reform school, where it is claimed he was raped by other inmates. He escaped only to be re-sentenced when he attacked a teenage girl with a hammer. During his time in prison, he was raped again and 'owned' by another prisoner. He escaped again only to be recaptured and re-released in 1961.

'All I could think about is how I could do anything I wanted to her.' - Gaskins, in his memoir, about a female hitchhiker he killed in 1969.

He claimed to have picked up his victims on the new American highway systems and killed for pleasure potentially once every six weeks at his peak. He tortured and mutilated his victims while keeping them alive as long as he could. He was arrested in 1975 and led police to his home where they found the remains of eight of his victims, some of whom have never been identified.

In May 1976, he was convicted of one of the murders and sentenced to death, under the assumption that the other seven were also confirmed to have been killed by him but would not change the outcome of the ultimate sentence. In 1982, while on death row, he killed another death row inmate. Over the years, a total of 15 victims have been positively linked to Gaskins. He was executed in the electric chair in South Carolina on September 6th 1991.

THE FACTS

Born: March 31st 1933 | Active: 1953-1982

Arrested: December 1975 | Country: USA (South Carolina)

Victims: 15 | AKA: Pee Wee

Sentence: Death penalty | Status: Executed in 1991

Georgiev, Hristo Bogdanov: The Sadist

On August 28th 1980, in Sofia City, Bulgaria, serial killer Hristo Bogdanov Georgiev, AKA: The Sadist, was executed for the murders of five women between 1974 and 1980. His final victim was in March of 1980 when he attacked Angelo Pantova on a train line. He stabbed her in the back but she managed to crawl over 30 metres, before Georgiev walked up behind her, raped her, and then strangled her to death.

LUIS GARAVITO

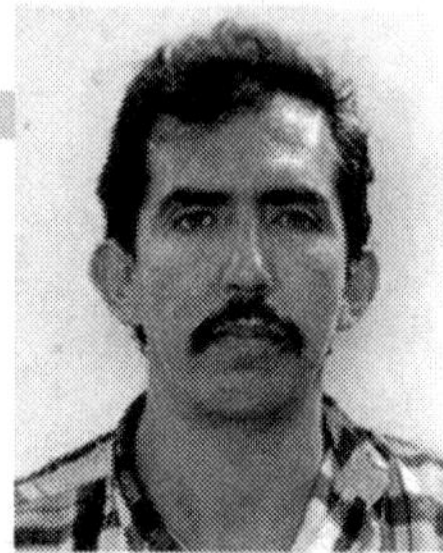

(ATTRIB A109)

(ATTRIB A111)

CHARLENE GALLEGO

(ATTRIB A110)

GERALD GALLEGO

(ATTRIB A112)

MICHAEL THOMAS GARGIULO

CARLTON GARY

(ATTRIB A113)

The murders had begun in 1974 and were only connected in 1979, when connections between the victims were found. Georgiev was arrested in April of 1980 and fast-tracked through the courts. He was known as The Sadist, due to the brutal way he claimed his victims. He was executed by firing squad on August 28th 1980.

After his arrest and execution, investigators discovered an underworld of major criminals, sex parties, mentally ill suspects, and murder linked to Georgiev, which led to the arrests of multiple people over the course of just one year.

In 2021, an engineer named Hristo Georgiev learned from a friend that his image was being used on a Google info-box displaying a Wikipedia page in relation to Hristo Bogdanov Georgiev. He reached out to Google, who removed the Wikipedia page entirely from their search listings.

THE FACTS

Born: 1956 | Active: 1974-1980

Arrested: 1980 | Country: Bulgaria | Victims: 5

AKA: The Sadist | Status: Executed in 1980

Gilbert, Kristen Heather

A former nurse, soccer-mom, and serial killer, Kristen Heather Gilbert killed at least four patients who were under her care at the Veterans Affairs Medical Centre (VAMC), in Massachusetts. She killed them by injecting their IV bags with epinephrine, which resulted in cardiac arrest.

To show herself as a heroine, she would respond to the emergency herself and aim to resuscitate the patient. On some occasions she would succeed. When she was growing up, Gilbert was known as a life-long manipulator and liar, who faked suicide attempts in order to gain sympathy and subsequently manipulate people around her.

She gained a nursing diploma when she was 21-years-old, in 1988, and married in the same year. She joined the VAMC site in 1989 and almost immediately was suspected of being the cause of an increasing number of deaths.

In 1996, three nurses at the centre reported their suspicions to authorities and an investigation began. Gilbert even tried to derail the investigation by phoning in a bomb threat, and then checked herself into various psychiatric hospitals to throw people off the scent. She was arrested on July 11th 1996.

In January of 1998, she was convicted firstly of making a bomb-threat and then for some of the murders that could be attributed to her. Staff at the hospital suggested that Gilbert was responsible for at least 80 deaths and at least 300 medical emergencies, in which she tried to show herself as the hero.

In March 2001, Gilbert was convicted of four counts of murder and two counts of attempted murder. She received four consecutive life sentences and an additional 20 years, to be served without the possibility of parole. She was transferred to a special federal prison for females with medical or mental health needs in Texas, where she has been ever since.

THE FACTS

Born: November 13th 1967 | Active: 1989-1996

Arrested: July 11th 1996 | Country: USA (Massachusetts)

Victims: 4 | Sentence: Life in prison | Status: Incarcerated

Gillis, Sean Vincent: The Other Baton Rouge Killer

EXTENDED CASE FILE

In Louisiana, American serial killer Sean Vincent Gillis, stalked, kidnapped, raped, murdered, and mutilated eight women over a ten year period. Born in 1962, it was claimed by his mother that his upbringing had been healthy and sociable and that he was a well-behaved child who got good grades in school. It was a far cry from the murders he committed later in his life.

Yet, his father had left the family the year he was born and it was something that infected his formative years, resulting in mental illness and alcoholism. From his later teens, he began drinking and taking drugs, and was arrested in 1980 for driving under the influence.

He was also prone to outbursts of anger and violence, with one witness saying he would go outside at three in the morning and start punching garbage cans to release his tension. He committed his first murder in 1994, when he was 30-years-old, and would later testify that he killed because he was stressed.

Just before the first murder, his mother moved away to take a job in Atlanta, and for the first time in his life, Gillis was forced to live alone. The loneliness he found himself in, saw him turn to pornography in a big way and he became obsessed with it. He became angry at his mother for leaving and would sometimes be heard screaming in the middle of the night.

His neighbours would often hear banging and cries of anguish in the early hours of the morning. On one occasion, he was caught spying on one of his female neighbours through their window. His obsession with porn led him to discover the dark side of the early mainstream internet. He consumed images of rape, dead bodies, and torture of women. But despite all of this, he still managed to find a girlfriend.

In March 1994, he attempted to rape 81-year-old Ann Bryan in her own home. When she screamed, Gillis claimed he had become scared and killed her to stop her screaming. He cut her throat and stabbed her over 50 times. He refrained from killing again for five years but during that time he began stalking joggers and other women across the county, watching their every move.

On May 30th 1999, he drove his car into 52-year-old jogger, Hardee Schmidt, who he had spotted three weeks earlier. The force of the collision threw her into a ditch. He then dragged her body into his car, drove to a remote area and raped her multiple times. After stabbing her to death, he dumped her body in a shallow grave.

As the murders continued, the police couldn't find any connections, as the victims were random and no evidence of a suspect was forthcoming. It meant that Gillis carried on killing for another five years. Some of his victims would have their hands or feet chopped off and other body parts would be removed. On one occasion, the local sheriff claimed that one of his victims had been so brutally hacked to pieces that it was difficult to believe they were looking at a human being. One of the victims was left in a ballet pose next to a sign that read; Dead End.

His final victim came in February 2004, when 43-year-old Donna Bennett Johnston was raped and strangled to death with a nylon tie. As she lay dead in front of him, Gillis sliced off her nipples and mutilated her breasts with a knife in a ritualistic fashion. He then sliced off one of her tattoos and cut off her left arm. Her body was found a few days later in a drainage canal near Louisiana State University.

In April of 2004, tyre tracks near the body of Johnston matched to Gillis's vehicle. Due to the specific type of tyre, only 90 purchases had been made in the area over a three year period which made it easier to track him down. Later in the same month, Gillis was arrested and charged with multiple smaller crimes, so the investigators had time to find further evidence against him.

Gillis confessed to eight murders but police were struggling to prove them all. When they searched his vehicle, they found 45 digital images on his computer of Johnston's body. There were also photos of her corpse in the trunk of his car. Then the investigation hit a goldmine of evidence when they found photos of other victims. Some of the photos were used in the subsequent trial.

Through all of his years killing women, his girlfriend had no idea that she was living with a serial killer. When they searched his home, they discovered various body parts, which he used in conjunction with the photographs to fantasise about the killings.

'What he is, is a narcissistic, self-centred, ego-maniac serial killer.' - Prosecutor Prem Burns, at the trial of Gillis.

In 2008, Gillis was convicted of three murders and sentenced to life without parole. He confessed to an additional five victims which were later proven to have been killed by him. While under arrest and awaiting his sentencing, he exchanged letters with a friend of his final victim, in which he was apologetic but also referred to himself as evil. He particularly regretted mutilating the bodies.

'If anything in my useless life comes out, help the little girls today not to be the premature corpses of tomorrow.' - Sean Vincent Gillis.

The reason Gillis was known as 'The Other Baton Rouge Killer', was because another serial killer was already operating in and would be caught during Gillis's campaign. The Baton Rouge Serial Killer, AKA: Derrick Todd Lee, was arrested in 2003, and at the time, the area breathed a sigh of relief, believing Lee to be responsible for all the murders. Lee killed at least seven women from 1992 to 2003 and was sentenced to death in 2004. He died of a heart failure in 2016 while awaiting his execution. Gillis remains incarcerated at the Louisiana State Penitentiary, AKA: The Alcatraz of the South.

THE FACTS

Born: 1963 | Active: 1994-2004

Arrested: April 29th 2004 | Country: USA

Victims: 8 | AKA: The Other Baton Rouge Killer

Sentence: Life imprisonment | Status: Incarcerated

Gilyard, Lorenzo Jerome: The Kansas City Strangler

Gilyard was a former trash company supervisor who raped and killed 13 women and girls but was convicted of six counts of murder in 2007. He raped his victims and left their bodies in secluded or isolated locations. His campaign of terror lasted from 1977 to 1993.

Most of the victims were sex workers in and around Kansas City, Missouri. All of them were strangled and had put up a struggle against him. Bizarrely, every victim was missing their shoes, and the bodies had been dumped in secluded locations around the city, but no effort apart from that was made to conceal the remains.

Almost all the victims had cloth or paper stuffed into the mouths, in a suspected attempt to silence them while he raped them. Back in 1969, for a five year period, he was linked to five more rapes but was never convicted for them. He also served an unlisted amount of time in prison for sexually abusing children.

Gilyard was arrested in 2004 after Kansas City police received a federal grant to reopen cold cases using advancements in DNA technology. Though confirmed to have killed 13, it is suggested many more victims could be attributed to Gilyard. He was sentenced to life in prison without the possibility of parole, where he remains to this day.

THE FACTS

Born: May 24th 1950 | Active: 1977-1993

Arrested: April 19th 2004 | Country: USA (Missouri)

Victims: 13+ | AKA: The Kansas City Strangler

Sentence: Life imprisonment | Status: Incarcerated

Glaze, Billy Richard: Jesse Sitting Crow

American serial killer Billy Richard Glaze AKA: Jesse Sitting Crow, was arrested on August 31st 1987, after a long investigation into his crimes. Glaze was a suspect in the murders of three Native American women in the Minneapolis, Minnesota area at the time and was arrested while driving under the influence of alcohol. The officers found a bloody shirt and a crowbar in the car.

Evidence in hair samples taken from the crowbar were used to convict him of the three murders and he was sentenced to life in prison. Glaze was suspected of involvement in a possible 50 murders in multiple states but with the evolution of DNA technology, Glaze's guilt was brought into question, and in 2014, various pieces of evidence were retested and showed they were not a match to Glaze.

It is suspected now that he was not involved in the crimes as DNA evidence points to an unidentified male in the murders. Glaze died of lung cancer in prison in December 2015 after spending 25 years inside, meaning the investigation into his crimes ended, and Glaze either took his secrets – or innocence – to the grave. His conviction for the three murders remains to this day.

THE FACTS

Born: July 13th 1944 | Active: 1986-1987

Arrested: August 31st 1987 | Country: USA (Minnesota)

Victims: 3 | AKA: Jesse Sitting Crow/Butcher Knife Billy

Sentence: Life imprisonment | Status: Died in 2015

Graham, Harrison

American serial killer Harrison Graham was convicted of the murders of seven females committed in 1986 but wasn't arrested until August 1987 when he was evicted because of the terrible smell coming from his apartment – the result of storing corpses.

On August 17th 1987, in Pennsylvania, Graham was arrested and charged with the murders. He said he killed all of them while he was under the influence of drugs and mostly at the same time as having sex with them.

He kept the bodies of his victims in his apartment, in the slum district of Pennsylvania, wrapping them in bedding and piling them up in his bedroom. The bodies were found after an eviction notice was served due to bad smells coming from the apartment. He turned himself in after a week on the run after his mother convinced him to.

Graham was arrested only months after another Philadelphia serial killer Gary M. Heidnik was arrested for similar crimes. A criminal justice professor named Anthony Walsh suggested that the lack of media attention to Graham's crimes was a media neglect of black serial killers in America. The general public of the day didn't really believe black people were capable of serial killing – except the 1980s were in fact witness to a large number of black serial killers.

Graham was convicted of seven murders and sentenced to death which was later commuted to life after an appeal regarding his mental health. As of 2022, he resides at the State Correctional Institution Coal Township (SCI Coal Township) in Pennsylvania.

THE FACTS

Born: September 9th 1959 | Active: 1986-1987

Arrested: August 17th 1987 | Country: USA (Pennsylvania) | Victims: 7

Sentence: Death penalty, later commuted to life | Status: Incarcerated

Greba, Alexander

A Russian serial killer sometimes known as 'The Goblin', though there is no data as to why he garnered that moniker. He first killed when he was just 16-years-old and would go on to murder five people. He was raised by a single mother with alcohol problems, who physically abused her children whenever she became angry, which was most of the time.

By the age of 10, Greba's criminal career had already begun and he began to shoplift and steal from people. In his early teens, he left home to live on his own in the forests surrounding the region of Oblast. In 1996, when he was 16, he broke into a house seeking refuge from the coldness of the winter months. He claimed that the woman who owned the house looked a lot like his own mother and so he murdered her in cold blood for that simple reason.

He was arrested in the same year and sentenced to eight years for the murder. He served the full sentence before being released in 2004. Just two weeks after he came out of prison, he broke into another house and killed the male owner. He went on to kill another three people in a similar fashion within a couple of months. He was arrested shortly after and convicted of the four murders. In March 2005, Greba was sentenced to life without the possibility of parole.

THE FACTS

Born: September 23rd 1980 | Active: 1996-2004

Arrested: July 6th 2004 | Country: Russia

Victims: 5 | AKA: The Goblin

Sentence: Life imprisonment | Status: Incarcerated

Greenwood, Vaughn Orrin: The Skid Row Slasher

In Los Angeles, California, Vaughn Orrin Greenwood, AKA: The Skid Row Slasher, killed at least eleven people and attacked at least one more victim, who went on to survive. In 1964, he killed two homeless men by slashing their necks from ear to ear. The victims were posed by Greenwood in a ritualistic fashion. As with all of his victims, there was salt found sprinkled around their bodies.

In 1966, in Chicago, Greenwood attacked a man with a knife but the man survived and Greenwood was arrested. He was sentenced for assault and served almost six years in prison. At the time, there had been no connection with the two homeless men in 1964. Upon his release, Greenwood went on a rampage.

From December 1974 to February 1975, he brutally killed at least nine more men, most of whom were homeless or staying in homeless hostels. As in the 1964 killings, Greenwood would kill them in a ritualistic fashion by posing their bodies and surrounding them with occult markings. In some cases, cups full of the victim's blood were found nearby leading to the suspicion that Greenwood was in fact drinking their blood.

Investigators on the case believed the man to be white but Greenwood was black, this was despite bringing in experts and psychics to assist them. Their mistakes in the profiling allowed Greenwood to get away with more killings than he should have done.

(ATTRIB A124)

SEAN VINCENT GILLIS

VINCENT DARRELL GROVES

(ATTRIB A125)

(ATTRIB A117)

LISA BREARLEY, WHO HAIGH STABBED 157 TIMES

(ATTRIB A126)

PAUL STEVEN HAIGH

He was arrested in 1975 and subsequently convicted of nine counts of murder but positively linked to another two. In 1977, he was sentenced to life in prison without the possibility of parole. Greenwood died of natural causes in prison on December 18th 2020.

THE FACTS

Born: January 19th 1944 | Active: 1964-1975

Arrested: February 1975 | Country: USA (California)

Victims: 11 | AKA: The Skid Row Slasher | Status: Died in 2020

Groves, Vincent Darrell

Groves killed seven sex workers over an 11-year period from 1977 to 1988 in Denver, Colorado. He was convicted of three but suspected of being involved in up to 17 murders. At the time he was killing, Denver was experiencing a raft of sex worker murders, leading to the press naming an unidentified killer the 'Denver Prostitute Killer.'

Between 1975 to 1995, up to 27 female sex workers were killed and were only grouped together in 2008, when cold case investigators made the links between them. Despite two other suspects who may have claimed one or two of the victims each, Groves has long remained the prime suspect but since he died in prison in 1996, and the bodies were mostly decomposed, the investigation hasn't moved forward.

In late 1977, 17-year-old Jeanette Baca was put into prostitution by Groves and for a while he became her pimp. One year later, her naked body was discovered in remote woodland, and although Groves was a suspect, there was no evidence to charge him. In 1978, he moved in with 21-year-old Norma Jean Halford, and less than one year later, her car was found abandoned. To this day, no trace of her has been found, dead or alive, but Groves was suspected in her disappearance.

On August 14th 1981, Groves killed 17-year-old Tammy Sue Woodrum while she was camping alone. He surrendered at the local police station and gave a full confession, which led to his 1982 conviction for murder and a 12-year sentence. Five years later, in February 1987, Groves was paroled to kill many more times.

Almost immediately upon his release, he began to kill again with three bodies discovered in 1987 alone. He would eventually be convicted of two more murders and sentenced to life in prison. Three murder convictions in total, seven confirmed murders, and as many as 17 suspected. In 1996, while investigations were still continuing, Groves died in prison, leaving behind a dark legacy that affected many lives.

THE FACTS

Born: April 19th 1954 | Active: 1977-1988

Arrested: September 1st 1988 | Country: USA (Colorado)

Victims: 7+ | Sentence: Life imprisonment | Status: Died in 1996

Grzesik, Tadeusz

In Poland, strawberry grower and serial killer, Tadeusz Grzesik, killed at least eight people as part of a gang known as the 'Moneychangers Gang'. The first confirmed murders took place in September of 1991, when he was involved in the shooting of two Ukrainian men and one Ukrainian women in a car park. Before he killed the woman, he raped her, and his DNA would later prove his involvement, 18 years after the fact.

The killings continued until 2007, and Grzesik was suspected of having killed over 20 people, with some of the bodies remaining undiscovered to this day. In 1998, he was suspected of having shot dead three men who were sitting at a table in front of a bar. In the same year, he was linked to the violent beating and stabbing of a 17-year-old clubber who was returning from a night out. The teenager's body was discovered the following morning.

In 2005, he created a gang to attack owners of exchange offices in the country. Up until 2007, the gang were linked to numerous robberies, at least five murders, and multiple attempted murders. In 2007, Grzesik was arrested, and DNA linked him to multiple murders and unsolved cases from 1991.

A lengthy trial led to his 2013 conviction for three murders and one rape, and he was sentenced to 25 years to life in prison. Some of the cases are still being investigated, and he has been positively linked to an additional five murders but is suspected of up to 20.

THE FACTS

Born: 1960 | Active: 1991-2007

Arrested: 2007 | Country: Poland

Victims: 8-20 | AKA: Moneychangers Gang (leader)

Sentence: 25 years to life | Status: Incarcerated

Haigh, Paul Steven

An Australian serial killer who shot and killed seven people in the late 1970s and then again in the early 1990s. In 1978, Haigh shot dead a 58-year-old Lotto Agency worker and a 45-year-old pizza shop operator, only two weeks after being paroled for multiple armed robberies.

A year later in 1979, he began killing people who he thought knew about his crimes. He killed an acquaintance named Wayne Keith Smith as he suspected he was about to contact with the police. He also shot dead Smith's 31-year-old girlfriend, Sheryle Gardner, and her 10-year-old son.

One of Haigh's most brutal attacks was committed against his girlfriend, 19-year-old Lisa Brearley, in the same year. Haigh stabbed her an astonishing 157 times after allowing another man to rape her at knifepoint. He believed she was sleeping with other men and needed to die for her sins. It was one of the worst murders ever committed on Australian soil.

He was caught later in 1979 and sentenced to life without parole, but claimed he suffered from Borderline Personality Disorder (BPD) and deserved a lower sentence because of it, despite never being diagnosed. In 1991, while in prison, he killed another inmate by hanging him from his neck. All appeals at reducing his sentence have fallen on deaf ears.

THE FACTS

Born: September 5th 1957 | Active: 1978-1991

Arrested: 1979 | Country: Australia | Victims: 7

Sentence: Life imprisonment | Status: Incarcerated

Hall, Archibald: The Monster Butler

Archibald Thomson Hall was known as The Monster Butler, who committed his crimes whilst working for the British upper class. He killed five people during his campaign. After being sentenced to prison for a number of crimes including robbery, he was released in 1975 and went on to kill his first victim shortly after.

He returned to his home country of Scotland and began working as a butler for Margaret Hudson who lived in Kirtleton House. In 1977, a man named David Wright began work at the house as a gamekeeper. It turned out that Wright and Hall had been in prison together and Wright threatened to tell the lady of the house about Hall's previous convictions. Hall then shot Wright dead while using a rabbit hunt as cover for the murder.

He then moved to London and began working for Walter Scott-Elliot and his wife. Hall's plan was to rob them of all their money and retire in a foreign country but when Mrs. Scott-Elliot walked in on Hall and an accomplice discussing their plan, the accomplice Michael Kitto suffocated her to death. They then drugged Walter and took him and his wife's body back to Scotland. They beat him to death, before enlisting the help of a local sex worker to assist with burying both bodies.

The sex worker was known only as Coggles. She had been seen wearing Mrs. Scott-Elliot's fur coat around town which Hall saw as drawing too much attention to herself, so Hall and Kitto killed her and buried her body in a barn. The final victim was his half-brother, Donald, a convicted paedophile just released from prison. Hall drowned him in the bath after having drugged him with chloroform.

Hall was subsequently captured in January of 1978 and attempted suicide while in custody. When it failed, he led police to the locations of the bodies. Kitto received 15 years to life in prison for his part in the crimes. Hall was sentenced to life imprisonment and died of natural causes on September 16th 2002.

THE FACTS

Born: July 17th 1924 | Active: 1977-1978

Arrested: January 16th 1978 | Country: United Kingdom

Victims: 5 | AKA: The Monster Butler

Sentence: Life imprisonment | Status: Died in 2002

Hance, William Henry

An American serial killer who is suspected to have killed four women in and around military bases before his arrest in 1978. Hance was killing at the same time as Carlton Gary; The Stocking Strangler, and so Georgia was playing host to a wave of serial killers.

In September of 1977, the nude body of 24-year-old Karen Hickman was discovered near Fort Benning in Georgia. She had been beaten to death and then run over with a car by Hance. Due to media attention being focused on Carlton Gary, Hance decided to take advantage of Gary's press by drawing attention away from his own murders.

He wrote a letter to the investigation claiming that he was part of a group of white supremacists called the Forces of Evil, and if they didn't catch Carlton Gary then a black woman would die at regular intervals. Hance had just killed a black sex worker named Gail Jackson but in his letter he claimed that the Forces of Evil were holding her hostage and would kill her if Gary wasn't captured – all in an attempt to deflect attention away from him.

After two more murders, police closed in on Hance, after realising early on that the culprit was from the nearby military base. He was arrested shortly after, found guilty and sentenced to life with hard labour. However, a review board did not agree with the sentence and a re-trial was ordered. Hance was ultimately convicted of killing three people and linked to a fourth that didn't go to trial. He was sentenced to death and executed in the electric chair in 1994.

THE FACTS

Born: November 10th 1951 | Active: 1977-1978

Arrested: April 4th 1978 | Country: USA (Georgia)

Victims: 4 | AKA: Chairman of the Forces of Evil

Sentence: Death penalty | Status: Executed in 1994

Hansen, Robert

An Alaskan serial killer who raped and murdered at least 17 women in Alaska between 1971 and 1983. He is suspected to have killed over 30. Most of his crimes took place in Anchorage and he preferred to hunt them in the wilderness with a gun and a knife. He would generally abduct them before killing them.

Born in Iowa, he became withdrawn from society at a young age and was known to have had a bad relationship with his aggressive father. He was bullied in school and grew up with a stutter that saw him struggle in social environments. He was jailed multiple times for various crimes, including burning down a local bus garage.

In 1967, he moved to Anchorage, Alaska with his second wife. He became well-liked in the area and was known to have involved himself with community events. He was jailed in 1977 for stealing a chainsaw but was released after a year when he was diagnosed with bipolar disorder.

From 1980, he began killing sex workers by paying for their services then flying them to his private cabin. He used his small private airplane that he had acquired at some point while in Alaska. When he got them to his cabin, he raped and beat them before releasing them into the open. Then he would stalk and hunt them with a rifle or hunting knife.

In 1983, the FBI were called in to assist with the investigation, as Alaska State Troopers were unsure what they were dealing with. It led to Hansen's arrest in the same year and he was subsequently sentenced to life in prison for 17 murders, after leading investigators to 17 grave sites. Hansen died of natural causes in prison in 2014, aged 75, and was suspected of killing up to 30 people in total. His killings were the subject of the film 'The Frozen Ground' with Nicholas Cage and John Cusack.

THE FACTS

Born: February 15th 1939 | Active: 1971-1983

Arrested: June 1983 | Country: USA (Alaska)

Victims: 17-30 | AKA: The Alaska's Serial Killer

Sentence: Life imprisonment | Status: Died in 2014

Harding, Donald Eugene

On September 17th 1979, in Arkansas, criminal and future serial killer Donald Eugene Harding escaped jail by sawing his way out. After his escape, he went on to kill at least six people and took part in numerous robberies and other crimes before his eventual recapture in 1980.

On December 10th 1979, in Dallas, Texas, Harding shot dead Stanton Winston Blanton during a robbery. One day later he kidnapped the entire Baker family before robbing their home and leaving with an unknown amount of cash and goods. He left the family tied up before moving out of the state to Waco, Texas, to continue his campaign of crime and murder across America's Southern and middle States.

After his recapture in 1980, he was charged, convicted and sentenced to death for his crimes including the murders of six people. Harding was executed in the gas chamber in Arizona on April 6th 1992.

THE FACTS

Born: March 1st 1949 | Active: 1979-1980

Arrested: January 1980 | Country: USA

Victims: 6+ | Status: Executed in 1992

Harvey, Donald

On October 26th 1987, American medical serial killer Donald Harvey, AKA: the Angel of Death, was admitted to the Toledo Correctional Institution in Ohio. This was after being convicted in August 1987 of killing 37 people. Harvey was a hospital orderly who claimed to have murdered 87 people between 1970 to April 1987 when he was arrested.

Harvey had worked in the medical profession from the age of 18-years-old. When he worked at the Marymount Hospital in London, Kentucky, he claimed to have killed at least a dozen patients there alone. Harvey said that he initially killed his victims because they enraged him but then he insisted it was because he didn't want to see terminally ill patients suffering.

He killed by administering many different types of drugs, mostly whatever was available at the time. He used arsenic, cyanide, insulin or morphine. He even suffocated some of them or drip fed them liquid tainted with HIV. Because he had worked in so many hospitals and his crimes didn't come to light for over 17 years, investigators suspected he could have killed hundreds of people.

Harvey claimed to have killed to ease the pain of his patients but stated that as time progressed, his enjoyment rose. In August 1987, Harvey was handed down 28 life sentences after pleading guilty to 37 murders, in order to avoid the death penalty. In 2017, he was savagely beaten in his cell and died of his injuries on March 30th of that year.

THE FACTS

Born: April 15th 1952 | Active: 1970-1987

Arrested: April 1987 | Country: USA (Ohio/Kentucky)

Victims: 37-87 | AKA: Angel of Death

Sentence: 28 life sentences | Status: Killed in prison in 2017

Hatcher, Charles Ray: Chucky

EXTENDED CASE FILE

May 27th 1978 is seen as a notorious date in St. Joseph, Missouri's, history. It was the day that four-year-old Eric Christgen was raped and killed by one of the worst killers to ever live in the United States; Charles Ray Hatcher. Hatcher was a one man crime wave who was born in 1929 and started killing when he was 40-years-old.

Over a 13 year period, he would go on to kill 16 people. He was born into a family with an abusive alcoholic father and was bullied at school. His oldest brother died when he was 16-years-old. After that moment, his parents split and his father left the family home. When Hatcher was 26-years-old, he moved to St. Joseph, Missouri, with his mother and her third husband. It was there that his life of darkness began.

Hatcher lived a life of crime before he first killed and he was able to fool the authorities by feigning mental illness. He is one of the world's worst criminals and his murders of many children were seen as some of the most horrific of all time. When Hatcher was six-years-old he witnessed an incident that some psychologists say would have affected him more deeply than people knew at the time.

In 1935, he was flying copper-wire kites with his older brothers. Just as his oldest brother was about to hand him the kite, it hit a high-voltage overhead line and electrocuted him. Arthur Allen Hatcher was killed instantly. Their father, Jesse, never got over the pain of losing his eldest son and turned to drink for solace. This downward spiral of grief and anguish finally led to his father leaving home and divorcing his mother. Hatcher's father was an ex-convict who had a violent streak within him. Whenever he drank, he became abusive towards his wife and children.

Hatcher became a prolific petty criminal after leaving school and was twice sent to the infamous The Walls prison in Missouri. After six convictions and served sentences, he was finally released back into the world on March 18th, 1959.

Only a few months after being out of Jail, Hatcher turned from a life of petty crime to those of a more serious nature. For most criminals, an escalation in what they do or perceive to love can sometimes be inevitable. The same can be said for most serial killers. Each kill is normally within a smaller time scale than the previous and usually more brutal or apparent.

In the Summer of 1959, again only a few months after being released, he attempted to abduct a 16-year-old newspaper boy, Steven Pellham. He tried to abduct him whilst waving a butcher's knife maniacally. It was unclear how Pellham managed to get away but he called the police and Hatcher was subsequently arrested yet again after being caught in a stolen vehicle.

Hatcher was sentenced to five years for the attempted abduction, along with the car theft. He was moved to maximum security after having spent most of his life behind bars. For the next two years, he would thrive on his criminal status within the prison until his release. One month after mankind landed on the Moon, hailing in a new era of technological and human marvels, Charles Ray Hatcher was strangling a young boy to death in a creek.

On August 27th 1969, he asked a 12-year-old boy to take a ride with him in his car. He drove to a local creek and strangled him until he died. He would later confess this at his trial. Only two days had passed when a six-year-old boy was reported missing. Hatcher had offered the little boy an ice cream to lure him away from his friends, who later spoke of the incident.

A passer-by walking his dog came across the horrific scene. Hatcher was caught red-handed sexually abusing and violently beating the young boy. He was arrested within a few minutes and fortunately, the boy survived the attack. It marked the beginning of Hatcher's game of multiple identities that he had most likely planned for a long time. He seemed to know, having spent most of his time in jail, how to game the system and the authorities. He refused to answer any questions and gave multiple names when asked who he was.

Before a judge in a Californian court, he would give the name of Albert Ralph Price. Because of this steadfast belief in another personality, the judge ordered Hatcher to be taken away for psychiatric evaluation. In 1970, Hatcher was diagnosed as unfit to stand trial with tendencies of insanity and notions of paedophilia. Although not one psychiatrist could actually agree on Hatcher's condition. Hospital staff felt that Hatcher was fabricating a lot of his mental suffering in order to stay out of prison and to make himself a more special case.

In the Winter of 1972 he was finally convicted of the murder and rape of Gilbert Martinez and was committed to the Californian State Hospital for the mentally insane. He was classed as a mentally disordered sex offender. In May of 1977, Hatcher was shockingly released to a halfway-house in San Francisco. This was because of the findings at a parole board hearing that stated Hatcher had improved dramatically during his time in prison. It stated that he was no longer a danger to the public. How wrong they were.

Almost immediately after release, he tried to stab a seven-year-old boy but the charges were dropped. His record of arrests, evaluations and sentences read like a horror book that surpassed even the worst criminals at the time. Hatcher was then considered a parolee at large and was not seen for an entire year. Until he returned to Saint Joseph, Missouri.

On May 27th 1978, four-year-old Eric Christgen was raped and killed by Hatcher. A search party found Eric's body in an area of weeds and marsh on the banks of the Missouri River. He had been molested and smothered to death. Eric's funeral was the largest ever held in the city and the public wanted an arrest. The police were all too happy to oblige and only one suspect came to the forefront of their investigations. It was not Charles Ray Hatcher but a man named Melvin Lee Reynolds, who was subsequently charged with the boy's murder.

The police had forced the arrest of Reynolds and he was sentenced to life in prison after nine months of intense interrogation where he signed a false confession. It was going to be another four years until the truth would come out. In September of 1978, Hatcher was arrested for sexually attacking another 16-year-old boy. Hatcher was placed into the Douglas County Mental Institution, in Omaha, Nebraska but again was released only a few months later.

Bizarrely, due to police procedures at the time, no one actually knew it was Hatcher. He had given a fake name to his arresting officers. Hatcher was subsequently released to continue his pattern of sexually abusing and killing young boys. On June 20th 1981, James Churchill was stabbed to death on the banks of the Missouri River, in Illinois. Hatcher would later confess to the murder stating that his desire to kill had gotten ahead of him. He said that he and Churchill had been drinking together and he snapped and then stabbed him ten times. He had left the knife sticking out of his chest near the heart.

On July 29th 1982, when Hatcher was 51-years-old, he killed an 11-year-old girl. Michelle Steele disappeared after a dentist appointment. A day later, under the name of Richard Clark, he checked himself into the Saint Joseph State Hospital. This was in an attempt to deflect attention from him or to rid himself of another prison sentence. At the same moment, a group of hikers stumbled across Michelle Steele's abused and broken body.

A few days later on August 3rd 1982, after matching his description to a man seen on the river bank the day of Michelle's disappearance, Hatcher was charged with murder in the first degree. But he was charged under the name of Richard Clark.

It would not be until April of 1983 when Hatcher was declared fit to stand at trial in the case of Michelle Steele. He was sent back to the Buchanan County Jail to await trial, whilst there, he gave a note to a young deputy.

'Please call the FBI and tell them I would like to see them today. Very important case.' - Hatcher's hand-written note.

When the FBI agents arrived, Hatcher told them everything and confessed to the murders of 16 people including many children. Apart from Michelle Steele, all of them were male. He drew a map to the body of Churchill and described burial grounds and positions of each corpse. In return for the information he was handing out, Hatcher pleaded for the death penalty.

On October 13th 1983, Hatcher was finally sentenced to life in prison for the murder of Eric Christgen. This was on the same day that Melvin Lee Reynolds was released from prison after being wrongfully convicted of the crime. A year later Hatcher was sentenced to another 50 years for the murder of Michelle Steele. Before the rest of his crimes could be brought to trial in separate cases, Hatcher hung himself in his cell in December 1984.

It has been suggested that Chucky from the Child's Play films was based on Charles Ray Hatcher and his murders. The name of the killer doll in the film is Charles Lee 'Chucky' Ray and the doll would attempt to kill children. Hatcher would sometimes wear a horizontally striped top, just like the character from the films.

THE FACTS

Born: July 16th 1929 | Active: 1969-1982

Arrested: August 3rd 1982 | Country: USA

Victims: 16 | AKA: One Man Crime Wave/Chucky

Sentence: Life imprisonment. | Status: Died by suicide in 1984

Heaulme, Francis: The Criminal Backpacker

Francis Heaulme, AKA: The Criminal Backpacker, was a French serial killer active from 1984 to 1992. He had the rare condition of Klinefelter's syndrome, which meant he had a supplemental X chromosome, was infertile, and had small testicles. In his formative years he was abused by his father and turned to drink before becoming suicidal.

At the age of 28, he left home to backpack around France, either by hitchhiking or cycling. Whatever money he earned was spent on drink and drugs. He would kill his victims with different methods and on random dates making his capture all the more difficult. In one such murder, he killed 44-year-old Aline Peres on a busy public beach in broad daylight, surrounded by people who witnessed nothing. Yet, it was because of the Peres murder that he was finally arrested.

ARCHIBALD HALL

IMAGE ATTRIB. A81

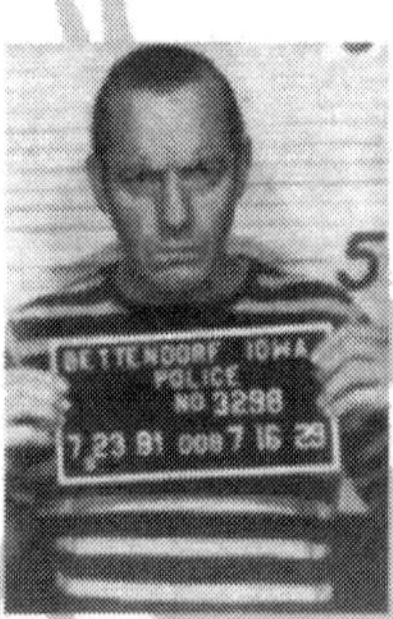

IMAGE ATTRIB. A80

CHARLES RAY HATCHER

PHILLIP CARL JABLONSKI

IMAGE ATTRIB. A82

IMAGE ATTRIB. A83

GILBERT PAUL JORDAN

Among others, he murdered two children in 1986 and dumped their bodies alongside a railroad track in Montigny-lès-Metz. A man named Patrick Dils was convicted of the crime and served 15 years in prison before being exonerated in 2002. Heaulme was arrested in 1992 and went on to describe each murder scene in detail.

He was sentenced to 22 years in May 1997, then subsequently sentenced to another 30 years in 2004 for three more murders, and life imprisonment in 2017 for the murder of two boys. As of 2022, he remains incarcerated, with many investigations into missing people and unsolved murders related to Heaulme still active. There are allegedly open cases in 87 different French police departments.

THE FACTS

Born: February 25th 1959 | Active: 1984-1992

Arrested: January 7th 1992 | Country: France

Victims: 9+ | AKA: The Criminal Backpacker

Sentence: Life imprisonment | Status: Incarcerated

Heidnik, Gary Michael

In less than six months from November 1986 to March 1987 in Pennsylvania, Heidnik had kidnapped, tortured, and raped six African-American women. During his childhood, Heidnik was emotionally abused by his father. He had long suffered with bed-wetting as he grew up and his father would punish him for it and humiliate him by hanging his stained bedsheets from his bedroom window in full view of the passing public.

Despite being arrested and convicted of various rapes before 1986, Heidnik was released into the world and kidnapped six women before his arrest, two of which he murdered. He would imprison his victims in a pit in the basement of his home and subject them to multiple rapes and tortures.

24-year-old Sandra Lindsay was kidnapped on December 3rd 1986 and killed in February 1987. She died of starvation and the effects of torture. Heidnik went on to dismember her body, cook her ribs in an oven, and boil her head. It was suggested he may have minced the flesh, mixed it with dog food and fed it to his other victims but those reports remain uncorroborated.

On January 2nd 1987, in Philadelphia, 23-year-old Deborah Dudley was kidnapped by Heidnik, and held captive before being murdered on March 19th. Heidnik was arrested five days later on March 24th, after a new captive managed to escape and call for help. Heidnik was convicted of two murders, six kidnappings, five rapes and multiple other crimes. He was sentenced to death and executed by lethal injection in July 1999.

THE FACTS

Born: November 22nd 1943 | Active: 1986-1987

Arrested: March 24th 1987 | Country: USA (Pennsylvania)

Victims: 3 | AKA: Brother Bishop

Sentence: Death penalty | Status: Executed in 1999

Hertogs, Jacobus Dirk

On April 5th 1979, in the Netherlands, the body of 18-year-old Emy den Boer was discovered by a hiker in a forest near Nistelrode. She had gone missing two days earlier and had been shot dead by Dutch serial killer Jacobus Dirk 'Koos' Hertogs.

A month later on May 11th, Hertogs abducted and murdered 12-year-old Tialda Visser, who was reported missing after failing to return home from ballet class at the Royal Conservatory of The Hague. Four days later her body was found not too far from where she had gone missing.

On September 29th 1980, Hertogs abducted and murdered 11-year-old Edith Post who disappeared while she was at school. She had left her classroom to get some study materials from a closet in the hallway but never returned to her class. Her body was found a few days later on October 2nd in the dunes of Wassenaar.

Unknown to police at the time, Hertogs was in a gay relationship with Cornelis Stolk, who was Vice President of the court in The Hague. This relationship allowed Hertogs to get close to his victims. But on October 3rd, Hertogs was arrested and charged with the three murders. He was caught after an anonymous tip led to his arrest.

In a press conference, the police claimed that his last victim, Edith Post, had bitten her attacker. A visitor to a nightclub noticed the bouncer had bite marks on his fingers. That bouncer turned out to be Hertogs, and he was sentenced to life in prison for the murders. Since his death by natural causes in 2015, there have been reports that the murders were committed by someone else and that Hertogs took the blame to cover up who the real culprit was – but it has never been proven.

THE FACTS

Born: 1949 | Active: 1979-1980

Arrested: October 1980 | Country: Netherlands

Victims: 3 | Status: Died in 2015

Hicks, James R

In Maine, American serial killer James Hicks went on to kill three people. His first murder was in 1977, when he killed his 23-year-old wife, Jennie Lynn Hicks. He dismembered her body and dumped the body parts in a nearby river, and in buckets of concrete near roadsides.

On October 16th 1982, he murdered 34-year-old Jerilyn Towers, who was last seen leaving a bar with him. He raped and murdered her, before dismembering her and dumping her in the same river as his ex-wife. The investigation into Jerilyn Towers' disappearance, meant that the Jennie Hicks's case was also re-opened, due to the similarities and location they lived in.

Hicks was arrested in 1983 and convicted of Jennie Hicks's murder. He wasn't charged with the Towers murder due to a lack of evidence, but for Jennie's murder, he was sentenced to 10 years in prison – only to be released six years later in 1990.

Shortly after his release, he began dating 40-year-old Lynn Willette, who he met at the motel they both worked in. They moved in together pretty quickly but on May 26th 1996, Hicks brutally murdered her and dumped her remains in the river. Due to a lack of evidence in her disappearance, he was not charged at the time.

In 2000, he moved to Levelland, Texas, and robbed a 67-year-old woman, holding a gun to her head and forcing her to write a cheque and suicide note. Fortunately, she had managed to escape and it led to his arrest. Hicks was convicted and sentenced to 55 years in prison. He had made a deal with authorities, that he would lead them to the remains of the murder victims in Maine, only if he could serve his time in Maine.

Some of the remains of his former wife and Towers were found buried at the side of the road near his former home in Maine. The remains of Willette were mostly found in concrete buckets, buried near to the river. The parts discarded into the river were never found.

THE FACTS

Born: 1951 | Active: 1977-1996

Arrested: April 2000 | Country: USA (Maine/Texas)

Victims: 3 | Sentence: 55 years in prison | Status: Incarcerated

Hojer, Ladislav

A Czechoslovakian serial killer and cannibal who killed five women over a three-year period. On December 1st 1978, he attacked and killed his first victim, known as Eva R. He dragged her into some bushes and strangled her, before abusing the corpse and masturbating onto her body.

He would kill again twice more in 1980 and twice in 1981 before his capture in the same year. In January of 1981, he committed a particularly brutal murder. He dragged a victim known as Ivana M, into a local park, where he attempted to rape her but failed, so he stabbed her and strangled her to death.

He cut off her breasts and genitalia with scissors and took them home in a plastic bag. Once home, he used the pieces of flesh in a sexual manner, and a week later he cooked them in salted water and ate as much as he could before feeling ill.

He was arrested after a mental health patient at a hospital where Hojer had spent time told police that Hojer had confessed to the murders. He was arrested in 1981, convicted of five murders, and executed by hanging in 1986.

THE FACTS

Born: March 15th 1958 | Active: 1978-1981

Arrested: March 1981 | Country: Czechoslovakia | Victims: 5

Sentence: Death penalty | Status: Executed in 1986

Holst, Thomas: Heidemörder

In Hamburg, Germany, on November 25th 1987, 21-year-old student Andrea Grube-Nagel went missing. She was the first victim to be abducted and murdered by German serial killer Thomas Holst, AKA: Heidemörder (Heath Killer).

As Andrea was leaving the Rissen Train Station, Holst had forced her into his car by putting a knife to her throat and threatening to stab her. He raped, tortured and dismembered her as he would his next two victims. Two days later, Andrea's remains were found by construction workers in the town of Kaltenkirchen, just north of Hamburg.

Over a two year period from November 1987 to November 1989, Thomas Holst abducted, raped and killed three women in Hamburg. Upon his arrest, a psychiatrist stated that he was 'untreatable and with extreme relapse probability.' He was sent to trial for the violent murders of three victims and subsequently sentenced to a high-security wing of a psychiatric hospital due to his mental condition.

Astonishingly, his therapist, Tamar Segal, helped him escape in 1995 as she had fallen in love with him. Holst gave himself up three months later and was detained at the

Hamburg Detention Center where he has been held ever since. In another bizarre twist, Thomas Holst married Segal while he was in prison in 1997 and by all accounts they are still married to this day.

THE FACTS

Born: February 18th 1964 | Active: 1987-1989

Country: Germany (Hamburg) | Victims: 3 | AKA: Heidemörder

Sentence: Life imprisonment | Status: Incarcerated

Hubal, Abdullah

A rare serial killer from the Yemen, Abdullah al-Hubal killed 13 people in the country from 1990 to 1998. In 1990 alone, Hubal killed seven people after Northern and Southern Yemen were reunited to make a singular country. He was arrested shortly after and sent to prison.

After a short prison sentence, he disappeared for a while until 1998 when he killed a couple in the area of Beit al Fakieh. He went on to murder three more people in the same area and become the country's most wanted man for a while. On August 16th 1998, when police tracked him down, he got into a firefight with them. He killed a police officer before being shot himself and remains one of the country's most notorious killers.

There have been only two other known serial killers in Yemen, Mohammed Adam Omar, a Sudanese morgue assistant who killed up to 51 women across Yemen and other countries from 1975 to 1999, and Dhu Shanatir, a Fifth Century Himyarite ruler who molested and killed young boys. Abdullah al-Hubal joined a very slim list indeed.

THE FACTS

Born: 1955 | Active: 1990-1998 | Country: Yemen

Victims: 13 | Status: Killed by police in 1998

Hughes, Michael

Michael Hughes was at one time known as the Southside Slayer, due to some murders in Los Angeles, but like other serial killers of the time and place, the moniker was given to many killers which confused investigations into the murders. He killed a total of seven females between the ages of 15 to 38 over a six year period from 1986 to his arrest in 1993.

He was first convicted in 1993 and given a life sentence without parole for the murders of four women who he had strangled to death. Then, due to advancements in DNA technology, Hughes was charged with an additional four murders in 2008. He had raped and killed two more women and two more teenage girls during his active years. One of the charges were later dropped as evidence wasn't as certain as the other murders, but it has still been attributed to him.

Some of the confusion with the victims was due to the fact that another serial killer was operating in the same area. Lonnie David Franklin Jr. AKA: The Grim Sleeper, who had left bodies in a similar fashion within the area. Hughes was convicted in 2011 and sentenced to death. As of 2022, he remains on death row at San Quentin State Prison.

THE FACTS

Born: 1957 | Active: 1986-1993

Arrested: December 1993 | Country: USA

Victims: 7-8 | Sentence: Death penalty | Status: Death row.

Ivanyutina, Tamara

A Ukrainian female serial killer who murdered nine people over an 11-year period. As most female serial killers tend to do, she used poisoning as her modus operandi. From 1976, she used thallium to poison those she simply didn't like, for there was no other reason. She would source the thallium by saying it was to kill rats in and around hers and her parent's properties.

In 1987, at a school where she was working at, several pupils and staff were hospitalised for extreme food poisoning. Two adults died and nine others went to intensive care. An investigation led to her arrest and subsequent confessions going back to 1976.

She claimed she targeted the school canteen because the sixth-graders refused to set up tables and chairs and so she decided to punish them. She was sentenced to death and executed by firing squad in 1987. Tamara was one of only three confirmed instances of a woman executed in post-Stalin Soviet Union.

THE FACTS

Born: 1941 | Active: 1976-1987

Country: Ukraine | Victims: 9 | AKA: The Kiev Poisoner

Sentence: Death penalty | Status: Executed in 1987

Jablonski, Phillip Carl

An American serial killer convicted of killing five women in California and Utah. On July 16th 1978, he killed Linda Kimball, his former partner, who was stabbed, strangled and beaten to death in their own home. He met her in February 1977 and lived with her before she gave birth to their daughter but he grew to hate her for reasons unknown.

Just ten days earlier, he had gone to her mother's house with the intention of raping her. He didn't go through with it but the rest of the family found out. Kimball left him a few days later and he killed her on July 16th. He was arrested, convicted and released in 1990 to sate his bloodlust even more.

In 1991, he killed his new wife and her mother along with two others. He would sexually assault all of his victims and either shoot or strangle them to death. In the case of fellow student Fathyma Vann, he had carved the words 'I Love Jesus' into her back. When her body was found, her eyes and ears were missing.

Some label Jablonski as a spree killer but his crimes and the sexual satisfaction he gained from them cannot be overlooked. He was sentenced to death in 1991 which was upheld in 2006. While on death row, he accepted and replied to pen-pal letters. He died of natural causes, two days after Christmas in 2019.

THE FACTS

Born: January 3rd 1946 | Active: 1978-1991

Arrested: April 28th 1991 | Country: USA

Victims: 5 | Sentence: Death penalty | Status: Died in 2019

Jackson, Elton Manning: The Hampton Roads Killer

In Virginia, serial killer Elton Manning Jackson, AKA: The Hampton Roads Killer, was convicted of one murder but confirmed to have killed 12 gay men. A suspected serial killer was stalking victims in the Norfolk gay community in the late 1980s and early 1990s, and he remained unidentified for many years until Jackson's arrest.

On July 22nd 1996, 38-year-old gay man, Andrew D. Smith, was strangled to death and his nude body was dumped on the side of a road in Chesapeake. Smith was considered to be the 12th victim of the then unidentified serial killer who had first killed in July 1987.

When he was arrested in 1997, Jackson wasn't immediately confirmed to have been the serial killer. Instead, the authorities only stated that the murder of smith was similar in fashion to the previous victims. The method of killing and the disposal of the body on the side of the road, matched all previous 11 murders, which led them to suspect Jackson was responsible.

The bodies were found at the entrance of major highway systems around the area, the men were gay or were those who had frequented gay establishments and were usually unemployed or of no-fixed-abode. Some of the men were known to have been male sex workers. Seven men were white and five were black, which profilers called a rarity, as a serial killer usually only killed a specific type of victim.

After Jackson's arrest, no further killings took place and evidence against Jackson began to mount up. In August of 1998, Jackson was found guilty of Smith's murder and sentenced to life in prison, where he has been ever since. With regards to the other 11 murders, Jackson remains the sole suspect and most investigators consider the cases closed.

THE FACTS

Born: 1956 | Active: 1987-1996

Arrested: May 6th 1997 | Country: USA (Virginia)

Victims: 12 | AKA: The Hampton Roads Killer

Sentence: Life imprisonment | Status: Incarcerated

Johnson, Martha Ann

An American female serial killer convicted of killing her 23-month-old but was positively linked with the murder of another three of her own children. Even by 22-years-old, she was already married for the third time, and had children from each of her three marriages.

In 1977, she killed her 23-month-old son, James William Taylor, by smothering him. She would do the same in 1980, 1981 and 1982 to her other daughters and eldest son, her eldest daughter was known to have died of asphyxia. She was linked to all four murders but convicted of only one.

Johnson horrifically killed her children by rolling her 250LB (113kg) body on them as they slept. She was arrested in 1989 and sentenced to death in 1990, which was later commuted to life. She is currently detained at Pulaski State Women's Prison in Georgia and has been the target of attacks from other inmates.

THE FACTS

Born: 1955 | Active: 1977-1982

Arrested: July 3rd 1989 | Country: USA | Victims: 4

Sentence: Death penalty, commuted to life | Status: Incarcerated

Jones, Genene

A female serial killer from Texas who killed up to 60 toddlers and children in her care when she was a nurse in the late 1970s and 1980s. She killed by injecting her victims with digoxin, heparin or succinylcholine. The drugs would cause paralysis of skeletal muscles which also means the patient wouldn't be able to breathe under their own control. In children, they would suffer heart attacks or stop breathing.

Unfortunately, the true number of victims remains unknown. The hospital deliberately misplaced her records to avoid further pressure on them but in doing so may have let Jones kill many more. Her motivation for the murders, like many 'angel of death' killers was to see herself become the hero.

She enjoyed putting small children in real danger and then jumping in to save the same child. Jones was arrested in 1982 and sentenced to 99 years in prison in 1985 for the murder of 15-month-old Chelsea McClellan, who she killed with succinylcholine.

Jones received an additional 60 years for the killing of another child, bringing her total sentence to 159 years in prison. She has since been linked to at least 60 murders in total. In 2021, she was due for parole but it was denied due to new murder charges being upheld against her. It's likely she will live out the rest of her days in a prison cell.

THE FACTS

Born: July 13th 1950 | Active: 1977-1982

Arrested: November 21st 1982 | Country: USA (Texas)

Victims: 60 | Sentence: 159 years in prison | Status: Incarcerated

Jordan, Gilbert Paul: The Boozing Barber

Known as The Boozing Barber, he was linked to the deaths of ten women over a 22-year period and used alcohol as a murder weapon. His other convictions were for rape, assault, kidnapping, hit and run and car theft.

On October 12th 1987, in Vancouver, Vanessa Lee Buckner's body was found naked on the floor of the Niagara Hotel. Buckner's death was caused by Jordan, a former barber, who supplied her with a fatal level of alcohol. For her death, Jordan was sentenced to 15 years for manslaughter in 1988 but served nine.

He was arrested multiple times but no murder charges could be brought against him because of the nature of the deaths. However it didn't stop police putting out a warning in relation to Jordan. The police warning was released by the Saanich Police Department on February 5th 2005. Release listed in partial form below.

JORDAN is currently in the Victoria area but has no fixed address. JORDAN has a significant criminal record including manslaughter and indecent assault of a female. He uses alcohol to lure his victims. JORDAN's target victim group is adult females. JORDAN is subject to court ordered conditions including:

1) Abstain absolutely from the consumption of alcohol.

2) Not to be in the company of any female person or persons in any place where alcohol is being either consumed or possessed by that person or persons.

He would seek out women in bars and ply them with drink, sometimes paying them for sex. Because some of his victims were alcoholics, the police paid little attention to them. Jordan was known to have drunk almost two bottles of vodka every day and was ultimately linked to the deaths of 10 women.

THE FACTS

Born: December 12th 1931 | Active: 1965-2004

Country: Canada | Victims: 8-10 | AKA: The Boozing Barber

Sentence: 15 years | Status: Died in 2006

Junco, Francisco del

In Miami, Cuban-American serial killer Francisco del Junco killed four female sex workers in less than one year between 1995 and 1996. Born in Cuba to a troubled family, he was taking medication for epilepsy at the age of three-years-old. He grew to suffer from delusions where he would hear people's voices and feel their negative influences.

When he was 16, he consulted black magic practitioners, including a high priestess. He began to withdraw from society and hide away from people who he believed were out to kill him, or who the voices said were going to kill him. In 1980, when he was 23-years-old, he moved to Miami with relatives and suffered even further with his delusions.

He was sectioned to a Miami mental health facility on three separate occasions from 1987 to 1992. Then from August 1995 to March 1996, he killed four black sex workers by bludgeoning them to death with iron bars. After he killed them, he set their corpses alight with gasoline and sat down next to them to watch them burn.

On June 3rd 1996, del Junco was arrested, after a speedy investigation. He was found by police and caught red-handed with a container of gasoline in his hand. A homeless women had contacted the authorities after he had become violent with her. He later confessed to the killings and was convicted in 2002 of four murders. He was handed down four life sentences and escaped the death penalty due to his mental illness.

THE FACTS

Born: 1957 | Active: 1995-1996

Arrested: June 3rd 1996 | Country: USA | Victims: 4

Sentence: Life imprisonment | Status: Incarcerated

MARTHA ANN JOHNSON

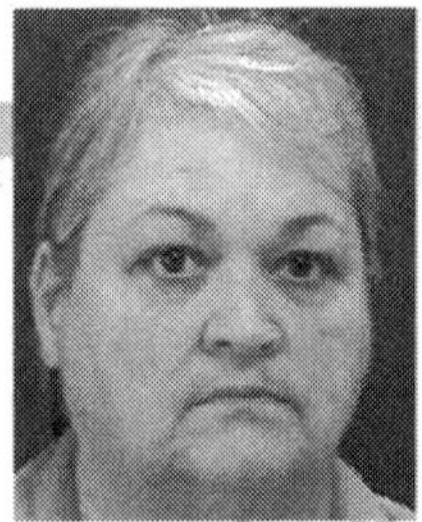

(ATTRIB A128)

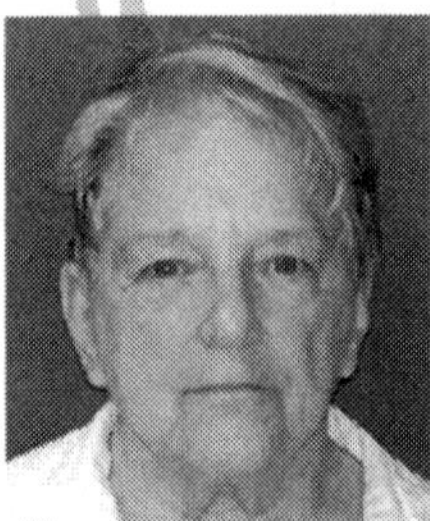

(ATTRIB A129)

GENENE JONES

FRANCISO DEL JUNCO

(ATTRIB A130)

(ATTRIB A131)

ISMO KULLERVO JUNNI

Junni, Ismo Kullervo

Born in 1943, Finnish serial killer Ismo Kullervo Junni would go on to murder five people from 1980 to 1988. Most of his crimes were committed at the Kivinokka summer camp area in Helsinki, and he became known for removing his victim's teeth.

Growing up, he had witnessed his father killing his mother by stamping on her head and dragging her body to their bathtub where she was mutilated. It was a traumatic experience that never left Junni's head, and throughout his formative years and into his adult life, he manifested a bizarre interest in cadavers and would often visit mortuaries.

In August of 1980, Junni killed his wife and then pulled out her teeth. He was investigated for the crime but due to insufficient evidence, the death was recorded as an accident. It wasn't until 1986 when he killed again. He murdered two of his colleagues at the summer camp and then set fire to the crime scene in order to hide the evidence.

In July 1986, Junni killed his friend, Matti Haapanen, by smashing a glass bowl over his head and setting fire to his summer home. Two years later, he claimed a fifth victim by burning them alive in their summer home. In 1990, when Matti's wife reported Junni's strange behaviour of telling stories about the fire, he was arrested and charged. Junni was convicted of four murders in addition to confessing to the murder of his wife. He was sentenced to life in prison where he died of natural causes in 1995.

THE FACTS

Born: June 1943 | Active: 1980-1988

Country: Finland (Helsinki) | Victims: 5

Sentence: Life imprisonment | Status: Died in 1995

Kibbe, Roger: The I-5 Strangler

EXTENDED CASE FILE

On September 17th 1987, American serial killer Roger Reece Kibbe killed 17-year-old runaway and sex worker Darcie Frackenpohl in California. He strangled her to death after raping and beating her. He went on to remove her hair and dumped her body near Echo Summit in California.

Darcie was Kibbe's final known victim as most of his murders took place in 1986. Most of the bodies were dumped on the side of the Interstate 5 (I-5), one of the longest road systems in the United States. Police discovered abandoned cars on the highway that belonged to some of the victims. At the time it was suspected that Kibbe patrolled the area searching out females with broken-down cars.

They were very much murders of the time which harks back to the notion that the highways opened up killing channels for serial killers to move back forth between states. Kibbe was born in 1949 to a violent mother who regularly beat him. He spoke with a stutter and was bullied by other children in school because of it. He developed an unhealthy view of women, most likely caused by the abuse he had received.

In his teenage years, he was arrested for stealing women's underwear from clotheslines. Unknown to the police at the time, Kibbe took pleasure in tying himself up with the underwear and taking sexual satisfaction in doing so. He would always cut up the items he stole with a pair of his mother's scissors, something that would be his modus operandi in years to come.

He married in his adult years to a dominant woman that reminded him of his mother, but not too much is known about that particular relationship. Kibbe's brother was a homicide detective and it was suspected he used his brother's knowledge about crime scenes to hide his true identity from any investigation that ensued. He learned how investigators would approach cases similar to his own murders. Because of this, no fingerprints or semen were found on his victims.

His first victim was in September of 1977, when he put a fake job advertisement in a business school, he did it with the sole purpose of finding a young female to rape and murder The job was for a secretary at a fake cosmetics studio, and 21-year-old student Lou Ellen Burleigh responded to the advertisement. Kibbe told her that his office was under construction and to meet in his van where he drove her to Lake Berryessa in Napa County.

He raped and strangled her before dumping her body near a riverbed. It would take 34 years for Burleigh's remains to be found. In 2011, a small bone was found in the area and DNA results confirmed it had belonged to her. Kibbe wouldn't kill again until April 1986, when he would kill five people in the same year.

It was Frackenpohl's murder that would lead to his arrest and conviction. Her body was discovered by a jogger two weeks after she was killed. After abducting, raping and strangling his victims he would proceed to cut open their clothes in irregular shapes with his mother's scissors. It was never clear why he did this but it stemmed back to his childhood fascination of cutting up the underwear he had stolen.

It has been proposed he did this to mentally cleanse himself of the crime. Another suggestion is that he touched the person in those areas and cut the clothing away to hide the evidence. Although this seems unlikely as it would have been easier to remove the clothing entirely, thus a deeper psychological reason must have been prevalent. He also removed the hair of some of his victims to remove the duct tape he had bound them with.

In April 1988, Kibbe was arrested and went to trial later in the year for Frackenpohl's murder. At the time there was insufficient evidence to link him to the other murders, even though police were sure he was the I-5 Strangler. In March of 1991 he was finally convicted of Darcie's murder and sentenced to 25 years.

When DNA technology advanced enough, further charges were brought to Kibbe and he made a plea bargain in 2009 to avoid the death penalty. He received six additional life sentences for the murders and was known to have killed eight people but has been linked to numerous more. Kibbe died of natural causes on February 28th 2021.

THE FACTS

Born: May 21st 1939 | Active: 1977-1987

Arrested: April 1988 | Country: USA (California)

Victims: 8+ | AKA: The I-5 Strangler

Sentence: Life imprisonment | Status: Died in 2021

Kirkland, Anthony

On May 20th 1987, Ohio serial killer Anthony Kirkland, murdered his 27-year-old girlfriend, Leola Douglas for refusing to have sex with him. After killing her, he set her body on fire and called police to make it look like an accident. He was convicted of manslaughter and served 16 years in prison until his release in 2004.

In the five years after his release, he would go on to kill another four females, including the aggravated murders and rapes of 14-year-old Casonya Crawford in 2006, and 13-year-old Esme Kenney in 2009, both of Cincinnati. He burned the bodies in an attempt to hide any forensic evidence.

He was caught near the scene of the Esme Kenney murder, where he was found to be in possession of her watch and iPod. He had dragged her into a secluded area as she was jogging around a lake then raped and brutally murdered her, before setting her alight. After various appeals and court proceedings, he was finally sentenced to death in 2018 and currently awaits his execution.

THE FACTS

Born: September 13th 1968 | Active: 1987-2009

Arrested: March 8th 2009 | Country: USA (Ohio)

Victims: 5 | Sentence: Death penalty | Status: Death row

Knychala, Jaochim: The Vampire of Bytom

A Polish serial killer sometimes known as 'The Vampire of Bytom' or 'Frankenstein', who killed five women over a five year period in Poland. As a child, his mother would neglect him and have sex with her many boyfriends in front of him. His grandmother would also violently and physically abuse him, and he grew up affected by the abuse.

Knychala killed all of his victims with an axe, butchering and dismembering their bodies afterwards, and his youngest victim was only 10. It is claimed that he was killing using the same methods as other serial killers who had already been caught to avoid detection but it is unclear who he was supposed to have copied.

However, Knychala's crimes are listed as some of the worst among Polish serial killers, though there are minimal records related to his crimes. It was also suspected that he drank the blood of some of the victims and copulated with their corpses. He was sentenced to death in 1985 and was hung three days before Halloween.

THE FACTS

Born: September 8th 1952 | Active: 1975-1982

Arrested: May 1982 | Country: Poland

Victims: 5 | AKA: The Vampire of Bytom/Frankenstein

Sentence: Death penalty | Status: Executed in 1985

Koltun, Julian: The Podlaski Vampire

Another Polish serial killer who was referred to as a vampire and suspected of drinking the blood of his victims. On August 31st 1980 in Podlaski, Poland, Julian Koltun, AKA: The Podlaski Vampire, claimed his first victim. She was an unnamed Russian female who was raped at knife point at the Polish-Soviet border and bitten multiple times in a frenzied attack. Fortunately, she went on to survive, but two others didn't.

Koltun was a railroad worker who was later arrested for raping seven women, killing two of them and drinking their blood. On September 17th 1980, he brutally murdered a teenage girl named Dorota. She had been so badly mutilated and beaten that the killer was labelled a vampire by the Polish press.

Koltun was active from 1980 to 1981 and has since been linked to at least six other disappearances in the region. He was arrested in January 1981 and sentenced to death in August of 1982 for the murders of two women, one of whom wasn't considered a murder case until Koltun confessed and led police to the remains. Koltun was executed in the same year.

THE FACTS

Born: 1950 | Active: 1980-1981

Arrested: 1981 | Country: Poland | Victims: 2-8

AKA: The Podlaski Vampire | Status: Executed in 1982

Komin, Alexander: The Vyatka Maniac

EXTENDED CASE FILE

When a Russian maniac built an underground textiles factory, he began recruiting females, not as workers, but to fulfil his twisted dream of owning an army of slaves. Alexander Komin, AKA: The Vyatka Maniac or Vyatskiye Maniac, was a Russian serial killer and criminal who killed at least four people over a two year period in the mid-1990s. The case became known as one of Russia's most disturbing crimes, so be warned on this next one!

From a young age, Komin had a thirst for unlimited power and control over others. In addition to the murders he carried out and ordered, he kidnapped and tortured many more. He also became known as The Slaveholder, due to the way he kept his victims in a nine-metre bunker under a garage on his property.

At various intervals over a two-year period, he had six slaves chained up in the dungeon. For the slaves under his control, it was pure terror, but for Komin, it was the fulfilment of a dream he'd had since he was a teenager.

The maniac had come from a poor background, born in 1950s Russia to a broken family of war-torn survivors and industrial workers. It was rumoured that he was left alone most of the time. At the age of 18, he was sentenced to three years in prison for vandalism and hooliganism.

While in prison, he met a fellow convict who had kept homeless people in his basement. The prisoner spoke of how he felt like God and had unlimited power and control over the people in his basement. Undisturbed by the nature of the man's crimes, Komin realised it was an experience that he wanted for himself.

A few years after being released from prison, he yearned for his own dungeon but knew he couldn't get away with it for too long without being found out. So he came up with the idea of creating his own textile production company. He would be able to create a legitimate business while keeping slaves at the same time.

He roped in some friends to help him build a bunker under his garage that could hold the necessary space to begin the company as a start-up. Suddenly involved with the business community of the town, he was given the funds to get the equipment necessary to start manufacturing. By 1995, the factory had multiple rooms, electric connections, ventilation, and a makeshift elevator designed to move goods up and down. Except it was to become more than just a workplace, and Komin seemed to be brazen about his plans for the facility.

One room had three bunk beds and an old television set while another had three sewing machines. Three trapdoors separated the bunker from the garage, with one of the doors having been stolen from a military base.

Komin ensured the steel ladder to the bunker was electrified so that his future slaves couldn't escape. He put up pictures of naked women, including hardcore images on the walls, to add to the bizarreness of the set-up, so that his slaves knew what to do.

In early 1995, Komin met Vera Talpayeva outside of a school and lured her back to the garage on the promise of easy money. Instead, he drugged her with clonidine laced vodka, and she garnered the unfortunate label of becoming his first slave and prisoner.

His next catch was a young tailor named Tatyana Melnikova who he lured back to his bunker. On the way back, they bumped into his first slave's boyfriend, Nikolai Malykh. Nikolai began asking the whereabouts of his girlfriend, and Komin gladly said he would show him. He took Tatyana and Nikolai back to the bunker where he drugged them both.

He decided he didn't want a man as a slave, and so after a couple of days, he poisoned Nikolai and knocked him out. He ordered the two female slaves to strip Nikolai of all his clothes. Komin then drove him to a remote field and watched as he died of exposure in the cold Winter weather. One week later, his body was discovered. It was suspected to have been an unfortunate accident at the time. Nikolai's clothes were alleged to have been rethreaded and resold to unknowing market sellers.

Now with two slaves in his bunker, he abused and raped both of them as and when he wanted. But his passion for keeping slaves grew and he wanted more workers for his business. Tatyana was the better tailor and put together various types of clothing that Komin would sell to other businesses, and at markets.

At the same time, he wanted to extend the bunker and fill it with more slaves. When his first victim, Vera, proved unable to carry out the structural works, he went looking for another victim.

Komin lured 37-year-old alcoholic Yevgeny Shishov to the bunker on the promise of more drink and easy paid work. A few days later, upon realising that Shishov was an electrician, Komin decided to kill him in case he worked out how to turn off the electrical current and escape through the doors.

If what Komin had done to that point was horrific enough, what he did next was simply barbaric. He created a makeshift electric chair purely to execute Shishov. He tied Shishov to the chair naked and secured him with exposed electric wires attached to his nipples, testicles, neck, face and stomach. He then ordered the two female slaves to push the two switches.

Shishov was barbarically electrocuted in front of them and his body was later removed and buried in the forest. Komin decided that because Vera was now an accomplice to murder, he knew she could be trusted. Komin convinced his slaves they were accessories to murder, and they fell under his barbaric spell.

Komin released Vera out into the open for the sole purpose of finding him a new prisoner. She had her back against a wall and followed Komin's orders to the letter. She brought another female back to the bunker named Tatiana Kozikova, a young local girl desperate for work. Komin then ordered the three of them to work 18 hours a day, creating dressing gowns and shorts for the business – which was doing rather well in the outside world.

The two latter prisoners suddenly decided to escape one day and managed to force Komin into one of the rooms where they jammed the door shut. But Komin wasn't trapped for long and he got himself out and dragged his slaves back before they had a chance to free themselves from the bunker.

For trying to escape, Komin gave the pair a choice of punishments; have their mouths cut to their ears or have the word slave tattooed on their foreheads. They both chose the tattoo over the slashing. From then on, Komin would regularly beat and rape his slaves to keep them under control. He had them wear collars and shackles and chained them to the wall.

A few months later, Vera was sent out to get another slave but she disappeared, deciding to runaway instead – much to Komin's annoyance. Though he had no concerns that she would let the world know what was going on in his bunker, she was an accessory to murder after all.

Komin then lured 27-year-old homeless person Tatyana Nazimova, giving himself three slaves with a similar forename, not that their names had mattered by that point. She jumped at the chance of being fed with a roof over her head. Komin then discovered that she was mentally and physically disabled, so he decided to only use her for sexual purposes.

Over the following year, the conditions in the bunker were becoming atrocious and disgusting. The prisoners begged Komin to give them more food, as he starved them on regular occasions. He responded by saying that if they wanted more food then he would cut up the body of a dead slave and feed it to them.

A year passed and Komin had become bored with his most recent sex slave and starved her for almost a week before injecting her with brake fluid. She died instantly. He put her corpse on a sled, drove to a nearby field and dumped her body in the open.

In January 1997, Komin's first victim, Vera, bumped into him while he was out looking for a new slave. Reports showed they chatted away like old friends. Astonishingly, Vera agreed to financial and sexual rewards for finding him new markets to sell at – and more slaves.

He got her on board by telling her that she had pressed the switch that killed Shishov in the electric chair. Two days later, Vera lured 22-year-old Irina Ganyushkina to the bunker, where she was drugged and added to his collection of slaves.

Komin attempted to fertilise Irina with injections in order to grow an army of slaves he could control. He had a vision that if Irina and any newer slaves were capable of giving birth then he wouldn't have to lure slaves anymore, he could create them.

At the same time, he decided to punish Vera for running away in the first instance. He tortured and beat her for half a day before giving her a choice of drinking antifreeze or having it injected into her. She chose to drink it and he made the other slaves watch her ordeal before she horrifically died of her injuries.

In what can only be described as a twisted twist, Komin claimed he fell in love with his latest prisoner, Irina, and wanted to marry her. The remaining two slaves, Tatyana and Tatiana suddenly saw an opportunity to escape and begged Irina to agree to the marriage.

In the Summer of 1997, Komin took Irina to his apartment to prepare for the wedding but she escaped and ran to the police. Komin was arrested shortly after. A friend of Komin's, Mikheyev, was arrested as an accomplice for helping him build the bunker in the first place, along with the knowledge that he knew what Komin was doing.

The two remaining slaves were rescued from the bunker. They had been underground for two years and had to wear a special bandage around their eyes, so their eyesight wouldn't be damaged by the light.

In 1999, Komin was sentenced to life imprisonment for four murders and various slave trade charges. Mikheyev was given 20 years in prison. Four days later, Komin killed himself by cutting the iliac artery at the base of his abdomen. He bled out before he could be saved.

When the two remaining victims had a fundraiser set up for them to remove the tattoos on their heads, not one person donated. In fact, the Russian public blamed the victims for their ordeal claiming that real women would have either died or killed their captor.

Many saw the victims as having brought it upon themselves, which later caused uproar when their story was published in the New York Times. Komin's story remains one of Russia's most disturbing crimes.

Fortunately, the maniac was caught before realising his full vision of an army of slaves. Unfortunately, he got away with it for so long. We can only begin to imagine the unwritten horrors that his slaves were subjected to – and the horrors he had planned for them next.

THE FACTS

Born: 1953 | Active: 1995-1997

Arrested: January 21st 1997 | Country: Russia

Victims: 4+ | AKA: The Vyatka Maniac/The Slaveholder

Sentence: Life imprisonment | Status: Died by suicide in 1999

Kraft, Randy: The Scorecard Killer

EXTENDED CASE FILE

On April 16th 1978, Randy Kraft abducted an 18-year-old Marine named Scott Michael Hughes. Hughes was plied with Valium before Kraft slit open his scrotum and removed one of his testicles. All before strangling him to death with a ligature and discarding his fully clothed body beside a freeway.

Randy Steven Kraft is sometimes known as the Southern California Strangler or The Freeway Killer. The Freeway Killer is generally considered to be a mistaken moniker. The name was coined by the media to describe a serial killer named William Bonin who was active from early 1979 and would go on to murder at least 21 young men until his arrest in the Summer of 1980.

The Southern California Strangler was the name that the investigation attributed to Kraft's murders. The Scorecard Killer attribute is given to Kraft because he kept coded references to his victims. He was convicted of 16 murders but it is suggested he may have been responsible for 67 killings during his campaign of terror.

He was born in 1945 at the tail end of World War Two. His childhood was better than one might have expected compared to others who went on to become a serial killer. There has never been any notion of abuse or trauma in his childhood save for the fallout of the war.

Kraft would also stand out as an anomaly amongst serial killers. Most serial killers are happy to discuss their crimes or prove their involvement in certain murders or disappearances. Kraft has never given any obvious reasons or motive for killing so many people. He also denied any involvement with his crimes and disregards the attention put on him as a serial killer.

Although he has never given reasons himself, there are things we know about him that might have led one to kill. His killings were about control and sating perversity, and his crimes show this many times over.

In 1964, he campaigned for presidential candidate Barry Goldwater, and joined demonstrations in support of the Vietnam War. At that time he became a bartender at a gay bar and started to use Valium heavily. A few years later, he earned a degree in economics. So far, there was nothing to think that he would go on to kill a possible 67 men.

His job at the gay bar would see him wrestle with his own sexuality. It was known that Kraft struggled with the possibility of being gay. In 1968, he joined the U.S. Air Force and was provided with high-level clearance. A year later, he openly came out as gay to his family and friends. He was discharged from the Air Force for medical reasons in 1969 and went back to bartending at the gay bar.

Although Kraft coming out as gay might not have had any link with the discharge, he was said to have felt forced out. The lack of belonging and somewhat isolation could have seen his mental state deteriorate.

Wayne Joseph Dukette was said to have been his first victim. Dukette's decomposing body was found near Ortega Highway in 1971 and had been there for months, his clothes were never found. Kraft is suspected to have killed from the early 1970s until his arrest in 1983. His victims were mostly homosexual men and he would torture and mutilate most of them, sometimes while they were alive.

The April 16th 1978 killing of Scott Michael Hughes would see Kraft go on to murder many more in the same year. Kraft had killed Scott with a ligature before throwing the body to the side of a freeway. It is suggested that he strangled Scott with his own shoelaces.

In June of the same year, he killed 23-year-old Roland Young. The victim's testicles and penis had been removed before being stabbed to death. In the same month, another Marine named Richard Keith was killed, he had been tied up by his wrists and strangled.

On July 6th, Kraft killed a hitchhiker named Keith Klingbeil. It was evidenced that the victim ingested a huge amount of paracetamol and alcohol before being strangled with his own shoelace. His left nipple had also been burned with a car's cigarette lighter. Klingbeil was found alive but died shortly after his arrival at hospital.

On September 29th, another hitchhiker, Richard Crosby, became Kraft's next victim, who was suffocated to death. As with other victims, his left nipple had been mutilated with a car's cigarette lighter. On November 18th, the body of Michael Inderbieten was found beside the San Diego freeway. He had been castrated, sexually abused, burned and suffocated to death.

Kraft was captured in 1983, was ultimately convicted of 16 murders, and sentenced to death. However, his coded 'scorecard' would take his suspected murder count to an astonishing 67. It was very clear that Randy Kraft could kill because of unlimited access to the highways and interstates. Maybe he thought the highways offered him anonymity with his killings which is why a lot of his victims would be hitchhikers. The interstates had offered the means with which to kill.

He has never shown any interest or given any assistance in clearing his name in unsolved murders and remains as tight-lipped about them to this day. As of 2022, he remains on death row in San Quentin State Prison in California.

THE FACTS

Born: March 19th 1945 | Active: 1971-1983

Arrested: May 14th 1983 | Country: USA

Victims: 16-67 | AKA: The Scorecard Killer

Sentence: Death penalty | Status: Death row

Krajcir, Timothy

An American serial killer who confessed to killing nine women; five in Missouri and four more in Illinois and Pennsylvania. He has spent most of his life in prison for various sex crimes he had committed. During the gaps when he was released, he acted on his dark desire to murder.

He travelled to different towns where he had no connection then stalked his victims before breaking into their houses and waiting for them to arrive home. Some victims were found tied to their beds, while others had been kidnapped and transported across state lines on the highway systems. Most would be raped and forced to perform demeaning sexual acts, and were either shot, stabbed or strangled.

Krajcir was linked to the murders in 2007 due to advancements in DNA technology and was arrested in the same year. As of 2022, he is currently serving 13 life sentences at the Pontiac Correctional Center in Illinois.

THE FACTS

Born: November 28th 1944 | Active: 1977-1982

Arrested: August 29th 2007 | Country: USA | Victims: 9

Sentence: Life imprisonment | Status: Incarcerated

Kuklinski, Richard: The Iceman

Known as 'The Iceman', Kuklinski holds a special place among serial killers as he is sometimes listed as a hitman, which is true, but he was also one of the worst serial killers in America's history. The classification of serial killer from the FBI is the unlawful killing of two or more people. The Iceman falls deep into the serial killer category.

He was convicted of murdering six people but it is suggested he may have claimed between 100 and 150 victims. He confessed to many more than he was convicted for. He was mostly a hitman for the American Mafia and was given the moniker of 'The Iceman' for freezing his victims to hide the time and date of death.

Mobsters came to call him 'The Devil Himself' due to his fearsome reputation and lack of emotion. At the time of his arrest, his family claimed to know nothing about his double life as a hitman and serial killer. He became sloppy in the disposal of his victims and it led to his arrest in 1986 and a life sentence in 1988. Some theories suggest he killed up to 250 people and by his own confession was the man behind the murder of Jimmy Hoffa. He died in prison of natural causes in 2005. The 2012 movie The Iceman starring Michael Shannon was based on the life of Kuklinski.

THE FACTS

Born: April 11th 1935. | Active: 1948-1986.

Arrested: 1986 | Country: USA.

Victims: 6-150+ | AKA: The Iceman/The Devil Himself

Sentence: Life imprisonment | Status: Died in 2005

Kukula, Henryk: The Monster from Chorzow

Polish serial killer Henryk Kukula, AKA: the Monster from Chorzow, raped and murdered at least four children over a ten year period from 1980 to 1990. He was only 14-years-old when he claimed his first victim.

During his childhood, Kukula showed signs of aggression towards people around him and was treated in a psychiatric hospital for suspected mental health issues. His mother allowed him to stop the medication and a year after he was discharged, he murdered a five-year-old girl then engaged in necrophilia with the body.

In 1984, he was sent to an educational facility where he beat a nine-year-old boy to death before having sex with the corpse afterwards. He was arrested and sentenced to 15 years in prison but was released only five years later. He claimed to have been raped multiple times by other inmates during his incarceration.

After his release in 1990, he raped and murdered two brothers aged five and seven. He was arrested again and sentenced to a further 25 years. Kukula was due to be released in 2020 but in January of that year, it was decided he would be transferred to the Regional Center of Forensic Psychiatry in Gostnin, where he would remain for an undefined length of time.

THE FACTS

Born: 1966 | Active: 1980-1990

Country: Poland | Victims: 4 | AKA: The Monster from Chorzow

Sentence: 25 years in prison | Status: Incarcerated

Lainz Angels of Death

In Austria, a group of four women killed their patients over a six year period from 1983 to 1989. Maria Gruber, Irene Leidolf, Stephanija Meyer, and Waltraud Wagner were the four who made up the serial killing group.

They were nurse's aides at the Geriatriezentrum am Wienerwald in Lainz, Vienna. They killed their victims by administering overdoses of morphine or by forcing water into the lungs. Because elderly patients were prone to having liquid in their lungs, the murders were virtually unprovable.

The investigation claimed the hospital refused to help them when they looked at one of the deaths in 1988 and that they could have stopped more murders from taking place. The group were caught when a doctor heard them talking about their latest murder while they were out drinking in a local bar.

When they were arrested, they all confessed to a total of 49 murders, and were sentenced to between 15 years and life in prison. By 2008, all four women had been released from prison and are supposed to be living in Austria under new identities.

THE FACTS

Active: 1980-1990 | Country: Austria | Victims: 49

AKA: Maria Gruber/Irene Leidolf/Stephanija Meyer/Waltraud Wagner

Sentence: 15 years to life in prison | Status: Released in 2008

Lee, Bruce George Peter

Lee was convicted of 26 murders and is one of Britain's most prolific serial killers. He would kill mostly by setting fire to people's houses with the owners inside. He was born with epilepsy and partial paralysis and grew up with his grandmother and then his mother until her husband left them.

He came out as gay in his teens and changed his name to Bruce Lee in honour of his favourite movie star. He associated the tingling in his fingers with starting fires, as if there were a subconscious trigger that meant it was time to start a fire.

IMAGE ATTRIB. A85

ROGER KIBBE

RANDY KRAFT

IMAGE ATTRIB. A86

TIMOTHY KRAJCIR

PEDRO LOPEZ

IMAGE ATTRIB. A6

He first killed in 1973 and then again in 1977 when 11 people died in a nursing home fire. It was suggested that he set fire to the nursing home because one of the residents had slapped him for kicking pigeons. That same man burned to death in his chair as he was unable to move freely by himself.

Lee killed a total of 26 people but mostly went unnoticed by media at the time. Because his convictions were manslaughter rather than murder, he was mostly forgotten about. It was also around the time that the trial of Peter Sutcliffe had taken precedent within the country.

THE FACTS

Born: July 31st 1960 | Active: 1973-1979

Arrested: December 4th 1979 | Country: United Kingdom

Victims: 26 | AKA: Peter George Dinsdale

Sentence: Committed to psychiatric care | Status: Incarcerated

Lee, Derrick Todd: The Baton Rouge Serial Killer

In Louisiana, Derrick Todd Lee, AKA: The Baton Rouge Serial Killer, murdered at least seven women over a ten year period. Another serial killer was operating in the region at the same time. Sean Vincent Gillis, AKA: The Other Baton Rouge Serial Killer, killed at least eight women around the same time period.

Gillis was known as the 'other' serial killer, as Lee was captured first and suspected of all the murders. But when Gillis continued his campaign, investigators realised they had two serial killers in the state. An urban legend surrounding Lee still perpetuates to this day. It claims that he would play the taped sounds of crying babies to lure his victims outside their homes.

Lee would stalk his victims before killing them, to get to know their routines and people associated with them. He was also caught looking into the homes of women but was ignored as a suspect because the police believed the killer to be white. He first killed in 1992 and claimed his last victim in 2003.

He was arrested on May 27th 2003, on suspicion of rape. When DNA was put through the system, it linked to one of the murder victims. Shortly after, DNA technology conclusively linked Lee to seven victims in Louisiana. In 2004, he was convicted of all the murders in separate trials and sentenced to death. In most trials, it took the jury just over one hour to come back with a guilty charge.

At the time, he was suspected of the other eight unsolved murders and would only come off the suspect list when Gillis was arrested and convicted of them. On January 21st 2016, Lee died of natural causes involving heart disease in a Louisiana hospital. He had been on death row awaiting execution.

THE FACTS

Born: November 5th 1968 | Active: 1992-2003

Arrested: May 27th 2003 | Country: USA (Louisiana)

Victims: 7+ | AKA: The Baton Rouge Serial Killer

Sentence: Death penalty | Status: Died in 2016

Lindholm, Jukka Torsten

Born in 1965 as Jukka Torsten Lindholm, the Finnish serial killer changed his name multiple times to be known as Michael Maria Pentholm and then Michael Penttila. His crimes had started in his early life and showed no signs of letting up. When he was 16-years-old, in 1981, he abducted a 16-year-old girl and dragged her into a basement where he beat and choked her.

The girl escaped and identified Lindholm as the attacker. He was sent to a youth prison in 1984 for one year for various other attacks and thefts. In 1985, upon his release, he killed his 48-year-old mother in the apartment they shared. Despite being a suspect, he was not charged with the murder.

In July of 1986, he lured two 12-year-old girls to his apartment for alcohol. He locked one of the girls in the bathroom as he choked the other one to death. When he released the girl in the bathroom, he raped and beat her but she escaped and ran from the apartment. Lindholm was caught shortly after whilst hiding out in a forest.

On March 17th 1987, he was found guilty of two charges of manslaughter along with other crimes. He was sentenced to nine years in prison but was released on parole in 1992 to kill again. He attacked more people in the year that followed, killed a 42-year-old woman, then escaped a police station in June of 1993. When he was recaptured, he was sentenced to another nine years in prison then sent to a psychiatric unit.

Astonishingly, he was released twice more in the years that followed only to attack more women and kill again. His final victim was on April 13th 2018 when he killed a sex worker in a Helsinki apartment. Lindholm, as Michael Penttila, was then sentenced to life in prison. Presumably until he is released on parole again.

THE FACTS

Born: July 1965 | Active: 1985-2018

Arrested: May 6th 2018 | Country: Finland

Victims: 4+ | AKA: Michael Maria Pentholm/Michael Penttila

Sentence: Life imprisonment | Status: Incarcerated

Lindsey, William Darrell: Bad Bill

Active in St. Augustine, Florida, William Darrell Lindsey AKA: Crazy Bill, was responsible for at least eight murders in the area over a 13 year period from 1983 to 1996. Lindsey became an orphan when he was just five-months-old, after his parents died in a car crash. He was quickly adopted into a household where suspicions of abuse were pointed towards the foster mother.

During his childhood years, he formulated an alter ego he would come to call 'Bad Bill'. The alter ego was a sadistic sexual deviant who would torture animals, be prone to violent outbursts, and go on to brutally murder at least eight women. It was known that he only became aroused when he was angry, leading to the violence against women.

'You've got to understand that there's a good Bill and a bad Bill. Good Bill is a decent person...Bad Bill is a person society needs to be afraid of.' - Lindsey, in a police interview.

He was known to have used sex workers regularly and found solace in the cocaine drug culture of Northeast Florida at the time. He was said to have killed for so long because his murders had no common links aside from the sex and drug ones. Lindsey was able to continue killing by floating through society unnoticed.

His first murder took place on October 9th 1983, after a drinking session at a bar known as the Tradewinds Lounge. He drove Lisa Foley to a local beach where an argument ended in murder, which wouldn't be solved until 14 years later when Lindsey confessed to the killing.

'We had intercourse and she wanted three hundred dollars. I said fifty dollars is all you're going to get. This started us fighting. I strangled her and took her body down to Pacetti Road and dumped her in a borrow pit down there.' - Lindsey's confession.

Lindsey would confess to another seven murders in the area and go on to describe them all in detail, though he often stated he didn't remember why he had become so enraged with each of his victims. He was arrested on suspicion of murder on December 29th 1996 and was linked to a possible 20 murders. He was sentenced to 30 years in prison, after bargaining his way out of a death penalty, and died of cancer in April 2001.

THE FACTS

Born: March 18th 1935 | Active: 1983-1996

Arrested: December 29th 1996 | Country: USA (Florida)

Victims: 8 | AKA: Bad Bill

Sentence: 30 years in prison | Status: Died in 2001

Lockhart, Michael Lee

American serial killer Michael Lee Lockhart was a multi-state killer who became infamous for receiving three different death sentences in three different states. He had killed in Florida, Indiana, and Texas.

In Indiana on October 13th 1987, Lockhart killed 16-year-old Wendy Gallagher. Her body was discovered in the bedroom of her family home by her sister. She was partially clothed with her hands tied behind her back and had been raped and mutilated, before being stabbed four times in the neck and 17 times in the upper body.

A large pool of blood surrounded her body. As she had been so brutally murdered, her intestines were exposed and hanging out. Forensics turned up fingerprints that matched Lockhart's but they couldn't find him as he had eloped.

In Florida, in January 1988, he killed 14-year-old schoolgirl Jennifer Colhouer in the same manner. He sexually assaulted her, mutilated her and left her body to be found by family. He shot dead a police officer who was trying to arrest him at a motel but was caught by other officers shortly after and ultimately sentenced to death for each of three murders he had committed.

> *'A lot of people view what is happening here as evil, but I want you to know that I found love and compassion here. The people who work here, I thank them for the kindness*

they have shown me and I deeply appreciate all that has been done for me by the people who work here. That's all, Warden, I'm ready.' - Lockhart's final words, December 9th 1997.

Lockhart claimed to have killed dozens of people during his reign, across many states and confessed to the murder of 16-year-old Kathy Hobbs in Las Vegas in 1987 but her case was never brought to trial. Although convicted of three murders, it is unclear how many Lockhart might have murdered. He was executed by lethal injection in 1997.

THE FACTS

Born: September 30th 1960 | Active: 1987-1988

Arrested: March 22nd 1988 | Country: USA | Victims: 3+

Sentence: Death penalty | Status: Executed in 1997

Long Island Serial Killer: The Craigslist Killer

EXTENDED CASE FILE

One of the most infamous unidentified serial killer cases in New York's history, the Long Island serial killer, AKA: The Craigslist Killer, is an unidentified serial killer who is suspected to be linked to at least 16 murders over a 17 year period from 1996 to 2013. Almost all the victims were sex workers, and their bodies were found on the South Shore of Long Island.

Many of the victims were discovered along the Ocean parkway which is near remote beach towns in the area, including Gilgo, Oak Beach, and Jones Beach. At one point, the killer was being referred to as the Gilgo Beach Serial Killer. Ten of the victims were not discovered until 2010 and 2011, when an investigation began picking up pace. Investigators concluded that all ten had been the victims of a single serial killer, and so more connections were made in relation to the killings.

In November of 2000, hunters discovered the body of a decapitated female in a remote wooded area. She had been placed in garbage bags and left out in the open. Four days later, in the same area, a nude male corpse was discovered, he had been strangled to death. Both bodies were discovered near the Long Island Expressway and would go on to become involved in the entire Long Island Serial Killer investigation.

Ever since the discovery of those two bodies, the Suffolk County Police Department (SCPD) has been under constant criticism for not doing enough to catch the killer. It has led to conspiracy theorists talking of a cover up within the SCPD. And as we continue down the rabbit hole of the investigation, it is clear that over the years the case has become more difficult.

It was left to the media to draw up a profile of the killer, who suggested that he was white, in his mid-20s to mid-40s, and was familiar with the South Shore of Long Island. The killer would also have access to burlap sacks, which was what he stuffed the bodies into before disposing of them. The media also claimed that the killer might have been a member of law enforcement, possibly involved with the SCPD.

In 2016, former SCPD Chief James Burke was suspected of having rough sex with sex workers on the same beach where the bodies were found. It was also claimed by a sex worker who was with him that Burke stated he had been involved in the killings.

In November of 2016, he was sentenced to four years in prison for violently beating a man who stole a bag from his car. The bag included various restraints, BDSM toys, and various pornography. It was also later proven that Burke stopped the FBI from getting involved in the Long Island Serial Killer Case. He had personally blocked all attempts from the FBI when they had decided to take the case and get involved.

Although many others were and have been suspected, Burke has long been the standout suspect for many. However, nothing has been proven and the case is still ongoing to this day. But a new twist emerged that was found within advertisements on the personal ad site Craigslist.

In December of 2010, four bodies and remains were discovered along the Gilgo Beach area of the region. Every victim had been strangled and placed in a burlap sack, then dumped or buried in a shallow grave in the area. All of them were later identified as sex workers who had also advertised their services on Craigslist.

The body of 25-year-old Maureen Brainard-Barnes from Connecticut, was among the victims. She was a sex worker who used Craigslist to advertise herself and was last seen on July 9th 2007. Shortly after she vanished, a friend of hers received a phone call where the caller claimed that Maureen was alive and 'working at a whorehouse in Queens'. Because Maureen was a mother who only rarely escorted, it was assumed the phone call had been from the killer to throw any investigation off track.

Another body found in the same month was that of 24-year-old escort Melissa Barthélemy, who lived in New York and had vanished a year earlier. She too had been advertising her sexual services on Craigslist across New York State. For an entire month after her disappearance, her teenage sister would get sexually vulgar calls from a man who was using Melissa's phone.

The man then claimed he had killed her sister and would relish seeing her rot. The calls were traced to Madison Square Garden in New York but no identification could be made. The other two bodies were 22-year-old Megan Waterman, from Maine, and 27-year-old Amber Lynn Costello, from New York. Both had used Craigslist advertisements to seek clients.

Costello's sister, who was also a sex worker, claimed that she was using Craigslist to catch her sister's killer, but has had no luck. In 2011, more bodies were discovered in the area. The community around South Shore of Long Island were outraged that the killer seemed to be uncatchable.

Back in 2003, the naked and dismembered body of 20-year-old sex worker Jessica Taylor from Manhattan, was discovered close to Gilgo Beach. She would be identified by DNA a few months later. In 2011, her skull and hands were discovered close to where the body had been found.

Over the course of 2011, multiple body parts and dismembered remains were discovered in the area. To this day, most have not been identified. The remains of four more young women and one young man became part of the same investigation. It is suspected that all five of them were sex workers. The male body was dressed in women's clothing and was killed in the same manner as the others.

Another six victims were added to the investigation in 2013 as they showed similarities to the other remains that had been found. One of the victims was linked by DNA to a set of dismembered legs that had been found in a garbage bag on April 20th 1996. It appeared the killer or killers had been active for at least 17 years.

Another connection was made in 1997, when the torso of a woman was found just off from Gilgo Beach. She had a tattoo of fruit on her body and was known from then onwards as Peaches. During the 2011 investigation of the shorelines, a dismembered skeleton was found, DNA proved they belonged to Peaches.

Later in 2011, the body of a two-year-old girl was discovered, DNA testing confirmed that the toddler was the daughter of Peaches. All of the body parts had been dispersed across County lines which could have been a deliberate attempt to confuse any resulting investigation.

Like the Texas Killing Fields, it has been suggested that there might be multiple serial killers who use the Long Island shoreline as a dumping ground for their victims. It could be that a lone serial killer knew of the police routines on the beach areas and worked around the gaps in their workforce.

What is clear, is that he would contact them mostly through Craigslist and arrange a meeting with the sex worker of his choice. He would then meet on his own terms and then brutally murder them. After their deaths he would dismember them and drive out to Ocean Parkway to dispose of the remains on the beaches.

It has since been claimed that the SCPD were responsible for the killer being active for so long and for having remained unidentified. The fact that the victims were sex workers led recent investigators to ascertain that it was because of their profession that investigations didn't move forward.

Fear and paranoia among locals was infesting the 2010 Summer tourist season and the SCPD still hadn't caught the killer. Frustrated by the lack of progress, many locals decided to take matters into their own hands and started their own vigilante groups to hunt the killer. One bought a disused bulletproof DEA van to spy on the beaches, and many more have started up their own websites dedicated to catching the killer. But as of 2022, the identity of the Long Island Serial Killer remains a mystery.

THE FACTS

Active: 1996-2010 | Country: USA (New York) | Victims: 16+

AKA: The Craigslist Killer/Gilgo Beach Serial Killer | Status: Unsolved

(ATTRIB A137)

OCEAN PARKWAY, NEAR TO WHERE THE FIRST BODY WAS FOUND

(ATTRIB A138-A140)

POLICE SKETCHES OF UNIDENTIFIED VICTIMS

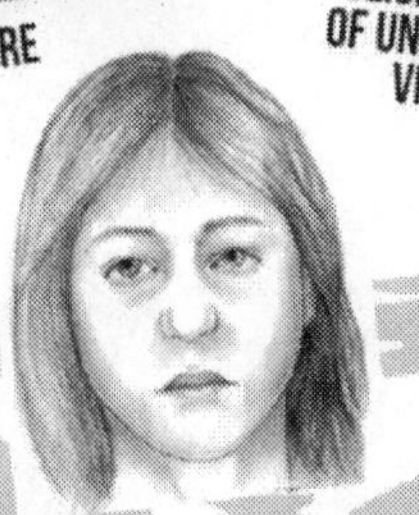

LONG ISLAND SERIAL KILLER

(ATTRIB A136)

MAP INDICATING THE LOCATION FOR WHERE MOST OF THE BODIES WERE DISCOVERED

Lopez, Pedro: Monster of the Andes

EXTENDED CASE FILE

On January 1st 1978, Colombian-born Pedro Alonso Lopez, known as the Monster of the Andes, was released from a Colombian state prison and went to Peru to continue his killings. Shockingly, there is a very slim chance that he still roams South America today, taking victims as he pleases.

His mother; Benilda Lopez de Casteneda, was a sex worker who was having an affair with the man who would be Lopez's father, who was shot and killed before Lopez was born. Lopez was the seventh of 11 children and his mother abused him from an early age, allowing him to watch her have sex with her punters. Lopez would claim that she let her clients hit her if they wished to.

When he was eight-years-old, he was caught abusing his younger sister and was thrown out of the house. It is said that he was found by a sex offender who took him into an abandoned house and raped him over and over. After the attack on him, he joined a street gang for protection and learned how to fight with knives and sticks.

In his late teens and early twenties, he stole cars and sold them for money, leading to his arrest in 1969 and a prison sentence of seven years. Prison was where the next level of Lopez's violence was formed. When he was 21 and serving time inside, he was violently gang-raped by three other inmates. It was said to be an event that traumatised him more than his childhood rape had done.

A few weeks later, he killed his rapists using a handmade weapon. As it was considered self-defence, he only received an additional two years on his sentence and was released on New Year's Day 1978. It was then that the Monster of Andes was born and he would take his revenge out on the world.

'I lost my innocence at the age of eight-years-old. So I decided to do the same to as many girls as I could.' - Pedro Lopez.

Upon his release and until his subsequent arrest in 1980, he killed on average three children every week. He preferred to kill girls between eight and 12-years-old and had no racial preference. He attempted to abduct and kill white foreign girls but he said they were too closely watched by their families.

The Monster of the Andes would roam the streets of Peru, Ecuador and Colombia, looking for 'good' girls to lure to their deaths, with the promise of gifts. He would prepare graves for the girls and generally take them from one area to a specific mass grave. Mostly, they were filled with the bodies of other small girls he had killed.

He claimed that he would make the child calm through the night, then at sunrise he would rape and strangle them. He chose strangling as he wished to see the child's eyes fade into nothing as they died in his hands. He always killed when the sun was out as he needed to see the eyes of his countless victims staring back at him.

Only then would he feel that the killing had been worthwhile. There was only ever a gap of a few days before he would hunt the next child to feed his pervasive and perverse desires. If the killings were bad enough, it was what he did after that proved him more of a monster. In Lopez's confession, upon his second capture in 1980, he told authorities details that would shock them to their core.

As he buried some of the children in one location, he would go back to the sites and position the corpses of the girls in a seated position on the edge the mass grave. He claimed he would hold tea parties and play other child-like games with them, talking to the dead as he did so.

He convinced himself that the corpses enjoyed his company and liked his games. But when the children didn't answer back or confirm their enjoyment then he would have to go and search for a new victim. He would sometimes ask the girls for directions and lead them off to his pre-meditated killing zone where the murders would take place.

He claims that he killed over 310 young girls in Colombia, Peru and Ecuador. The police deduced that the girls were either runaways or used as child sex workers. This was also due to the views on child abuse and child sex workers at the time. It wasn't only a United States or United Kingdom issue, most countries in the 1970s had a very lax view on those type of crimes.

After his confession, the police didn't believe he could have killed so many. So he offered to take them to some of the grave sites. They subsequently found the bodies of 53 young girls in one mass grave alone. For raping, killing, and mutilating over 100 confirmed murders of children, Pedro Lopez received life in prison. But life in prison in Ecuador, meant just 14 years.

He was released in 1994 but immediately arrested again and sent back to Colombia where he stood trial for the murder of a girl in 1979. In 1995, he was declared insane and sectioned to a psychiatric hospital instead of prison.

Unbelievably, in 1998 he was deemed fit for a return to normal society and was released. His conditions of release deemed he would continue his psychiatric treatment and report to the police once a month. He was never seen again.

No one truly knows what happened to Pedro Lopez beyond 1998. But in an interview from inside prison, he said he would happily return to killing young children upon his release. Indeed, he 'looked forward' to when he could get his hands around the throat of another child.

There are many theories, including the horrific one that he may still be alive and killing today. There's also the belief that he was caught by a vigilante gang and murdered. Another one suggests the authorities executed him in secret as they couldn't have him running amok but couldn't change their own laws. Lopez is one of the worst serial killers to have ever walked the face of the earth and his murder count is unparalleled.

THE FACTS

Born: October 8th 1948 | Active: 1969-1980

Arrested: March 9th 1980 | Country: Colombia/Peru/Ecuador

Victims: 300+ | AKA: Monster of the Andes

Sentence: 14 years in prison | Status: Unknown

Louis, Emile

A French serial killer who killed seven young girls during the 1970s. Over 30 women were said to have gone missing in the same area but Louis retracted his initial confession and remained silent until his death. There were suspicions that he did not act alone but no accomplice has ever been caught.

The seven confirmed victims were known to have had mental deficiencies and lived in homes for the handicapped and orphaned. It was assumed by law enforcement that the girls had simply runaway and no further investigations were needed. Louis was arrested in 2000 and led police to the remains of two of the seven girls.

Later efforts by a military investigator named Christian Jambert were blocked and the investigator subsequently took his own life. When his case was reopened it was confirmed that Jambert had been shot twice in the head.

He may have been murdered to cover up something potentially far more brutal; a potential secret criminal network that would pay to torture and rape young girls. Although it seems like fiction, many researchers suspect something bigger may have been going on in France at the time. Louis was sentenced to life in prison in 2004, where he died of natural causes in October 2013.

THE FACTS

Born: January 26th 1934 | Active: 1975-1979

Arrested: December 2000 | Country: France | Victims: 7+

Sentence: Life imprisonment | Status: Died in 2013

Lucas, David Allen

In San Diego, California, on May 4th 1979, serial killer David Allen Lucas brutally murdered 31-year-old Suzanne Jacobs and her three-year-old son in their home. He raped Suzanne and then slashed both their throats before leaving their bodies to be discovered by family and friends.

Between 1979 to 1984, he murdered between three to six people in total, in addition to kidnappings and attempted murders. On November 20th 1984, Lucas raped and murdered University of San Diego student, Anne Catherine Swanke. Her body was discovered four days later in a remote area of the Spring Valley. Her vehicle had run out of gas at the time of her disappearance.

Lucas was arrested shortly after the Swanke murder in 1984 and charged with her murder, along with the murders of Jacobs and her son. Due to ongoing investigations, the trial took another four years to complete, and in 1989, Lucas was sentenced to death for all three murders but was linked to another three. Lengthy appeals in 2016 and 2020, saw the death penalty upheld and he remains on death row to this day.

THE FACTS

Born: 1956 | Active: 1979-1984

Arrested: 1984 | Country: USA | Victims: 3-6

Sentence: Death penalty | Status: Death row.

Lucas, Henry Lee

A controversial name to put on the list but a serial killer nonetheless who was active over a 30-year period. Hundreds of unsolved murders were attributed to him in what was described as a 'clearing up' of old cases. He was convicted of 11 murders but sentenced to death for just one of them.

Lucas had lost an eye at ten-years-old, after an infection caused by fighting. His mother was a sex worker who would force him to watch her have sex with clients and would also force him to dress as a girl in public. His father, who had his legs amputated in a train accident, died in a blizzard when he was drunk.

In 1951, Lucas claimed his first victim when he strangled a 17-year-old girl named Laura Burnsley. She had apparently refused his sexual advances, although he later retracted his claim.

There have been many books and documentaries on Henry Lee Lucas, mostly because of the absurdity of the investigation and the clearing up of cases that surrounded him. He first claimed he killed over 100 people but it reached a figure 3,000 when cases from various states were attributed to him.

It is suggested that his real victim count comes in at around 40. Lucas died in 2001 of a heart attack, leaving his true dark legacy a mystery and a talking point that is still being discussed today.

THE FACTS

Born: August 23rd 1936 | Active: 1951-1983

Arrested: June 11th 1983 | Country: USA

Victims: 11+ | AKA: The Confession Killer

Sentence: Death penalty, commuted to life | Status: Died in 2001

Luptak, Juraj: The Strangler from Banska Bystrica

A Czechoslovakian serial killer who raped and murdered three women from the late 1970s to the early 1980s. The Strangler from Banska Bystrica was raised in an orphanage and fell into alcoholism in his teens, leading to multiple arrests for crimes committed while he was drunk.

On May 6th 1978, Luptak was working in a meadow when he saw 20-year-old Elena Adamova walking nearby. He hit her on the head with a stone, raped her and strangled her to death. Her shrivelled corpse was found in April 1979, hidden in thick bushes. At around the same time, Luptak was arrested for tax evasion and spent two years in prison.

In 1982, he was released from prison and saw 15-year-old Lýdia Rydlová going home from school. He dragged her into a secluded area, raped, and strangled her, before burying her alive in a shallow grave. Her decomposed corpse was discovered a month later with soil in her lungs. Shortly after Lýdia's body was discovered, he abducted 15-year-old Ivana Turová.

He knocked her unconscious and was about to rape her when he saw she was on her period. When she awoke, he beat her to death in anger. Due to media and police pressure, Luptak ran off into the mountains and lived in the wild for a week. He broke into a house for supplies but was arrested after being recognised from a description photo. He was sentenced to death for three murders and hung for his crimes on July 16th 1987.

THE FACTS

Born: January 2nd 1942 | Active: 1971-1982

Arrested: 1982 | Country: Czechoslovakia

Victims: 3 | AKA: The Strangler from Banska Bystrica

Sentence: Death penalty | Status: Executed in 1987

Maake, Maoupa Cedric: The Wemmer Pan Killer

South African serial killer and criminal, Maoupa Cedric Maake, AKA: The Wemmer Pan Killer, took the lives of at least 27 people from 1996 to 1997. The Wemmer Pan moniker came about because of the area of Johannesburg where he was claiming most of his victims.

It took a number of months for the Johannesburg Police Force to link some of the murders together and it was then they realised that they had a serial killer at large in the city. Maake would kill men and women using two distinct methods of tracking and killing. He would follow men or women who were walking alone then attack them from behind with a small rock to the back of the head. In the case of the men he would bludgeon them to death. In the case of the women, he would rape and abuse them first before killing them also.

The second targets were young couples in cars, in and around his local area. He would surprise the couple and then shoot the male in the head before dragging the female from the car and raping her, before shooting her dead.

Maake was arrested in December of 1997 and immediately confessed to some of the crimes, showing police the areas where he carried out the murders. He was charged with 36 counts of murder, 28 attempted murders, 15 rapes, and various other charges relating to robbery and assault.

He pleaded not guilty, but in September of 2000, he was convicted of 27 of the murders, 26 attempted murders, 14 rapes, and a raft of other charges. He was sentenced to 27 life sentences which along with the other charges amounted to 1,340 years in prison. As of 2022, Maake remains incarcerated in a South African prison.

THE FACTS

Born: 1965 | Active: 1996-1997

Arrested: December 23rd 1997 | Country: South Africa

Victims: 27+ | AKA: The Wemmer Pan Killer

Sentence: life imprisonment | Status: Incarcerated

Martynov, Sergei

A Russian serial killer, Sergei Martynov killed nine people in the Chelyabinsk Oblast region of the country. His first murder happened in 1992, when he raped and murdered a teenage girl. He was arrested shortly after and convicted of the murder. His sentence of 14 years was served out and he was released in 2005, when he began adding to his tally.

Only a few months after his release, he raped a teenage girl at knifepoint. He became a suspect straight away but had gone off-the-grid, so he remained on a wanted list for the years that followed. He wouldn't kill again until June 2007, when he raped and killed another woman, before dismembering her body and burying her in a shallow grave.

In July of 2007, he raped an eight-year-old girl and was suspected of further crimes in the same year but they could not be proven. He went on to kill a man during a robbery in 2008 and committed the rape and murder of a 70-year-old woman. Some of his victims had been mutilated and their breasts or sexual organs had been cut off.

His crimes were being committed all over the country, which made the hunt for him extremely difficult. He even left notes near some of his victims that taunted the police for not being able to capture him.

After his final murder in 2010, Martynov was arrested in November of the same year, when he had used a mobile phone belonging to one of the victims. After his arrest, he confessed to crimes across ten different regions of Russia, including multiple rapes and eight murders.

He claimed that his motivation for the crimes was simply to rid the country of undesirables in what he called the cleansing of society. When he was awaiting sentencing, he requested to have another inmate in his cell purely so he could kill him out of boredom. In 2012, Martynov was convicted of an additional eight murders and sentenced to life in prison.

THE FACTS

Born: June 2nd 1962 | Active: 1992-2010

Arrested: October 2010 | Country: Russia | Victims: 9

Sentence: Life imprisonment. | Status: Incarcerated

Mashiane, Johannes: The Beast of Atteridgeville

Another South African serial killer, Johannes Mashiane, AKA: The Beast of Atteridgeville, killed 13 people over a 12 year period from 1977 to 1989. His first victim in 1977 was his girlfriend who he strangled to death. He was caught shortly after and sentenced to only five years before being released in 1982.

From his release until his death in 1989, he raped and killed at least 12 small boys. He would either strangle them or stone them to death and would sodomise them before and after their deaths. Mashiane was caught red-handed while molesting his fourteenth victim but police were informed and gave chase through a large Pretoria suburb.

Before he could be caught he threw himself in front of a bus and was killed instantly. His suicide robbed the victims' families of motive and justice. He was known as The Beast of Atteridgeville due to the area within Pretoria where he carried out his crimes.

THE FACTS

Active: 1977-1989 | Country: South Africa | Victims: 13

AKA: The Beast of Atteridgeville | Status: Died by suicide in 1989

Mason, David Edwin

Mason was an American serial killer who killed at least four elderly people during 1980 in Oakland, California, and also killed his cellmate in 1982. On August 18th 1980, a 75-year-old male was beaten and strangled to death by Mason during a home invasion robbery.

Mason knew most of his victims and found it easy to access their properties before killing them. He took on small jobs as a gardener or maintenance man, getting to know his victim's routines and habits. He was also wanted in Butte County for shooting and killing his male lover while he was sleeping.

He was arrested in 1982 at a Holiday Inn following a warrant that had been put out for his arrest. While awaiting trial, he and an accomplice killed his cellmate and hung him from the showers to make it look like a suicide. Mason was later convicted of five counts of first-degree murder and sentenced to death. He was executed in the gas chamber on August 24th 1993.

THE FACTS

Born: December 2nd 1956 | Active: 1980-1982

Arrested: 1982 | Country: USA | Victims: 6

Sentence: Death penalty | Status: Executed in 1993

Matteucci, Andrea: The Monster of Aosta

Italian serial killer Andrea Matteucci, AKA: The Monster of Aosta, killed at least four people from 1980 to 1995. His childhood was marred by a criminal father who abandoned Andrea the year he was born. His mother was a sex worker who allowed him to watch her liaisons with clients, a common theme among those who grow up to be serial killers. Matteucci then grew a hatred of women who were paid to be with men.

He killed his first victim on April 30th 1980. Matteucci met a man at an abandoned Roman Theatre but the man made sexual advances towards him which angered Matteucci, so he stabbed him to death. From then on, Matteucci grew a second hatred for people who had affairs or sexual contact with others while having a family of their own.

It remains unclear whether he killed anyone else before 1992 when his second confirmed victim was confirmed. Going against his own ideals, he met a sex worker named Daniela Zago but they argued about the cost of her services, so Matteucci shot her in the head.

Two years later, a Nigerian sex worker died at his hands, apparently over an argument relating to what he called her unsatisfactory performance. He beat her before shooting her dead. He then proceeded to engage in necrophiliac acts with her corpse before taking the body home and dissecting it with a kitchen knife.

All of his victims remains were burned which made the investigation difficult. On June 26th 1995, he was arrested in connection with the disappearance of his final victim. He confessed to all the murders and was sentenced to 28 years. In March 2017 he was released from prison and sent to a psychiatric hospital. As of 2022, it is unclear whether Matteucci still remains there or has been released into the public domain.

THE FACTS

Born: April 24th 1962 | Active: 1980-1995

Arrested: June 26th 1995 | Country: Italy

Victims: 4+ | AKA: The Monster of Aosta

Sentence: 28 years in prison | Status: Released in 2017

Maudsley, Robert: Hannibal the Cannibal

EXTENDED CASE FILE

Known as the real Hannibal the Cannibal, Britain's most dangerous prisoner was confined to a specially built glass isolation cage in the basement of one of the country's most notorious prisons.

Considered one of Britain's most dangerous prisoners, Robert John Maudsley killed four people, three of them while in maximum security facilities. To protect other inmates, a special glass cell was constructed in the basement of HMP Wakefield which became known as The Cage.

Born in 1953, Maudsley had 11 siblings growing up and spent most of his time in an orphanage due to the broken relationship with his parents. When he was eight, Maudsley was physically and sexually abused by his parents.

He had been raped as a child and didn't escape the rotating door of abuse until social services stepped in and removed him from his parents' care when he was 10. His broken childhood led him to a deep drug addiction in his teenage years, which inevitably sent him down a spiral of self-abuse.

To subsidise his addiction, he turned to prostitution, and moved to London when he was 16. He attempted suicide on many occasions, which led to him receiving temporary psychiatric care, where he was diagnosed with a deep-rooted depression. He told doctors he was hearing voices telling him to go back and kill his parents, which he later claimed would have been the right thing to do.

'If I had killed my parents in 1970, none of these people need have died.' – Maudsley

In 1974, a punter named John Farrell picked Maudsley up for sex but he had darker fantasies he wanted to share with the then 19-year-old. Farrell showed Maudsley photographs of the children he had sexually abused.

Enraged by images of child abuse which had brought back memories of his own upbringing, Maudsley killed Farrell by strangling him with a garotte, stabbing him multiple times, and hitting him over the head with a hammer.

Not long after, Maudsley surrendered to police and asked for psychiatric help. It became clear to the authorities that Maudsley was not only a danger to others but to himself, having attempted suicide multiple times before Farrell's murder.

Because of his personal history, psychiatric issues, and extenuating circumstances, in 1977 he was found unfit to stand trial and sent to Broadmoor Hospital, a high-security psychiatric facility, which has been home to some of the country's most notorious criminals, including The Yorkshire Ripper, Charles Bronson, Ronnie Kray, and the Freddy Krueger Killer.

While there, he and another patient, John Cheeseman, locked themselves in a prison office with a known convicted paedophile, David Francis. They tied him up with electrical cord and tortured him over a period of almost ten hours, before Maudsley strangled him to death.

When they surrendered, one of the guards who was first into the room claimed that Francis's head had been cracked open and a spoon was sticking out of his skull. It was widely reported that a piece of his brain was missing, and that Maudsley had cannibalised it.

Though it remains a point of contention, it has never been conclusively proven either way whether Maudsley had eaten part of the brain. As the story began to do the rounds, Maudsley earned the unfortunate nickname of Hannibal the Cannibal, despite reports to the contrary that the cannibal aspect of the killing was false.

Maudsley was convicted of manslaughter and not murder due to diminished responsibility but was deemed to be of relatively sane mind. As such, he was sent to Wakefield Prison, commonly known as Monster Mansion due to it's unfortunate roster of dangerous criminals.

Inmates known to have been resident at Monster Mansion include Harold Shipman (Doctor Death), Ian Huntley, Colin Ireland, Robert Black, Ian Watkins (former frontman of Lost Prophets), and USSR spy Klaus Fuchs, among countless others.

Other prisoners in Wakefield were already aware of Maudsley's reputation and he was given the nickname 'Spoons' due to the story of the spoon sticking out the skull of Francis.

On July 28th 1978, Robert Maudsley told other inmates that he was going to kill two people that day. His case is a unique one in that he would kill more people in prison than he did on the outside.

On that fateful day, Maudsley lured wife-killer Salney Darwood, into his cell. He tied a garotte around his neck and smashed Darwood's head repeatedly into the wall. He hid the body under his bed and tried to lure other prisoners into his cell.

When no one came in, he prowled the prison and walked into the cell of Bill Roberts before stabbing him to death with a shiv, a homemade blade. After having killed the two men, he calmly walked into a prison guard's office and placed the bloody handmade weapon on the table.

He looked up at the guard and said; 'there'll be two short when it comes to the next roll call.' Maudsley surrendered to the guards and was transferred to solitary confinement to await trial, where he was convicted of both murders and sentenced to life at Wakefield Prison.

Maudsley had killed three people while inside a high security psychiatric facility and a maximum security prison. He was considered such a dangerous criminal that the prison service decided to build a unique isolation cage to house him.

In 1983, a specially-constructed cell was designed in the basement of Wakefield Prison, where he has resided ever since. The glass cage, 5.5metres by 4.5metres, has bulletproof windows and an entire team of prison officers assigned to watch him.

In order to access The Cage you would have to go through an astonishing 17 locked steel doors. The only furniture is a cardboard table and chair, a bed made up of a thin mattress on a concrete slab, and a toilet and sink bolted to the floor.

The Cage, though rarely seen, has been likened to the Hannibal Lecter cell in the Silence of the Lambs movie. Thomas Harris, the author of the Hannibal Lecter series, wrote Silence of the Lambs in 1988, five years after Maudsley's cage had been built.

He wrote the first Hannibal Lecter book, Red Dragon, in 1981, four years after the story of Maudsley eating part of a brain while in prison. Harris based some elements of the character of Hannibal Lecter on Maudsley's case, specifically the cannibal part of the story and the glass isolation cell.

Unsurprisingly, this led to Maudsley gaining the moniker of Hannibal the Cannibal in the British press, something which has never gone away. Maudsley is also known to have a high intelligence and has a passion for high art and classical music. Those who are allowed to be in close contact with him, have long claimed that he is a gentleman to be around, much like Hannibal Lecter.

Maudsley remains in The Cage for 23 hours a day and is fed through a glass drawer on the front. When he is allowed his one hour a day for exercise, he is escorted to the yard by no less than six prison officers and is banned from interacting with any other inmate.

Unsurprisingly, there are some people who see Maudsley as a hero vigilante, who killed paedophiles and wife beaters. There is still an active campaign to move Maudsley out of The Cage where he has resided for most of his life.

His family have long claimed that his isolation is detrimental to any rehabilitation and that he lives in a cloud of depression. In 2000, his defence team appealed to relax his solitary confinement measures or that he be allowed to end his own life with a cyanide capsule. Both were denied.

In the 1990s, notorious inmate Charles Bronson, who had also come from Broadmoor, decided to try and befriend Maudsley by sending him a watch via a prison guard. Maudsley told the guard to throw it out with the rubbish, leading to Bronson calling Maudsley an 'ungrateful bastard'.

He went on to say that he hoped to one day bump into Maudsley and that he wouldn't need a blade to overpower him. He ended his tirade with, 'nobody rips my heart out or eats my brain, especially a nutcase like Bob Maudsley.'

In 2010, Maudsley petitioned officials to let him play board games with guards to pass the time. His request was denied because of the murders committed behind bars, and the suspicion that Maudsley was still violent.

Their beliefs were backed up in March 2022, when the then 68-year-old Maudsley claimed in a letter to his nephew that he would kill again the moment he was released, and that he was content to remain in solitary confinement for the rest of his life.

There are some mixed beliefs as to whether Maudsley should have been given the label of serial killer. In Britain, a serial killer is someone who has killed three people over a period of time. In America, the FBI use the murder of two people in two separate incidents as their classification.

By both standards, Maudsley is a serial killer. Whether he is a vigilante or not depends on how much one believes Maudsley had killed because his victims were child abusers or wife beaters, something which he hated.

Though some journalists and researchers write about the tragedy of Maudsley and how he was driven to kill out of revenge for the 'true' bad people in the world, it remains a fact that he has killed four men, three behind bars.

His childhood was tragic, forged in the darkness of abuse, lack of foundation, and hate over love. In his adult life, Maudsley chose to kill four others, whether out of revenge, hate, circumstance, or because of psychiatric issues. Either way, he was deemed to be Britain's most dangerous prisoner and remains in the basement of Monster Mansion, feared by guards and other inmates. His case has shone a light on long term prisoners who wish to end their own life and if the law might be changed to allow it but there has been no progress since 2000.

No photo of Maudsley exists past 1983 and no images of The Cage have ever been released to the public. No one really knows if there truly was a spoon sticking out the skull of one of his victims but the legend perpetuates to this day.

If the prison service have deemed Maudsley dangerous enough to remain isolated in The Cage, and that Maudsley himself claims he will kill again if ever released, then maybe Maudsley is where he needs to be.

THE FACTS

Born: June 1953 | Active: 1974-1978.

Arrested: 1974 | Country: United Kingdom.

Victims: 4 | AKA: Hannibal the Cannibal/Spoons

Sentence: Life imprisonment | Status: Incarcerated

Maust, David Edward: Crazy Dave

An American serial killer who committed his crimes in West Germany and the United States. He killed five boys and men aged between 13 and 19. He was sent to a mental institution at nine-years-old at the request of his mother, who claimed to be mentally suffering herself and was clinically psychotic. It was said that his mother had dumped him into mental health care, neglecting him on purpose.

A few years later, Maust choked two of his friends but didn't kill them. The incidents were not lost on his brother, who later said that Maust would beat squirrels to death with a baseball bat. Maust was also abused by other boys in a children's home when he was 13-years-old.

DERRICK LEE TODD

(ATTRIB A132)

(ATTRIB A133)

JUKKA TORSTEN LINDHOLM

HENRY LEE LUCAS

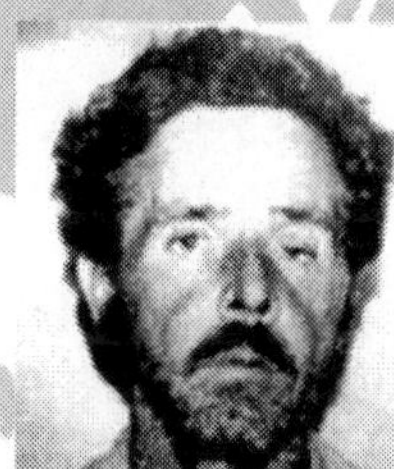

(ATTRIB A134)

(ATTRIB A135)

ROBERT MAUDSLEY

In 1974, while based in Germany, Maust killed a 13-year-old boy by sexually assaulting and stabbing him to death. He was sentenced to four years in a military prison. He then requested not to be freed but was released in 1977 anyway. Two years later he stabbed a friend while he was sleeping.

He was arrested and held for trial in 1982 but wasn't convicted until 1994. Maust was sentenced to 35 years but was released five years later in 1999, due to time spent inside. Upon his release, he killed three more boys and men before being arrested again. While awaiting the next trial in 2006, he killed himself in prison.

THE FACTS

Born: April 5th 1954 | Active: 1974-2003

Arrested: December 9th 2003 | Country: Germany/USA

Victims: 5 | AKA: Crazy Dave

Sentence: Life imprisonment | Status: Died by suicide in 2006

Maxwell, Bobby Joe: The Skid Row Stabber

In mid-1978, Maxwell, AKA: The Skid Row Stabber, was sentenced to just two months in jail for mild offences. Shortly after his release, from October 1978 to December 1978, Maxwell was alleged to have brutally killed 10 people in a violent rampage that tarnished Los Angeles.

On December 14th 1978, police arrested him for concealing a weapon on his person and he was only sentenced to two months in prison as they didn't know he had killed 10 people. After his second release, on January 21st 1979, Maxwell killed 26-year-old Luis Alvarez. On April 4th 1979, Maxwell was arrested for the final time after having been under surveillance for two months.

There had been a two-month gap in the Skid Row stabbings and that gap just happened to coincide with the two-month prison sentence that Maxwell had received in late 1978. Armed with this and fingerprints from one of the murders, Maxwell was finally captured. He was charged with 10 of the 11 murders but convicted of two and later sentenced to two life terms. In prison, he confessed to another inmate that he killed 'to obtain the souls for Satan.'

Thirty years later in 2010, Maxwell's lawyers proved that most of the witnesses to Maxwell's killings had given false statements to the police as they had been pressured by investigators. The courts overturned Maxwell's convictions in the same year which led to a new trial. In late 2017, while the new trial was ongoing, Maxwell suffered a massive heart attack which resulted in a coma.

In 2018, due to the condition of Maxwell, the prosecutors dropped all charges against him and the trial was thrown out of court. His convictions and sentence were labelled as a miscarriage of justice. Maxwell died in April 2019 while still in a coma. He never recovered to hear that he had been found innocent after nearly forty years. Despite Maxwell claiming his innocence, some investigators believe he was the true culprit and would have been convicted again, but officially, the true identity of the Skid Row Stabber still remains unsolved.

The Skid Row Stabber is sometimes confused with Vaughn Orrin Greenwood, AKA: The Skid Row Slasher. Greenwood was active from 1964 to 1975 and killed eleven people along with one victim who survived. He was arrested in 1975 and subsequently convicted of nine counts of murder. In 1977, he was sentenced to life and remains incarcerated in a Californian prison.

THE FACTS

Born: 1945 | Active: 1978-1979

Arrested: April 1979 | Country: USA | Victims: 11

AKA: The Skid Row Stabber | Status: Died in 2019

McDuff, Kenneth

An American serial killer who murdered at least nine people. By 1966, he had already made claims of raping and killing two women and was convicted in the same year of the murders of three teenagers. He raped one of them so violently that he broke her neck with a broom handle.

He received three death sentences and was due to be executed in the electric chair but his accomplice, Roy Green, was released after 11 years in prison. In 1977, McDuff's sentence was commuted to life. He then hired a lawyer who amassed a huge amount of evidence to prove that Green was the real killer.

Unbelievably, the parole board deemed McDuff fit for society and he was released in 1989. He would then go on to a kill at least another six victims. The ones he would be convicted of were raped, tortured and strangled. In 1992, he was arrested, sentenced to death, and executed by lethal injection in 1998.

THE FACTS

Born: March 21st 1946 | Active: 1966-1992

Arrested: May 4th 1992 | Country: USA | Victims: 9+

Sentence: Death penalty | Status: Executed in 1998

McGown, Richard Gladwell

Richard Gladwell McGown was a Scottish-Zimbabwean murderer and suspected medical serial killer. He was convicted of the murders of two children from 1986 to 1992 but had been linked to at least three more. He had injected an overdose of morphine into their bloodstream which killed them within minutes.

Back in 1981, McGown had started to hold his own medical experiments to test new drugs and anaesthetics. He did this in Zimbabwe where he had been settled since the 1960s. Without the knowledge of his patients he is said to have experimented on at least 500 Zimbabwean children. Some of those children would later die from his experiments.

He was arrested in 1993 and an investigation into his conduct took place. A group of Zimbabwean students turned up outside the court and threatened to kill white people if the doctor wasn't sentenced. The case caused uproar in the country and a lead prosecutor stated that McGown was a 'messenger of death stalking our hospitals.'

He was charged with five murders but convicted of only two. It was unclear why the other charges were dropped. McGown was referred to as a Nazi and racist by the Zimbabwean media and the general public.

Despite being convicted for two murders, he was only sentenced to one year in prison which was reduced to six months. He was told to pay $1,250 USD to the families of the victims, who called the case and sentence a mockery of justice.

After his release, he returned to the United Kingdom and even went as far as appealing his medical license in a British Court. The British General Medical Court banned him from entering a medical profession or practising medicine anywhere in the world. Since 1995, Richard McGown has been free to live among us.

THE FACTS

Born: 1937 | Active: 1986-1992

Arrested: 1993 | Country: Zimbabwe | Victims: 5+

Sentence: One year in prison | Status: Released in 1995

McGray, Michael Wayne

Canadian serial killer Michael Wayne McGray was convicted of killing seven people but claimed to have killed 11 more. He killed over a 13 year period between 1985 and 1998. The first murder was in May of 1985 when McGray was only 19-years-old. He picked up a 17-year-old hitchhiker named Elizabeth Gale Tucker then drove her to a remote wooded area in Nova Scotia, where he brutally killed her and dumped the body in a shallow grave.

On November 14th 1987, McGray robbed a taxi driver with two newfound accomplices. It is claimed that McGray killed the driver, but evidence was thin on the ground. A trial for one of his accomplices, Norm Warren, ended with a not-guilty verdict. McGray was however sentenced to five years for the robbery and couldn't be charged in the taxi driver's death due to his plea.

On March 30th 1991, he was given a three-day parole pass to a halfway house in Montreal. The day he was paroled he was invited back to a gay man's house where McGray stabbed him multiple times in the throat and chest. A day later on March 31st, he went back to a gay meeting area and was invited back to another man's house.

He stayed the night before waking up and stabbing the man to death. A day after that, he killed another gay man, which meant he had killed three victims in three days. He returned to prison over a month late but the authorities had no idea what he had done. Upon his official release, he went on to kill many more.

More confirmed victims came in 1998 when he killed a mother and daughter in their apartment. Joan Hicks and her 11-year-old daughter Nina were living in New Brunswick when McGray broke into their home. Joan was beaten to death and her throat had been cut. Nina was discovered in her bedroom closet hanging by her neck.

The next day, he was arrested and confessed to all the murders and more. He claimed 18 victims across the entirety of Canada and one in Seattle but was convicted of seven. While in prison he killed another inmate and was transferred to a high security prison to live out the rest of his life sentence without parole.

He said if he was ever released that he would kill again. In Nova Scotia on July 12th 2019, cold case investigators confirmed another female victim from 1995. Shockingly, her boyfriend had been convicted and spent 17 years in jail for a crime he didn't commit. That case is now active and ongoing.

THE FACTS

Born: 1965 | Active: 1985-1998

Arrested: October 1999 | Country: Canada | Victims: 7-18

Sentence: Life imprisonment | Status: Incarcerated

McRae, John Rodney

Serial killer and paedophile John Rodney McRae, killed up to five young boys between 1950 and 1997, and was known as a psychopath with sadistic tendencies. He never admitted to his murders and refrained from ever speaking about them.

Back in 1950, when McRae was only 16-years-old, he killed his eight-year-old neighbour and was subsequently sentenced to life in prison, only to be paroled in 1972. Up until his second arrest in 1998, many children had gone missing that would soon be linked to him.

On September 15th 1987, in Michigan, 15-year-old Randy Laufer vanished. His bones were discovered on McRae's former Michigan property in 1997 and McRae was arrested shortly after. In 1998, he was sentenced to life for the Laufer murder but is suspected to have been involved in the disappearance of at least five boys in total. In 2005, McRae died in prison of natural causes, taking any secrets he had to the grave.

THE FACTS

Born: November 20th 1934 | Active: 1950-1997

Arrested: October 1987 | Country: USA | Victims: 5+

Sentence: Life imprisonment | Status: Died in 2005

Metheny, Joseph Roy

An American serial killer who is said to have killed ten people but was convicted on two counts of murder. He was an alcoholic and drug addict, as were most of his victims. He joined the U.S. Army in 1973 and claimed to have served in Vietnam although this was never substantiated.

He also claimed to have first killed in 1976 and was linked to more murders in the late 1970s. He would deliberately hunt women with drug or alcohol problems and in 1994 he killed a sex worker named Cathy Ann Magaziner.

He buried her body in a shallow grave and then returned six months later to dig up her corpse and remove the head. He unceremoniously threw the head in the trash. Her body would remain undiscovered for another year and a half.

In 1996, the decomposed body of Kimberly Spicer was discovered under a trailer just ten feet from Metheny's own trailer, she had been stabbed and strangled to death. Metheny was arrested for her murder and convicted of two murders in total but positively linked to five. He was sentenced to death which was later commuted to life in prison without the possibility of parole.

It is claimed that Metheny dismembered some of his victims' bodies and stored the 'meat' in his freezer. Then he would combine the flesh with a mixture of beef and pork to make burger patties. He sold the burgers on a small barbecue stand at the side of the road on the weekends.

During his trial, he said he committed the murders because he enjoyed it and got a rush out of it, making him a prime example of a thrill killer. He also claimed he had no real excuse other than he liked killing. He was found dead in his cell in 2017, having apparently died of natural causes.

THE FACTS

Born: 1953 | Active: 1976-1995

Arrested: December 15th 1996 | Country: USA | Victims: 5-10

Sentence: Death penalty, commuted to life | Status: Died in 2017

Mfeka, Samuel Bongani: The Kranskop Killer

Another South African serial killer to make the list, Samuel Bongani Mfeka, AKA: The Kranskop Killer, raped and killed six women in the KwaZulu Natal area of the country between 1993 and 1996. He was also accused at one point of being the Nasrec Strangler, who had left 15 bodies in his wake around the same time.

On September 8th 1996, the body of Mfeka's final victim was discovered, and on the same day Mfeka was arrested on a rape charge. While in custody, Mfeka confessed to six murders and told police he would show them where the bodies were. Four of the victims were unearthed nearby to where Mfeka lived, and most bodies were in a severe stage of decomposition.

One of the victims dated back to 1993 and was said to have been Mfeka's first murder. There were similarities between the victims of Mfeka and the Nasrec Strangler, and the investigation went on longer than expected. Mfeka was convicted of the six murders and sentenced to life. He was known as The Kranskop Killer due to the township in which he committed the murders.

He was one of a number of black serial killers in South Africa during the 1990s, who raped and killed an extremely high number of women between them. These included David Selepe, Sipho Thwala, and Moses Sithole, among others. Sithole alone murdered at least 38 women from 1994 to 1995. Mfeka's current status is unknown.

THE FACTS

Active: 1993-1996 | Arrested: September 8th 1996

Country: South Africa | Victims: 6 | AKA: The Kranskop Killer

Sentence: Life imprisonment | Status: Unknown

Mikhasevich, Gennady

A soviet serial killer, Mikhasevich murdered 36 women from the 1970s to the 1980s but confessed to 43. He strangled and smothered his victims, mostly in secluded locations. He would rape them or sexually assault them before and sometimes after the murders before robbing them of all their belongings.

He had joined the army at a young age and served in various locations around the country but returned home one day to find that his girlfriend had left him and was married to another man, all without his knowledge. He would later claim it was the trigger that sent him into a violent rage.

On May 14th 1971, he had planned to kill himself by hanging but had met a young girl waiting on the side of the road as he walked home. He decided in that moment to take out all his anger on her by killing her in a brutal frenzy. From that moment, killing became easier, so he decided not to kill himself but to kill women as an outlet for his rage.

He was arrested in 1985 after a large investigation tracked him down and he was ultimately sentenced to death. His case became known as The Vitebsk Case which went on to unveil corruption within law enforcement agencies in the process. Mikhasevich was confirmed to have killed 36 women. He was executed by firing squad on February 3rd 1988.

THE FACTS

Born: 1947 | Active: 1971-1985

Arrested: December 9th 1985 | Country: Soviet Union

AKA: The Vitebsk Case | Victims: 36-43

Sentence: Death penalty | Status: Executed in 1988

Minghella, Maurizio: The Valpocevera Strangler

EXTENDED CASE FILE

On April 18th 1978 , Italian serial killer Maurizio Minghella killed a sex worker named Anna Pagano. The corpse was found by shepherds, her head had been bashed in and a ballpoint pen was embedded in her anal cavity. He would kill again on July 8th, July 18th, August 22nd and November 1978. In separate killing spans, he would kill a total of 15 women before his arrest in 2001 with five of them in 1978 alone.

The Italian press gave him the nickname Killer of Prostitutes. Sex workers are more likely to be targeted by serial killers than any other female. Yet, in Italy, serial killers were not as common as they were in the United States, Russia or even the United Kingdom.

Minghella was born in Genoa in 1958 and was raised from the age of six-years-old by his single parent mother. She then married a new man who would subsequently beat her and Minghella's four siblings. It was later confirmed that Minghella's stepfather was an abusive alcoholic who would brutally beat every member of the family.

Minghella was failing in school because of the abuse and started to bully other pupils. He would get them in headlocks or push them by their necks. Sometimes he would drag them by their noses or mouths. Beyond his school life he had taken on many small jobs and had been seen with plenty of girls on his arm. He had then been nicknamed the Travoltino of Val Polcevera due tohis affection for women and disco music. Travoltino translates to Travolta.

Beyond his bit-part jobs he would steal motorbikes and small cars to charge around the streets of Val Polcevera. Shortly after, his brother was killed in a car crash, and it is suggested that this event had a huge psychological impact on him. Afterwards, he developed a morbid fascination with dead bodies but somehow held off from killing.

He married a 15-year-old girl named Rosa Manfredi. Although that might shock a lot of people in other countries, the age of consent in Italy was 14-years-old in 1977 and remains the same today. The law even stretches to 13-years-old if their partner is under the age of18-years-old.

Rosa died shortly after their marriage of a drug overdose, related to suffering depression after a miscarriage. She was already dependent on psychotropic drugs when they had met. Her death just a few months after their marriage had an even deeper psychological impact on Minghella's own mental health.

He began to visit sex workers more so after Rosa's death, but even while they were married. At the beginning of 1978, he was briefly under the care of a psychiatric clinic in Genoa, but they failed to see the path he was going to take.

On April 18th 1978, he killed 20-year-old sex worker, Anna Pagano. He attempted to divert any following investigation by writing messages related to the Red Brigades on her body. It is said that the police didn't take notice of it and saw it as misdirection immediately.

On July 8th 1978, he killed another sex worker and hid her body in an abandoned car. Just ten days later, he would kill 14-year-old Maria Catena Alba who had gone missing the previous day. Her nude body was found tied to a tree by her neck. She had been raped and abused before and after her death.

Two more victims were raped and murdered before his arrest in December of 1978. He confessed to two immediately but pleaded not guilty on the others. The writing on the body of his first victim and the pen in the victim's anus was enough to link him directly with that crime.

On April 3rd 1981, he was sentenced to life in a maximum security prison for the five murders. He then proclaimed his innocence and in a twist of fate he was released to community care in 1995, which acted as a gateway between prison life and full freedom.

But Minghella was a killer, he had killed before out of sexual perversity and would kill again. There was no doubt of this in the minds of some psychologists who were against his soft-release. In March of 1997 he killed a 53-year-old sex worker in Turin. It was his new first victim of his second era of freedom. He would kill again in 1997, 1998, and in 1999.

'I hated him a lot, I often dreamed of killing him, pulling a rope around his neck from behind his back.' - Minghella in an interview, speaking about his stepfather.

His last victim was in February 2001, when he killed 27-year-old Florentina Motoc. Her face and head had been bashed in and she had been sexually abused. He attempted to burn her clothing but failed to get rid of all of his DNA. He was subsequently arrested, just six years after his release.

Beyond the DNA, the investigation had used mobile phone tracking technology to place Minghella in the area where Motoc had been discovered. In that six year period, he had killed a suspected ten more women.

After a brief escape in 2003, he was only convicted of four murders but linked with ten. He was sentenced to life in prison in Pavia, where he is currently incarcerated. It is suspected he had killed at least 15 sex workers over the course of his life.

THE FACTS

Born: July 16th 1954 | Active: 1978-2001

Arrested: March 2001 | Country: Italy

Victims: 15 | AKA: The Valpocevera Strangler

Sentence: Life imprisonment | Status: Incarcerated

Mmbengwa, David: The Lover's Lane Killer

Another South African serial killer, David Mmbengwa, AKA: The Lover's Lane Killer, would be convicted of seven counts of murder in 2001. Mmbengwa first killed in 1991 during a robbery, and he was arrested and sentenced to six years in prison for culpable murder.

After four years, Mmbengwa was released from prison, and went on to kill seven more people. Most of his killings came about from robberies and were couples who were making love in their cars, hence the moniker the press attributed to him. Among his victims, he claimed a Police Inspector, a Police Sergeant, and a Government Agriculture Official.

He was arrested on November 14th 1996 but managed to escape the Silverton Police Station. He was recaptured a few hours later and 23 counts of murder were laid at his feet. He was convicted of seven murders and given a life sentence for each of them. He also received another 46 years for various other crimes including robbery. As of 2022, he remains incarcerated.

THE FACTS

Born: October 10th 1966 | Active: 1991-1996

Arrested: November 14th 1996 | Country: South Africa

Victims: 8+ | AKA: The Lover's Lane Killer

Sentence: Life imprisonment | Status: Incarcerated

Monster of Florence

The mysterious murders in Florence, Italy, over a 17-year period from 1968 to 1985 still baffle investigators to this day. They deduced that the murders were not committed by just one person but a group of people. The victims were generally young couples parked in isolated areas and were either shot or stabbed. The female victims also had their sex organs removed.

One of the connected 14 murders happened when a young couple were killed in September of 1974. They had been shot and stabbed to death in a country lane near Borgo San Lorenzo, while having sex in their car. The female had been raped with a grapevine stalk and disfigured with 97 stab wounds. Various other victims also suffered brutal attacks and deaths.

The Monster or Monsters of Florence would claim at least 14 victims. Due to the dates and the methods of killing, it has been suggested that the Monster of Florence and the Zodiac Killer could have been the same person but it has never been proven. The murders of the Monster of Florence remain unsolved.

THE FACTS

Active: 1968-1985 | Country: Italy

Victims: 14 | Status: Unsolved

Morus, Henryk

In Poland, serial killer Henryk Morus killed seven people in a six year period from 1986 to 1992. His first murder in 1986 was 60-year-old shop owner Teresa Grabowska, who was killed in her own shop. He went on to kill another six people including a young couple in their home where the woman was pregnant, two more business owners, and a pensioner.

PHOTO OF STEFANO BALDI AND SUSANNA CAMBI, VICTIMS OF THE MONSTER OF FLORENCE, KILLED OCTOBER 23, 1981

FLORENCE, ITALY

PHOTO OF HORST WILHELM MEYER AND JENS-UWE RüSCH, VICTIMS 0 THE MONSTER OF FLORENCE, KILLED ON SEPTEMBER 9TH 1983

PHOTO OF JEAN-MICHEL KRAVEICHVILI AND NADINE MAURIOT, VICTIMS OF THE MONSTER OF FLORENCE, KILLED BETWEEN 7TH AND 8TH SEPTEMBER 1985

IMAGE ATTRIBUTIONS
(ATTRIB A32) (ATTRIB A33)
(ATTRIB A34) (ATTRIB A84)

MONSTER OF FLORENCE

According to those who knew Morus, he was a caring husband and a good man, hiding his true evil from those around him. For four of the murders, he was sentenced to death which was later commuted to life. For the other three, he was sentenced to life along with other crimes.

He died in 2013 in a prison hospital when he was 70-years-old. Up until his death he had been a model inmate and had repeatedly apologised for his crimes. He died of a suspected heart attack and was buried by the prison as his family refused to have the corpse collected. He was the last person to be sentenced to death in Poland.

THE FACTS

Born: 1943 | Active: 1986-1992

Country: Poland | Victims: 7

Sentence: Death penalty, commuted to life. | Status: Died in 2013

Mulaudzi, Mukosi Freddy: The Limpopo Serial Killer

In Limpopo, South Africa, serial killer Mukosi Freddy Mulaudzi, AKA: The Limpopo Serial Killer, murdered at least 13 people from 1990 to 2006. Mulaudzi was originally convicted for two murders and an armed robbery in 1990 but managed to escape Baviaanspoort Prison in Pretoria in 1996.

He carried on a life of crime and murder until his re-arrest in July of 2006. A year before his arrest, he raped and killed four young girls at the same time. 19-year-old Ndivhuwo Winnity Tshilimandila was raped and then hacked to death. Her cousins aged seven, 10, and 14, were also raped and brutally murdered. It was a quadruple murder that shocked South Africa.

A few months later, in Tshsdza Village, he killed a mother and her two young children in their home. He stabbed 30-year-old Phophi Tracy Radzilani to death then tied her two children to their bed, before setting fire to the house. Five-year-old Moses Mushiana and seven-year-old Rotondwa were burned alive in their bedroom.

His last victim was in 2006, when he killed Shonisani Thinandavha in Mulodi. She had been found partially cannibalised. Her breasts, right hand, left ear, and lips had been sliced off. Mulaudzi was captured shortly after. At his trial in 2006, he was sentenced to 11 life sentences for 13 murders. As of 2022, he remains incarcerated in a prison in Limpopo, South Africa.

THE FACTS

Born: 1962 | Active: 1990-2006

Arrested: July 2006 | Country: South Africa

Victims: 13 | AKA: The Limpopo Serial Killer

Sentence: Life imprisonment | Status: Incarcerated

Murphy, Donald

On December 15th 1980, American serial killer and sex offender Donald Murphy was arrested and charged with six murders of sex workers in Detroit. On the evidence available to the jury in his trial, he was convicted of two murders and sentenced to 30 years for each of them. But the bodies had been piling up.

On April 19th 1980, the body of 24-year-old sex worker Jeanette Woods was discovered on a sidewalk on Melrose, near the I-375. She had been raped, beaten, and strangled before having her throat cut. She had left her mother's house the evening before to meet with an unidentified boyfriend but never returned. She had previously been admitted twice to the Detroit Osteopathic Hospital for injuries suffered from beatings.

Two months later on June 15th 1980, the nude body of 22-year-old Diane Burks was discovered by a dog walker at a known lover's lane area. Burks' hands had been tied behind her back and she had been strangled to death by Murphy. She had last been seen leaving her sister's boyfriend's house and heading towards her home.

On August 19th, the nude and battered body of 17-year-old Cassandra Ann Johnson was discovered in a field by a 14-year-old neighbour. She had gone missing the day before and was last seen entering a store after leaving her boyfriend's house. Johnson had been beaten to death by Murphy and had died of head injuries as a result.

A couple of months after that on October 8th, the body of 26-year-old former cheerleader Betty Jean Rembert was discovered under some hedges on a vacant lot. She had died from a stab wound to the neck and head injuries that had caused a fractured skull.

In the same month on the 23rd, the body of 23-year-old sex worker Cynthia Angela Warren was discovered a few blocks away from the red-light district of Eight Mile Road, where she worked. A man flagged down a police car to inform them he had found a body. Warren had been stabbed and beaten by Murphy and he was convicted of her murder.

Murphy was never convicted of the Rembert murder and her death remains listed as unsolved. Despite being linked to the Woods murder, he was never convicted and her death also remains listed as unsolved.

In the late 1970s and 1980, 18 sex workers were killed in Detroit. It led investigators to believe that two serial killers had been active in the area at the same time as Murphy. The other, if there was another killer, remains unidentified. Murphy was sentenced to two concurrent sentences of 30 years in prison, where he remains to this day.

THE FACTS

Born: 1944 | Active: 1980

Arrested: December 1980 | Country: USA | Victims: 2-6

Sentence: 30 years in prison | Status: Incarcerated

Nance, Wayne: The Missoula Mauler

Wayne Nance was one of the rare serial killers to have been killed by his final intended victim. It is claimed he killed more than five people over a minimum 12-year period. He was a truck driver from Montana who had been known as the local 'weirdo' ever since his teens.

He boasted of worshipping Satan and had once used a hot coat hanger to burn himself with satanic symbols and occult signs. He claimed his first victim in 1974, a woman named Donna Pounds, who was held captive in her own basement, raped and tied to a chair then shot in the head at point blank range. Nance joined the U.S. Navy in the same year and left in 1977, leading investigators to suspect he killed more during that time.

From 1980, Nance was linked to at least another five victims including 15-year-old Devonna Nelson, whose decomposed body was found on a road bank in Missoula, Montana, in January 1980, leading the press to call the killer The Missoula Mauler.

In September 1986, Nance attempted to murder Doug and Kris Wells. He asked if he could borrow a torch in order to get inside their house, then he hit Doug in the head and stabbed him in the chest, leaving him in his basement. Nance took Kris to the bedroom to rape her but Doug escaped from the basement with his rifle and shot Nance, who died of his injuries the next day.

Due to the botched murders, Nance was then positively linked to the Pounds and Nelson murders, in addition to unsolved murder cases from 1974, 1980 and 1985. Both Doug and Kris went on to recover from their injuries and became instrumental in the capture of a serial killer.

THE FACTS

Born: 1955 | Active: 1974-1986

Country: USA (Montana) | Victims: 5+

Status: Killed in 1986

Naso, Joseph: Double Initial Killer

Naso was convicted of the death of six women in California from 1977 to 1994 but was positively linked to a total of ten victims. On August 13th 1978, a decomposing nude body was found on the Carquinez Scenic Highway, later identified as Carmen Colon, one of Naso's victims.

In an uncanny twist, a victim attributed to 'The Alphabet Killer' a few years earlier in 1971 to 1973, was also named Carmen Colon but the women were not related. Naso was subsequently ruled out of being The Alphabet Killer as he was not in the area at the time. Those murders remain unsolved.

Naso ended up claiming victims with the same letter on their first and second name, much like The Alphabet Killer. It has long remained unclear if that was his selection choice for victims but he was given the moniker of the Double Initial Killer.

Naso was arrested in April 2010 after a search of his home uncovered a list of names in a diary, four of which were linked to murder victims. In 2011, he was charged with the four murders but the investigation uncovered two more victims from his list in 2013 and Naso was ultimately convicted on six murders and sentenced to death. The other four women on his list remain unidentified.

THE FACTS

Born: 1934 | Active: 1977-1994

Arrested: April 11th 2011 | Country: USA (California)

Victims: 6-10 | AKA: Double Initial Killer

Sentence: Death penalty | Status: Death row

Nighttime Killers, The

In Kiev, Ukraine, between 1991 and 1996, two men murdered 16 people, together they became known as the Nighttime Killers. Vladyslav Volkovich and Volodymyr

Kondratenko were charged and convicted of 16 murders and claimed they had started killing as practice to becoming contract killers.

Their victims were killed in a number of different ways. Most were killed with a rifle but others were stabbed or bludgeoned to death. They killed mostly homeless people as 'practice' before they could kill for profit. It remains unclear how they thought they would become contract killers.

On June 18th 1996, 44-year-old Yevheniy Osechkin was shot dead near a railway station in Kiev. Robbery was ruled out as motive as Osechkin still had cash in his pockets. Investigators then began looking at other murders in the area and noticed a pattern of homeless people being shot or stabbed to death, including one who was found dead just 100 metres from Osechkin.

On July 2nd, a well-liked doctor named Oleksandr Yehorov was shot dead in his car. One hour later, another male victim was found just a few streets away. He too had been shot with the same weapon and also stabbed. As more victims piled up, the investigation increased its manpower. But although they had DNA, there was no match on the database.

In October 1996, the pair were caught after the investigation collated all the information they had gathered. The day they were arrested, they had planned to kill a security guard. Two more men were also arrested as co-conspirators in some of the crimes. Not long after the trial began, Kondratenko killed himself by taking an overdose of painkillers.

'They were nothing to me, not people, just items in a list. Killing them made me feel like a superman.' - Volkovich in his confession, regarding his victims.

In 2000, Volkovich was convicted of 16 murders. The pair had originally claimed 20, but four of them were homeless victims who couldn't be proven. After Kondratenko died, Volkovich attempted to blame him for everything. Even so, Volkovich received a sentence of life in prison, as did the two co-conspirators.

THE FACTS

Active: 1991-1996 | Arrested: October 1996

Country: Ukraine | Victims: 16 | Sentence: Life imprisonment

AKA: Vladyslav Volkovich/Volodymyr Kondratenko

Status: Kondratenko (died by suicide)/Volkovich (incarcerated)

Nilsen, Dennis: The Muswell Hill Murderer

EXTENDED CASE FILE

The sickening tale of British serial killer Dennis Nilsen, who killed 15 young men, and dissected some of their remains – before flushing them down the toilet and blocking the sewers with flesh.

Dennis Nilsen is one of Britain's most infamous serial killers. Some see him as the British version of Jeffrey Dahmer, and in a lot of ways, the similarities are striking. They both killed gay men and they made their first kill within five months of each other in 1978. Nilsen killed 15, Dahmer killed 17, and they both carried out necrophilia acts upon the bodies of their victims.

Because of the United Kingdom's different legal system to that of the United States, Dennis Nilsen was sentenced to life, as since 1969, the country no longer carries the death sentence.

Nilsen would request parole hearings for immediate release up until his death in 2018 when he died of natural causes. He reached out from within his cell with now banned autobiographies and interviews to sate the appetite of the curious public.

He murdered 15 young men in London over a five year period and kept the victims' bodies for a certain amount of time after he had killed. Then he dissected them and either burned the remains or flushed them down the toilet.

During his life, he worked as a military chef, police officer and civil servant. Not the usual career progression to serial killer. To stand in such esteemed positions in work and life and then go on to kill is one that has produced conflicting reports from psychologists and experts alike.

Nilsen was only four-years-old when his parents divorced due to his father's drunkenness, and his mother remarried soon afterwards. The disruption in the British Isles after the dust of World War Two had settled was felt throughout the nation, more so on the children born into that era.

The fallout of World War Two across many countries is considered one of the reasons for the rise of the serial killer in the Seventies and Eighties. For Nilsen, the break-up of his family at a time of national hardship was crippling.

In his trial and subsequent interviews, Nilsen claimed there was an event in his life, at the age of six-years-old, that was to shape him for many years to come. After his mother remarried, she sent him to live with his grandparents.

It was there he found a kinship with his grandfather, Andrew Whyte, but after a couple of years he was returned to his mother. In the Autumn of 1951, Nilsen's grandfather died of a heart attack.

Some serial killers have attributed the death of a grandparent as a turning point in their lives. Alexander Pichushkin, the Russian Chessboard Killer, confirmed that after the death of his grandfather, he turned to vodka, and then to murder.

What didn't help Nilsen's fragile tendencies at the time was that his mother made him view the body of his grandfather due to her strong religious beliefs. Nilsen later stated that the first time he knew of his grandfather's death was when he saw the corpse.

He said, 'it caused a sort of emotional death inside me.'

Two years later, when he was eight-years-old, Nilsen almost drowned in the seas close to his hometown. An older boy who was on the coast at the time saw what was happening and went in to rescue him. Nilsen later said that the boy masturbated over his body. He awoke from his experience with near death to find ejaculate on his stomach.

Afterwards, he withdrew into himself, hiding away from the world. He was a loner and kept himself to himself but he was never disliked and had many friends at the time. Yet, he preferred to be with his own company.

He had never killed small animals or exhibited a cruel streak towards living things and was never aggressive or violent towards his peers. He was for all intents and purposes, a good and well-loved child, and the opposite of what a potential serial killer was supposed to have been.

On one occasion he helped in the search of a local man who had gone missing. As fate would have it, it was a young Nilsen and a friend who found the man's body on a riverbank. He later said it had reminded him of seeing the body of his grandfather and upon coming across the corpse he had felt no emotion towards it. He never had a sexual encounter, nor suffered abuse during his childhood or teenage years. It would be almost two decades later when Nilsen would record his first kill.

He joined the British Army at 17-years-old and stayed there for 11 years. During his time in the military he said he carried with him a huge weight of loneliness. When he was allowed a private room he would lay down in front of a mirror so he couldn't see his own head in the reflection. He would then masturbate to the sight of what he viewed as an unconscious body.

This might in some part have been carried over from his experience on the beach. In 1972 he left the military of his own accord and returned to civilian life. He went on to join the Metropolitan Police in London but only served eight months as an officer before once again leaving of his own accord.

He often witnessed autopsied bodies in close proximity. It fascinated him and he revelled in that part of the work but he left because he felt the job didn't fit him well, having come from the military. In 1974 he went on to work as a civil servant in a job centre in London and became active in trade unions. Then the fantasies he'd long held started to seep into his reality.

There are infamous addresses where killers and murderers have carried out their crimes and lived but none more so than 195 Melrose Avenue. The address in the London area of Cricklewood, would claim 12 victims. He had access to a large garden and was able to burn many of the remains in bonfires. Some of the entrails were thrown over the fence so that local wildlife would consume them.

Nilsen had moved into 195 Melrose Avenue, sometimes listed mistakenly as Melrose Place, with a man named David Gallichan. It was said to have been a purely platonic relationship. Nilsen wanted more however, he wanted real commitment and after a series of casual sexual encounters, his bizarre corpse fantasies started to become more prominent.

When he positioned himself in front of a mirror so that his head appeared as missing, he would start to add fake blood to his corpse to look as though he had been killed. He fantasised someone would take him away and bury him and he started to believe that his corpse was the perfect state of his human body.

There was nothing more emotionally and physically pleasing to him than fantasising about his own dead body. After a rough and stressful relationship with Gallichan, Nilsen forced him to leave but was aware of the consequences of being alone.

'Loneliness,' he wrote, 'is a long unbearable pain.'

A day before New Year's Eve in 1978, Nilsen claimed his first victim, 14-year-old Stephen Holmes, who had been refused alcohol at a local pub. Nilsen took the opportunity to invite him to his flat on Melrose Avenue to drink alcohol with him.

'He was to stay with me over the New Year period whether he wanted to or not.'

After going to bed together, Nilsen woke at dawn and became aroused at the sight of his new friend's sleeping body. Holmes was sleeping on his front when Nilsen straddled him and slipped a tie under his neck. He subsequently drowned the young boy in a bucket of water by resting his head over the edge of a chair.

After the bubbles stopped rising from the water, Nilsen rested him on the floor realising that he had just killed a man whose name he did not know. He was also suddenly fearful of the consequences of his actions. Again, a trait not carried by most serial killers.

Nilsen said later that he just sat there staring at the boy's fresh corpse, shaking with the fear and stress of the situation. He made himself a coffee and smoked some cigarettes to ease his nerves. After washing the corpse in the bathroom he returned Holmes to the bed and was fascinated by the limpness of the corpse.

'It was the beginning of the end of my life as I had known it, I had started down the avenue of death and possession of a new kind of flat-mate.'

The concept of keeping corpses as flat-mates was now embedded into Nilsen's psyche. He thought the sight of the corpse was beautiful and not appalling in anyway whatsoever. He hid the body under the floorboards, but after a week had gone by, curiosity had got the better of him – he wanted to see whether the body had changed in anyway.

As he was carrying the body back to the living room, he felt himself becoming aroused and subsequently masturbated onto the corpse's stomach. He even trussed him up by the ankles for an undisclosed amount of time before putting the corpse back under the floorboards.

It would be almost eight months later when Nilsen removed the body to burn it in a bonfire in his garden. He burned rubber to hide the smell and raked the ashes into his garden. Most of his victims were homeless or homosexual men who he would lure to his home with offers of food, alcohol, or a place to rest their heads.

His victims were normally killed by strangulation or drowning during the course of the night. He then proceeded to use his butchering skills, learned in the British Army, to help him get rid of the bodies.

He would keep them in various different locations around his home but usually under the floorboards and would constantly engage in sexual activity with the corpses. Over the next three years, Nilsen would murder another 11 men in the ground floor apartment at Melrose Avenue. Of these 11, only four were ever identified.

Kenneth Ockendon was a Canadian tourist he had met at a local pub for lunch in 1979. Nilsen claimed he enjoyed the company of Ockendon and it was the thought of him leaving that drove him to kill again. He strangled him with a headphone cord before washing the body and taking it to bed with him.

Nilsen said he never had sexual intercourse with the corpses but that he did carry out sexual acts with them. He enjoyed masturbating on the corpses and pleasuring himself on certain parts of their bodies. He placed Ockendon under the floorboards and would take the corpse out several times to watch the television with him.

Nilsen said he would sometimes go into a killing trance and didn't always remember the act of murder. The feeling of control over the corpses of his flat-mates thrilled him and he held a certain fascination with how they deteriorated over time. He believed he was appreciating them more dead than alive.

When the investigation started after Nilsen's arrest, police investigators found over 1000 bone fragments in the garden of 195 Melrose Avenue. He had used the small garden as his own personal burial ground.

Through his butchering career in the British Army he learned the art of butchery so well he would use this skill to rid the house piece by piece of the corpses that remained. He would strip to his underwear and cut them up on the stone floor of his kitchen. He would then place the organs in plastic bags.

His fantasy progressed to removing the head and then heating it in a large pan of water to boil off the flesh of the skull. He would burn the rest of the remains over time, sometimes close to the garden fence. He was constantly amazed that he was never caught or that no one ever questioned him and his strange activities.

Nilsen one day decided to leave Melrose Avenue and move into a new place in the city. In some part to leave the murderous part of his life behind and in others to escape from the torment he had inflicted. Before Fred and Rose West's 25 Cromwell Street was known to the public, 195 Melrose Avenue was the darkest house of horrors in the British Isles.

In 1981, Nilsen moved to 23 Cranley Gardens in Muswell Hill, London, and it proved to be his undoing. He found it difficult to get rid of the bodies in his new home and ended up with black bin-liners full of human organs in his wardrobe. He would kill three more at Cranley Gardens over the next year and a half.

The last victim was dissected in the same way as the previous ones. The head was boiled and the limbs and organs were placed into bags, ready for disposal. But without access to a garden, Nilsen had to come up with different methods of disposal.

One of the other five tenants who lived in the block complained to the landlord the toilet was not flushing properly. Nilsen had apparently tried to clear the blockage with acid and it mostly worked but it didn't clear the blockage in the external drain.

A local plumber called in a specialist team to get a second opinion, and one of the technicians, Michael Cattran, went into the drains beneath the house. He found a gooey sludge blocking a part of the sewer coming from a pipe linked to the property.

It appeared to be various pieces of animal flesh and so he immediately reported it to his superiors. When the sewer team left, Nilsen went down into the sewers and started removing the lumps of flesh that had congealed together. But some of the other tenants noticed his movements and strange actions and reported it to the police.

At the same time, the results came back from the analysis of what was assumed to be animal remains. The results were unquestionable; they were human. Detectives paid a visit to the house the following evening.

DCI Peter Jay waited at the scene with two officers for Nilsen to return from work, they followed him into the block of flats and they immediately smelled rotting flesh. Nilsen asked why the police were interested in the drains. They told him they had found human remains.

"Good grief, how awful," Nilsen said.

"Don't mess about, son, where's the rest of the body?" DCI Jay responded.

Nilsen remained relaxed and calmly said that the remains of the bodies were in two plastic bags in the wardrobe. When they drove him to the police station, they asked him how many bodies he was actually talking about.

"Fifteen or sixteen since 1978."

He pleaded guilty with diminished responsibility but on November 4th, 1983, he was sentenced to life imprisonment. He was convicted of six murders and two attempted murders. The Home Secretary later imposed a whole life tariff, which meant that he would never be released and would subsequently be denied any requests for parole.

Nilsen died of natural causes in 2018. His disturbing crimes have been made into various movies, TV series, multiple books, and thousands of articles, each trying to uncover the madness behind the eyes of one of Britain's worst serial killers.

THE FACTS

Born: November 23rd 1945 | Active: 1978-1983

Arrested: February 9th 1983 | Country: United Kingdom

Victims: 12+ | AKA: The Muswell Hill Murderer

Sentence: Life imprisonment | Status: Died in 2018

Onoprienki, Anatoly: The Beast of the Ukraine

EXTENDED CASE FILE

On April 16th 1996, Ukrainian serial killer Anatoly Onoprienko, AKA: The Beast of the Ukraine, was arrested at his girlfriend's house in Zhitomir. The arrest came after an estimated 2,000 police officers and 3,000 military troops were involved in the investigation. The Beast had already killed at least 52 people.

He was born in the Summer of 1959, in what was then called the Ukrainian SSR, part of the Soviet Union. His mother died when he was just four-years-old, and he was handed off to his grandparents. Their father was a decorated World War Two veteran who had been suffering mental trauma from the effects of the war but he decided to keep Onoprienko's older brother at his home.

CRANLEY GARDENS, MUSWELL HILL, WHERE NILSEN KILLED AND DISMEMBERED SOME OF HIS VICTIMS

IMAGE ATTRIBUTIONS
(ATTRIB A35) (ATTRIB A36)

DENNIS NILSEN

BITSEVSKY FOREST IN BITSA PARK WHERE PICHUSHKIN KILLED SOME OF HIS VICTIMS

IMAGE ATTRIBUTIONS
(ATTRIB A11) (ATTRIB A38)

ALEXANDER PICHUSHKIN

Onoprienki grew to hate his father for leaving him alone with others. There was a time, shortly after, when his grandparents handed him over to an orphanage where he saw a side of life that his brother did not see. Onoprienko later claimed that being raised partially in an orphanage put him on a pre-defined route of violence. He would later claim that voices had tipped him over the edge and he listened to their commands to kill others.

The first confirmed murders happened in 1989, when Onoprienko was 30-years-old. He had been a regular at a gym in his local area and met a man there who would become his short-term accomplice. Together they robbed a house in the middle of the night but the family who lived there woke up and a fight ensued.

By the end of the night, the two parents and all eight of their children had been murdered by the pair of murderous burglars. They would both later claim it was in self-defence. Later in 1989, five more people, including a young boy, were shot dead while sleeping in a car, before their bodies were burned on the side of the road. Onoprienko acted alone that time and again stated that he only intended to rob them.

After committing multiple crimes there came a five year gap where he was said to have been silent. Yet, as he lived mostly off the grid, there could have been many more crimes attributed to him. It was 1996 when Onoprienko began to take lives on an epidemic level. Over a three month period, he slaughtered entire families.

On January 5th 1996, four people became victims of the Beast of the Ukraine. In Oblast, two businessmen named Odintsov and Dolinin were shot dead as they sat in their broken-down vehicle. A couple of hours later, just down the road from the double murder, a pedestrian and a police officer were shot dead. Onoprienko later claimed the death of the latter two was to kill off any witnesses to the prior murders.

Just one day later on January 6th, on a nearby highway, four more people were shot dead in individual incidents. The victims were a Navy officer, a taxi driver, a chef, and an unidentified man. One of the cars was already stationary while the other cars had been flagged down by Onoprienko before he shot them dead. The rampage struck fear into the hearts of the Ukrainian public at the time. But Onoprienko was only getting started.

'I just shot them. It's not that it gave me pleasure, but I felt this urge. From then on, it was almost like some game from outer space.' - Onoprienko, in his confession.

On January 17th, the entire Pilat family were slaughtered and their bodies burned. All five members were shot dead when Onoprienko entered the home in the early morning. He then set fire to the house, burning the bodies within. Two witnesses saw him committing the crime and he went after them. The witnesses; a female rail worker and a train passenger were shot dead as they walked down a nearby street.

On January 30th, four more people died at the hands of Onoprienko, he used a shotgun to shoot dead a female nurse and her two sons. In a separate incident, he also pulled over another car and shot dead a 32-year-old visitor to the area. On February 19th, he killed all four members of the Dubchak family.

He stormed into their home and immediately shot dead Mr. Dubchak and his son. Then he took a hammer and beat Mrs Dubchak to death in front of her daughter. Onoprienko ordered the daughter to give him money and expensive belongings. According to his later confession, she had refused, and so he also beat her to death with a hammer.

On February 27th, the entire Bodnarchuk family were killed in their home in Malina. Upon entering the home, he shot dead both parents and took their seven-year-old and eight-year-old daughters to one side before hacking them to death with an axe. Just one hour later, one of the family's neighbours wandered too near to the house, and Onoprienko charged outside and killed him with the same axe. He then proceeded to chop him into pieces.

On March 22nd, the final confirmed victims were killed. The Novosad family were killed in their own home. All four members were shot dead and then Onoprienko set the house on fire to supposedly eliminate any traces of evidence.

'To me it was like hunting. Hunting people down. I would be sitting, bored, with nothing to do. And then suddenly this idea would get into my head. I would do everything to

get it out of my mind, but I couldn't. It was stronger than me. So I would get in the car or catch a train and go out to kill.' - Onoprienko, in his confession.

In April of 1996, Onoprienko moved in with one of his cousins, Pyotr Onoprienko. Pyotr discovered a large number of weapons and suddenly realised they were similar to the ones used in the massacres that were bringing the country to its knees. After kicking him out of his home, Pyotr immediately called the police.

A few months before Onoprienko's April 1996 arrest, the investigation had been focused on another man named Yury Mozola. Due to the mounting pressure and public outcry, the Ukrainian Security Service (USS) tortured Mozola for a confession. All the time, Mozola maintained his innocence but the torture continued and after a few days, he died from the injuries of his ordeal. Seven members of the USS were subsequently convicted of his death.

After one of the largest investigations in Ukrainian history, involving thousands of police and military, Onoprienko was finally arrested on April 16th 1996, where upon he confessed to the murders.

His trial was also one of the largest in the country's history, where an estimated 100 volumes of evidence were compiled, along with 400 witnesses. Public reaction was understandably violent and full of anger. Hundreds of people were outside the court room every day and would spit and throw things at the very mention of his name.

Onoprienko was sentenced to life in prison which caused further outrage. Ukraine had just entered the EU treaty of abolishing the death penalty and so Onoprienko could not be sentenced to death. The resulting sentencing caused a further debate within the country regarding the abolishment of capital punishment. On August 27th 2013, Onoprienko died of a heart attack in his prison cell.

THE FACTS

Born: July 25th 1959 | Active: 1989-1996

Arrested: April 16th 1996 | Country: Ukraine

Victims: 52+ | AKA: The Beast of the Ukraine

Sentence: Life imprisonment | Status: Died in 2013

Pandy, Andras: The Family Killer

The Belgian-Hungarian serial killer András Pándy, AKA: The Family Killer was convicted for the murders of six family members in Brussels between 1986 and 1990. He has since been linked to at least another eight murders. His two former wives and two children disappeared mysteriously and it has long been suspected that Pandy had killed them and disposed of the bodies.

It is claimed that he killed them all with the help of another daughter named Ágnes. He had been involved in a violent incestuous relationship with Ágnes since she was a youngster and it had continued into adulthood. In 1984, he began another incestuous relationship with another of his daughters and had Ágnes beat her in the basement when she didn't comply. The other girl later escaped to live a new life elsewhere in Hungary.

From 1986 to 1990, multiple children of both his daughters also disappeared, when family members returned from holiday, Pandy told them their siblings had gone to live elsewhere. In reality, Pandy had killed them and disposed of their bodies.

In 1997, both Pandy and Ágnes were arrested. It was the confession of Ágnes that sealed both their fates. She claimed she had helped her father kill most of her disappeared relatives but was solely complicit in the murder of her own mother. They both killed the family members by shooting or hitting them in the head with a sledgehammer.

The bodies were cut into pieces and taken to a bathtub in the basement of their home where they dissolved them with acid and other chemicals. Any remaining bones were taking to a local slaughterhouse for disposal.

In 2002, Pandy was convicted of six murders and the rape of three of his daughters and sentenced to life without parole. Ágnes was sentenced to 21 years for being an accomplice in five murders and one attempted murder.

She later claimed to be completely under her father's control and had no way to get out of the situation she found herself in. In 2013 András Pándy died from natural causes in a Bruges prison. As of 2022, Ágnes remains incarcerated, awaiting parole.

THE FACTS

Born: June 1st 1927 (András) | Active: 1986-1992

Arrested: October 20th 1997 | Country: Belgium

Victims: 6-14+ | AKA: The Family Killer

Sentence: András (life imprisonment)/Ágnes (21 years)

Status: András died in 2013/Ágnes remains incarcerated

Parker, Gerald: The Bedroom Basher

On December 1st 1978 in California, American serial Killer Gerald Parker, AKA: The Bedroom Basher, claimed his first victim. The body of 17-year-old Sandra Fry was discovered by her flat-mate in Anaheim late at night. She was nude from the waist down and her blouse was pulled up, exposing her bra.

She had been raped by Parker then hit in the face and head with a blunt object, fracturing her skull. She was barely alive when found and died shortly after in the emergency room. A sixth woman survived Parker's attack but she was pregnant at the time and her unborn child died.

His victims were killed by being beaten to death with wooden poles, a hammer, or a baseball bat, in their own homes, leading to the media labelling him as The Bedroom Basher. The husband of the sixth woman was Kevin Lee Green, who was convicted of the unborn child's murder and spent 16 years in prison as an innocent man.

He was only exonerated when improvements in DNA forensics proved that Parker was involved. Parker brutally murdered six people from 1978 to 1979, was convicted in February of 1999, and sentenced to death. Despite an appeal in 2017, he remains on death row.

THE FACTS

Born: 1955 | Active: 1978-1979

Country: USA | Victims: 6 | AKA: The Bedroom Basher

Sentence: Death penalty | Status: Death row

Paulin, Thierry: The Monster of Montmartre

On November 25th 1987, French serial killer Thierry Paulin brutally murdered 79-year-old Rachel Cohen. She would become one of his 21 confessed murders. Later on the same day he attacked 87-year-old Berthe Finalteri but she would go on to survive and give a description that would result in the capture of Paulin. The killing of Genevieve Germont on November 27th 1987 would be his final victim.

Thierry Paulin had contracted HIV in the years prior and then AIDS. His killings sped up as he realised he was under a biological death sentence and set out to cause as much carnage and chaos as possible. He organised large and expensive parties that were all paid for with stolen credit cards along with the financial gains from his murders.

He was arrested on December 1st 1987 and charged with 18 murders but he confessed to 21 in total. Just over a month later, Paulin fell ill due to AIDS complications. He was subsequently hospitalised and died on April 16th 1989.

THE FACTS

Born: November 28th 1963 | Active: 1984-1987

Arrested: December 1st 1987 | Country: France | Victims: 18-21

AKA: The monster of Montmartre | Status: Died in 1989

Peiry, Michel: Sadist of Romont

Swiss serial killer, Michel Peiry, AKA: the Sadist of Romont, killed 11 hitchhikers between 1981 and 1987. He is said to be the worst serial killer in the country since World War Two. He would abduct or lure teenage hitchhikers then tie them up and rape or abuse them. Afterwards he would violently murder them and burn the corpses.

Peiry was raised in an unhappy home and his father was violent to both he and his mother. He grew up to lead a relatively normal life until he began to repress his homosexuality. Out of this, he leaned towards violent sexual fantasies which he acquired through a love of bondage. He claimed that sexuality and violence became inseparable.

His first victim was on September 1st 1981 when he travelled to the United States and killed a Canadian backpacker named Sylvestre whose body was never found. Realising he could get away with murder and having developed his modus operandi, he claimed his second confirmed victim in France in 1984.

A year later, he killed his only female victim, who has since remained unidentified. Over the next two years, he travelled across Europe and claimed another eight lives. He was arrested in May 1987 after a man survived his attack in Switzerland and informed authorities. Peiry was ultimately sentenced to life in prison and was positively linked to 11 murders in total.

THE FACTS

Born: February 28th 1959 | Active: 1981-1987

Arrested: May 1st 1987 | Country: Switzerland/France/Italy/USA

Victims: 11 | AKA: The Sadist of Romont

Sentence: Life imprisonment | Status: Incarcerated

Pennell, Steven Brian: The Route 40 Killer

American serial killer Steven Brian Pennell, AKA: The Route 40 Killer, killed five people in the state of Delaware. He is infamous for being Delaware's only known serial killer. His victims mostly consisted of hitchhikers who he picked up in his work van along Route 40 in Delaware.

One such murder took place on November 29th 1987, when he picked up Shirley Ellis and promised her money for sex in his van. He then tied her up, brutally raped her, beat and mutilated her body, which he dumped near Route 40.

The carpet of the van proved to be a vital piece of evidence in his capture as small fibres from the carpet were found on the body of the first victim. The carpet fibres were removed from the van by an undercover policewoman who was posing as a sex worker. She managed to pull some from it when she pretended to admire his carpet, before deciding not to go with him.

While the fibres were being forensically tested, Pennell was placed under surveillance. He was arrested in 1988 and convicted of two murders. He pleaded no contest on three more murders on the condition that he be executed as a preference. There was another murder in 1988 that he was also linked to but was never proven.

He claimed that it would be easier to execute him rather than have his family see him in jail for the rest of his life. In 1992, Pennell got his wish and was executed by lethal injection, the first person to be executed in Delaware since 1946.

THE FACTS

Born: 1957 | Active: 1987-1988

Arrested: November 29th 1988 | Country: USA

Victims: 5-6 | AKA: The Route 40 Killer

Sentence: Death penalty | Status: Executed in 1992

(ATTRIB A141)

ANATOLY ONOPRIENKO

GERALD PARKER

(ATTRIB A141)

(ATTRIB A143)

STEVEN BRIAN PENNELL

VINKO PINTARIC

ARTIST IMPRESSION FOR WANTED POSTER

(ATTRIB A136)

Pichushkin, Alexander: The Chessboard Killer

EXTENDED CASE FILE

Born in Russia on April 9th 1974, Alexander Pichushkin would go on to be convicted of 49 murders. He then asked if he could have another eleven added to his body count, bringing it up to 60. After his arrest, officials discovered a chessboard with specific dates on 62 of the 64 squares. Pichushkin claimed he was aiming for 64 murders, to complete his chessboard, and that if he wasn't caught then he would have succeeded in his macabre mission.

When Pichushkin was a child, he fell off a park swing, and the edge of the seat hit him hard in the forehead. From that moment, he turned from a well-liked child with a bubbly personality to a withdrawn individual who was known to have become anti-social. Brain damage was a term thrown around during his trial, used by media outlets and his lawyers as a soft defence of his crimes.

They suggested that the event may have damaged the frontal cortex of Pichushkin's brain. Damage to the brain in that area is well known to produce poor impulse regulation, along with an aggressive nature that may or may not have been evident before. But the very nature of the brain damage has never been proven and remains conjecture to this day.

After the accident, and because of his change in nature and emotion, his mother chose to remove him from his school. She transferred him from his public school to a special facility for children with learning disabilities. Because the facility was in the same area as his previous school and because of the social climate at the time, Pichushkin was bullied both physically and verbally.

Later, Pichushkin claimed he had learned to hold back his anger at being bullied, he internalised his quiet rage until it materialised in the most of heinous of ways just a few years later. Pichushkin's grandfather became frustrated with the new school, as they didn't push the children to grow beyond their means. And so he introduced Pichushkin to the game of chess, to increase his intelligence.

Pichushkin's grandfather was a chess player himself and knew that the game would be able to focus his grandson's emotions. Little did he know that the mundane action of introducing him to the game of chess would be used for an entirely different purpose. It didn't take long for Pichushkin to be shown the public exhibition games in Bitsa Park, also known as Bitsevski Park.

Bitsa Park is set in over 18 square kilometres of land with a stretch of 10 kilometres from North to South. It is one of the largest natural parks in Moscow and has extensive trails running through the forests, alongside the Bitsa and Chertanovka River. The area of beauty was to become synonymous with one of the most notorious serial killers of recent times.

Pichushkin claimed he enjoyed living with his grandfather, as his intellect was respected and he was allowed to progress where others had held him back. It was then fate that his grandfather suddenly died and Alexander had to return to live with his mother. Almost as soon as he returned to his mother's, he was bullied again by the locals. Even as he grew into a young man, he was still being bullied whenever he was outside and this only led to a larger build-up of anger and aggression.

He subsequently turned to drinking vodka in large quantities. Over the years, he became so dependent on vodka that others suggested he had become immune to its effects. He would sometimes drink huge amounts of alcohol and then go and play chess in Bitsa Park. He would still win a majority of his chess games and he found the ability to focus through the veil of alcohol. It was to play a part in his murders as he was often intoxicated when he killed.

It has also been alleged but never proven that his one aim was to outdo the body count of Andrei Chikatilo, who had recently been convicted for the murders of 53 children and women. The media furore around Chikatilo's case was one that might have influenced Pichushkin's decision to kill.

When Chikatilo was on trial in 1992, Pichushkin at the age of 18-years-old, claimed his first victim. When he was still a student, he pushed another boy out of a window, who fell to his death. It has never been clear whether the other boy had bullied or was bullying him at the time, but the death was recorded as suicide. However, Pichushkin spoke of the murder in detail at his trial.

'This first murder, it's like first love, it's unforgettable.' - Pichushkin in an interview with police.

It would be another decade until he would kill again. During that time, his murderous tendencies remained hidden from view and he learned to control his anger and conceal the rage within. In 2001, Pichushkin began a campaign of murder that would strike fear into the heart of Moscow. He would kill those who were said to be on the fringe of civilised society. His victims consisted of homeless men, runaways, sex workers and lonely alcoholics.

It started with elderly homeless men who resided in or around the vicinity of Bitsa Park. He would lure them away from their troubles with offers of free vodka. He would befriend and drink with them until they were intoxicated, then he would hit them on the back of the head with a hammer, to avoid spilling blood on his clothes. Many of his victims were unidentifiable, because of their wounds or because they had been off the grid for far too long.

As Pichushkin gained confidence in his killing blueprint, he began increasing the intensity of his crimes. He would push a vodka bottle into the open wound of his victim's heads, through the skull and into the brain itself. His obsession with murder slowly moved him away from elderly homeless men to younger men, women and children.

'In all cases I killed for only one reason. I killed in order to live, because when you kill, you want to live. For me, life without murder is like life without food. I felt like the father of all these people, since it was I who opened the door for them to see another world.' - Pichushkin's confession.

When he began his campaign of murder, he would crudely hide the bodies by dropping them down into the many sewers inside the park. But as the killings increased, he would leave his victims in the open, in the exact location he killed them. This led to a frenzy within the city, and a knowledge that a serial killer was on the loose.

Around 2003, Moscow's citizens began to fear a killer the media had described as the Bitsevsky Maniac or The Bitsa Beast. It was only in 2003 that the investigation really started to take hold. Pichushkin wouldn't be a suspect for another three years.

In the Spring of 2006, the body of his final victim, 36-year-old Maria Moskalyova was found in Bitsa Park, with a bottle of vodka sticking out of her head. Detectives found a Moscow Metro train ticket on her person and traced her on surveillance footage. After following her route, they discovered that Pichushkin was accompanying her a few hours before she died.

While they were hunting Pichushkin, another body was found. Pichushkin had murdered one of his colleagues from a supermarket where he worked. She had left a note for her son that said she was going for a walk with Pichushkin. Unaware of the letter in her home, he killed her and left the body in the park.

It wasn't until his arrest that police discovered the now infamous chessboard with dates on all but two of its squares. At his trial, Pichushkin's confession was aired on Russian TV stations.

'For me, a life without murder is like a life without food for you.' – Pichushkin.

In October 2007, it took a jury only three hours to find him guilty of 49 counts of murder and three counts of attempted murder. The death penalty in Russia had recently been abolished and so he was sentenced to life in prison with the first 15 years in solitary confinement. The debate surrounding a return of the death penalty in Russia is still debated to this day.

Pichushkin has been interviewed on many occasions and has offered incredible insight into the mind of a killer. His thoughts on the very nature of human life comes from that of a man obsessed with belittlement and appearing as a higher form of human.

'Human life is not too long. It is cheaper than a sausage. My lawyer: I would cut him open like a fish. I would have killed him like an insect, and I would receive much pleasure from the process. I would cut him up and make belts out of his flesh. But as for remembering everyone I killed, who and when and where, that, I don't remember. I don't even care to remember.'

His nonchalance for human life is characteristic of a sociopathic personality, believing that he is better off and more powerful than everyone around him. The feeling of playing god is a trait of a serial killer that often shows up. He later revealed that he did have a dog and the dog's death hit him harder than he could have imagined.

'She died. It was my fault. I treated it, how to say, not very well. She could have been saved. It was a bad situation, it left something in my subconscious.'

The feeling of something being left in his subconscious, his dreams at night, could have been the only strand of guilt that Alexander ever felt. He blamed himself for his dog's death and felt bad about it. Yet the multiple destruction of human life was not as important as the loss of that which was close to him. Pichushkin has gone on record many times to say that he does not regret anything he ever did.

'No, I do not regret it. So much strength and time spent. Repent? I do not repent, this is again a dull formality. It will not change my sentence. Since I was very young, I dreamed. Everything was different back then. And it all turned out the way I wanted it to.'

Like Ted Bundy before him, Pichushkin sometimes spoke of himself in the third person, whether to remove himself of the guilt of the crimes, or to look upon his crimes from an outsider's perspective.

'Even someone wrote: Pichushkin himself doesn't know yet that the history of criminology is changed, that it didn't account for someone such as him, that he will go down in history, forever.'

Pichushkin was baptised when he was three-months-old but claimed that he did not want it. When speaking of religion he is on record as saying that he does not think that anyone is there. As of 2022, Pichushkin remains in solitary confinement. More quotes from Pichushkin taken from confessions and interviews:

'I will not either read the Bible or write an autobiography. I have never prayed to God, never will. This is a beautiful fairy tale for the weak.'

'I didn't take anything else of value from them. Money, jewellery, I didn't need it. I felt like God.'

'I tried to collect their spirits, their souls, I felt no emotion when I killed them.'

THE FACTS

Born: April 9th 1974 | Active: 1992-2006

Arrested: June 14th 2006 | Country: Russia | Victims: 49-62

AKA: The Chessboard Killer/Bitsevsky Maniac/The Bitsa Beast

Sentence: Life imprisonment | Status: Incarcerated

Pickton, Robert: The Pig Farmer Killer

EXTENDED CASE FILE

One of Canada's worst cases of serial killing began in 1983 and continued for 19 years until 2002. Robert Pickton, AKA: The Pig Farmer Killer, was responsible for at least 49 murders. Even though he was only convicted on six of them. He was arrested in 2002 and charged with the deaths of another twenty women.

Forensic detection proved difficult because most of the bodies had either been decomposing for a long time or had been consumed by insects and pigs on the farm. The investigation included heavy equipment and even had 15-metre-long conveyor belts and soil sifters to find evidence of human remains.

In 2004, the Canadian Government confirmed that Pickton may have ground up human flesh and mixed it with pork to be sold to the public and to the wholesale trade. In conjunction with the Health Authority, they issued a warning about meat that had originated from the region.

Almost all of Pickton's victims were prostitutes from the Vancouver area, and in some cases it was suggested that he fed the bodies to his pigs. He was sentenced in 2010 to 25 years in prison without the possibility of parole in what was the maximum sentence for murder under Canadian law. He confessed to 49 murders but wished to kill another to make it a round fifty.

During the trial, laboratory workers confirmed that 80 unidentified DNA profiles had been detected on the evidence provided to them. Excavations at the farm continued for a year and cost upwards of $70million CAD. The area is now fenced off and all properties belonging to the farm have now been destroyed.

Born in 1949, Robert Pickton came from a family of pig farmers based in Port Coquitlam, British Columbia, just 17 miles east of Vancouver. Pickton and his two brothers grew up on the farm and inherited it from their family. In the mid-1990s, they sold parts of the farm for a few million dollars.

A worker at the farm named Bill Hiscox described the remaining part of the farm as a creepy-looking place. He described Pickton as a bizarre individual who would draw attention to himself through any means possible. By 1996, Pickton had already murdered an unknown number of victims. It was in 1996 that things took an even greater turn for the worse.

After selling off parts of the farm, the Pickton brothers neglected the farming operations and looked at events as a way to bring in money. They registered a non-profit company called the Piggy Palace Good Times Society. The operation involved the running and managing of events, including functions, dances, shows, and exhibitions on behalf of service and sports organisations.

Mostly it was a way to host raves and mega parties in a converted slaughterhouse on the farm, which sometimes attracted upwards of 2,000 people a night. Clientele included Hells Angels and Vancouver sex workers. The set-up provided all the victims that Pickton needed.

The raves were against the law as they would sell illegal drugs and alcohol without a license to party-goers, they also charged an entrance fee. It has been suggested that the Piggy Palace Good Times Society was merely a front for their illegal operations.

Pickton had been linked with missing people and murders all the way back to 1978 but was only convicted of murders that took place between 1997 and 2001. A total of 65 women had disappeared in the area from 1978 to 2001. After the largest investigation in Canadian history, investigators are still unsure as to which missing person was the first of his murders.

Prostitutes on the Downtown Eastside area of Vancouver were plentiful in the time that Pickton was killing. The red-light district was known for drug users, prostitutes and crime. Pickton had his pick of victims and it was reported that almost all of his victims were involved in drug use or prostitution. That a murdered prostitute is difficult to investigate, Pickton went unnoticed for two decades.

Before the illegal raves brought a raft of potential victims his way, he would lure the women to his pig farm where no one would hear them scream. He either strangled them with ligatures or shot them dead – before feeding them to the pigs.

Pigs can eat through a human body with ease, it is known that feeding a body to pigs was also used by the Italian Mafia at one point in their history. Because the farm processed the meat on site, Pickton had an easy method of disposal at his hands. It is also unclear whether he fed his victims to the pigs whilst they were dead or alive.

By 2001, Bill Hiscox began to notice that women would be seen entering the farm and never leaving. He finally raised his concerns to police and Pickton was arrested after women's items were found on the farm. In 2006, he pleaded not-guilty to 27 counts of murder. It is also claimed he attached a dildo to the end of his gun in order to use it as a silencer. It was then suggested that he inserted the dildo into one of the women before shooting them through it.

One of Pickton's friends, Scott Chubb, claimed that Pickton spoke to him about the best ways to kill hookers. He said that if she was a heroin addict then you could inject her with windscreen washer fluid. He even told Chubb that he killed prostitutes by handcuffing them and strangling them. He claimed he would bleed and gut them dry before feeding them to the pigs.

Pickton was convicted of six murders and the rest were discontinued. The court said that even if the rest were convicted then it wouldn't change the sentence Pickton had received. The difficult lack of evidence in most cases was hard to convict him on. Even though he claimed a total of 49 murders.

After his arrest, a witness named Lynn Ellingsen came forward to claim she had seen Pickton skinning a small woman hanging from a meat hook on his farm. She didn't tell anyone at the time as she had been blackmailing Pickton about it ever since. In 2010, Pickton was sentenced to life with no parole for 25 years, which is the longest possible sentence under Canadian law.

THE FACTS

Born: October 26th 1949 | Active: 1983-2002

Arrested: February 2nd 2002 | Country: Canada

Victims: 26-60 | AKA: The Pig Farmer Killer

Sentence: Life imprisonment | Status: Incarcerated

Pintaric, Vinko

A Croatian serial killer who murdered five people over a 17-year period between prison escapes and police stakeouts. He spent a lot of the time hiding in the northern regions and as such was considered an outlaw who engaged in various crimes.

He was born in 1941 during World War Two when his father was out fighting with the Partisan resistance. At one point, Vinko's father was beaten in front of his family, then killed not too long after. Vinko's mother remarried and his new stepfather physically and emotionally abused him. From then on, Vinko spoke about avenging his father.

AERIAL VIEW OF THE PICKTON FARM IN PORT COQUITLAM

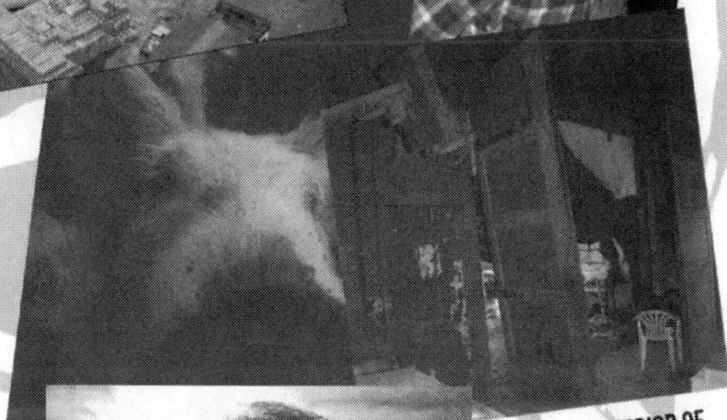

INTERIOR OF PICKTON'S SLAUGHTERHOUSE

IMAGE ATTRIBUTIONS (ATTRIB A9) (ATTRIB A10) (ATTRIB A75) (ATTRIB A76) (ATTRIB A77)

ROBERT PICKTON

On April 26th 1973, he killed his first victim after drinking heavily in a local bar. When he arrived home, he got into an argument with his neighbour before shooting him dead and injuring his neighbour's tenant. He surrendered to police 18 days afterwards. He was subsequently committed to a psychiatric institute but escaped and went into hiding, before killing his wife in a drunken rage on October 24th.

Police surrounded the house on January 20th 1974 and arrested him without resistance. Vinko admitted to all his crimes but pleaded not guilty due to intoxication by alcohol when committing them. He was sentenced to death which was later commuted to 20 years in prison. After multiple escapes and subsequent prison time, he was killed in 1991 during a police shoot out.

THE FACTS

Born: April 3rd 1941 | Active: 1973-1990

Arrested: 20th January 1974 | Country: Croatia | Victims: 5

AKA: Čaruga of Zagorje | Status: Killed by police in 1991

Popkov, Mikhail: The Werewolf

EXTENDED CASE FILE

Mikhail Popkov, AKA: The Werewolf, is Russia's worst ever serial killer. For many years, researchers have assumed that Andrei Chikatilo or Alexander Pichushkin were the worst, but as of 2022, Popkov is suggested to be linked to over 200 murders. He has already been found guilty and convicted on 78 counts of murder.

In 2015, Popkov was convicted on 22 counts of murder, and three years later in 2018, he was convicted of another 56 counts of murder, with many more waiting in the pipeline. Born on March 7th 1964, it is claimed that Popkov was abused by his mother, although not much information on his childhood is known. He became a police officer in the Irkutsk region of Russia and also worked as a security guard at the Angarsk Oil and Chemical Company, along with private contracts.

His wife and daughter claim to this day that he is innocent of the crimes that he has been found guilty for, and stand by him, protesting his innocence at every turn. However, Popkov has been with investigators when he explicitly showed them how he killed some of his victims and where their remains were buried.

Almost all of his victims were women between the ages of 15 and 50. He also killed a fellow male police officer but the motive has never been forthcoming. Most of the victims were sex workers, homeless or drunk. They were people that Popkov considered immoral and of a lower social standing than himself. He chose himself to be judge, jury, and executioner.

While pretending to be on-the-clock in his police uniform, he would lure his victims into his car before killing them in the vehicle or in remote locations around the region. He used knives, axes and baseball bats to kill them. His axe, in particular, had been used to kill at least 17 women.

He killed one of his victims by stabbing her over 170 times. The brutality of his murders and the way in which he completely ripped his victims apart, earned him the moniker of The Werewolf, as the bodies appeared to have been ripped apart by a vicious animal.

One victim was beheaded and another had her heart ripped out of her chest and thrown to the side of her body. Some people who knew Popkov claimed that a lot of the victims had a similar look to his own mother, and it has been suggested that he may have been taking revenge on her by killing those with a similar appearance.

Ever since 1992, Popkov had been taking victims in a similar manner. The Russian police force was involved in the case from 1994, investigating murders of women across a large region of the country. It was at a time when the trial of fellow Russian serial killer, Andrei Chikatilo, had infested the national psyche. At the same time, Alexander Pichushkin, a Russian serial killer said to be influenced by Chikatilo, had already claimed a victim, and was building up to a campaign of terror in the Russian Capital.

After two decades, the investigation found patterns in the vehicle tracks near to the remains of some victims. They were the same as the off-road vehicles used by the police force and similar authorities. In 2012, DNA testing of 3,500 current police officers and former police officers in the Irkutsk region, resulted in Popkov's arrest.

"I had a double-life. In one life I was an ordinary person, I was in the service in the police, having positive feedback on my work. I had a family. My wife and daughter considered me a good husband and father, which corresponded to reality. In my other life I committed murders, which I carefully concealed from everyone, realising that this was a criminal offence. My wife and daughter never knew about the crimes I committed and did not even suspect this." - Popkov, in his confession to police.

There were also two survivors, and one of them would speak in detail about her experience. One survivor was attacked, left for dead, and subsequently awoke in a morgue. She had been raped, beaten and repeatedly thrown into a tree. When her battered body crumpled to the ground in a pool of her own blood, Popkov left her, assuming she had died. It remains unclear how she came to awake in a morgue.

In October of 1998, two more victims were discovered by shepherds. 19-year-old Yulia Kuprikova was found next to her friend, 20-year-old Tatiana Martynova. They had attended a concert in the area and then went out for a drink afterwards. After Tatiana failed to return home, her husband, Igor, called the police and a search was undertaken.

Both Yulia and Tatiana had been raped, beaten and mutilated. Popkov was also accused of engaging in necrophilia with the corpses. Tatiana's eldest brother flew from Moscow to the region, to identify his sister's corpse. It is claimed that when he exited the coroner's room, he became sick and could not speak as to what he had seen.

In January of 2015, Popkov was sentenced to life in prison on 22 counts of murder, alongside two attempted murders. At the time, a Russian investigator claimed that Popkov could have murdered up to 200 people. As of 2022, 14 of the victims remain unidentified due to their personal histories or the way in which the bodies had been mutilated.

On December 10th 2018, Popkov was convicted of another 56 counts of murder. There were three more that he confessed to but due to a lack of evidence, they were not pursued in the courts. The convictions only added to his life sentences. At that time, another investigator claimed that there could be an additional 122 victims, bringing the total body count to the already suggested number of 200.

During his trial, Popkov referred to himself as a cleaner. He claimed to be punishing young women for immoral actions and behaviour.

'They left their husbands and children at home and went out drinking as if for the last time. Of course nobody is without sin. But one must not hurt one's dearest.' - Popkov interview in the Russian newspaper Komsomolskaya Pravda (2015)

Psychiatrist reports list the motive of the murders as purely psychopathic, they claimed he simply had an irresistible urge to kill and got away with it for so long due to his connections with law enforcement. Popkov was sent to the Black Dolphin facility to serve his sentence, a high-security prison to Russia's East, on the border of Kazakhstan.

After the end of the death penalty in 1996, the Black Dolphin prison holds Russia's most brutal and heinous criminals. In July 2020, Popkov confessed to more killings, bringing the total number of admitted victims to 83. As of 2022, Popkov is the country's worst known serial killer by brutality and body count.

THE FACTS

Born: March 7th 1964 | Active: 1992-2010

Arrested: June 23rd 2012 | Country: Russia

Victims: 83-200 | AKA: The Werewolf

Sentence: Life imprisonment | Status: Incarcerated

Price, Craig Chandler: The Warwick Slasher

On July 27th 1987, in Warwick Rhode Island, serial killer Craig Chandler Price claimed his first victim, and he was only 13-years-old at the time. He would be arrested before he even reached his 16th birthday and by then he had already murdered four people.

On the evening of July 27th, he broke into a house only two doors away from his family home. He took a knife from the kitchen and killed the occupant; 27-year-old Rebecca Spencer, by stabbing her an astonishing 58 times. He would kill his victims usually when high on marijuana and LSD.

His murders were so violent that the handles would break off the knives with the blades still embedded in the victims. He killed one of his neighbour's eight-year-old daughter by crushing her skull and stabbing her over 30 times. Price was arrested in 1989 when he was just 15 and sentenced to life in prison.

Price continues to be violent in prison, having stabbed a prison officer in 2009 and another inmate in 2017. He has never shown any remorse for his crimes and remains incarcerated for at least another 25 years.

THE FACTS

Born: October 11th 1973 | Active: 1987-1989

Arrested: 1989 | Country: USA (Rhode Island)

Victims: 4 | AKA: The Warwick Slasher

Sentence: Life imprisonment | Status: Incarcerated

Profit, Mark Antonio: The Wirth Park Killer

In Minneapolis, Minnesota, serial killer Mark Antonio Profit, AKA: The Wirth Park Killer, would be convicted of one murder, with three more confirmed. From the age of 15, Profit had been outside of prison for a combined total of only one year. Over three months in 1996, he killed three women and one trans man.

Just 17 days after his release from a halfway-house in Minneapolis, he claimed his first victim, and the one he would be convicted for. On May 23rd 1996, the nude body of 30-year-old sex worker Renee Bell was found floating face down in a creek in Theodore Wirth Park. She had been dead for a couple of days before her discovery.

She had been gagged, raped and strangled to death with a ligature. The material would prove instrumental in Profit's conviction, as fibres from it were found in his vehicle upon his arrest. Profit had gone as far as packing mud onto and into her body in a supposed failed method to see the body decompose quicker.

Then on June 3rd, the burned nude body of 43-year-old Deborah LaVoie was found in the same park. On June 19th, another body, that of 36-year-old Avis Warfield was discovered near to Wirth Park, she had been stabbed and the body and been burned. And then on July 29th, the body of 21-year-old Keooudorn Photisane was discovered in bushes near the park's golf course and bike trail.

Profit was arrested in October, and a year later on June 2nd 1997, was sentenced to two life terms for the murder of Renee Bell and the rape of another woman. For the murder of Avis Warfield, Profit claimed to have been in a County Jail when the murder happened, but authorities confirmed that he had not yet been arrested by that point. He was also placed at the scene of the crime.

In August 2001, while at the start of his sentence, he attempted to kill a prison guard and was charged with attempted murder. Just two months later in early October, Profit was found dead in his cell at the Minnesota Correctional Facility. No cause of death was provided.

THE FACTS

Born: 1964 | Active: 1996

Arrested: October 3rd 1996 | Country: USA (Minnesota)

Victims: 4 | AKA: The Wirth Park Killer

Sentence: Two life sentences | Status: Died in 2001

Psicopata, El (The Psychopath)

On July 14th 1987, sex worker Ligia Camacho Bermudez was murdered in her home as she was laying on her bed reading a book. She had been shot from outside her house, through the window. When ballistics were run, it showed the murder was carried out by a notorious Costa Rican serial killer known as The Psychopath (El Psicopata).

Between 1986 and 1996, The Psychopath was responsible for the murders of at least 19 people in major cities across the country. The last known murders of El Psicopata were on October 26th 1996, a young couple who were parked beside a road near San José.

The killer forced them at gunpoint to get out and leave their car behind, he then marched them away from the road and shot them both in the head. It was never clear what happened to the killer after the final murders.

In 1996, a suspect was identified by the Civil Police but never found. Due to the Costa Rican statute of limitations having passed, even if a suspect was found today, he could not be tried for the murders. This effectively means that the culprit would get off scot-free.

THE FACTS

Active: 1986-1996 | Country: Costa Rica | Victims: 19+

AKA: The Psychopath | Status: Unsolved

Quansah, Charles: The Accra Strangler

A rare serial killer from Ghana, Charles 'Papa' Kwabena Ebo Quansah, AKA: The Accra Strangler, strangled to death at least nine women from 1993 to 2000. On January 19th 1996, the body of Akua Serwaa was discovered just outside the Kumasi Sport Stadium. She had been strangled to death by Quansah.

He would be convicted of her murder while in custody for killing his girlfriend, Joyce Boateng in 2000 but it was far from his first kill. From 1993, the bodies of multiple women began turning up across Accra, the capital city of Ghana. A serial killer was suspected but the investigation was getting nowhere and Quansah carried on killing.

He was a mechanic who lived in the Adenta region of the city and was already under suspicion due to previous convictions and prison time for rape in the 1980s. He was under police surveillance as a suspect in some of the murders. When he was arrested in 2000, 34 victims had been attributed to the then unknown serial killer.

Although Quansah would be convicted on nine murders, he was strongly linked to the other 25. In July of 2002, he was convicted of the nine killings and sentenced to death by hanging. He claimed he was coerced into a confession by police who tortured him. Until his execution shortly after, he proclaimed his innocence at every turn.

THE FACTS

Born: 1964 | Active: 1993-2000

Arrested: July 2000 | Country: Ghana

Victims: 9-34 | AKA: The Accra Strangler

Sentence: Death penalty | Status: Executed in 2002

Quick, Thomas

Born Sture Ragnar Bergwall in Sweden, he is more commonly known as Thomas Quick. He is suspected of having killed up to 30 people over various periods of time between 1964 and 1996. He killed in various Scandinavian countries including Sweden, Finland, Denmark, and Norway.

While he was sectioned in psychiatric institutions, he confessed to his murders but claimed it was different parts of his personality that had killed them. He then withdrew his confessions at a later date and the case has since been under the scrutiny of the Swedish press and public. It has been claimed that a cult of psychologists coerced Quick to give false confessions.

He took his mother's surname of Quick when he was 14-years-old and went on to a life of crime involving the sexual abuse of children and various assaults on other people. He would ultimately be convicted of eight murders over different trials. He confessed to abducting and killing nine-year-old schoolgirl Therese Johannessen in 1988.

He gave instructions to police that would lead them to her remains, and even went as far as describing her wristwatch in great detail. Investigators then found bone fragments in the exact place where Quick claimed to have buried her. Then came the outrage as Quick claimed that his confessions were false and forced upon him.

He publicly took back his confessions in 2008. Bizarrely, because each trial had rested on his confession alone, each conviction was quashed, with the last conviction finally overturned on appeal in 2013. There was even no evidence beyond a confession in the murder of Johannessen.

What is clear, is that Quick was a criminal in his younger years, and that he did originally confess to the murders of 30 people. What is unclear, is the exact nature of his mental state before, during, and after the murders. Quick has since been released from psychiatric care and is suspected of living a free life somewhere in Sweden.

His treatment plan has been wrapped up in secrecy and cannot be revealed to the press or researchers. Interestingly, from the uncensored portions of his files, it seems that Quick is no longer taking medication and hasn't been since his release. Even though he had been on medication for most of his life. As of 2022, Quick's whereabouts are known only to a few. He is the only known serial killer to have all of his murder convictions quashed due to failures in the legal system.

THE FACTS

Born: April 26th 1950 | Active: 1964-1996

Arrested: March 1996 | Country: Sweden/Finland/Denmark/Norway

Victims: 8-30 | AKA: Sture Ragnar Bergwall

Sentence: Convictions quashed | Status: Unknown

Rader, Dennis: The BTK Killer

EXTENDED CASE FILE

Born on March 9th 1945, Dennis Rader grew up in a normal household and went on to a happy marriage with children and a dream job at a security company. But Rader had been dreaming and having thoughts about restraining women so he could abuse and torture them. He killed from 1974 to 1991 and had claimed at least ten victims within that period.

Knowledge gained from his security job at ADT made it easier for him to cut the phone lines of his victim's homes. Around the time of the last murder in 1991, technology was on the rise, home computers were becoming popular, and more was known about technology in general.

Dennis Rader was one of the rare serial killers who it seemed wanted to become famous and it was Rader himself who created his own serial killing moniker. He would write letters to police and goad them constantly. He referred to himself as The BTK Killer, which stood for 'Bind. Torture. Kill'.

On January 15th 1974, Rader murdered four members of the Otero family, the parents and two children, in Wichita, Kansas. Their bodies were discovered by the family's eldest child, Charlie Otero, as he returned home from school. It wasn't until Rader's arrest in 2005 that he would confess to the murders.

He claimed that in October 1974, he wrote a letter that he stashed inside a book in the Wichita Public Library. It detailed the killing of the family and was to be the start of his demand for media attention. The following is a copy of a letter sent to a television station in 1978, it is displayed here as written with no editing. As such, the grammatical and spelling errors remain and are the style of Denis Rader.

ONE OF THE MANY BIZARRE SELFIES THAT RADER TOOK OF HIMSELF

(ATTRIB A145-146)

DENNIS RADER

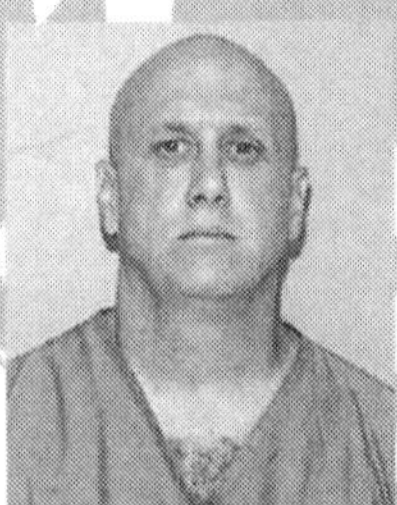

(ATTRIB A147)

JAMES MICHAEL RANDALL

TERRY PEDER RASMUSSEN

(ATTRIB A148)

"How many do I have to Kill before I get a name in the paper or some national attention. Do the cop think that all those deaths are not related? Golly -gee, yes the M.O. is different in each, but look a pattern is developing. The victims are tie up-most have been women-phone cut- bring some bondage mater sadist tendencies-no struggle, outside the death spot-no witness except the Vain's Kids. They were very lucky; a phone call save them. I was go-ng to tape the boys and put plastics bag over there head like I did Joseph, and Shirley. And then hang the girl.

"God-oh God what a beautiful sexual relief that would been. Josephine, when I hung her really turn me on; her pleading for mercy then the rope took whole, she helpless; staring at me with wide terror fill eyes the rope getting tighter-tighter. You don't understand these things because your not under the influence of factor x). The same thing that made Son of Sam, Jack the Ripper, Havery Glatman, Boston Strangler, Dr. H.H. Holmes Panty Hose Strangler OF Florida, Hillside Strangler, Ted of the West Coast and many more infamous character kill. Which seem s senseless, but we can't help it.

"There is no help, no cure, except death or being caught and put away. It a terrible nightmare but, you see I don't lose any sleep over it. After a thing like Fox I come home and go about life like anyone else. And I will be like that until the urge hit me again. It not continuous and I don;t have a lot of time. It take time to set a kill, one mistake and it all over. Since I about blew it on the phone-handwriting is out-letter guide is to long and typewriter can be traced too. My short poem of death and maybe a drawing;later on real picture and maybe a tape of the sound will come your way. How will you know me. Before a murder or murders you will receive a copy of the initials B.T.K. , you keep that copy the original will show up some day on guess who?

"May you not be the unluck one! P.S. How about some name for me, its time: 7 down and many more to go. I like the following How about you?

"THE B.T.K. STRANGLER', WICHITA STRANGLER', 'POETIC STRANGLER', 'THE BOND AGE STRANGLER' OR PSYCHO' THE WICHITA HANGMAN THE WICHITA EXECUTIONER, 'THE GAROTE PHATHOM', 'THE ASPHIXIATER'. B.T.K"

The statement in the letter above proves that above all else, Rader was a narcissist and showed how much he craved attention. It is then assumed that he was fully aware of people's fascination with serial killers and the macabre, due in some part to the media putting serial killers in the limelight.

Rader was the perfect family man between murders, alluded to in a book written by his daughter, Kerri Rawson. She says that he was perceived as a pillar in the community and a family man who had a positive outlook on life with his wife and children. We already know with Ted Bundy that some serial killers are capable of great love for women they hold in high esteem and yet capable of such violence towards those they do not.

Internally, Rader was holding off the desire to kill for months and sometimes years at a time. He would engage in autoerotic fantasies until the desire to kill became too strong. He confirmed later he knew the public would want to know more about him and they would want to know how he did it and what his motivations were. He was deliberately appealing to society's appetite for murder stories.

In another letter to authorities, he claimed he could not stop killing and society should be thankful to him for holding back the monster. He fantasized more and more about killing and held off by using the trophies of his victims in a sexual manner while masturbating with them.

He claimed to be seeking victims all the way through the late 1970s to the 1980s. In the killing of the Otero family, he used many methods. He strangled the father by putting a cord around his neck then he put a bag over nine-year-old Joseph Otero's head. He strangled the mother but she 'came back to life' and so he strangled her harder than before.

He killed the daughter, 11-year-old Josephine Otero last, by dragging her into the basement and tying a noose around her neck. He hung her and watched her die in front of him all the while saying that she would be joining her family in heaven. Then he ripped off some of her clothing and masturbated over the girl's legs.

The last murder was in January of 1991 when he murdered 62-year-old Dolores Davis. He claimed that as he had aged – he was 45 when he killed Dolores – he had become weaker and as such needed weaker victims to kill. He stalked Dolores before realising that she lived alone and seemed like a perfect victim. He was a leader on a boy scout trip at the time and had left the campsite to kill her. He went to his parent's house and got changed into his 'killing clothes' then drove to a church parking lot. He then walked to her house and broke in by smashing the window on the back door.

She came down the stairs and saw Rader waiting for her. He later claimed Dolores said she was waiting for someone to arrive at her house shortly, but it didn't stop him. He killed her and then used her own car to drive to a lake where he dumped her body. He then cleaned down the car, left it back at her house, returned home to get changed and went back to the boy scout camp as if nothing had happened.

In a twist of fate, it was Rader's obsession with himself and his desired celebrity status that caught him. In one of his final letters to police, he asked if a floppy disk could be traced if he put confessions and writings onto one and sent it to them. The police answered in a newspaper ad in the Wichita Eagle stating that it would be safe and couldn't be traced.

When they received it in 2005, police found metadata in a deleted Microsoft Word document that included reference to a 'Dennis' and 'Christ Lutheran Church'. An internet search linked them as Rader was on the church council, and along with other evidence compiled, he was subsequently arrested. He finally got his wish as the Wichita Police announced that the BTK Killer had been caught. He is currently serving ten consecutive life sentences at El Dorado Correctional Facility in Kansas.

THE FACTS

Born: March 9th 1945 | Active: 1974-1991

Arrested: February 25th 2005 | Country: USA

Victims: 10 | AKA: The BTK Killer

Sentence: 10 life sentences | Status: Incarcerated

Rand, Andre: The Pied Piper of Staten Island

Suspected American serial killer Andre Rand, AKA: The Pied Piper of Staten Island, kidnapped and killed children from 1972 to 1987. It is claimed that he kidnapped them to be used in Satanic rituals. Rand was the prime suspect in the disappearance of five-year-old Alice Pereira, who vanished in 1972 in Staten Island, New York. No trace of her has ever been found, dead or alive.

Rand was also the suspect in the 1981 abduction of seven-year-old Holly Ann Hughes when he grabbed her off the street and threw her into his car as her friend watched nearby. In 1983, 11-year-old Tiahease Jackson disappeared near Mariner's Harbor Motel in Staten Island, less than two weeks after Rand was released from prison for stealing a school bus packed with children.

In 1984, 22-year-old Hank Gafforio disappeared after last being seen in a local diner with Rand. On July 9th 1987, 12-year-old Jennifer Schweiger went missing. After an intense and widespread search that lasted 35 days, her body was found in a shallow grave in an area of woodland near her school. She had been raped and brutally killed by Rand and would be the last of his known victims.

Rand was arrested in August of 1987 and was sentenced to 25 years to life in prison for the murder of Schweiger. Due to the statute of limitations he couldn't be tried for the murder of his earlier victims and was due for release in 2008. However he was convicted on further kidnapping charges, which are not restricted by the statute.

He was convicted of the kidnapping of Holly despite her body never being found. Some researchers suspected he may have been kidnapping young girls to hand over to Satanists for use in rituals – which has never been proven. As of 2022, Rand remains incarcerated and is now due for paroled release in 2037.

THE FACTS

Born: March 11th 1944 | Active: 1972-1987

Arrested: July 1987 | Country: USA

Victims: 1-5+ | AKA: The Pied Piper of Staten Island

Sentence: 25 years to life in prison | Status: Incarcerated

Randall, James Michael

American murderer and suspected serial killer, James Michael Randall, was active in Massachusetts and Florida from 1984 to 1996. He raped numerous women and killed at least two in the Tampa Bay area. The first murder he was linked with was the 1984 death of Holly Cote, who was strangled to death.

She had been a friend of the family and was last seen alive close to where Randall resided at the time. Randall also alluded to the murder in numerous interviews with psychiatrists, however he was never charged with it. In 1986, he beat his wife, Linda Randall, so badly that he was arrested and sentenced to a minimum of five years for assault.

He was released in 1992 and moved to Florida, where his blood lust only grew. Randall had developed a fascination with erotic asphyxiation, which meant that he enjoyed choking his sexual partners during sex. Some of his former girlfriends and former wife confirmed that he would hit them and take enjoyment from it. He was also known to have visited sex workers regularly, and when he did, he choked and beat them too.

On October 20th 1995, Florida sex worker Wendy Evans was strangled to death. Her nude body was discovered on the side of a road by a delivery driver the next morning. Three months later on January 18th 1996, another Florida sex worker, Cynthia Pugh, was strangled and her body dumped on the side of the road.

Immediately, Randall became a suspect, due to his previous convictions and that his tyre marks matched his vehicle. On June 27th, police went to interview Randall at his house. Shortly after, he sped off in his vehicle, causing police to go after him. After a high-speed chase, Randall jumped out of his car and ran off but was arrested and charged four days later on July 1st.

Less than a year later, in April of 1997, Randall was convicted on two charges of murder for the deaths of Wendy Evans and Cynthia Pugh and was handed down two death sentences. After an appeal in 2000, the death sentences were commuted to life in prison.

Randall has long been suspected of killing more sex workers and continues to be a suspect in various cold cases across Florida. Though none have been proven, as of yet, investigators believe he may be responsible for at least four more murders. When charges of two murders were laid at his feet, he looked at the detectives and said, 'is that all?'

THE FACTS

Born: August 28th 1954 | Active: 1984-1996.

Arrested: July 1st 1996 | Country: USA | Victims: 2-6

Sentence: Death penalty, commuted to life | Status: Incarcerated

Rasmussen, Terrence Peder: The Chameleon Killer

AKA: The Chameleon Killer, Rasmussen was an American serial killer who took the lives of at least six people. He was known for having used multiple aliases for at least 20 years across many states and was able to hide within different communities using his various identities, leading to him becoming The Chameleon Killer in the press.

Born in 1943, he joined the U.S. Navy at a young age and was discharged for unknown reasons in 1967, when he was 24. After getting married and having four children, Rasmussen suddenly eloped in Christmas of 1974. He moved around the country and lived in at least seven different States, from Virginia to Hawaii.

He used multiple identities to remain off-the-grid and took work under different names. Curtis Mayo Kimball, Gordon Jensen, Larry Vanner, and Gerry Mockerman were among some of his more used names. Because of recent genetic genealogy testing, we know more about what Rasmussen did in the early years. A lot of the following information was discovered in 2019, nine years after his death.

In 1978, Rasmussen's then girlfriend, Marlyse Honeychurch, her six-year-old daughter and her one-year-old daughter went missing on Thanksgiving. In 1985, their decomposed bodies were found in two barrels, along with two other victims. They became known as the Bear Brook murders and wouldn't be identified until

2019, except the one-year-old who couldn't be named, but DNA testing proved it to be the child of Rasmussen. He had murdered them all in cold blood.

On Thanksgiving of 1981, while under the name of Bob Evans, Rasmussen is suspected of having murdered his then girlfriend Denise Beaudin, whose body has never been found. He claimed that she had run off due to financial reasons. He then took custody of their six-month-old daughter, who he abandoned shortly after.

He was sentenced in 1986 for child abandonment, served four years, and then vanished again in 1990. Another known murder came in 2002 when he killed and dismembered his then wife; Eunsoon Jun. He was arrested in 2002 and confessed to the murder. Under the name of Larry Vanner, he was sentenced to 15 years to life. Fingerprint and DNA then began matching him to other names in different states, and a new investigation began drawing up a much larger map of his crimes.

But in 2010, Rasmussen died in prison of natural causes, taking his secrets to the grave – or so he thought. Genetic genealogy testing of cold cases and suspected murders linked him to at least five more murders across multiple states. Rasmussen was considered unique in that he generally killed those who were close to him. It went against the usual victim selection type for serial killers, who mostly prey on strangers rather than those close to them.

THE FACTS

Born: December 23rd 1943 | Active: 1978-2002

Arrested: November 2002 | Country: USA

Victims: 6+ | AKA: The Chameleon killer

Sentence: 15 years to life in prison | Status: Died in 2010

Ray, David Parker: The Toy Box Killer

EXTENDED CASE FILE

From the 1950s to 1999, American serial killer and torturer David Parker Ray, AKA: The Toy-Box Killer was suspected to have killed up to 60 people. Astonishingly, no bodies have ever been found, but his accomplices statements combined with missing persons reports assured police that Ray was potentially one of America's worst serial killers.

He soundproofed and kitted out a truck trailer with instruments of torture and sexual devices and called it his toy box. By the end of the trial in 2001, Ray had been convicted of kidnapping and torture but was never convicted of murder. In recent years, due to advancements in DNA technology and investigatory procedures, he has been positively linked to 14 murders.

For the victims he raped and tortured but didn't kill, he used drugs and brainwashing techniques so the victims wouldn't remember what happened to them. The FBI later stated that the true extent of his crimes might have been stratospheric and that he was kidnapping and killing up to six women every year while he was active.

In the mid-1950s, when he was just a teenager, he developed a fascination with bondage and BDSM. When his violent alcoholic father left him and his sister with their elderly grandfather, Ray was known to have had secret fantasies about tying people up and murdering them. His father would supply him with pornographic magazines depicting bondage and BDSM which carved out an image of women he took into his adult years. He was also bullied by other school children for his shyness around girls.

When he was in his late teens, he abducted a woman and tied her to a tree, then tortured, mutilated, and killed her before dumping the body in the woods. He married shortly after to a woman named Peggy, who claimed she knew of his fantasies but not that he was acting on them. At the time he was married, Ray became addicted to using sex workers and took part in BDSM relationships with them.

His sole child, a daughter from the marriage, Glenda Jean Ray, had previously reported him to the FBI in 1986. She said that her father was kidnapping women and selling them to buyers in Mexico. The FBI didn't believe her story, saying it was too far-fetched with not enough details. It would be another 13 years before Ray was finally arrested. The FBI never commented on their mistake in not following up on the report.

The town he lived in was called Elephant Butte which is a small town in New Mexico. He had positioned the toy box trailer in a static location for many years, next to a large lake and area of New Mexico parkland. It has been suggested that bodies could easily be dumped in the area, due to its remoteness but the area has never been excavated. Ray also had extensive knowledge of the parkland, due to his position as a maintenance man for the New Mexico Parks Department. It is claimed that his knowledge of the land allowed him to hide bodies all over the place. The toy box was his life's work and he spent all his earnings on it. Inside, there were detailed and intricate torture devices and machines designed to maximise pain and keep his victims restrained with minimal movement.

He would source his victims from rundown bars in the area, sex workers, or drifters and runaways. Then he would torture his victims by using sexual instruments and industrial items. These included saws, blades, straps, clamps, whips and chains. He also had multiple accomplices, some of whom have never been named. Together they raped dozens of women.

He also kept detailed illustrations regarding his various techniques for torture and restraint. He even had an electrical generator that he used to torture his victims. He would put them in large contraptions that kept them bent over in one position and placed a mirror in front of them. Then he would bring in dogs to rape them.

Ray kept a detailed journal which contained information on his victims with dates of abductions and murders. It is claimed that without it, there wouldn't have been any prosecution at all. However, the FBI had built up a large case against him and three trials took place for the kidnap and torture of three victims. He was subsequently sentenced to 224 years in prison.

In 2002, as part of his plea agreement, he agreed to show investigators where the bodies were buried. Just before he was about to, he died of a heart attack. In doing so, he took the locations of the bodies to his grave. As of 2022, no bodies have ever been discovered.

THE FACTS

Born: November 6th 1939 | Active: mid-1950s-1999.

Arrested: March 22nd 1999 | Country: USA (New Mexico/Arizona)

Victims: 14-60+ | AKA: The Toy-Box Killer

Sentence: 224 years in prison | Status: Died in 2002

THE TOY BOX TORTURE TRAILER WHERE PARKER RAY TORTURED HIS VICTIMS

DAVID PARKER RAY

IMAGE ATTRIBUTIONS
(ATTRIB A87) (ATTRIB A88)
(ATTRIB A5)

GARY RIDGWAY

LOREN HERZOG

WESLEY SHERMANTINE

IMAGE ATTRIBUTIONS
(ATTRIB A47A) (ATTRIB A47B)

SPEED FREAK KILLERS

Reddy, Umesh

Umesh Reddy is an Indian serial killer and rapist who was convicted of killing nine females and the rapes of an additional 22 girls and women. He confessed to 18 murders but police suspected he had been involved in the deaths of at least 20 women across various regions in the country. He was also a transvestite who was often found wearing female underwear underneath his clothing.

In November 1996, Reddy attempted to rape a high school girl in the Chitradurga district but the girl escaped his clutches by hitting him in the head with a stone. She remains one of his only victims to have escaped. Reddy generally targeted housewives in the middle of the day, as there was less chance of a male being in the house. He would knock on the door and ask for directions before forcing his way into their home with a knife.

On December 6th 1996, Reddy raped, beat, and murdered a 16-year-old girl known as Rupa. She lived in the same area as the previous victim and was attacked as she returned home from school. Reddy was arrested and escaped custody an astonishing four times until 2002, when he was caught and convicted of nine counts of murder and rape.

In 2007, he was sentenced to death for the 1998 rape and murder of a 37-year-old woman in front of her son before he repeatedly had sex with her corpse. He told her son that an evil spirit had entered her mother's body and he was exorcising the demon within. Despite a lengthy appeal in 2021 to commute the death sentence to life, Reddy remains on death row in India.

THE FACTS

Born: 1969 | Active: 1996-2002

Arrested: 2002 for the last time | Country: India

Victims: 9-20+ | AKA: The Bangalore Serial Killer

Sentence: Death penalty | Status: Death row

Reinstrom, Lutz: The Acid Killer

German killer Lutz Reinstrom, AKA: The Acid Killer, murdered at least two people in his underground bunker from 1986 to 1988. He built the bunker in the grounds of his terraced house in Rahlstedt, Hamburg.

In 1986, he abducted a 61-year-old lady who was known to him as the wife of his teacher. He took her belongings, cleared her accounts, and stole items worth a total of about 40,000 DEM (approx. $20,000 USD at the time). Then he raped, tortured and dismembered her over the course of a week.

The other known victim was on 5th October 1988 when he abducted a 31-year-old female known as Annegret B and locked her in the bunker. He emptied her bank accounts before raping and torturing her for four weeks. Reinstrom made video recordings and took multiple photos of her ordeal before ending her life and dismembering her corpse.

He made his victims write farewell letters and postcards to their relatives claiming they wanted to begin a new life in another country. Reinstrom would then travel to the countries and post the letters. It wasn't discovered until later that the victims had secretly added cries for help within their words.

Another kidnapping in 1991 was botched when his wife came home from vacation early. He let his 53-year-old victim go but she became instrumental in his arrest in September of that year. During the search of Reinstrom's property, five canisters of hydrochloric acid were found, along with a barrel full of human remains. He used the acid to both torture his victims and break down their remains. He was convicted of two murders and sentenced to life in prison.

THE FACTS

Born: March 29th 1949 | Active: 1986-1991

Arrested: September 17th 1991 | Country: Germany

Victims: 2+ | AKA: The Acid Killer

Sentence: Life imprisonment | Status: Incarcerated

Resendiz, Angel Maturino: The Railroad Killer

Mexican serial killer and lifetime criminal Angel Maturino Resendiz, AKA: The Railroad Killer was confirmed to have killed 16 people but suspected of at least 23 across Mexico and the United States between 1986 and 1999. Most of the murders were committed near railway tracks, which is where he gained his moniker.

The first murder came in 1986 when he shot dead an unidentified female in Texas before dumping her body in an abandoned farmhouse. He claimed that he killed her because she had disrespected him when he picked her up to join him on a road trip. He pulled over, let her out, then used her as target practice with his gun, where he shot her four times.

"Evil contained in human form, a creature without a soul, no conscience, no sense of remorse, no regard for the sanctity of human life." - From the wife of one of his victims. (2006).

After the Texas shooting, he illegally rode the railways across Mexico and the United States, where he would jump on and off, selecting victims at will. He killed using rocks, a pickaxe, lumps of wood, a sledgehammer, and other blunt objects. His victims were killed at random which made him difficult to capture with an age range between 16 and 80.

On June 15th 1999, his final victims were killed. He robbed and ransacked a house near to a railway track in Illinois. There, he shot dead an 80-year-old man in the head with a shotgun and used the same weapon to beat to death a 52-year-old woman later that day. Investigators found the man's vehicle 60 miles away and discovered DNA linking Resendiz to the murder.

He surrendered to police in July 1999 and was convicted of one murder within Texas, that saw him get a death sentence. Instead of extraditing him to other states to face trials that would have resulted in a lesser or same sentence, he was executed by lethal injection, in Texas in 2006.

THE FACTS

Born: August 1st 1960 | Active: 1986-1999

Arrested: July 12th 1999 | Country: USA/Mexico

Victims: 16-23+ | AKA: The Railroad Killer

Sentence: Death penalty | Status: Executed in 2006

Retunsky, Vladimir: The Povorino Maniac

The Soviet-Russian serial killer Vladimir Nikolaevich Retunsky, AKA: The Povorino Maniac, killed at least eight women between 1990 and 1996. He was also heavily linked to four more but they could not be proven at the time. In 1990, aged 30, he claimed his first victim. Retunsky was a truck driver who picked up hitchhikers, or lured women into his truck with drink or drugs. Once they were in the passenger side, they couldn't get out due to the passenger door having no handle.

He raped and beat his victims before stabbing or bludgeoning them to death, then dumping their bodies on the roadside or in shallow graves. Some of the victims had body parts removed and most were mutilated, though it remains unclear why he did this or if he consumed some of the body parts.

In 1996, he claimed his final confirmed victim. When he picked her up, she had a puppy Rottweiler with her, so after raping and killing her, he decided to keep the dog and took it back home with him. Suspicions were raised when reports of a woman going missing with her dog, ran on the news. When neighbours saw that Retunsky had a similar dog where he had no dog before, a search warrant for his house was issued.

Inside, the investigators found a large collection of pornographic VHS tapes and images, along with notebooks detailing the murders of each of his victims. He called the murders, his 'work'. The hatred towards him grew in the public domain, and there were reports he had to be guarded by multiple security teams so he wasn't attacked and lynched by angry mobs. The trial was held in a closed court and he was sentenced to death for eight murders.

Unbelievably, the sentence was commuted to only 15 years, after an appeal. At the time there were no life sentences in Russia, and 15 years was the maximum. In 2012, Retunsky was released from prison to live with his sister and remained under a strict curfew from 10pm until 6am every day. He was arrested later in 2012 for stealing cash and sentenced to an additional five years in prison. On July 22nd 2015, Retunsky was released from prison for a second time and now lives freely within Russia. His whereabouts are currently unknown.

THE FACTS

Born: 1950 | Active: 1990-1996

Arrested: February 1997 | Country: Russia

Victims: 8-12 | AKA: The Povorino Maniac

Sentence: Death penalty, commuted to 15 years | Status: Released in 2015

Rhoades, Robert Ben: The Truck Stop Killer

American serial killer Robert Ben Rhoades, AKA: The Truck Stop Killer, is suspected of killing at least 50 women. He was convicted of three murders and was due to be convicted of more until the victims' families dropped the charges to save them the pain of further trials, because he had already been convicted of three and his life sentence without parole was deemed good enough.

It is suggested that he raped, tortured and murdered more than 50 women over a 15 year period 1975 to 1990. The investigation arrived at that number due to the routes his truck-driving job took him on with the correlations of missing people around the same time as he was in those locations.

Rhoades had created a torture chamber in the sleeping area of the truck and would keep women tied up in there for days and sometimes weeks as he travelled around.

He tortured and raped his victims before either shooting or strangling them to death and dumping their bodies on the roadside or in secluded locations. Upon his arrest in 1990, it was discovered he was heavily into the BDSM lifestyle and had been killing for at least 15 years.

He also took many photos of his victims. The most infamous is the disturbing photo of 14-year-old Regina Kay Walters, who was his last known victim. She had run away with her boyfriend before Rhoades picked them up. The investigation found that Rhoades had killed the boyfriend and kept Walters as his sex slave for up to a month before killing her. The last photo of her was taken only a few minutes before her death.

In 1994, Rhoades was convicted of Walters' murder and sentenced to life without parole. In the past few years he has been extradited to various states across America to be charged in separate murder cases. As of 2022, he remains incarcerated and is said to be assisting cold case investigators with missing persons cases.

THE FACTS

Born: November 22nd 1945 | Active: 1975-1990

Arrested: April 1st 1990 | Country: USA

Victims: 3-50+ | AKA: The Truck Stop Killer

Sentence: Life imprisonment | Status: Incarcerated

Ridgway, Gary: The Green River Killer

EXTENDED CASE FILE

Gary Ridgway, AKA: The Green River Killer, was an American serial killer who was convicted of 49 murders and has been linked to many more since. He is one of the country's most prolific killers who killed teenage girls and women across the state of Washington between 1982 and 2001.

Born Gary Leon Ridgway in 1949, a few years after the end of the Second World War, he was raised in a home of violent arguments, and grew a hatred for his mother who had a dominant personality. His father was a bus driver, and it is claimed he constantly moaned about the large number of sex workers he would see on any given shift.

Ridgway later claimed that he felt a sexual attraction to his mother and as such often fantasised about killing her. Up until the age of 13, Ridgway was a regular bed-wetter and his mother made a point of telling others about it. The humiliation only continued as his mother would make a point of washing his genitals afterwards.

Bed-wetting is one of the elements of the Macdonald Triad, which cites three factors during childhood that may be markers to violence later on in life. These include bed-wetting, harm to animals, and setting fires. First proposed by psychiatrist J.M. Macdonald in 1963, it has since evolved to various different factors associated with childhood behaviour and later violence.

When Ridgway was 16-years-old, after being held back for a year in school, he lured another pupil into the woods and stabbed him. The boy survived but Ridgway went unpunished. In 1969 he married his 19-year-old girlfriend then joined the U.S. Navy. He was subsequently sent to Vietnam where he was involved in combat. While he was in Vietnam, his wife cheated on him and their marriage ended within 12 months.

But Ridgway wasn't any less innocent at the time, he had encounters with various sex workers while in the military and took multiple partners. The resulting under-achievement of the Vietnam War infected the national psyche like a plague, including personal and national failures, wasted lives, and a divide that reached the political parties.

Most of the American military were drinking lots of alcohol or doing drugs. Some took part in violent rapes and senseless murders on the basis that they would get away with it and most did. Some were psychologically affected by their experiences and returned to the United States with their mental disturbances. More on the effects of the Vietnam War can be found in the Why Serial Killers Kill section of this book.

Ridgway's second marriage ended in a similar manner with his wife cheating on him. During that time, he found God and fell into religion in a big way, taking part in sermons and reading the bible daily. Regardless of his religion, he continued to use the services of sex workers, due to an insatiable appetite for sexual contact.

There was a noticeably clear paradox at work; Ridgway hated the presence of sex workers in his area but would use their services more and more as time went on. Soon he began to hate them so much that he refused to pay them.

"I picked sex workers as my victims because I hate most sex workers and I did not want to pay them for sex."

His first known victim was in 1982, when he killed 16-year-old Wendy Lee Coffield. Ridgway would earn the trust of a sex worker by showing a picture of his son, before either taking them home, to his truck, or to a secluded area. Then he would rape them and strangle them to death from behind. For a while he used his hands to kill them but after a dozen or so victims, he moved to using a ligature to prevent any bruising to himself.

From 1982 to 1998, he had a confirmed victim count of 49 victims, all teenage girls and women, though he later confessed to at least 71. In the early 1980s, the King County Sheriff's Office created the Green River Task Force to investigate the murders. Two task force members; Robert Keppel and Dave Reichert, had famously interviewed Ted Bundy in 1984. And it was Bundy himself who offered a profile on The Green River Killer.

He suggested the killer was revisiting the burial or dumping sites to have sex with his victims. He said that if police found a fresh grave, then they should stake it out and wait for him to come back. Astonishingly, Ridgway would return to the places where he dumped the bodies just as Bundy had said. He dumped the bodies in 'clusters', mostly in wooded areas and would return to the bodies to engage in acts of necrophilia with the corpses. He later claimed that having sex with a corpse stopped him from killing someone else at that very moment.

"I placed most of the bodies in groups which I call clusters. I did this because I wanted to keep track of all the women I killed. I liked to drive by the clusters around the county and think about the women I placed there."

Ridgway married again in 1988 and claimed to have loved his new wife more than anything. In the time after his third marriage, he only killed a suspected three more victims until his final arrest in 2001 which meant he had killed most of his victims from 1982 to 1987, approximately one every six weeks. DNA samples collected in 1987 proved to be vital to his arrest and conviction.

At his trial in 2003, he entered a plea bargain to plead guilty to 49 charges of murder instead of the seven he was originally charged with. This allowed the families of 42 more victims to find resolution. He later confessed to 71 murders in total but is suspected of up to 90. He was sentenced to life in prison, and as of 2022 is incarcerated at the Washington State Penitentiary in Walla Walla. He is constantly being made available for information relating to open murder investigations and remains one of the most notorious serial killers in the United States.

THE FACTS

Born: February 18th 1949 | Active: 1982-2001

Arrested: November 30th 2001 | Country: USA (Washington)

Victims: 49-90 | AKA: The Green River Killer

Sentence: Life imprisonment | Status: Incarcerated

Robinson, John Edward: The First Internet Serial Killer

EXTENDED CASE FILE

Serial killer John Edward Robinson was a life-time criminal, involved in kidnapping, forgery, assaults, and murder. He was convicted of eight murders but is connected to others. All his post-1993 victims came from online chatrooms, leading him to be known as the first serial killer who used the internet to select victims.

Born in Illinois, he and his four siblings were raised by an alcoholic father and strict mother. In 1957 he was enrolled at a private boy's school for those wishing to become priests. He was removed after a year due to behavioural issues. He then enrolled in medical school but dropped out there after two years.

Robinson was first arrested in 1969 after forging over $30,000 (USD) from a medical practice where he worked as an X-ray technician. He was convicted of embezzlement and given a three-year suspended sentence. Up until 1975, he was connected with two more frauds in different companies in different States, with a fraudulent company he had set up.

By 1980, he was becoming well-known around his Kansas City community by involving himself in every possible way. He became a local baseball coach, a Sunday School teacher, and a director of a charity. While working with the charity, he forged letters to the Kansas City Mayor and named himself Man of the Year within the charity. His desire for power was becoming all too evident.

In 1982, he was sentenced to 60 days in jail for another fraud, along with cheque forging. When he was released, he set up another fake company and swindled people out of their money. He claimed it was for his wife's medical care as she was seriously ill – which she wasn't.

In the mid-1980s Robinson claimed to have joined a cult called the International Council of Masters. It was a secret BDSM cult, whose mission was to lure young women to be tortured and raped by the cult members. In 1984, he set up another company and hired 19-year-old Paula Godfrey, to work in sales. He then sent her away for 'training'.

After a few days, Paula's parents reported her missing, and Robinson claimed he had no idea what had happened to her. A few days later, her parents received a letter from their daughter claiming that she was okay but did not want to see anyone again. The police stopped their investigation as the letter was believed. Paula was never seen again, and it is suspected that she was Robinson's first murder victim.

In 1985, he met Lisa Stasi at a women's refuge. He offered her a job and took her away. Lisa had a four-month-old daughter and so Robinson contacted his brother who had been unable to adopt a baby. He forged documents and solicited over $5,000 USD for legal fees and gave his brother the child. Lisa vanished and was never seen again. She too became a victim of the internet's first serial killer. Later, in 2000, the child was tested, and DNA confirmed that she was the daughter of Lisa.

Then in 1987, he hired 27-year-old Catherine Clampitt for a fake job. She vanished a few weeks later and was never seen again. After breaking his probation and being arrested again for multiple fraud incidents, he was sentenced to various prison sentences in Kansas and Missouri. From 1987 to 1993, he remained incarcerated on various charges.

Upon his release, John Edward Robinson discovered something that changed the way he selected his victims – the internet. He used the burgeoning BDSM chatroom culture to look for women who enjoyed submissive sex. Robinson went by the name of Slave master and found a 45-year-old woman named Sheila Faith.

He pretended to be a wealthy businessperson and offered to help pay for her disabled daughter's healthcare. In 1994, Sheila and her 15-year-old wheelchair-bound daughter, vanished from the face of the earth. Robinson carried on forging their documents and received pension cheques for another seven years.

"He's maintained the secrets about what he's done with the women, he won't ever tell, it's the last control that he's got. There are other barrels waiting to be opened, other bodies waiting to be found." – An investigator in a 2010 interview with Cold Case Files.

By 1999, he was well-known within the growing online BDSM community. In the same year he solicited 21-year-old Polish immigrant Izabela Lewicka, after meeting her in the chatroom. She claimed she wanted a BDSM relationship and the Slave master obliged. He married her under false pretences and got her to sign a slave contract that listed over 100 elements she had to do to please him. Later that year, she too vanished without a trace.

About the same time, nurse Suzette Trouten, gave up her life to travel the world as a submissive sex slave to Robinson. But she too vanished without a trace. Letters that were sent to her family after her disappearance were supposed to have come from various foreign countries but instead had the Kansas City postal stamps.

Although the internet's first serial killer was becoming known to police, there wasn't enough evidence against him, and without a body or a crime scene, it became impossible to link him to anything. It wasn't until an unnamed woman accused him of stealing her sex toys in 2000, that Robinson would be arrested.

Much to the investigators delight, it was enough for a warrant to search Robinson's large farm and farmhouse. The team discovered two decomposed bodies within two chemical drums. They were the remains of Polish immigrant Lewicka, and nurse Trouten. They then searched his storage properties in Missouri, where they discovered three more decomposed corpses in similar looking chemical drums.

The bodies were that of Sheila Faith and her 15-year-old daughter, along with 49-year-old Beverly Bonner, who had been the prison librarian at the same prison where he had been incarcerated. The five victims had been killed with a powerful blow to the back of the head. The other three missing women have never been found but Robinson was the only suspect in their disappearances.

In 2002, after the longest criminal trial in Kansas history, John Edward Robinson was found guilty of three murders, and sentenced to death. In Missouri, he pleaded guilty by way of a statement and was convicted of five murders there. For each of the five murders, he received additional life sentences. Missouri was known at the time to actively pursue death sentences, whereas Kansas was not. By pleading guilty in Missouri, Robinson avoided the death penalty there.

Four years later, in 2006, while Robinson was on death row, the decomposed body of a young woman was found in a chemical barrel in Iowa. Even with DNA testing, the victim has never been identified and may have been inside the barrel for two decades or more.

Investigators then claimed that Robinson's whereabouts for many years were unknown, and he had set up businesses all over the country. But the internet's first serial killer has long remained tight-lipped and silent on the murders and his involvement. It is the only control he has left.

THE FACTS

Born: December 27th 1943 | Active: 1984-2000

Arrested: June 2nd 2000 | Country: USA

Victims: 8+ | AKA: First Internet Serial Killer/Slave Master

Sentence: Death penalty | Status: Death row

Rogers, Ramon Jay

On February 18th 1996, in California, actor and heavy-metal drummer Ramon Jay Rogers, claimed his third victim. Rogers, who appeared in an episode of 'Renegade', brutally murdered his Polish ex-girlfriend, 32-year-old Beatrice Toronczak, when she visited him at the apartment complex that he managed.

It is claimed she had threatened Rogers with taking their son back to Poland. Days later, body parts were discovered in a storage locker. Teeth and fingers were identified as Toronczak's, and Rogers was arrested for her murder in March of 1996. The arrest led investigators to reopen two other missing persons cases of Rogers' former girlfriends and friends.

Previously, the limbs and jaw of one of his previous partners had been discovered but no evidence was found to make an arrest. In a grim portent about what was to come, Rogers had previously played roles in Crime Stoppers TV shows, where he played all manner of criminals, including murderers.

In 1997, Rogers was convicted of three murders; his ex-girlfriends Beatrice Toronczak and Rose Albano and the second degree murder of his friend Ron Stadt, but it has long been claimed he may have killed more. Rogers was sentenced to death, and an appeal in 2009 failed to commute his sentence. He remains on death row at the Centinela State Prison in California.

THE FACTS

Born: 1959 | Active: 1993-1996

Arrested: March 13th 1996 | Country: USA

Victims: 3+ | Sentence: Death penalty | Status: Death row

Romanov, Vladimir: The Kaliningrad Maniac

Russian serial killer and paedophile Vladimir Ivanovich Romanov, AKA: The Kaliningrad Maniac, killed at least 13 people from 1991 to 2005, but is suspected of killing at least 20 and raping numerous more. Born in 1950 and raised in the Kaliningrad Oblast, Romanov grew up in a rough household and took a liking to young girls.

In 1991, he killed two teenage girls and buried their bodies in shallow graves close to where he lived. They were listed as missing persons until Romanov's confession in 2006. In the same year, he raped a 12-year-old girl who survived the attack and gave a description that led to his first arrest in 1991. He was convicted of the rape and sentenced to 10 years in prison. It was claimed he was raped by another inmate whilst serving his sentence.

For ten years, Romanov had been dreaming of killing again, and in 2001 he was released with a plan in mind. From 2001 to 2005, he killed at least 11 more young girls between the ages of 12 to 19. He viciously raped all of them before strangling them to death and burying their bodies in forests or burning their remains.

In 2006, he attempted to rape a young-looking 24-year-old, who fought him off and escaped. Two days later, he was arrested, and confessed to 13 murders in total, with hints that he had killed more. While in solitary confinement, awaiting trial in 2006, Romanov hung himself with his bed sheets, shortly after leaving an apologetic suicide note to his own family. He denied families of the victim's true justice for his crimes.

THE FACTS

Born: December 1950 | Active: 1991-2005

Arrested: September 2006 | Country: Russia | Victims: 13-20+

AKA: The Kaliningrad Maniac | Status: Died by suicide in 2006

Rose, Lindsey Robert

An Australian serial killer who killed five people from 1984 to 1994. The first murders were in 1984, when he shot dead Edward John Cavanagh and Cavanagh's girlfriend, Carmelita Lee, in their home in Sydney. He claimed it was out of revenge for Cavanagh beating up one of his friends a few years before. He killed Carmelita as he did not want any witnesses to the murder.

Three years later, on January 19th 1987, Rose broke into a house in the West Ryde area of New South Wales. It was the home of William Graf, a known businessman, who wasn't home at the time. Rose had intended to rob the property of some of the pricier belongings but was caught in the act by Graf's partner Reynette Holford. Rose stabbed Reynette multiple times with a screwdriver and a vegetable knife. He tied her up after he had attacked her before running from the property, leaving her to die of her injuries.

On Valentine's Day 1994, Rose claimed two more victims when he shot and killed Fatma Ozonal while gaining access to a massage parlour where he then stabbed and killed Kerrie Pang. Pang's partner Mark Lewis was arrested for both murders and sentenced to life in prison as he had arranged for Pang to be murdered by Rose. Ozonal was simply in the wrong place at the wrong time.

Lewis was found guilty because he had organised Pang's murder even though he hadn't actually carried out the act himself. For another three years, Rose got away with it. He was caught in 1997 and was ultimately convicted of five murders between 1984 and 1994. As of 2022, he remains in prison in Australia serving five consecutive life sentences.

THE FACTS

Born: 2nd May 1955 | Active: 1984-1994

Arrested: 1997 | Country: Australia | Victims: 5

Sentence: Five life sentences | Status: Incarcerated

Rylkov, Oleg: The Tolyatti Ripper

Over a five year period in the city of Tolyatti in Russia, Olga Rylkov, AKA: The Tolyatti Ripper, raped 39 young girls and killed six people. All of his victims were between the ages of six to 13, and the victims would mostly be attacked in their own homes. He waited for the parents or adult guardians to leave before knocking on the door, raping the victim and robbing the home.

The first confirmed murder happened on February 7th 1996, when he killed a seven-year-old boy named Ruslan Tkachev. He lured the boy to a small village on the outskirts of the city and violently stabbed him to death. When the body was discovered, the boy's genitals, eyes, ears, tongue and fingers had been cut off. The body had been so badly mutilated that the gender of the corpse couldn't be confirmed until later.

On July 20th 1996, Rylkov lured a young girl from the streets and brutally raped and murdered her. He left her body in an abandoned military bunker near the city. When he abducted the girl, there were witnesses who gave his description to police. When they went to arrest him, Rylkov pretended to be someone else, and the police believed him, so he escaped arrest.

In October of the same year, another Russian serial killer named Alexander Spesivtsev was arrested for the murder and rape of at least 20 people. For a while, police believed Spesivtsev to be the culprit of the Tolyatti murders, and Rylkov escaped justice. But in 1997, Rylkov murdered a 40-year-old woman with an axe, which led to his arrest as the two had often been seen together.

Rylkov went to trial and was found guilty of six murders and numerous rapes. In 1998, he was sentenced to death which was commuted to life because of a change in the death penalty in Russia at the time. He is currently an inmate at the infamous Black Dolphin Prison on the border of Kazakhstan, where he continues to confess to further murders and rapes.

THE FACTS

Born: December 21st 1966 | Active: 1992-1997

Arrested: July 1st 1997 | Country: Russia

Victims: 6+ | AKA: The Tolyatti Ripper

Sentence: Death penalty, commuted to life | Status: Incarcerated

Sakharov, Nikolay Alexandrovich: The Vologda Ripper

In February 1979 in Vologda Oblast, Soviet Union, Nikolay Alexandrovich Sakharov, AKA: The Vologda Ripper, was executed by firing squad for the murders of three girls. In 1977, the former police officer was known to have brutally raped three young girls on three separate occasions, before beating them to death with a hammer.

He went on to burn the bodies and shatter the skulls into smaller pieces, before wrapping their remains in cloth and discarding of them in a local river. He even kept trophies of some of the victims and handed them out to his various mistresses. Despite killing three young girls, at least five in total had gone missing from the region in 1977.

The number of the missing wasn't helped by locals who exaggerated the number of missing girls. At one point it was claimed that dozens of girls had fallen victim to the ripper. On December 15th 1977, Sakharov was arrested after witness statements led to police tracking his vehicle. In January 1978, Sakharov confessed to the murders of Tatyana Svetina, Natalia Vinogradova and Marina Mukhina.

He said he would dress up as a police officer in order to lure girls into his car. Then he would take them to a remote location, usually a forest, where he raped them before beating them to death. His trial during 1978 was one of the largest the region had ever seen, leading to a massive police presence in the area for fear that lynch mobs would overrun the courts. Sakharov was sentenced to death and executed by firing squad on February 5th 1979.

THE FACTS

Born: April 22nd 1954 | Active: 1977

Arrested: December 15th 1977 | Country: Soviet Union

Victims: 3 | AKA: The Vologda Ripper | Status: Executed in 1979

Saldivar, Efren

In California, American 'Angel of Death' serial killer, Efren Saldivar, murdered at least six of his patients, but confessed to 50. It was suspected by investigators that he may have been responsible for at least 200 deaths in total. When he was 19, he started work as a night shift respiratory therapist at the Glendale Adventist Medical Center.

He killed his victims by administering a paralytic drug which would lead to respiratory or cardiac arrest. Most of the time, he used an overdose of morphine to end their lives and was able to get away with it as the night shift had fewer staff working at the time. He chose victims who were already close to death, which made catching him even more difficult.

Ten years later in 1998, he quit his job and made a voluntary confession in which he claimed he had killed 50 patients under his care. To get the evidence they needed, the resulting investigation exhumed 20 bodies and found six that had unusually high levels of the drug that Saldivar said he had used.

In 2002, he was convicted on six counts of murder and sentenced to six consecutive life sentences, without the possibility of parole. An internal investigation at some of the hospitals where Saldivar had worked, disclosed that it might have been likely that 200 patients died at his hands. The deaths couldn't be proven because most of the victims had been cremated, leaving no physical evidence behind. The number remains conjecture to this day.

THE FACTS

Born: September 30th 1969 | Active: 1988-1998

Arrested: March 13th 1998 | Country: USA (California)

Victims: 6-50+ | AKA: Angel of Death

Sentence: Six life sentences | Status: Incarcerated

JOHN EDWARD ROBINSON

(ATTRIB A149)

NIKOLAY ALEXANDROVICH SAKHAROV

(ATTRIB A150)

ALTEMIO SANCHEZ

(ATTRIB A151)

TOMMY LYNN SELLS

(ATTRIB A152)

Sanchez, Altemio: The Bike Path Killer

EXTENDED CASE FILE

Altemio Sanchez was an American serial killer, also known as The Bike Path Rapist/Killer, who was active over a 25-year period. He was confirmed to have killed at least three women and raped at least 10 girls and women in the Buffalo region of New York.

Sanchez was born in Puerto Rico and moved with his family a couple of years after his birth to Florida. After his father died young and his mother married again, Sanchez moved to Buffalo to be a factory worker. There was nothing untoward in Sanchez's childhood that suggested he would go on to become a serial killer.

In 1980, when he was 22, he married and had two sons. His wife had no idea of Sanchez's secret life and divorced shortly after his conviction. Sanchez had embedded himself into the local community, working as a baseball coach and gardener. He even joined a fun-run in memory of one of his own murder victims.

All in all, he was a well-liked individual, but somewhere along the line he developed a hatred for women. From the mid-1980s, he had begun stalking and raping women at random and whenever the opportunity arose. In the early 1990s, Sanchez began using sex workers on regular occasions and was arrested in 1991 and 1999 for the solicitation of prostitution.

His first known murder victim came on September 28th 1990. 22-year-old University student Linda Yalem was raped and strangled to death by Sanchez. The attack happened on the Ellicott Creek Bike Path, one of many cycleways and public paths that Sanchez used as hunting grounds.

In November 1992, 32-year-old sex worker Majane Mazur, was murdered near rail tracks. Sanchez had grabbed her from behind, raped her then strangled her to death. The last known murder victim was on September 29th 2006, when Sanchez murdered 45-year-old Joan Diver.

Sanchez would patiently wait for the right moment to attack and chose secluded areas of cycleways or pathways that were close to wooded areas. He would then attack them from behind and drag them into the wooded area to rape them. He would use a ligature or his own hands to strangle them into submission.

He then used duct tape or medical tape to cover his victim's eyes, nose and mouth. All of the attacks took place from May to November and all of his victims were of slim build, between the ages of 14 to 45. His 14-year-old rape victim came in October of 1994, when he grabbed the schoolgirl from behind a junk yard.

While Sanchez was still attacking victims from the 1990s, a special Bike Path Task Force was set up by the Erie County Sheriff's Office, with assistance from the FBI. Sanchez was a suspect from the early 2000s but there was no evidence against him. While he was under surveillance, police watched him eat at a Latin restaurant, and when he had finished, they covertly took his glass, cutlery and a napkin to obtain DNA.

Immediately, the DNA matched eight victims of rape or murder. While they were still investigating Sanchez, they connected him to another six rape victims in the area. On January 15th 2007, Sanchez was arrested and confessed to three murders. Due to the absurdity of the Statute of Limitations, which sets out time limits on how long after a crime a person can be prosecuted, Sanchez escaped many of the rape charges. Murder, however, was not time-limited by the same statute, and Sanchez was convicted of three murders.

In August 2007, Sanchez was sentenced to 75 years to life in prison. It has long been claimed by investigators that he may have killed more but he has never confessed. And yet, Sanchez's crimes would go on to be infamous for more than just his convictions. Back in 1985, Anthony Capozzi, a man suffering from schizophrenia, had been convicted of the rapes of two women.

After Sanchez was convicted, police looked at rapes with similar circumstances and discovered Capozzi's convictions. DNA from Sanchez matched Capozzi's two victims, and it appeared that they had convicted the wrong man. Capozzi, who had maintained his innocence for over two decades, was released after 22 years in prison. He later won a $4.25million USD lawsuit for wrongful conviction and imprisonment.

After this, new laws were introduced that would speed up similar lawsuits, and the legislation became known as Anthony's Law, named after Capozzi. The fact that New York had to create a new law to speed up lawsuits for those who have been wrongfully convicted, is disturbing enough. It is also a damning indictment for the absurdity of the Statute of Limitations. As of 2022, Sanchez remains incarcerated at a New York prison.

THE FACTS

Born: January 19th 1958 | Active: 1975-2006

Arrested: January 15th 2007 | Country: USA

Victims: 3+ | AKA: The Bike Path Rapist/The Bike Path Killer

Sentence: 75 years to life in prison | Status: Incarcerated

Satish: The Bahadurgarh Baby Killer

In Bahadurgarh, Haryana, India, a serial killer known as Satish killed at least ten young girls between the ages of five to nine, from 1995 to 1998. He was positively linked to the abduction and rape of another four children, which earned him the moniker of The Bahadurgarh Baby Killer.

During Satish's reign of terror, the local communities lived in fear but also claimed the police were not doing enough to find the killer of children. The police force came under immense pressure to arrest the culprit and get a conviction, which resulted in riots caused by the local residents.

In order to placate the growing anger, the police arrested and convicted three innocent men. Each man was arrested one after the other as another murder took place while the previous one had been convicted. Satish wasn't arrested in connection with the murders until 1998, when he was only 25-years-old.

On January 9th 1996, six-year-old Sweta left her home with her sister to meet her friends and play with other children. Her sister ran back home shortly after, in a panic, and told her mother that a man on a bicycle had kidnapped Sweta. The man had been wearing a shawl and couldn't be identified. Sweta was raped and murdered and her body was found a day later on January 10th.

On June 12th of the same year, seven-year-old Janno was abducted from the front of her house as she slept. Her sleeping parents were only a few metres away from her when she was taken. Just a few hours later, her body was discovered in a ditch, she had been raped and murdered by Satish.

In 1998, one of his victims was left for dead in a wooded area. When the young girl was found in a delirious state two days later, she led police to the house where she was being kept, where Satish was subsequently arrested. A $10,000 USD reward for the capture of the killer, put up by the Delhi Police Force, was later given to the young girl in recognition of her bravery and information that led to Satish's capture. As of 2022, Satish remains incarcerated at an Indian prison, despite calls of replacing his life sentence with death.

THE FACTS

Born: 1973 | Active: 1995-1998

Arrested: November 20th 1998 | Country: India (Bahadurgarh)

Victims: 10-14 | AKA: Bahadurgarh Baby Killer

Sentence: Life imprisonment | Status: Incarcerated

Schaefer, Gary Lee

On December 13th 1979, in Springfield, Vermont, the skeletal remains of 13-year-old Sherry Nastasia were discovered in a shallow grave in a remote area. She was the first victim of serial killer Gary Lee Schaefer who killed three people between 1979 and 1983. Nastasia had been abducted near to an apartment complex where she lived with her parents. The same apartment complex that Schaefer's brother was managing.

In 1981, Schaefer abducted Theresa Fenton as she was riding her bike near to her home. He took her to a wooded area close to the Connecticut River where he raped and beat her before partially burying her near a small hill. A search party found her a few hours later but she died of her injuries in hospital.

In 1982, 17-year-old Deana Buxton survived an assault by Schaefer. He trapped her in his car but when he stopped to buy beer at a nearby shop, Buxton managed to escape and call for help. Her victim statement pointed to Schaefer as the attacker but police claimed there was no evidence to support her claim.

On April 9th 1983, Schaefer abducted 11-year-old Catherine Richards while she was walking with her friend Rachel Zeitz. Rachel ran off to call for help but Catherine was driven to a remote location, where Schaefer raped her and crushed her skull with a rock. The body was discovered the next day. Witness reports once again pointed towards Schaefer and he was finally arrested in late April.

He was ultimately sentenced to 30 years to life in prison for the murder of Catherine Richards and the kidnapping of Deana Buxton. Due to his plea deal in the murder of Richards, he couldn't be charged with the Theresa Fenton murder but confessed multiple times. He was also charged with the Sherry Nastasia murder but a judge dropped the charges due to procedural errors and her murder officially remains unsolved. Due to the court placing a gag order on the trial, Schaefer's current whereabouts are unknown.

THE FACTS

Born: 1951 | Active: 1979-1983

Arrested: September 1983 | Country: USA | Victims: 3

Sentence: 30 years to life | Status: Unknown

Scheanette, Dale Devon: The Bathtub Killer

In Texas, Dale Devon Scheanette, AKA: The Bathtub Killer, killed at least two people in 1996 alone. In her Arlington, Texas, apartment on September 17th 1996, the nude body of 26-year-old Christine Vu was discovered lying face down in her bathtub. She had been tied up with duct tape, raped, strangled, and then drowned.

Scheanette had left his fingerprints at the scene and DNA on Vu's body but it didn't match any suspects on the police or federal databases, and so Scheanette was free to kill again. On December 24th 1996, another murder happened in the exact same apartment block where Vu lived, and in the exact same manner.

The body of 20-year-old Wendie Prescott was discovered face down in her bathtub. She too had been restrained with duct tape, raped and strangled to death. The murders became referred to in the media as the Bathtub Killings but no suspect was found and the murders remained unsolved for another four years. In 2000, the Arlington Police Department ran the fingerprints through the system again and this time they found a match.

Scheanette was arrested shortly after and subsequently linked to further attacks of four other women in their own homes. In 2003, Scheanette was sentenced to death for the murder of Wendie Prescott. On February 10th 2009, Scheanette was executed by lethal injection. His final meal consisted of two spicy chicken legs, two spicy fried pork chops, and French fries. He refused to acknowledge the witnesses to his death.

THE FACTS

Born: May 7th 1973 | Active: 1996

Arrested: 2000 | Country: USA (Texas)

Victims: 2+ | AKA: The Bathtub Killer

Sentence: Death penalty | Status: Executed in 2009

Schiffer, Egidius: The Strangler of Aachen

German serial killer, Leo Egidius Schiffer, AKA: The Strangler of Aachen, killed five young women between 1983 and 1990. His crimes also became known as the Disco-Murders or Hitchhiker Killings but the German media eventually settled on the strangler moniker.

He claimed his first victim in 1983 when he was only 27-years-old. In Alsdorf, 18-year-old Marion Gerecht was waiting at a bus stop when Schiffer approached and attacked her. She fought with him and broke his windscreen but she was eventually stripped naked and strangled to death before her body was dumped in a fishing pond.

In 1984, Schiffer killed 15-year-old Andrea Wernicke when she was walking home alone from a nightclub. He raped her before strangling her and dumping her body near a dirt track. In the same year, he murdered 17-year-old hitchhiker Angelika Sehl who was walking back to her accommodation from a different nightclub. Her partially clothed body was found in a forest shortly after.

In 1985, he abducted 18-year-old Marion Lauven from a bus stop, before raping and killing her. Schiffer drove across the country with Lauven's body in the trunk until he found a suitable forest to dump her corpse. It is unclear if Schiffer killed again before his final murder victim in 1990 but many more murders have since been linked to him.

Schiffer was finally arrested in 2007 when he was caught stealing scrap metal. He voluntarily gave a saliva sample which was conclusively linked to five murders. He confessed to the murders and was sentenced to life in prison a year later. He told the court he received a massive amount of sexual pleasure in killing the girls. On July 22nd 2018, Schiffer was found dead in his cell. He had been using electrical cables in a sexual manner and had accidentally electrocuted himself to death.

THE FACTS

Born: 1956 | Active: 1983-1990

Arrested: March 2007 | Country: Germany

Victims: 5 | AKA: The Strangler of Aachen

Sentence: Life imprisonment | Status: Died by suicide in 2018

Seel, Manfred

A German serial killer, sometimes known as 'Jack the Ripper of Scwalbach', was suspected of killing five people and linked to another four. He died of cancer in 2014 before he was caught and before the full extent of his crimes were uncovered. He killed his victims by using what the media described as 'harsh violence in sexually relevant zones'.

Most of his victims were either homeless, sex workers, or drug addicts and he was known for drug use in his personal life. He was also known to have violent outbursts, attacked women, and could not keep his anger under control, which some suspect was born from his addiction to using sex workers. Seel enjoyed hurting and dehumanising sex workers as a way to control them.

With each of his victims, he would remove organs from their bodies or other body parts such as genitals, arms or legs and keep them as trophies. It is suspected he returned to their corpses for sexual gratification. Shockingly, the victims all had different body parts removed. An investigator told a press conference that 'if you put the missing parts together, you could actually make a new body by doing it'.

When Seel died in 2014 before his capture, his daughter and her partner discovered human remains in a garage that Seel was renting. Police discovered over five terabytes of violent porn in images and videos on his various hard drives. Seel would perceive his victims as objects for his sadistic fantasies. German investigators called it the most inexplicable and unfathomable case known to them.

THE FACTS

Born: September 30th 1946 | Active: 1971-2004

Country: Germany | Victims: 5-9

AKA: Jack the Ripper of Scwalbach | Status: Died in 2014 before arrest

Segundo, Juan

An American serial killer who was sentenced to death for the 1986 rape and murder of 11-year-old Vanessa Villa. She was living in Fort Worth, Texas, with her mother and siblings when she was abducted, raped, and killed. On that fateful Sunday, she went to help out at a Dallas flea market and returned home later that day. It was suggested that Segundo had followed Villa to her home unseen.

That same night, Segundo broke into her home and raped her before strangling her to death. Segundo was known to be a family friend and was never suspected until

DNA evidence linked him to the murder almost 20 years later. It is also claimed that he even attended Villa's funeral. Villa's mother even defended him when he became a suspect, informing the investigation that he was not the type to kill people.

On October 6th 1987, in Fort Worth, Texas, an unnamed woman awoke in the middle of a sexual attack by Segundo. He carried on the attack and then physically assaulted her before fleeing the property. The unnamed victim survived the ordeal but at least three others died at the hands of Segundo.

He was sentenced to ten years in prison for the attack and burglary of the house but was released only one year later. In 2005, following a cold case investigation into Villa's murder, advancements in DNA technology confirmed that Segundo was the killer. He was also linked by DNA evidence to three more murders between 1994 and 1995. Segundo is currently on death row awaiting execution.

THE FACTS

Born: January 25th 1963 | Active: 1986-1995

Arrested: April 19th 2005 | Country: USA

Victims: 4 | Sentence: Death penalty | Status: Death row

Sells, Tommy Lynn

On November 18th 1987, in Illinois, police descended on a mobile home in the village of Ina. Inside, they discovered an entire family has been slaughtered. 29-year-old Russell Keith Dardeen was found in a nearby field, he had been shot dead and his genitals had been mutilated.

His pregnant wife, Ruby Elaine Dardeen, and their son who were in the mobile home were beaten to death. Ruby was so badly beaten that the attack had forced her into labour. Shockingly, the new-born was also beaten to death. They had been murdered by American serial killer Tommy Lynn Sells.

Tommy first killed in 1980, when he was just 15-years-old. He had broken into a house to discover an adult man performing oral sex on a little boy. Tommy then killed the man in a haze of anger and violence. He was known to have been abused by his mother's partner and later claimed that he would relive the abuse while committing his crimes.

His last murder was on New Year's Eve, 1999, in Del Rio, Texas. He lured and raped two small girls, 13-year-old Kaylene Harris and 10-year-old Krystal Surles. He stabbed to death Harris and cut the throat of Surles. Miraculously, Surles survived and stumbled 500 metres along a road to her house while holding her throat in place. She then gave a description to the police and Tommy was finally arrested a few days later on January 2nd 2000. Surles went on to make a full recovery and was instrumental in the capture of one of America's most prolific serial killers.

While on death row for two separate murders, Tommy confessed to the killing of the Dardeen family. Despite being convicted of two murders, investigators connected Tommy to at least 22 but he himself confessed to over 70 victims. He was executed by lethal injection on April 3rd 2014.

THE FACTS

Born: June 28th 1964 | Active: 1980-1999

Arrested: January 2nd 2000 | Country: USA

Victims: 22-70+ | AKA: The Cross-country Killer

Sentence: Death penalty | Status: Executed in 2014

Shankariya, Kampatimar

On May 16th 1979, in Jaipur, India, one of the country's most notorious serial killers was executed by hanging. Kampatimar Shankariya killed at least 70 women and men from 1977 to 1978 by beating them to death with a hammer. He usually hit them on the side of the head just under the ear because he found it to be more effective at killing.

He later told investigators that he killed purely because he took great pleasure in doing so. He also claimed that there were probably more than 70 victims but he could not remember them all. Very little is known about Kampatimar aside from a handful of newspaper articles, probably as the Indian press didn't want to spread too much information about a monster, something which is the opposite in Western media.

Due to the lack of information in the Indian press, we are left to assume that many more Indian serial killers may have been hidden from the public eye. We don't know where Kampatimar was born or where he grew up but we do know he was executed by hanging on May 16th 1979. Just before his execution he said that he had murdered in vain and that no one should become like him.

THE FACTS

Born: 1952 | Active: 1977-1978

Arrested: 1978 | Country: India

Victims: 70+ | Status: Executed in 1979

Shawcross, Arthur: Genesee River Killer

An American serial killer known as the Monster of the Rivers or the Genesee River Killer, he killed 14 victims in New York from 1972 to 1989. His first murders were of a young boy and girl in Watertown, during 1972. He raped and killed 10-year-old Jack Blake after luring the boy to a local wooded area then four months later, raped and killed eight-year-old Karen Ann Hill.

Born in 1945, he was raised in Maine before his family moved to New York, where he suffered from intellectual disability, was a known bed-wetter, and was abused by his mother. He also claimed to have had an incestuous relationship with his sister. He became a bully at school and was violent to everyone around him and would set fires to sexually satisfy himself.

After the murders of Blake and Hill in 1972, he was swiftly caught and sentenced to 25 years in prison. After an early release in 1987, he went on to kill 12 more women, mostly sex workers in Munroe County. On January 5th 1990, two days after the body of his final victim was discovered, Shawcross was arrested.

He confessed to all the murders, and in a later interview, he bragged about removing and eating the vulvas of three of his victims. He was sentenced to life in prison without the possibility of parole on a 250-year term, despite having multiple mental health issues. He died in prison of natural causes in 2008. An autopsy found a cyst pressing on the temporal lobe of his brain which may have resulted in a lack of decision making and self-control.

THE FACTS

Born: June 6th 1945 | Active: 1972-1989

Arrested: January 5th 1990 | Country: USA

Victims: 14 | AKA: Monster of the Rivers/The Genesee River Killer

Sentence: Life imprisonment | Status: Died in 2008

Shermantine, Wesley & Herzog, Loren: The Speed Freak Killers

EXTENDED CASE FILE

The Speed Freak Killers is the moniker attributed to serial killing duo Loren Herzog and Wesley Shermantine. They were suspected to have been involved in as many as 72 murders in California from 1984 to 1999. The pair disposed of bodies in old mine shafts, remote hills, and some beneath a trailer park.

Herzog and Shermantine became friends when they were children. They were born and lived in the small town of Linden, California. They quickly became addicted to amphetamines and methamphetamine's and made their first kill together when they were only 19-years-old.

They were arrested separately in 1999, when they were both 33. Herzog was charged with the 1998 abduction and murder of 25-year-old Cyndi Vanderheiden, along with four other murders dating back to 1984. It appeared that the investigation had only scratched the surface of the terror that the pair had inflicted in the region.

Shermantine was also charged with Vanderheiden's murder, and together they were convicted of the murder of two drifter killings in 1984. 31-year-old Paul Raymond Cavanaugh and 35-year-old Howard King were found shot dead in their car on a remote area of road. Both Herzog and Shermantine would have been only 19 at the time.

Herzog was also linked to and charged with the 1984 murder of 41-year-old Henry Howell, who had been shot dead near Highway 88. Another victim was the 1985 murder of 24-year-old Robin Armtrout. His naked body had been discovered near a creek and he had been stabbed more than 10 times.

Shermantine was charged individually for the murder of 16-year-old Chevelle Wheeler. The schoolgirl had decided to skip school for the day but never returned home. DNA in her home was linked to Shermantine, but her remains are still undiscovered. The investigation believed that Shermantine alone killed at least 20 people, with bodies scattered in old mine shafts and his own trailer park.

Multiple witnesses testified against his character. Five women came forward and stated that he had violently raped and abused them. One of them was a babysitter who had visited him to collect money that he owed her. A former wife of Shermantine claimed that he beat her for years, even while she held children in her arms.

"Listen to the heartbeats of people I've buried here. Listen to the heartbeats of families I've buried here." – Shermantine, to a woman in his trailer park.

It was their heavy amphetamine use that birthed the moniker of the Speed Freak Killers. They killed for the thrill of killing and it was claimed that they killed for sport. Shermantine stated that he hunted humans as the ultimate thrill kill. During the trial, both men pointed the blame at each other and implicated one another in further killings.

FBI also seized over $40,000 worth of firearms from Shermantine's parents' house. A large number of technicians and forensics experts studied the weapons to see if they could link them to further murders. In 2004, an appeals court overturned the convictions of Herzog due to the fact that his confessions were coerced. A retrial was ordered but never took place.

Herzog instead pleaded guilty to manslaughter in the death of Cyndi Vanderheiden and had his life sentence commuted to 14 years. He was paroled in 2010, causing an outcry in California. There was so much opposition that no county in the state would house him and so he was paroled to a trailer at the gates of the High Desert State Prison in Susanville.

In Linden, California, in February of 2010, investigators were led to a well where over 1,000 bone fragments were unearthed. Shermantine had been writing letters to his sister while waiting on death row and explained where the abandoned well was. The owner of the property at the time stated that the well had been sealed up long before the murders.

It took another two years for the site to be excavated and the amount of bone fragments shocked even the most hardened investigators. In March of 2012, the FBI's Evidence Recovery Team was drafted into the investigation, mostly because of the way the excavation of the well was actioned.

In the same year, before more victims were found, Herzog took his own life by hanging himself inside the trailer. The identity of some of the remains were found to be that of two Californian teenage girls who disappeared in 1984 and 1985. Another unidentified victim was found along with the remains of a foetus. More bodies were discovered in the same year at a property owned by Shermantine's parents.

Later in 2012, Shermantine was allowed into police custody to show them four more abandoned well sites where he claimed more bodies would be found. No remains were unearthed but wild animals in the area may have consumed the bodies, had they been there in the first instance.

In 2018, the San Joaquin County Police Department re-opened the case of the Speed Freak Killers, in the hope that a new investigation with modern technology would link the killers to more bodies and give families of missing people a greater sense of closure. Between them they were confirmed to have killed 19 people but are suspected of over 70. As of 2022, Shermantine is on death row at San Quentin State Prison.

THE FACTS

Born: December 8th 1965 (Herzog)/February 24th 1966 (Shermantine)

Active: 1984-1999 | Arrested: March 17th 1999

Country: USA | Victims: 4-70+ | AKA: The Speed Freak Killers

Sentence: Shermantine (death penalty)/Herzog (life, commuted to 14 years)

Status: Shermantine (death row)/Herzog (died by suicide in 2012)

Shemyakov, Eduard: The Resort Maniac

Ukrainian-born, Russian serial killer Eduard Vasilyevich Shemyakov, killed at least 10 people over a two year period from 1996 to 1998. He was known as The Resort Maniac due to the locations he killed victims, with some near campsites. He claimed he was ordered to kill by the voices in his head.

Shemyakov was bullied in the army for living with his parents and being awkward around girls. He discharged himself shortly after and became fascinated with a 1972 Russian film called 'The Dawns Here Are Quiet'. It was an anti-war film that focused on a regiment of women in the Russian Army. He became enraged after watching it, and combined with the growing voices in his head, decided he needed to kill women.

He carried out his crimes in and around St. Petersburg, and would rape his victims, decapitate them and dismember their corpses. On at least one occasion, he ate some of the body parts. His youngest victim was a girl aged 11-years-old who he raped and mutilated before cutting her up into small pieces.

Shemyakov killed his sister's girlfriend, which led to his mother discovering a half-eaten piece of human flesh in his fridge. He was arrested without trouble, later the same day. In 2002, due to the nature of his crimes, he was deemed insane and detained in a psychiatric hospital. Despite appeals from the victim's families, he currently remains within the hospital's walls.

THE FACTS

Born: September 30th 1975 | Active: 1996-1998

Arrested: 1998 | Country: Russia

Victims: 10 | AKA: The Resort Maniac

Sentence: Institutionalised | Status: High-security psychiatric hospital

Shipilov, Sergey: The Velsk Chikatilo

Sergey Aleksandrovich Shipilov, AKA: The Velsk Chikatilo, is a Russian serial killer born in 1959, who took the lives of at least 14 people, mostly in his hometown of Velsk. Shipilov first killed in 1995, claiming he robbed and then stabbed to death an unknown female which he confessed to in 2016.

In 1996, he killed at least three more people. In April of that year, he murdered a female hitchhiker after raping her, and made no effort to hide her corpse, dumping her near a fence on an industrial estate. She had been stabbed so hard in the heart, that the knife broke inside of her. The DNA he left in and on her body would be crucial in bringing him to justice in 1999.

Over the Summer of 1996, he killed two more women in a similar fashion and buried them in shallow graves around the Primorsky District. One victim escaped from him after he had raped her and she went straight to the police. He was arrested on rape charges and sentenced to eight years in a regime colony. At the time, he was never suspected of the murders until that point.

At the colony, some prisoners were allowed outside the walls on special leave, which enabled Shipilov to kill again in 1998. He killed a sex worker and covered her body with branches instead of burying her in a shallow grave. He continued to rape and kill in this fashion for another year, and in 1999 he killed four people in 16 days.

He was held on suspicion of murder in late 1999, and in 2000 was convicted of all 12 murders and an additional nine rapes. In 2016, he confessed to two further murders. As of 2022, he remains incarcerated in isolation at Arkhangelsk Central Prison in Northern Russia.

THE FACTS

Born: May 17th 1959 | Active: 1995-1999

Arrested: October 10th 1999 | Country: Russia

Victims: 12-14+ | AKA: The Velsk Chikatilo

Sentence: Life imprisonment | Status: Incarcerated

Shipman, Harold: Doctor Death

EXTENDED CASE FILE

On August 7th 1978, Harold Shipman killed Sarah Hannah Marsland, one of his patients. It was one of four confirmed murders in 1978 alone. It was also one of 215 convicted murders and he was suspected of killing over 250. He would kill three more times in 1978, again in August and two more in December.

On New Year's Day 2000, a jury found Harold Shipman, who became known as Doctor Death, guilty of the murder of 215 patients under his care. It is the highest convicted murder count in the world with claims that more victims were attributed to him. Although Pedro Lopez claimed 310 victims, not all of them were confirmed and most were suspected or by using his own claims.

Because the United Kingdom does not have a death penalty, Shipman was sentenced to life in prison but hung himself in 2004. He killed his first victim in March of 1975, Eva Lyons, who was one day shy of her seventy-first birthday. Then in February 1976, he was convicted of obtaining the drug; pethidine, by deception to feed his drug addiction. Later he managed to obtain enough morphine to kill an estimated 360 people. He received treatment in York before appearing as a GP in the Manchester area of Hyde.

He would kill his victims by injecting them with diamorphine which is a medical version of heroin. He managed to get away with killing 71 patients at the Donnebrook Medical Practice in the town. He killed the rest of his victims, mostly at his surgery in Market Street. Shipman killed 171 women and 44 men. The youngest was 41-years-old and the oldest was 93-years-old. There was suspicion in later investigations that some of his victims were children but it has never been substantiated.

When we think of serial killers, we generally don't think of medical practitioners, at least not in the way that Harold Shipman was. Our likely belief of a serial killing doctor tends to look like Jack The Ripper, were he of course to have been a doctor. Shipman wasn't killing out of sexual perversity, he wasn't mutilating his victims and he wasn't having to worry about hiding corpses. But he still murdered 250 people.

"The police complain I'm boring. No mistresses, home abroad, money in Swiss banks, I'm normal. If that is boring then I am." - Harold Shipman, in a letter to a friend from prison.

Because Shipman killed himself in prison in 2004, he robbed the world of understanding how he could have killed so many. Some people suggest that he was avenging the death of his mother as medical practitioners were unable to save her. Whereas some considered that he was even easing the burden on the National Health Service (NHS). Though this might have been the case in his early murders, it would have changed as he continued at such a prolific rate.

Some psychiatrists have concluded that he killed simply because it gave him control. Although he wouldn't physically dominant or possess his victims as Ted Bundy would have done, he did control their life and death. Possibly, he just couldn't resist playing God. It wasn't until the case of Harold Shipman that British medical law was reviewed and majorly changed in the wake of his killings.

What he got away with from the 1970s to the late 1990s would not be possible in the medical world beyond his conviction. He was fired from Todmorden Practice for forging prescriptions and got a fine but was not struck off the medical register. Instead, the General Medical Council (GMC) sent him a warning letter – and that was it.

It wasn't until 1998 that Hyde Undertakers became suspicious at the large number of his patients that were dying under his care. Another medical practice in the town learned that Shipman's death rates were almost ten times higher than their own. Concerns were raised with a coroner and then the Greater Manchester Police who became involved.

An investigation followed but the police failed to run even basic checks. It might have been because the image of a general practitioner in the 1990s was linked with someone of high-esteem within the community. The police did not check his criminal record or contact the GMC at all. They didn't even speak to Shipman himself or the family of his patients.

It wasn't until he forged the will of one of his victims, Kathleen Grundy, that he would be caught, as Shipman had become greedy. He killed her on June 24th 1998 and ticked the cremation box but she was fortunately buried instead. A local solicitor informed her children of the will and the doubts of its authenticity. It had apparently been made by Kathleen Grundy herself but it voided her children from the will and instead left £386,000 to Shipman.

Her body was exhumed and was found to contain traces of diamorphine. Shipman claimed she was an addict but a police search on his computer showed that he falsified hers and others medical records. The subsequent review into the Shipman murders saw changes sweep across the medical industry in the UK.

The British Government even changed the constitution of the General Medical Council to ensure that the previously independent body was no longer dominated by its elected medical practitioners and instead would be made directly accountable to parliament.

Harold Shipman's legacy is alive to this very day. His giant victim count stands as one of the largest in recorded history for a serial killer. For a relatively small geographical country such as the United Kingdom, Doctor Death continues to dominate documentaries, books, and historical records.

THE FACTS

Born: January 14th 1946 | Active: 1975-1998

Arrested: September 7th 1998 | Country: United Kingdom

Victims: 215-250+ | AKA: Doctor Death

Sentence: Life imprisonment | Status: Died by suicide in 2004

IMAGE ATTRIB. A46

HAROLD SHIPMAN

JOSEPH MICHAEL SWANGO

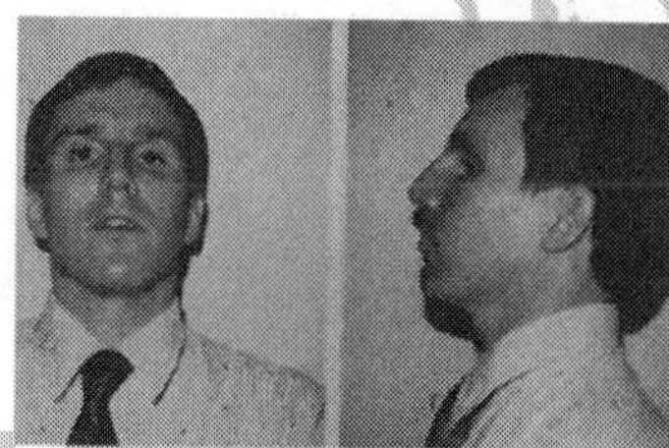

IMAGE ATTRIB. A40

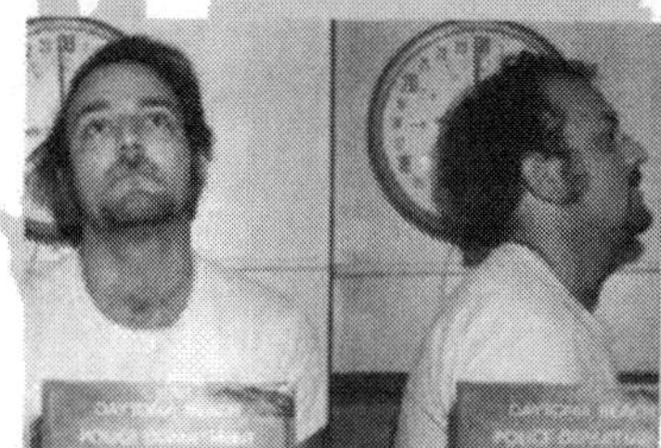

IMAGE ATTRIB. A42

GERALD STANO

ANATOLY SLIVKO

IMAGE ATTRIB. A43

Shulman, Robert Yale

Robert Yale Shulman was an American serial killer who was arrested on April 6th 1996. He was a postal worker from Long Island, New York, who was convicted of the murder of five sex workers between 1991 and 1996. He has also been a suspect in numerous other cold cases.

His first known victim came in 1991 when he murdered 24-year-old Lori Vasquez. Her dismembered body was later discovered in a trash can. Another dismembered body of an unidentified woman was discovered in a similar trash can in 1992, near to where Lori's remains had been found.

Three more victims followed in 1994 and 1995, and all had been dismembered. The final victim on December 8th 1995, had her hands sliced off and had been discovered wrapped in a sleeping bag. While investigators went door to door, they discovered that hotel managers had seen a man in a blue Cadillac canvassing the streets on various occasions.

Shulman became a suspect and was arrested in 1996, with evidence from the sleeping bag and his car. A search of his bedroom resulted in hundreds of bloodstains that hadn't been cleaned properly. It was suggested then that Shulman had killed them in his home before dumping their bodies around the city.

Shulman was sentenced to death for one of the murders and life in prison for the other four. His death sentence was later reduced to life after an appeal in 2004. Shulman's attorney had argued that Shulman suffered from depression and had a 'weak grasp of reality' – which was no excuse to have murdered five women. On April 13th 2006, Shulman died in prison of natural causes.

THE FACTS

Born: March 28th 1954 | Active: 1991-1996

Arrested: April 6th 1996 | Country: USA | Victims: 5

Sentence: Death penalty, commuted to life | Status: Died in 2006

Sikder, Ershad

Bangladeshi serial killer Ershad Sikder, killed at least seven people and committed numerous other crimes over an eight period in the 1990s. After moving to the Khulna District in his teens, he became a railway worker and began robbing trains. After a few run-ins with local gangs, he went on to form his own gang and became known as Ranga Chora across the community.

He then left the gang he had created and formed another called Ramada Bahini. The group became involved in terrorism, theft and violent assaults. Amazingly, beyond that, he entered the world of politics, and in 1988 was elected as Commissioner of Ward 8 of the Jatiya Party.

With more power at his fingertips, he began to take possession of various properties and escalated his criminal activities. He purchased an ice factory and went on to use it as his own personal torture facility, where he was suspected of having tortured over 60 people, mostly those who spoke out against him or were involved in other gangs.

After a large investigation, Sikder was arrested in 1999 on the suspicion of 43 murders in the region from 1991 onwards. He was convicted of seven killings and sentenced to death, along with an additional four life sentences. He was executed by hanging on May 10th 2004 and has since been linked to at least 60 murders.

THE FACTS

Active: from 1991-1999 | Arrested: August 11th 1999

Country: Bangladesh | Victims: 7-60+ | AKA: Ranga Chora

Sentence: Death penalty | Status: Executed in 2004

Silveria Jr., Robert Joseph: The Boxcar Killer

American serial killer Robert Joseph Silveria Jr. AKA: The Boxcar Killer, murdered between nine and 28 victims. Over a period of 15 years from 1981 to 1996, Silveria rode the freight train routes and claimed to have killed 28 people. He was part of the Freight Train Riders of America (FTRA).

They were suspected to be a criminal group that committed crimes by moving between freight trains all over the United States and Canada. Some of them were thought to have been involved in train derailments. The FTRA was created by a group of Vietnam War veterans who were distraught at their treatment by the United States government. They slept in box cars, under bridges, and train yards.

Silveria was linked to the murders of homeless people and runaways along the freight rail routes. He would shoot or stab them before leaving their bodies in the open. He was also known as 'Boxcar Bob'. Because of these murders, the FTRA received nationwide attention and a large investigation began.

An FTRA member named Michael Elijah Adams, was also eventually caught and was linked to 17 murders. Another FTRA member, Robert James LeCou, was convicted of killing three people in Montana, and was subsequently sentenced to 300 years in prison.

Silveria was arrested in 1996 and was sentenced to double life sentences without parole for the murders of Charles Randall Boyd in Kansas and Willie Clark in Florida. He remains imprisoned in a Medium Correctional Institution in Wyoming and has been linked to over 30 murders across the United States.

THE FACTS

Born: March 3rd 1959 | Active: 1981-1996

Arrested: March 2nd 1996 | Country: USA

Victims: 2-30+ | AKA: The Boxcar Killer/Boxcar Bob

Sentence: Two life sentences | Status: Incarcerated

Simons, Norman: The Station Strangler

EXTENDED CASE FILE

South African serial killer Norman Avzal Simons was suspected of killing at least 22 young boys between 1986 and 1994. He was convicted on one of the murders and is still part of an ongoing court process to this day. By 1994, the residents of Mitchell's Plain were haunted by the plague of a serial killer known as The Station Strangler.

South Africa in 1994 was going through a process of rebirth and struggle. Apartheid had fallen and the country was about to celebrate the news by holding its first democratic elections. For a large number of families, the new freedom meant very little because their children were dead, and the killer was still walking their streets.

During his childhood, Simons was deemed to be an intelligent boy who played classical instruments such as the piano. He also learned to speak seven languages and went on to have a career in teaching. He taught grade-five students, who are generally children aged between 10 to 11. It is no surprise then that most of his victims were around that age group.

He is known to be South Africa's Andrei Chikatilo and was even inspired by the stories coming out of Russia. Chikatilo was a Russian serial killer who killed young boys and girls by mostly luring them away from train stations. Simons utilised the same method and thus became known as The Station Strangler. He is to this day, one of South Africa's most notorious serial killers.

Simons claimed that during his formative years, his older stepbrother raped him on many occasions. His stepbrother was an alcoholic Rastafarian who was murdered in 1991 in a separate incident. Simons also claimed that he heard his stepbrother's voice in his head, ordering him to kill others.

His stepbrother then moved from voices to possession. Simons claimed that his spirit jumped into his body and lived inside him, ordering him to kill. He claimed that the voices and delusions began when his stepbrother started to rape him. He refrained from acting on the voices until 1986.

He claimed his first victim in that year when he was just 19-years-old. He lured 14-year-old Jonathan Claasen away from Modderdam Station, before raping and killing him. Claasen's body was discovered on October 3rd 1986. Generally, Simons would tie his victim's hands behind their backs and strangle them with their own underwear. He would dump the bodies near to the stations in shallow graves with the corpses lying face down.

The area of Mitchell's Plain is 20 miles from Cape Town and is one of South Africa's largest suburbs. It was a large housing area that quickly became an urban ghetto. The transition from housing projects to ghetto came about because of poverty, drugs and a rising criminal underclass. Children were still free to roam and play around until the bodies began to pile up.

On January 7th 1987, the body of 10-year-old Yussuf Hoffmann was discovered. He had been killed in the exact same manner. Hoffman had been raped and strangled to death with a piece of his own clothing. His hands were tied behind his back and his face had been pushed into the sand in the area of Rocklands.

Two weeks later, the body of 13-year-old Mario Thomas was discovered in Kuilsriver, less than 20 miles away from the location of Hoffman's body. It was already becoming clear that a perverse serial killer was stalking the streets of Mitchell's Plain. In June of that year, 12-year-old Freddie Cleaves was discovered near Belhar Train Station, just six miles away from the body of Mario Thomas.

In August 1987, the body of 14-year-old Samuel Ngaba was discovered at the exact same station as Cleave's body. On October 1st 1987, the seventh victim was discovered almost a year to the day of the discovery of the first victim. The unnamed boy was found in exactly the same location as Simons very first victim, at Modderdam Railway Station.

By the beginning of 1988, nine young boys had been found murdered in the same fashion, and the community of Mitchell's Plain was in a state of panic and fear. Serial killers were and are rare in South Africa, despite the huge amount of crime in the country. And so the local detective assigned to the case had no experience or training in how to solve serial killing cases.

Because of the public knowledge of the killings, the murders ceased for a number of years until 1992 when The Station Strangler returned to his old stomping ground of Mitchell's Plain and began killing again. The body of an 11-year-old boy was found in October of 1992, face down on a local beach.

It wasn't until January 1994 that he would kill again in what came to be known as the month of horror. It began on January 13th, when the body of an unidentified young boy was discovered in the remote Weltevrede Dunes outside of Cape Town. The dunes were considered remote enough that bodies would be hard to find.

Like the Texas Killing Fields in the United States, the Weltevrede Dunes became The Station Strangler's very own killing fields. Every victim from then onwards would be found in the dunes. Even up until 2022, they have become synonymous with the murders.

Once the first body had been found, more bodies began turning up on the dunes. The community was in shock and demanded action, so the police began searching the area themselves. Over the month of January 1994, in conjunction with the South African Army, the police discovered a total of 11 bodies in shallow graves on the Weltevrede Dunes.

On January 27th alone, six bodies were uncovered there. One was an adult male killed in the same fashion and the other 10 were of young boys. In February 1994, a special task team consisting of 14 men was set up, called the Station Strangler Squad. The task team was given every resource available and even had help from FBI serial killer profiler Robert Ressler.

Ressler was set on heading to South Africa to assist the team but the political unrest in the country at the time put him off and in the end he remained in the states. Ressler reviewed some of the profiles drawn up about The Station Strangler and mostly agreed with what had been written. He would later go to a South African press conference where he would praise the investigatory team on their work.

On April 13th 1994, Simons was arrested in connection with another murdered boy who had been discovered on the Weltevrede Dunes in March. He would go on to confess that he had been killing young boys since 1986. An officer with no knowledge of the case was brought in to accompany Simons as they undertook a walk-through of the dunes.

Simons pointed out where the bodies had been found and even showed him areas where other bodies should have been. No body was found there but items of clothing were recovered. It was also known that wild animals would come to the dunes to hunt and it was suggested that more bodies may have been consumed by them.

"I am nothing. I am dirty. I am filthy and not worthy. I am sorry for letting you down. Don't get caught in the same thing. I really regret everything. It's hard to be possessed by unknown forces. These forces cannot be explained by medication." - Norman Simons, from his confession.

The trial began in 1995 and lasted three months. Because of lack of evidence due to decomposition of the bodies, they were only able to convict him on the final victim in March of 1994 based on eye-witness reports. He was sentenced to life and is currently incarcerated at the Drakenstein Maximum Correctional Facility in Paarl, the same prison where Nelson Mandela was imprisoned.

Further prosecutions were ruled out and Simons repeatedly appealed his conviction but the sentence was upheld at every juncture. An inquest in 2005 led Simons defence team to claim his innocence in the crimes. There is now a public perception that the wrong killer may have been caught and that Simons was merely a copycat killer.

It was alleged that even during his trial, more boys had gone missing and more bodies were found. Although this is in hearsay, there is a huge belief in it and also in the conspiracy that authorities covered up the subsequent murders to not look inept in the eyes of the community. However in 2008, the inquest ended and it was suggested there was sufficient evidence for Simons being the killer in at least some of the murders.

In 2014, a man who testified to being a surviving victim of The Station Strangler, claimed that Norman Simons was not the man who had attacked him. He and a friend were lured to a remote area and raped before an attempt to strangle them. When the man had fallen asleep, they both managed to escape. Because their friends knew Norman Simons, they were sure that he was not the man who attacked them. The man who attacked them was apparently known to police but was never questioned in the investigation for the murders.

A short while later, a radio station in Cape Town was debating the case live on air when they received a phone call from one of the prosecutors, Mike Stowe, who was involved in the original trial. He claimed live on air that he was sure they had convicted the wrong man. He claimed that witness statements didn't add up and that no one had seen Simons near the train stations when the boys had gone missing. He also cited further information that he felt was inconclusive.

Stowe's conversation and admission of possible innocence sent shock waves through the country and especially the area of Mitchell's Plains. Family members of the victims were in uproar and suddenly the entire Station Strangler story was thrown into confusion.

In 2016, 58-year-old Brian Shofer killed himself in his police cell. Shofer was a convicted South African paedophile who had been arrested just two days prior for the rape of a 17-year-old boy. The boy in question had been living with Shofer since he was 12-years-old. Shofer spent a lifetime surrounding himself with children and taught children in his home, or theirs, under a private tutorship.

Shofer was a resident in Mitchell's Plain at the same time that The Station Strangler was active. Shofer claimed that he was violently abused as a child and that his uncle raped him on numerous occasions. His father knew of the abuse and allowed it to happen. He also claimed that from this abuse, he grew to prefer children as sexual contacts.

Shortly after a 2010 conviction for sexual assault, he began working at a primary school in the Cape Town area. He left shortly after when his landlords claimed that Shofer had been in a relationship with a 16-year-old girl. Both of them happened to believe that he was the real strangler. Even as far back as 1994, Shofer had been found guilty of multiple rapes on young boys under the age of 15-years-old.

Before he killed himself, Shofer was about to be charged with 18 cases of sexual assault involving homeless children and runaways. After his death, criminal profilers came forward who suggested there were two serial killers, who had exactly the same process of killing young boys.

The inquest into Norman Simons concluded that there was sufficient evidence to link him to at least six of the murders but not good enough evidence to link him to the rest. But because he had pointed out the murder scenes and one other where clothes were found, then it is generally assumed that Simons is The Station Strangler, regardless of the minimal evidence that convicted him.

If there was a second strangler or an accomplice then it is also generally assumed to be Shofer. However, he now takes his secrets to the grave and the end of the story remains solely with Norman Simons – The Station Strangler.

THE FACTS

Born: 12th January 1967 | Active: 1986-1994

Arrested: 1994 | Country: South Africa

Victims: 6-22+ | AKA: The Station Strangler

Sentence: Life imprisonment | Status: Incarcerated

Sinclair, Angus: The World's End Murderer

EXTENDED CASE FILE

On 20th November 1978, the body of 17-year-old Mary Gallacher was found on waste ground near a footbridge at Barnhill Railway Station, in Glasgow, Scotland. She would come to be known as a victim of one of Britain's worst serial killers but it took another 23 years to bring the killer to justice.

The judge who first sentenced Angus Sinclair told him he was 'a dangerous predator capable of sinking to the depths of depravity.' No truer words were spoken about the man who would become known as The World's End Murderer. In 1961 at the age of just 16, Sinclair killed his seven-year-old neighbour Catherine Reehill.

She was visiting family in Glasgow's Woodlands when she went to a nearby shop only to never return. Sinclair lured her to his family home where he raped and strangled her to death. Even at such a young age, his callousness was well known. After killing Catherine, he threw her body down the stairs then called an ambulance and claimed she had fallen in an accident. The police saw right through his evil ways and arrested him for murder.

Unfortunately for his future victims, he was able to strike a plea deal where he was sentenced to a lesser charge of culpable homicide. He was released six years into a ten year sentence and was allowed to kill again – and again. Upon his release, in his early twenties, he got married and had a son, nothing was seemingly untoward for a short while.

On 15th October 1977, two teenagers named Helen Scott and Christine Eadie were seen leaving the World's End Pub on Edinburgh's Royal Mile. The next day, Christine's naked body was discovered by hikers in East Lothian. Helens' body was found over six miles away in a corn field. They had been raped, abused, beaten, and strangled to death with their bodies left in the open without any attempt to hide them.

The murders of Helen and Christine would later become known as the World's End Murders, and Sinclair; The World's End Murderer. Due to the media running with the story in a big way, some witnesses suggested they had seen the girls with two men that night. This claim was backed up by police who said that both girls had been tied with different knotting methods.

As a possible link between two men was made, the investigation garnered widespread attention and over 13,000 witness statements were taken. 500 suspects were drawn up but no culprit was identified at the time. At the time of the World's End murders, the police had failed to make a connection with four other women who had been found and killed in a similar fashion throughout the same year.

A cold case investigation discovered that during 1977, six young women had disappeared after nights out across the central belt of Scotland, which is generally referred to as a fifty mile stretch from Glasgow to Edinburgh. Along with Helen and Christine, four other victims were later linked to Sinclair. 37-year-old Frances Barker disappeared outside her home in Maryhill in July 1977 after getting a taxi home from visiting family in Parkhead.

When her body was found at a waste ground, 44-year-old sex offender Thomas Young was arrested and convicted of her murder. At every step of the way, he protested his innocence, and it wouldn't be until his death in prison in 2014 that Sinclair was linked to Barker's murder.

20-year-old Glasgow brewery worker Anna Kenny disappeared in August 1977 after leaving the Hurdy Gurdy bar in the city. She was raped and strangled, and her decomposed remains were found two years later in Skipness, Argyll.

In October 1977, 36-year-old Hilda McAuley was raped, beaten and found dumped on wasteland in Langbank, Renfrewshire. In December, 23-year-old Agnes Cooney disappeared after a night out at the Clada social club in Govanhill. She was tortured, stabbed 26 times and dumped on moorland at Caldercruik. Sinclair was later linked to all four murders but justice was decades away.

In May of 1978, the investigation was scaled down. The World's End murders, at least for a while, fell into dark Scottish legend. As the investigation dwindled, Sinclair saw opportunity to kill again. His inability to control his urges would lead to the 1978 killing of 17-year-old Mary Gallacher on a footpath in Glasgow.

She was abducted under cover of darkness, raped and strangled to death with a ligature made from the leg of her trousers before her throat was cut for good measure. She was found dead on a dumping ground, nude from the waist down, exposed to the elements. Sinclair would not be convicted of that particular murder until 2001, when DNA matching cold cases connected him to the crime. It had remained until then, one of Scotland's most mysterious murders.

The Gallacher murder deepened the divide between Glasgow and Edinburgh as the investigation into her death was not as large as the two Edinburgh murders the year before. It was assumed by some that murders in Glasgow were not deemed as important as those in Edinburgh, due to the poverty and cultural divide between Scotland's two largest cities.

Gallacher's murder led Sinclair to change the way he chose his victims. There had been a witness to her abduction and the police were closing in, albeit to the wrong people but Sinclair turned his attention elsewhere. Psychologists believed it was the witness that led Sinclair to devise different tactics. Unfortunately, it led him to start preying on children. Between 1978 to 1982, Sinclair raped, sexually abused, or assaulted dozens of young girls in the Glasgow area.

He was arrested in 1982 and pleaded guilty to the rape and sexual assault of 11 girls between the ages of six to 14-years-old. He was sentenced to life in prison for the abuse but it was almost 20 years later that he would be charged with murder. A 2000 cold case review of Mary Gallacher's murder linked Sinclair's DNA to her death, leading to his conviction of her murder in 2001, 23 years later, and getting him another life sentence.

In 2004, realising Sinclair may have murdered more, three Scottish police forces came together and formed Operation Trinity, to review all the 1977 murders and hundreds of others before and after. Forensic experts proved that the other four murders of 1977 showed they had a unique signature belonging to Sinclair. Incidentally, Sinclair had provided his DNA voluntarily while in prison.

It was also claimed he carried out some of the murders with his brother-in-law Gordon Hamilton who died in 1996 before justice could find him. Recent evidence showed that Hamilton was implicit in at least one of the murders. By 2007, the World's End murders had been attributed to him but the trial was to collapse in an extraordinary miscarriage of justice. Sinclair's lawyers had put forward two special defences, one that included the belief the two girls had consented to sexual intercourse with Sinclair.

The second being that anything that happened after that – the murders – were the actions of Gordon Hamilton. Because there was insufficient evidence to prove any sexual encounter had not been consensual then the judge infamously dismissed the case. The news of the verdict caused mass outcry in Scotland and widespread criticism of the police and justice system. The resulting shift in Scottish Law was felt internationally as the Scottish Parliament managed to legally circumnavigate the double jeopardy law.

It was a law which used to mean that one couldn't be tried for the same crime twice. But in 2011, the Scottish Parliament passed the Double Jeopardy Act 2011. It had made various provisions for circumstances when a person convicted or acquitted of an offence could be newly prosecuted. As such, in 2014, there was a controversial retrial of the World's End murders, which involved the jury visiting the locations where the bodies were found.

Sinclair was then found guilty of Helen and Christine's murders in November 2014. He was sentenced to life in prison on top of his convictions for abuse and the murder of Mary Gallacher. Sinclair was the first person in Scotland to be given a retrial of the same crimes under the new law. His parole date would have been when he was 108-years-old, meaning he was never going to be released from prison.

Sinclair died of natural causes in HM Prison Glen Ochil on 11th March 2019. He was never charged with the four additional murders of 1977 but they have since been linked to him through DNA evidence and cold case reviews. He killed at least seven people and abused at least 11 more but he had left behind many more deaths in his wake. The family of Hilda McAuley suffered from a suicide relating to the case.

Anna Kenny's parents died young, as did her brother, supposedly due to the stress of losing a family member. Other family members of the dead still hold a grudge against a police investigation they say failed them.

Angus Sinclair was one of Britain's most notorious serial killers, with additional murders linked to him using modern research techniques. Gordon Hamilton, it seemed, managed to get away with murder, but if they had worked together as a pair, it seems certain there are many more victims out there. Ultimately, for the families of the dead, the monster who took their loved ones is long gone, confined to the corridors of hell for eternity.

THE FACTS

Born: 1945 | Active: 1961-2005 | Victims: 4+

Country: United Kingdom |AKA: The World's End Murderer

Sentence: Life imprisonment | Status: Died in 2019

Sinclair, Charles Thurman: The Coin Shop Killer

On July 14th 1987, in Spokane, Washington, coin shop owner Leo Cashatt was shot dead and his coin shop was robbed. He was one of the victims of Charles Thurman Sinclair, AKA: The Coin Shop Killer.

Sinclair was an armed robber, murderer, and rapist of women and was active from the early 1980s. He left a trail of bodies across the Western states of America and parts of Canada. Investigators followed his crimes across the country and he was arrested in Alaska in August of 1990.

Upon his arrest, Sinclair was suspected of eight murders. When the investigation searched a storage shed owned by him they found the evidence they needed. Maps, false ID machines, C-4 explosives, land-mines and an entire stash of rare coins were the tip of the iceberg.

He was subsequently linked to at least 11 murders and two rapes. He would specifically target coin shops to rob, before killing the owners to hide any witnesses. In October 1990, while in custody, he died of a heart attack, leaving the investigation at a standstill and justice going unserved.

THE FACTS

Born: 1946 | Active: 1980-1990

Arrested: August 13th 1990 | Country: USA

Victims: 11+ | AKA: The Coin Shop Killer | Status: Died in 1990

Sleepy Hollow Killer

In South Africa, an unidentified serial killer known as the Sleepy Hollow Killer, raped and killed at least 16 sex workers, from the early 1990s to at least 2007. The killer would strangle his victims using their own underwear, a trait shared with three victims in 2007, which were linked to the same killer.

Before that date, the killings supposedly stopped in 2001, leading some to believe that they belonged to a copycat killer. As all murders are still open and active cases, the three from 2007 have been attributed to the Sleepy Hollow Killer. All victims had been raped and their bodies were discovered along the N3 Highway in Pietermaritzburg.

It wasn't until 2001, that an investigation was opened, and seven of the unidentified victims were exhumed from their graves, to see if modern technology could help identify them. No matches or new evidence was found and the investigation shut down in the same year. The three 2007 victims were found on the same stretch of highway, with the same murder method, over a six month period.

Around the same time, more victims were discovered further away from the region, all had the same methods of killing. A special task force was set up to look for connections and examine the evidence, in order to catch the killer. As of 2022, the investigation is still ongoing and no charges have been brought to any one person. The Sleepy Hollow Killer remains unidentified but has at least 16 victims to their name.

THE FACTS

Active: 1990-2007 | Country: South Africa

Victims: 16+ | Status: Unsolved

Slivko, Anatoly

A Russian serial killer who murdered seven people over a 19-year period. Slivko witnessed a violent automobile death of a teenage boy in 1961 and it acted as a catalyst for his own murders. He would kill young boys in an attempt to recreate what he had witnessed as it had sexually aroused him.

When Slivko worked at a children's club, once or twice a year he would befriend a young boy and lure them into an experiment. Whereby he would hang them in a controlled environment to stretch the spine. But when they passed out he would strip them naked and sexually abuse them.

Over a period of many years, he persuaded 43 boys to take part in the experiment. Seven of them he would kill, dismembering their bodies and pouring gasoline over the remains, to remind him of the death he had witnessed in childhood. He killed purely out of sexual sadism. He was caught in 1985 and executed by firing squad in 1989.

THE FACTS

Born: December 28th 1938 | Active: 1964-1985

Arrested: December 1985 | Country: Soviet Union

Victims: 7 | Sentence: Death penalty | Status: Executed in 1989

Slovák, Jozef: The Genius Murderer

A Slovakian serial killer who killed at least five women from 1978 to 1991. On August 22nd 1978, Slovák killed his first victim who he'd met on a train, known only as Blažica P. They went into the Bratislava Woods together and he tried unsuccessfully to have sex with her. She refused further advances and fought back, so Slovák choked her to death.

He then dragged her body deeper into the forest and covered it in light foliage and branches. He burned some of her clothing within the woods but disturbingly gave some of her belongings as gifts to his girlfriend. In 1982, he was captured and sentenced to 15 years for the murder but was released early in 1990.

He then went on to kill four more women, with his second murder coming only three months after his release. His second victim he killed by shooting her eight times before crushing her skull with a heavy lump of wood. He then returned to the body a week later to leave a train ticket in an attempt to confuse police.

Two days after his last murder in 1991, Slovák was arrested and sentenced to life in prison. Psychologists who interviewed him later, found him to have a high IQ, and noted he was the holder of several electronic patents, giving him the moniker of The Genius Murderer. They also found him to be a narcissistic psychopath.

THE FACTS

Born: April 7th 1951 | Active: 1978-1991

Arrested: July 18th 1991 | Country: Czech Republic/Slovakia

Victims: 5 | AKA: The Genius Murderer

Sentence: Life imprisonment | Status: Incarcerated

Smith, Lemuel

An American serial killer who was already in prison for the murders of five people when he murdered a female prison guard in Green Haven Correctional Facility, in New York in 1981. He holds the unfortunate title of the first convict to have killed an on-duty female corrections officer. The murder brought scrutiny on the New York prison systems at the time.

Back in 1958, he robbed and beat to death Dorothy Waterstreet, when he was only 16-years-old at the time. The following year, after being arrested for a different offence, he was charged for the murder and would serve almost 20 years in prison, only to be released in 1976.

In the same year he brutally murdered two people the day before thanksgiving, Robert Hedderman, and his secretary, Margaret Byron. Their bodies were discovered in the back of Hedderman's religious store in Albany. Hair and blood evidence from the scene later proved instrumental in convicting Smith.

In December of the same year, 24-year-old Joan Richburg was raped, murdered and mutilated in her car at the car park of the Colonie Center Mall. In July 1977, 30-year-old Maralie Wilson was strangled to death and her corpse was mutilated and abused. Some investigators who saw the body said it was the worst they had ever seen.

After another victim escaped a few weeks later, Smith was arrested in August 1977 and ultimately convicted of four murders, despite claiming insanity. He was sentenced to death which was later commuted to life. After the murder of the prison guard in 1981, he was transferred to isolation at Five Points Correctional Facility in New York, with six murders to his name. As of 2022, Smith is still considered one of the most dangerous prisoners in the city and is held in isolation for 23 hours a day.

THE FACTS

Born: July 23rd 1941 | Active: 1958-1991

Arrested: August 19th 1977 | Country: USA | Victims: 6

Sentence: Death penalty, commuted to life | Status: Incarcerated

Smithers, Samuel: The Deacon of Death

In Florida, on May 12th 1996, Samuel Smithers, AKA: The Deacon of Death, murdered his first victim, sex worker Denise Roach. He killed her at the vacant Whitehurst estate, that he was taking care of at the time. Smithers claimed that Roach had been loitering around the property on at least two occasions. On May 12th, he asked her to leave but she had refused.

She had apparently hit Smithers in the arm and threw a potted plant at his vehicle. He claimed that he pushed her into a wall and a small plank of wood fell from a shelf and hit her head, killing her. He returned the next day and hid the body in the pond. Unfortunately for Smithers, his story didn't match up with the subsequent coroner's report. Roach had been hit at least 16 times in the head, most likely with an axe. She also had fractures to her face and injuries consistent with strangulation.

Two weeks later, on May 28th, Smithers murdered his second known victim, sex worker Cristy Cowan, who he killed at the same vacant estate. Smithers told varying stories of how he had come to kill her. In an attempt to cover his own back, he claimed that he saw a car parked on the side of the road and went to help. He then drove Cowan to a nearby store where she demanded money or she would accuse him of rape.

He took her to Whitehurst and gave her all his money but she was angered at the amount and threw a drink over him. Smithers claimed he reacted badly, picked up an axe and smashed it into the side of her head. He then dragged her to the estate's pond. A coroner's report later confirmed she had died of strangulation combined with massive head trauma.

At the same time, the owner of the property, Mr. Whitehurst, dropped by to check on the house and saw Smithers cleaning an axe over a pool of blood on the carpet. Smithers claimed someone had killed an animal in the house. Whitehurst contacted the local police department, who went to the property later that day.

The blood had gone but the drag marks remained. They followed them to the pond where they found Cowan's body floating. After a further search, they found the decomposed body of Denise Roach. Evidence found at the scene and on CCTV in the local area, led to Smithers' arrest.

After the arrest, the true nature of a the 'kind-hearted' Baptist deacon, came to light. Other sex workers in the area recognised Smithers as a previous customer of theirs. Smithers claimed he was innocent through all the initial interviews but failed a polygraph test. He later subsequently confessed to the two murders but changed his story every time he could.

He was convicted of two murders and sentenced to death. As the years passed, various cold cases have been linked to Smithers, including the unsolved murder of Roslin Kruse, who had lived with Smithers at the time. Some investigators have stated that Smithers may have killed many more and hid their bodies in various parts of the country. As of 2022, he remains on death row.

THE FACTS

Born: January 30th 1953 | Active: 1996

Arrested: May 28th 1996 | Country: USA

Victims: 2+ | AKA: The Deacon of Death

Sentence: Death penalty | Status: Death row

Snowtown Murders: The Bodies in the Barrels

EXTENDED CASE FILE

In Snowtown, Australia, a master manipulator convinced others to help him commit serial murder and dispose of their victims' bodies in barrels of acid, leaving 12 dead, and a town forever tainted by infamy. Before 1999, Snowtown in Adelaide, Australia, was known for its location on the main road and rail routes between Adelaide and Perth. With a population of a little under 500, the region relied on its crop economy and nearby salt mine.

That all changed when the town became the location where the remains of eight bodies were found in barrels of acid kept in a disused bank vault. Though only one of the murders took place there, Snowtown quickly found itself becoming a hub for true crime enthusiasts and dark tourism.

Between 1992 and 1999, John Bunting, Robert Wagner and James Vlassakis killed at least 12 people between them. A fourth member, Mark Haydon, was convicted on conspiracy to murder as he had helped dispose of the bodies. Each of the victims had been dismembered and left to rot. Most of the victims were the killer's own family members or acquaintances that one of them knew. The discovery and resulting trial made Snowtown famous for all the wrong reasons.

The Snowtown Murders, more commonly known as the Bodies in the Barrels, are one of the most infamous cases in Australian history, a series of killings carried out by three serial killers, operating as part of a gang. John Bunting, born in 1966 Queensland, claimed that each of the victims were either paedophiles, gay men, or simply considered inferior, traits that angered him. He made the others believe that murder was the right way to do things, to rid the world of true evil, as he saw it.

Before they killed their victims, they subjected each of them to horrific torture. All the victim's identities were stolen, and their bank accounts were emptied. Bunting was the ring-leader of the serial killing gang and instigated all of the murders. When he was eight-years-old, he was violently beaten and raped by one of his friend's family members. The abuse he received was linked to him wishing to kill those who attacked children, and he made it his life's mission.

In Australia, the slang for a paedophile is rock spider. In one of the rooms of his home, Bunting created a rock spider wall of information, where he stuck the names and photos of people he suspected to be paedophiles or gay men. He bundled gay men under the same rock spider banner, as he saw them as immoral and dirty, and linked to child abuse. He had managed to convince himself that gay men were as bad as child abusers, and that any men who showed weakness should be punished.

Bunting was known to be socially active and easy to talk to, this allowed him to bring people in close and manipulate others. This gave him a level of control over others who wanted to help him out or do things for him, but his darker side would shine through more often than not. When he was in his early twenties, he worked at an abattoir and bragged to his friends and family about how he could skin and slice up any animal with ease. His love of butchery carried over into his everyday life.

He once killed a friend's dog simply because he wanted to see how the body functioned, claiming he was curious about the anatomy of animals and humans. He also told others that he skinned cats alive and enjoyed slaughtering animals whenever he found the opportunity.

In 1991, Bunting and his new wife moved to North Salisbury in South Australia, where his animal killings escalated into human murder. The first murder took place in 1992. Bunting invited 20-year-old Clinton Trezise over for a drink at his place and accused him of being a paedophile. After a fiery argument, Bunting beat Trezise to death with a shovel, and buried the body in a shallow grave, it was a murder that paved the way for Bunting to claim more lives.

Clinton's body was discovered two years later in 1994 near the tiny town of Lower Light, but due to the decomposition, there was little evidence to suggest how he had died or who had killed him. It was later never proven that Clinton was a child abuser. His was one of two bodies not found in the barrels or in Bunting's garden. The other was Thomas Trevilyan, who was found on the same day he had been killed in November 1997, again with little evidence pointing to a suspect.

It led many later researchers to suggest that Bunting would use the paedophile or gay angle as an excuse to kill, and as a lure for the other men he roped into killing. Bunting's neighbour, Robert Joe Wagner, was befriended by him in 1991, and was encouraged to take part in the murders from 1995. At first, Robert thought he was helping as a vigilante but as time went on, Bunting's murders became less focused, and incredibly violent.

Wagner had just ended a relationship with Vanessa Lane, a transgender woman with a history of paedophilia. Formerly Barry Lane, they had started their relationship when Robert was only 14. The age gap was something that later enraged Bunting.

Bunting was married to Elizabeth Harvey, who had a son from a different marriage named James Vlassakis. He convinced James to help him kill those who deserved it, and James also went on to suggest victims. It was later discovered that Elizabeth assisted in at least one of the murders.

Mark Haydon lived near to the Bunting household, and he too was befriended by Bunting, and brought into his circle of killers and torturers. Haydon's cousin, Jodie Elliott, also helped out with claiming insurance and welfare benefits. With the gang growing in size, the murders escalated.

Many victims were subjected to horrific torture. This included knives, ropes, gloves, pliers, a shotgun, metal rods and an electric shock tool, which was used on the genitals of the men they killed. On some of their victims, they crushed the toes with pliers, shoved lit sparklers into their genitals, burned their ears and nose with cigarettes, and beat them with clubs and metal rods. The killers ordered their victims to refer to them by many controlling names, including Master, God, or Lord.

Some of the victims were killed in their own homes, and the gang would rampage through their houses, smashing things up before killing them. They would also trash the homes of other people they believed to be gay. Most victims however were lured to Bunting's home, where they were tortured before being dismembered. One of these was Vanessa Lane, Robert's ex-partner, who they decided deserved to be killed for having involved herself with Robert at such a young age.

It was Robert who instigated much of the torture on her. Lane's new partner, Thomas Trevilyan, who was part of the group for a short while, was also killed just weeks after Lane in 1997. One of Bunting's ex-girlfriend's was also killed, along with Elizabeth Haydon, Mark's wife. Many of the gang ended up killing members of their own family.

The group also tortured and killed James' friend, his half-brother, and the final victim, James' stepbrother, David Johnson. By this point, the group had rented a disused bank building in Snowtown. To hide the remains of their victims, they stored them in barrels full of acid, which they moved around to avoid detection.

James had lured the final victim to the bank building where the others were waiting. They tied him down and told him to read from a pre-written script, which included fake crimes and false confessions of things that Johnson had never done. They went to empty Johnson's bank account from an ATM and when they returned, he had died from his injuries.

This upset Robert, who claimed they hadn't made the most of their time torturing him. To appease him, everyone helped dismember Johnson's body and sliced off parts of his flesh, then they fried the body parts and sat down to feast on Johnson's remains.

Eight of the bodies were found in giant plastic barrels that were full of acid. Two of the bodies had been pushed into just one of the barrels. They stored the barrels in the old bank vault, and Bunting would return to them on regular occasions to see how well they were being dissolved in the acid.

Bunting said, 'they're rotting very nicely,' when remarking on the first victim to be put in a barrel. He enjoyed watching the bodies dissolve and made notes on how long it took each body part to rot away.

Though David was the last victim, the group were ultimately caught as a result of the investigation into the disappearance of Mark's wife, Elizabeth Haydon. She had been killed because Bunting claimed she had made sexual advances towards him and he saw this as immoral and dirty – thus she needed to die.

She was killed without Mark knowing about it. When he was shown the body in the barrel, Mark reportedly huffed and smiled to himself. Enquiries into Elizabeth's disappearance ultimately led investigators to the old bank where they found the barrels. Police suspected the group moved the barrels around to avoid detection, mostly because they knew they were being investigated. When police searched Bunting's home, they found two more bodies buried in his garden.

On 21st of May 1999, Bunting, Robert, James, and Mark were arrested on suspicion of murder. The subsequent trials were among the lengthiest and most expensive in Australian history. Bunting showed no remorse for his crimes and spoke about the torture of the victims in such an open manner that three of the jury members walked out with their hands over their mouths. He also ignored the proceedings, instead reading a book, and refusing to listen to what was going on around him.

They were all sentenced in 2003. Bunting received 11 life sentences without the possibility of parole, for the murders of 11 people. The body of his ex-girlfriend, Suzanne Allen, who was killed in 1996, was found shortly after the barrels were discovered.

Due to her case being tried beforehand with suspects who were innocent, it was decided not to try her case again due to the agreed conclusion that Bunting had killed her, and that it wouldn't affect his overall sentence. Hence why Bunting was convicted of 11 murders and not 12.

Robert got life without the possibility of parole for his participation in nine murders. For his involvement in the crimes, Jamie was sentenced to life with a 26-year minimum term, after striking a plea deal to testify against Bunting and Robert.

Mark got 25 years in jail with a minimum term of 18 years. He struck a plea deal where he would not be charged with murder, but for helping the group of serial killers dispose of some of the bodies. Other people involved who helped in some way, struck plea deals to testify against Bunting. It's not uncommon to read about serial killing couples or pairs, but rarer to find a case about a gang of serial killers. Bunting was at the heart of the mission to destroy gays, paedophiles, and weak men, and he was able to manipulate other men into killing as part of his mission.

Snowtown is now synonymous with the murders, and at one point, the community had voted to change the name to Rosetown, but for whatever reason, it didn't happen. However, the murders gained such infamy that tourist shops in the area began selling Snowtown murder souvenirs.

The rise of dark tourism and true crime enthusiasm meant that some shops in Snowtown never stopped selling bizarre souvenirs related to the murders. With the salt mine and crop industry giving diminishing returns, the dark tourism one unexpectedly took off, and solidified Snowtown's place in true crime infamy.

THE FACTS

Active: 1992-1999 | Arrested: May 21st 1999

Country: Australia | Victims: 12+ | AKA: Bodies in the Barrels

Sentence: 25 years to life | Status: Incarcerated

Solomon Jr., Morris: The Sacramento Slayer

On March 19th 1987, In Sacramento, the body of 18-year-old sex worker Maria Apodaca was discovered. She had been bound, wrapped up in bedding and then buried. She had been raped and killed by American serial killer, Morris Solomon Jr. AKA: The Sacramento Slayer.

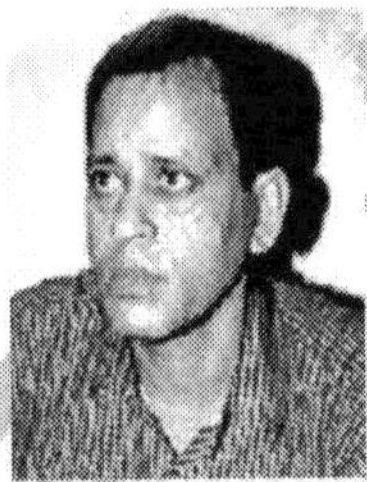

(ATTRIB A153)

ERSHAD SIKDER

ROBERT JOSEPH SILVERIA JR.

(ATTRIB A154)

(ATTRIB A155)

SAMUEL SMITHERS

MORRIS SOLOMON JR.

(ATTRIB A156)

Born in 1944, Solomon had been raised in rural Georgia by an abusive grandmother. She would beat him and his brother daily if they wet the bed, spoke with bad grammar or cried during a beating from the day before. There were times when she beat them for no other reason than it had become a normal routine.

She also made Solomon remove all his clothing and stand on a stool in the corner where she beat his naked body until he bled. On one occasion, she tied him to a pole so he couldn't escape her violence, before whipping him with electrical cord, permanently scarring his body.

On April 20th 1987, the body of 26-year-old sex worker and drug-user Cherie Washington was uncovered on Solomon's property. He had given police permission to search the car in his yard and upon doing so they noticed a depression in the ground nearby. Believing something to be untoward, they borrowed a shovel, excavated a small area of and uncovered Washington's body.

She had been raped and killed by Solomon, before being bound, wrapped in bedding and then buried. This method became his modus operandi. On April 22nd, Police discovered two more bodies on the property. 24-year-old Linda Vitela and 17-year-old Sheila Jacox were unearthed, they had been tied up and buried in bedding. Both victims were sex workers and drug-users, and their bodies had been in the ground for a year before being uncovered.

On April 29th, another body was discovered on the property; 29-year-old Sharon Massey was discovered buried and wrapped in bedding. Massey had been raped and murdered by Solomon and had been dead for approximately six months before her body was unearthed. Solomon was ultimately convicted of six murders but positively linked to one more, bringing his total to seven. He is currently on death row at San Quentin Prison in California.

THE FACTS

Born: March 15th 1944 | Active: 1986-1987

Arrested: April 22nd 1987 | Country: USA (California)

Victims: 7 | AKA: The Sacramento Slayer

Sentence: Death penalty | Status: Death row

Spencer, Timothy Wilson: The Southside Strangler

EXTENDED CASE FILE

On November 22nd 1987, 15-year-old high school student Diane Cho, was found dead in her family's home in Chesterfield County. She had been raped and strangled by serial killer Timothy Wilson Spencer, AKA: The Southside Strangler. She had been killed in her bedroom while her family slept nearby in the other rooms, and duct tape had been put across her mouth to stop her from crying out.

Spencer would be convicted of five murders from 1984 to 1987 and was the first serial killer in the United States to be convicted on DNA evidence. His case also involved the first person to be found innocent of a crime they had previously been convicted for, all because of the advances in DNA technology.

Born in 1962, Spencer was raised in the Green Valley area of Arlington, Virginia. At the time, it was generally a black neighbourhood and known as a lower-income region area prone to violence. In 1984, Spencer claimed his first victim, Carolyn Hamm, from Virginia. Her body was discovered face down near the door to her garage. She had been raped, tied up and hung with a cord from a Venetian blind.

Her murder was in an area where violent crime was considered rare, and due to media attention, an arrest was made quickly. A confession was obtained and charges were brought to David Vasquez. Vazquez was wrongly convicted and served five years of a 35 year prison sentence before the conviction was overturned in 1989. He was the first person to have his conviction overturned due to advancements in DNA technology.

On November 27th 1987, five days after Cho's murder, Spencer killed 44-year-old Susan Tucker who was strangled to death in her condominium. The body wasn't discovered until December 1st. In a similar fashion to the 1984 murder of Hamm, a cord had been taken from a nearby Venetian blind and used to strangled her. She had also been raped and her body had been found nude, partially covered by a sleeping bag.

In both cases, the killer had entered the properties through a first floor window and it was suggested that due to the prevalence of semen stains that Spencer had masturbated over the bodies. An investigation then linked three more murders that were carried out in 1987, over a hundred miles away in Richmond

On September 19th 1987, in Richmond, Debbie Davis was found dead in her first floor apartment which she lived in alone. She had been strangled with a sock that had been tied around her neck and twisted tight with a small section of pipe. Spencer had left multiple semen stains on Davis as well.

Just two weeks later and less than a mile away from the Davis crime scene, Dr. Susan Hellams was found dead in her bedroom closet. She had been killed in a remarkably similar fashion to Davis and the other victims. It took a large effort by lead investigators to convince different departments that the murders were linked.

This is referred to as linkage blindness and makes serial killing cases difficult to investigate. The lead investigator, Joe Horgas, then connected various rape and burglary cases in the region. In one incident of burglary, Spencer had climbed through a basement window of a woman's apartment and left porn magazines in the house along with a cord from a Venetian blind on her bed. It was suggested that Spencer was waiting for her to come home but for some reason decided to leave.

After following up the burglary and rape cases, Horgas determined that Spencer's methods had been perfected over many years. Beginning with burglaries then rape and then finally moving onto murder. The pattern was becoming obvious as the crime scenes were starting to look very similar.

Spencer was arrested on January 20th 1988 for the rape and murder of Susan Tucker. He became the first person in Virginia in which DNA was successfully used to prove an offender's identity. Over various trials in different counties, Spencer was convicted of four murders, and positively linked to Hamm's murder by DNA evidence. He was sentenced to death and executed in the electric chair on April 27th 1994.

THE FACTS

Born: March 17th 1962 | Active: 1984-1988

Arrested: January 20th 1988 | Country: USA (Virginia)

Victims: 5 | AKA: The Southside Strangler

Sentence: Death penalty | Status: Executed in 1994

Spesivtsev, Alexander: The Siberian Ripper

EXTENDED CASE FILE

Russian serial killer Alexander Nikolayevich Spesivtsev, AKA: The Siberian Ripper, was convicted for the murders of four people in the city of Novokuznetsk in 1996. He has been accused of killing up to 19 people but police evidence recently suggested he may have killed as many as 80.

Astonishingly, Spesivtsev was assisted by his mother, who helped him abduct homeless children and young women across the region. The victims would be lured into the apartment they shared, where they would be brutally murdered. It was also proven that Spesivtsev ate some of his victims which earned him the additional moniker of The Novokuznetsk Monster.

Born in 1970, he was constantly ill as a child after having been birthed prematurely. As he grew up, he remained unsociable and isolated, preferring his own company instead of making friends. He was bullied by other school pupils and returned home to an abusive alcoholic father. It has been suggested that his mother may have persuaded Spesivtsev to kill in the first instance. As he was growing up, and at an influential time of his life, she would share a bed with him and show him pictures of dead bodies and autopsies from true crime books and magazines.

He did get a girlfriend in his late teens but he would often show an aggressive streak and she broke up with him soon after. Spesivtsev didn't take it too kindly and kidnapped her. He took her to his apartment where he proceeded to abuse and torture her for an entire month. He was arrested for the prolonged attack and sent to a secure psychiatric unit in the area.

He was discharged three years later, in 1991, and fell down a rabbit hole of loathing and paranoia. He developed a hatred of homeless children and began associating with street people in order to get close to the younger ones. He then began luring victims to the apartment, and shortly after, his mother began luring victims for him.

All of his victims were street children, runaways, or those from poor areas. The collapse of the Soviet Union meant that construction sites and abandoned industrial factories were left to rot. Many children played in those areas and Spesivtsev began selecting his victims from them.

In the apartment, he would torture the children and then slaughter them, with most of the victims cannibalised to some degree. Any remaining body parts were put into buckets by his mother, who would dispose of them in a local river, in the middle of the night. As time passed and cases of missing children began to rise, more and more body parts were being discovered in the area.

They ranged from severed heads, torsos, arms and legs of small children, with most of the remains washing up on the banks of the river his mother had been dumping them in. It took a while for the authorities to believe they were dealing with a serial killer. At first, investigators assumed they were dealing with organ smugglers who sometimes operated on the city's boundaries.

They had police officers searching baggage on outward flights and infiltrating criminal gangs in the region. Pressure from local communities and the amount of body parts being found, pushed the investigation forward and then they realised that it could be the work of a single serial killer.

Witnesses had spotted Spesivtsev's mother with some of the victims before their disappearances, and police managed to track her down. She claimed that her son was still under psychiatric care at a hospital outside of the city but she was arrested anyway and questioned for three days.

While she was under arrest, a neighbourhood officer and a maintenance man contacted the police, and the investigation turned a corner. They claimed they had visited a communal apartment block to unclog the drainpipes and needed access to the Spesivtsev apartment. Alexander Spesivtsev had answered the door and claimed that he was a mental patient who was being forced to remain in the apartment.

When the two men caught wind of a putrid smell coming from the apartment, they forced their way in. Spesivtsev ran to the building's roof and disappeared. The two men were left in the apartment, and they found a place of horrors. 15-year-old Olga Galtseva was laying on the floor, bleeding from a single deep stab wound to the chest, fighting for her life. In the bathroom, a decapitated body was found in the bathtub with its arms and legs missing. Various blood stains and the smell of rotted flesh adorned the entire apartment.

Spesivtsev was arrested a week later, a day before Halloween in 1996. He was found on the streets, suffering from cold and hunger. He had kept a detailed journal of the murders and it was this that partially led to his conviction. When the apartment was searched, 82 items of blood-stained clothing were found, along with various other souvenirs, including jewellery and photos of the victims.

But it was too late for 15-year-old Olga Galtseva, who died the following day from the stab wound to her chest. On October 5th 1999, Spesivtsev was declared insane and committed to a mental hospital by a court for the rape and killing of four young girls. His mother was sentenced to only 13 years in prison for being an accomplice in the murders.

Though he was convicted of four murders, Spesivtsev confessed to 19, but investigators suggested there could have been as many as 80 victims. As of 2022, Spesivtsev remains committed at the Kamyshin Regional Hospital, a locked neuropsychiatric specialised hospital. He is likely to remain there until his death.

THE FACTS

Born: March 1st 1970 | Active: 1991-1996

Arrested: October 30th 1996 | Country: Russia

Victims: 4-80+ | AKA: The Siberian Ripper

Sentence: Institutionalised | Status: High-security psychiatric hospital

Stafford, Roger Dale

An American serial killer who was convicted of nine murders and implicated in a total of 34 across various states. Stafford began killing in 1974 when he shot dead an assistant manager working at a McDonald's in Alabama, before robbing the place of approximately $1,500.

Four years later on June 22nd 1978, Stafford, along with his wife, Verna, and brother, Harold, flagged down a vehicle on the side of Interstate 35 in Oklahoma. Stafford then robbed and murdered the entire Lorenz family; Melvin, Linda and their 12-year-old son. Their bodies were left on the side of the road and were found the next day.

Only three weeks later in July, Stafford killed six employees at a Sirloin Stockade restaurant in Oklahoma City during a robbery. Six days after the robbery, Harold was killed in a motorbike crash. Verna went to view his body at the funeral and was followed home by police where she remained under surveillance until she and Stafford were arrested.

In October 1979, Stafford was convicted of nine murders after Verna testified against him. She was convicted for her part in the crimes and sentenced to two life terms. Stafford was sentenced to death and executed by lethal injection in 1995. Verna would later implicate Stafford in the killing of 34 people.

THE FACTS

Born: November 4th 1951 | Active: 1974-1978

Arrested: March 13th 1979 | Country: USA | Victims: 9-34

Sentence: Death penalty | Status: Executed in 1995

Stano, Gerald Eugene: The Boardwalk Serial Killer

EXTENDED CASE FILE

On August 5th 1978, Sandra DeBose was found shot dead in West Cocoa, Florida. She was one of many victims of a horrific serial killer named Gerald Stano. If ever there was a case of nature versus nurture and nature winning out then Stano is it. He is Florida's worst serial killer confirmed to have killed 41 people and has been linked with up to 90 murders.

His beginnings were more than brutal. He was born Paul Zeininger in 1951, in New York, to a mother who already had four other children, three of whom she had given up for adoption. Paul was also then put up for adoption. He was adopted by Eugene and Norma Stano whose hearts went out to the malnourished and neglected boy.

When he was just 13-months old, a team of psychologists and social workers examined him and determined that he would be unable to be adopted due to severe neglect. According to psychologists at the time, the 13-month-old was functioning with animalistic behaviour. It was written that he would remove his own diaper and play with his own excrement. Clearly, the neglect from his birth mother had been so bad, that the boy had been dehumanised from birth.

Undeterred, the Stano's adopted him six months later. We do know that many serial killers suffer abuse during childhood, but not much research has been carried out on abuse on babies and the psychological effects on their development. Being adopted also comes with its own dangers, with the FBI claiming that 16% of all serial killers had been adopted at some point in their childhood.

The lost identity in being adopted sometimes leads to the child questioning who their parents actually were and then they might paint a morbid picture of their parents in their heads. There is also very few studies on the impact of adoption in serial killer cases.

Fitting into the McDonald Triad, Stano was a bed wetter up until the age of ten and was emotionally distant from everyone. During his teens, he was isolated, preferring to be alone which made him a target for bullies in school. Teenage girls, specifically, would make fun of him and use him as the basis for belittlement and emotional bullying.

In 1967, the family moved to Pennsylvania in the hope that Stano's behaviour might get better but it worsened. His adoptive parents were still sure that they could give him the life he deserved and the love he never received. They still believed there was good in him. Stano killed his first two victims in 1969, in Pennsylvania. The rest of his alleged 41 victims were between 1973 and 1980, in the Florida region.

After a graduation when he was 21-years-old, he moved into a motel and then got a job at a hospital but was fired for stealing money again. He then moved with his parents to Florida and found himself drifting from job to job, mostly because of being fired for theft, or lack of attendance.

He married a local woman in 1975 and for a while things were going well. However, he began drinking heavily and only a few months after being married he started abusing his wife, physically and emotionally. She quickly filed for divorce and he moved back in with his parents again.

He would later receive the death penalty for stabbing to death 17-year-old Cathy Lee Scharf in Brevard County, in 1973. Stano preyed on sex workers and hitchhikers whose ages ranged from 13 to 35. They were killed either by shooting, stabbing, or strangulation. Because none of his discovered victims were raped, it was concluded by psychiatrists that his motives arose from simply enjoying the act of killing.

"I can't stand a bitchy chick." - Stano's reply to an officer when asked his reason for the murders.

In April 1980, Stano was arrested after an intended victim managed to escape from him. She had fallen into a police station with stab wounds, dripping in blood, but later surviving the attack. Her evidence was vital in catching him, and it was said that if she had not managed to escape then many more lives would have been lost.

In his confession, Stano directed the investigation to the buried remains of 24 identifiable victims and two Jane Does. There is a theory that officers were feeding him information about the murders but it doesn't quite stack up because if they knew where the bodies were, then they wouldn't have waited for Stano to tell them. He also described wound details that would only later become known in coroner's reports.

By December 1983, he had provided details of 41 victims and had already been sentenced to eight life terms before the death sentence received for his 1973 killing of Cathy Lee Scharf. It is suggested that he may have killed more than 41 people and even as many as 90.

It's also suggested that he was coerced into confessing crimes he didn't commit. An investigation into his murders and other crimes in the area at the time is still being undertaken. The evidence was stacked against him and he was finally executed in the electric chair in 1998.

THE FACTS

Born: September 12th 1951 | Active: 1974-1986

Arrested: April 1st 1980 | Country: USA

Victims: 41-90 | AKA: The Boardwalk Serial Killer

Sentence: Death penalty | Status: Executed in 1998

Steinwegs, Kurt-Friedhelm

A German serial killer convicted of six murders in a seven-year period, he is also known as 'The Monster from Lower Rhine'. He was the fifth of eight children and his mother died when he was 10. His father and his new partner gave some of his siblings up for adoption which left Steinwegs alone and angry.

Steinwegs was placed into a youth centre, where he killed a 59-year-old man named Ernst Dorf by hitting him over the head with a stone. He was only linked to the murder later on when he confessed to it. In 1978, when Steinwegs was 18, he killed 13-year-old Andrew Robinson, whilst he was living with his father.

Shortly after, he was committed to a psychiatric hospital where he killed four other patients, taking great care in removing the genitalia of his victims. He was arrested inside the facility in 1984 and confessed to six murders in total but may have killed more. Upon his arrest the press named him 'The Beast' due to the viciousness of his murders.

He was found unfit to stand trial and was institutionalised. As of 2022, he remains imprisoned in a forensic clinic in Germany. Being sent to a forensic clinic in Germany means the patient has been found unfit to be detained in a prison or mental health facility. It is likely that Steinwegs will live out the rest of his days there.

THE FACTS

Born: December 5th 1960 | Active: 1974-1983.

Arrested: 1984 | Country: Germany | Victims: 6+

AKA: The Monster from Lower Rhine

Sentence: Institutionalised | Status: High-security psychiatric institute

Stoneman, The

In India, over a four year period from 1985 to 1989, at least 13 homeless people were killed during their sleep by an unidentified killer known only as The Stoneman. The murders took place in Calcutta but at the same time, another 13 homeless people were killed in a similar fashion in Mumbai, two cities over 1,200 miles apart.

The same moniker was also given to the Mumbai killer whose victims were killed from 1985 to 1988. It has since been suggested that the killings were committed by the same person, which meant that The Stoneman was responsible for at least 26 murders.

It still remains unclear why the homeless people were killed, or if they were murdered by one individual or a group. The victims were all killed in the same fashion. The killer or killers found a homeless person sleeping alone in a dark area of the city. Then they would crush the victims head with a single stone that weighed as much as 30 kilograms.

Almost all of the victims remain unidentified and it wasn't until the sixth murder that the police began to see the connections. As of 2022, all the murders remain unsolved and no one has ever been linked with the killings.

THE FACTS

Active: 1985-1989 | Country: India

Victims: 13-26+ | Status: Unsolved

Storozhenko, Vladimir: The Smolensk Strangler

Vladimir was a soviet serial killer also known as 'The Smolensk Strangler' who killed 13 people from 1978 to 1981. Born in 1953, Vladimir quickly fell into a life of crime and by the time he was a teenager, was already known to the police for petty theft and the torture and killing of cats and dogs.

He also developed a hatred for girls and belittled them wherever he could, though it was unclear where the hatred had come from. His crimes were carried out in the city of Smolensk in Russia. From 1978 to 1981, there were more than 20 violent sexual attacks on women and girls in the city, 13 of which resulted in murder.

Although he was called a 'strangler' he would always brutally torture his victims before killing them. One of his younger victims, a 12-year-old student from a local school, was discovered in a sand pit and had been mutilated before and after her death. Before he was captured, four innocent men were arrested and accused of the attacks and murders.

His final victim managed to escape in 1981 and recognised one of Vladimir's tattoos when shown photos of suspects. Vladimir was found guilty of 13 murders and many more sexual assaults in the city. He was sentenced to death and executed by firing squad in 1984.

THE FACTS

Born: April 11th 1953 | Active: 1978-1981

Arrested: July 21st 1981 | Country: Soviet Union

Victims: 13 | AKA: The Smolensk Strangler

Sentence: Death penalty | Status: Executed in 1984

Suradji, Ahmad: The Sorcerer

EXTENDED CASE FILE

A shaman known as The Sorcerer planted 42 victims on his sugar cane plantation, with their heads sticking out of the ground facing his home, believing he would gain magical powers.

In Indonesia, on 24th April, 1997, a 21-year-old female named Sri Kemala Dewi needed spiritual assistance to help with the turmoil in her life. She believed there was only one person who could help her and one person the community spoke of in whispers. This mystical healer was known locally as The Datuk. His real name was Ahmad Suradji, and he went by many nicknames including Nasib Kelewang, Datuk Maringgi, or The Sorcerer.

But for Sri Kemala, The Datuk's name didn't matter, what mattered was that he could help her in ways that others couldn't. Sri Kemala was a secretive woman, preferring to keep her life private. She asked a 15-year-old rickshaw owner named Andreas Suwito to take her to The Datuk but begged him to keep it a secret and never tell a soul where he had taken her.

He dropped her off near the residence of The Sorcerer and pedalled away as fast as he could after hearing strange stories about the place. Andreas would go on to break his promise because Sri Kemala's decomposing corpse was found buried in a sugar cane field three days later. She had become the 42nd and final victim of Ahmad Suradji.

Between 1986 and 1997, Suradji killed at least 42 young girls and women between the ages of 11 to 30, as part of an ongoing ritual that saw him requiring 70 victims. Suradji lived in Medan, in the North Sumatran region of Indonesia, where he worked as a cattle-breeder. He claimed to be a dukun, which is a class of shaman who are supposed to hold supernatural powers.

Word spread around local villages of his healing powers, so more people came his way to gain advice or assistance. Before he would give guidance, or healing, he charged each of his victims the going rate for the ritual which was approximately £200 GBP ($300 USD). For those who wished to be more sexually attractive to men, he would charge more.

Belief in sorcery and the supernatural is common across Indonesia, especially in poor, rural areas where education levels are low. In 1986, Suradji's deceased father visited him in a dream and commanded him to drink the saliva of 70 dead females as part of a larger black magic ritual. Believing it to be a real commandment, he began the ritual.

He said it would have taken too many lifetimes to encounter 70 dead women and so he decided to kill in order to drink their saliva and speed up the process of gaining more magical powers. He married three sisters, who lived with him on the plantation and appeased his every need. He told them of the visitation from his father and what needed to be done. He claimed that by killing 70 women, he would become more powerful and be able to perform more elaborate and compelling acts of supernatural magic, including becoming a mystical healer.

"My father did not specifically advise me to kill people. So I was thinking, it will take ages if I have to wait to get seventy women. I was trying to get to it as fast as possible, I took my own initiative to kill." - Ahmad Suradji.

For many women, they felt their time with Suradji had been beneficial, but at least 42 of them were strangled and buried in the ground up to their necks, on his sugar cane plantation. He chose the victims from the women that came to visit him for spiritual guidance and magical assistance. Enough women were coming to him but when he had a gap with no victims, he purposely went out to seek prostitutes and homeless women.

He took them into the nearby sugar cane fields where he had the victims dig a hole before burying them up to their necks. They believed it was all part of a magical healing ritual, not realising they were digging their own graves.

When they couldn't move out of the mud, Suradji strangled them until they were dead and drank the saliva from their mouths. Then he removed the clothes of the victims and planted them in such a way that their heads were facing his house, believing their positions imbibed him with extra powers. Many skulls were later found on the plantation that suggested he had indeed planted his victims.

There had been many reports of missing people in the area but only tentative connections to Suradji. Because many of the victims were so secretive about visiting a mystical healer, it was difficult to link Suradji to any of the missing. Until the body of Sri Kemala was discovered.

A couple of days after her discovery, Andreas the rickshaw driver heard about the discovery and knew he had to say something. He went to police and told them he had dropped Kemala off at the home of Suradji. On 30th April 1997, police visited the property and found items belonging to Kemala, including her handbag. Suradji was arrested and didn't put up a fight. He confessed to her murder and the murders of at least 42 other females in the same manner.

"We are all human beings, we have our own strengths and weaknesses. If I remember correctly, I have murdered 42 women. I did not suspect I was going to get caught. I did not try to run away when I saw the police, because I had resigned to my fate."

When the investigation turned to excavating the sugar cane plantation, 42 bodies were found with some so far along the decomposition process that they could not be identified. Suradji's three wives were investigated after the murders were discovered but only one was charged as his accomplice. Tumini went on trial at the same time as Ahmad. She received the death penalty but it was later commuted to life in prison. His other two wives apparently had no knowledge of the murders or ritual, and later eloped from the area.

Suradji was sentenced to death and was executed by firing squad on 10th July 2008, despite a last minute appeal by Amnesty International. He was allowed one last liaison with his convicted wife, Tumini, before he was led out to the firing range. Authorities were forced to cancel a plan to bury Suradji's body in a public cemetery because up to 100 relatives of his victims were waiting there, planning to disrupt the funeral.

Although he was linked to 42 murders, there were reports at the time that over 80 people had gone missing in the area and that he may have reached his target of 70.

"The black magic came from God. I don't have it anymore, I have repented. I hope I have a chance to live." – Suradji, in a final interview before he was executed.

THE FACTS

Born: January 10th 1949 | Active: 1986-1997

Arrested: April 30th 1997 | Country: Indonesia

Victims: 42+ | AKA: The Black Magic Killer/The Sorcerer

Sentence: Death penalty | Status: Executed in 2008

Sutcliffe, Peter: The Yorkshire Ripper

EXTENDED CASE FILE

On January 21st 1978 Yvonne Pearson, a 21-year-old sex worker from Bradford, UK, was bludgeoned to death by The Yorkshire Ripper. Her body would not be found for another two months. After appearing at Peter Sutcliffe's car window, they had quickly agreed a price of only £5 for her services. They ended up at a waste ground where Sutcliffe hit her over the head with a hammer.

But the story itself was to have more twists and turns than expected. The following details are from Peter Sutcliffe's confession in 1981. Regarding the murder of Yvonne Pearson. The interview was recorded on January 5th, 1981 from 9:50am to 3:15pm.

"She stepped straight up to the car as I stopped and tapped on the window. She asked me if I wanted business. This was one time when I was genuinely going home as it happened, but I still had a hammer in the car on the floor, under my seat. I told her to get in. She suggested that I turn the car round and she told me where to drive.

"I drove back along Lumb Lane, past Drummond Mill, turned right down a road onto White Abbey Road, and I was directed to turn by Yvonne left into a street behind Silvios Bakery. I drove to the very end of this street where there was a large open space like a parking space and parked the car.

"I asked her how much she wanted. She said, 'It depends how much you can afford.' 'A good time £5, more than a good time £10.' She had very few words to say after

that, the last words she said was, 'Shall we get into the back?' We both got out and she went round to the back door of the car on the nearside, she tried to open it but it was locked. I opened the front passenger door, reached in, and opened the rear door catch.

"As she opened the door, I hit her from behind twice on the head with the hammer. She fell down and started to moan loudly. I dragged her by the feet on her back about 20 yards or so to where there was an old settee lying on its back on some spare land. When I got her to the settee she was still moaning loudly. At that moment, a car drove up and parked next to my car.

"I saw there was a blond woman in the car and a man driving. To stop her moaning, I took some filling from the settee, I held her nose and shoved the straw into her mouth, then I shoved it down her throat. I was kneeling behind the settee, hiding from the motor car, keeping hold of her nose.

"I let go after a while to see if she was still making a noise through her nose, but when I did, she started again, so I took hold of her nose again. The car seemed to be there for ages before it drove away. I stayed still, petrified with fear while the car was there.

"When the car had gone I was seething with rage. Her jeans were nearly off, because she had undone them at the car, and when I was pulling her by the feet I nearly pulled them off. I pulled her jeans right off. I think I kicked her hard to the head and body. I was senseless with rage and I was kicking away furiously at her.

"After this, I remember acting very strangely, I talked to her and apologised for what I had done, but she was dead. I put the settee on top of her. I was very distraught and I was in tears when I left her. This was the first time I had apologised to someone I had killed. I drove home, I cannot recall the time, but it was after 9:00pm. I can't remember if Sonja was in the house or not.

"I remember stopping on the way home and I just sat in the car trying to work out why I had done this killing. My mind was in a turmoil."

He ended this section of his confession with an important line:

"*...I didn't dare go back to where she lay, there was no reason to go back.*"

There is a mystery regarding Peter Sutcliffe and the Ripper murders and it's as mysterious as those of Jack The Ripper. On March 26th, Easter Sunday in 1978, Yvonne Pearson's body was discovered under the sofa where Sutcliffe had left her. Her body had been putrefying for two months and had started to rot. She was spotted by a passer-by because her arm was sticking out from under the sofa.

Police were shocked that her body had not been found earlier in such an obvious position. There was also a copy of the Daily Mirror wedged underneath one of her arms, it appeared as though it had been deliberately positioned there. The newspaper was dated February 21st, exactly one month after the murder but Sutcliffe confirmed that he never returned to the body's location.

Regarding the body of Yvonne Pearson, Professor David Gee's examination of her led him to believe an alternative theory. He claimed that the injuries to her head were caused by a large rock or boulder and not a hammer. He concluded that it wasn't a victim of The Yorkshire Ripper.

Of course, this goes against Peter Sutcliffe's own confession, in stating that he apologised to Yvonne's corpse. It would seem pointless to lie about not going back to the body and so it remains a mystery to this day, although Sutcliffe was charged with her death. As the murders escalated from 1977 until 1980, over 350 detectives from three counties had been involved at some point. The Ripper murders had cost the British taxpayer over £4million throughout the investigation.

There has been a theory put forward by Noel O'Gara, that Peter Sutcliffe was a copycat Yorkshire Ripper and the real Yorkshire Ripper was killing around the same time and after Sutcliffe's imprisonment. He went on to state that subsequent murders were covered up by the police as they couldn't risk the public knowing that the Ripper was still out there. Again, this is a theory and the evidence surrounding it is rather thin but it remains out there in the public domain.

Yet, Sutcliffe was convicted for killing 13 people and the attempted murder of seven others over a period of five years. He later claimed the voice of God had sent him on a mission to kill sex workers. He was sentenced to life in prison without the possibility of parole.

In 2017, further investigations were underway looking at unsolved murders from 1964. Sutcliffe was a lorry driver who regularly went to Europe with his work. The investigation spread to Northern Europe and looked at possible links with the unsolved murders of sex workers in the region. No additional victims have yet been found. On 13th November 2020, while in prison custody aged 74, Sutcliffe died of COVID-19 related complications.

THE FACTS

Born: June 2nd 1946 | Active: 1975-1980

Arrested: January 2nd 1981 | Country: United Kingdom

Victims: 13+ | AKA: The Yorkshire Ripper

Sentence: Life imprisonment | Status: Died in 2020

Swango, Joseph Michael

American physician and serial killer Joseph Michael Swango is estimated to have killed at least 60 people through poisoning of patients and some of his colleagues. He admitted to four deaths but the investigation linked him to dozens more. Swango joined the Marine Corps but received a discharge in 1976 for an unknown reason.

He went to train at a medical school at Southern Illinois University School of Medicine (SIU). While there he went through a strict regime of physical training and was known to punish himself with push ups and jogging if he got something wrong. From the moment he got a surgical internship, patients began mysteriously dying around him.

He would kill his victims by injecting them with drug overdoses. His crimes didn't stop at patients and he would drug his colleagues by preparing the food for them and lacing them with overdoses of sedatives. By 1994, the medical community and an investigation was on to him so he changed his name and moved to Zimbabwe of all places.

IMAGE ATTRIBUTIONS
(ATTRIB A41) (ATTRIB A78)

PETER SUTCLIFFE

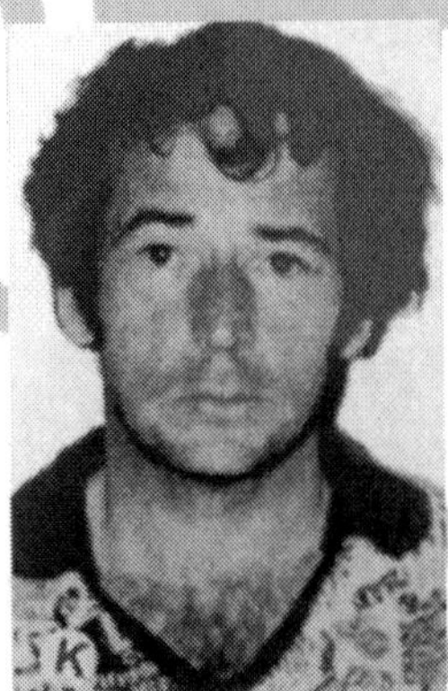

WORLD'S END PUB, HIGH STREET, EDINBURGH, WHERE SINCLAIR'S VICTIMS WERE LAST SEEN ALIVE

ANGUS SINCLAIR

IMAGE ATTRIBUTIONS
(ATTRIB A41) (ATTRIB A78)

There, he got a job in a hospital and continued to kill patients and colleagues. He was arrested in 1997 while boarding a flight to Saudi Arabia. First sentenced in Zimbabwe, he was subsequently extradited to the United States to be sentenced to three life terms with no parole. As of 2022, he remains incarcerated at the ADX Florence supermax prison near Florence, Colorado.

THE FACTS

Born: October 21st 1954 | Active: 1981-1997

Arrested: June 1997 | Country: USA/Zimbabwe

Victims: 4-60+ | AKA: David J. Adams/Jack Kirk/Michael Swan

Sentence: Three life sentences | Status: Incarcerated

Thwala, Sipho

Sipho Mandla Agmatir Thwala is a South African rapist and serial killer who murdered at least 16 women and raped an additional 10. He began his killing spree in 1996, in South Africa's KwaZulu-Natal province.

He would lure young local women into the sugar cane fields just outside of the town of Phoenix, with the offer of employment. He would then attack them from behind, tie them up with their own underwear and rape them. Afterwards he would strangle or beat them to death and leave them to be burned in the sugar cane fields.

He was arrested a year later in 1997 after DNA from one of his victims matched his from a previous arrest. In 1999, he was found guilty of 16 murders and 10 rapes and sentenced to 506 years in prison. As of 2022, he is incarcerated at a prison in Pretoria, South Africa. There is minimal information available in his case.

THE FACTS

Born: 1968 | Active: 1996-1997

Arrested: August 14th 1997 | Country: South Africa

Victims: 16+ | AKA: Phoenix Strangler/Cane field Killer

Sentence: 506 years in prison | Status: Incarcerated

Tinning, Marybeth

Nine children would die under American serial killer, Marybeth Roe Tinning's care, during a 14 year period from 1971. She was convicted of only one murder, that of her ninth child, four-month-old Tami Lynne, in 1985 who she smothered to death with a pillow. She was suspected of being involved in the deaths of her eight previous children.

Six autopsies were carried out on most of the children and their causes of death varied from natural to unnatural. Tinning was released on parole in August 2018 and vehemently denied all the murders except Tami Lynne's in 1985.

Her husband believed Tinning to be innocent and stood by her all the time she was incarcerated. He was there to meet her at the gates of the prison upon her release. Her story has been the subject of numerous books, articles, films, and documentaries.

THE FACTS

Born: September 11th 1942 | Active: 1971-1985

Arrested: February 4th 1986 | Country: USA | Victims: 1-9

Sentence: 20 years to life in prison | Status: Released in 2018

Tkach, Serhiy Fedorovich: Pavlohrad Maniac

Over a 25 year period, from 1980 to 2005, Ukrainian serial killer Serhiy Fedorovich Tkach killed at least 37 women and girls but confessed to over 100 more murders at his trial. Tkach targeted young female victims between the ages of 8-years-old and 18-years-old. He would rape them before suffocating or strangling them.

He would engage in sexual acts with his victim's corpses, before leaving their bodies at random locations throughout the country. In a chilling comparison with fellow Soviet serial killer, Andrei Chikatilo, Tkach chose victims near railway lines and especially those that had recently been installed.

The tar of the tracks covered the scent of some of the bodies, meaning that police dogs were thrown off course. In 2005, Tkach had the gumption to attend the funeral of one of his victims. It was other children at the funeral who raised the alarm as they had seen Tkach with the victim shortly before her abduction and death.

He was arrested shortly after and confessed to over 100 murders. In 2008, he was sentenced to life without parole for the murder of 37 victims. Ten years later on November 4th 2018, Tkach died of natural causes and was buried by prison staff. Thus ending the life of one of Ukraine's most notorious serial killers.

THE FACTS

Born: September 15th 1952 | Active: 1980-2005

Arrested: August 2005 | Country: Soviet Union/Ukraine

Victims: 37-100+ | AKA: Pavlohrad Maniac/Polohy Maniac

Sentence: Life imprisonment | Status: Died in 2018

Tobin, Peter: Bible John

EXTENDED CASE FILE

Three murders in the late 1960s linked to the mysterious Bible John remain unsolved to this day, with a strong suspicion that serial killer Peter Tobin was the man behind the unidentified murderer. For many years, there was a seemingly obvious connection between a serial killer and various unsolved murders, but decades later, it seems the connections have been cut and there could have been two serial killers in Scotland in the late 1960s, one of whom has never been caught.

Scottish serial killer and rapist Peter Britton Tobin killed three women over an extended period of time and raped many others. On 10th February 1991, 15-year-old schoolgirl Vicky Hamilton vanished from a bus stop in Falkirk, Scotland, and was stabbed to death by Tobin. Realising heat was on him, he fled Scotland to a new flat at 50 Irvine Drive, Margate, Kent, and in a macabre display of ownership, took Hamilton's body with him. He later buried her corpse in the back garden of the property.

Six months later, in Essex, England, 18-year-old student Dinah McNicol vanished while hitchhiking with her boyfriend, who was dropped off at a different location while McNicol stayed in the car. Tobin was later confirmed to have been the driver and her eventual killer. In the months that followed, regular withdrawals were made from her bank account to the maximum amount of £250 each time. Tobin had forced McNicol to hand over her PIN before killing her, though his motive for murder was primarily sexual and not robbery.

She too was buried in the back garden near to the decomposed corpse of Hamilton. It would be another 16 years before their remains were uncovered following Tobin's subsequent arrest for their murders. In 1993, two years after escaping justice for the murders, he raped two 14-year-old-girls at his new flat in Leigh Park, Havant, a large residential area just north of Portsmouth. The two girls went to visit a neighbour who wasn't in so asked to wait in Tobin's flat.

He then held them at knifepoint, forced alcohol down their throats and raped them. He stabbed one of them and turned the gas on in the house to kill them. The two girls survived the attack and went straight to the police. Tobin went on the run immediately as the girls had identified him and were obviously found to have been raped in Tobin's home. To avoid police he joined a religious sect in Coventry, named the Jesus Fellowship. Also known as the Jesus Army, the group – or cult, as some called them – were part of the British New Church movement and were founded in 1969 to spread the Christian message to people directly by using street-based evangelism.

By 2007, there were said to be an estimated 3,500 followers in 24 separate congregations. By 2019, the group came under fire for its leaders having committed sexual assaults against children and young women during the 1970s.

Fitting then, that Tobin was part of the group, living on one of their communal properties, hidden from the long arm of the law. Today, there are still around 200 followers who live in communal buildings owned by the group.

While on a trip to Brighton, when his car was spotted parked up on the seafront, Tobin was arrested for the attacks on the two girls. In 1994, he was sentenced to 14 years in prison but only served 10 and had escaped justice for the murders of Hamilton and McNicol, as he was never connected to them at the time.

He was released in 2004 and sent back to Scotland, where he disappeared from the authorities by exploiting open-door policies at various churches and religious groups. He went by many different names in order to remain off-the-grid and hid the fact he was on the sex offenders' register.

He became an expert at hiding himself among fringe religious groups, but there was a darkness inside of Tobin that saw him needing to commit more crimes, and it would come at the expense of the groups that veiled him from the world.

In September 2006, less than two years after his release, he attacked and killed 23-year-old Polish student Angelika Kluk, who was staying in the accommodation building of a church that Tobin was working at.

She was raped, beaten and stabbed to death in a frenzied attack that the coroner claimed was one of the worst he had ever seen. Tobin hid her body in an underground chamber in the floor of the church, near to the confessional booth, but his haphazard attempt at dumping the body led to his downfall.

A few days later, Kluk's body was discovered, after a churchgoer noticed the flooring had been disturbed. The coroner later confirmed that Kluk may have been alive when she was buried in the chamber.

Knowing police were closing in on him, and in an attempt to trick authorities, Tobin admitted himself to hospital under a false name, and with a fictitious complaint. But police were already aware of what Tobin looked like, and word was put out to various authorities around England. He was arrested shortly after Kluk's body was found.

Tobin was charged and went to trial in the Spring of 2007, where he was found guilty of the rape and murder of Kluk and was sentenced to a minimum of 21 years in prison. He believed he had escaped justice for the murders of Hamilton and McNicol – until investigators looked closer.

Realising Tobin had already been convicted of rape and attempted murder, the investigation looked at older cases that he might have been involved in. Due to the number of properties that Tobin was known to have lived in, forensic searches of numerous houses and flats were undertaken across the country, including one at the seaside town of Southsea, Hampshire.

On 14th November 2007, police confirmed that human remains had been unearthed at Tobin's former residence at 50 Irvine Drive. The first remains to be discovered were that of 15-year-old Hamilton. At the same time, Essex Police opened a cold case for Dinah McNicol and linked up with the Tobin investigation.

A few days after Hamilton's remains were discovered, McNicol's remains were discovered in the grounds of the same property. The then owners of the house had no idea they were living with the corpses of two teenage girls.

In November 2008, Tobin was transferred to a court in Dundee, Scotland, where he was convicted for the murder of Hamilton. After a trial which lasted a month, Tobin had his 21-year sentence increased to a 30 years minimum.

'Yet again you have shown yourself to be unfit to live in a decent society. It is hard for me to convey the loathing and revulsion that ordinary people will feel for what you have done.' – The judge in Hamilton's murder trial.

For McNicol's murder, Tobin went to trial in 2009, in an Essex court. Unusually, Tobin's defence offered no evidence in his favour. It took less than 15 minutes for the jury to find him guilty, and he was sentenced to an additional life term.

On the same day that Tobin was convicted of his third murder, police reopened multiple cold cases under the banner of Operation Anagram. Investigators came to believe that Tobin may have been involved in at least 13 more murders.

It was then he was linked to the Bible John Murders in Glasgow, which remain unsolved to this day. The three murders from 1968 to 1969 were similar in style to Tobin's method of killing, and he would have been in and around the area at the time.

The artist photofit of Bible John matched photos of how Tobin looked at the time. Eyewitnesses claimed that the suspect had one tooth missing on the right-hand side of his mouth. Tobin had one tooth removed in the late 1960s, in the same place that matched eyewitness accounts.

He got the name of Bible John because it was suspected that he went to rape his victims but found them in the middle of their menstrual cycle, so he killed them instead. Tobin also left Glasgow just a few weeks after the final known Bible John murder. But was Tobin the victim of Henry Lee Lucas syndrome or really the beast behind Bible John?

Bible John's victims were picked up from the Barrowland Ballroom in Glasgow, that remains open today as The Barrowlands. Despite one of the longest manhunts in Scottish history, the murders remain unsolved and the suspect unidentified.

The Bible John murders made Scottish crime history when a composite of the suspect was released publicly for the first time. Unfortunately, police recently confirmed that DNA evidence from the three Bible John murders had deteriorated due to incorrect storage of the samples.

This means that if Tobin was Bible John, then without a confession, it would be difficult to now prove. Operation Anagram hit full speed in 2010, as police forces across the United Kingdom checked DNA against cold cases and followed up on missing people that might have been connected with Tobin.

In the end, multiple murder cases of teenage girls and women were reopened. During interviews with Tobin, psychiatrists and profilers suggested he most likely had killed many more, beyond the three he had been convicted for.

On Wednesday 15th May 1980, 22-year-old Eastbourne College student Jessie Earl had disappeared from her bedsit and failed to return home the next morning. The London born student was known to take long walks up to Beachy Head where she would read and write about nature.

So when she disappeared, and a police search turned up no trace of her, it was suggested she had become part of the saddening suicide statistics that had haunted Beachy Head for centuries. Until her remains were discovered on the cliff top nine years later.

Her death was included as one of the cold cases in Operation Anagram. Though similarities were found between Earl's case and Tobin's confirmed victims, there was not enough solid evidence to convict him of the murder, which to this day remains unsolved.

The operation diminished in 2011 when they failed to positively link any more victims to Tobin. While in prison, Tobin boasted to a psychiatrist that he had ended the lives of 48 people.

But if Tobin was not Bible John, as the evidence suggests, then who was? At the time of the murders, a man calling himself John White was suspected to be the killer but because his teeth didn't match that of the eye-witness accounts, he was discounted.

John White was a fake name, he had been seen arguing with women, made regular visits to the Barrowland Ballroom, and fitted the profile of the killer. However, in 2005, 'White' came forward to offer a DNA sample which then removed him from the suspect pool.

In 1983, police received an anonymous phone call from a Dutch man who claimed his friend was Bible John. He believed it because of his friend's demeanour, activity in Glasgow around the time of the killings, and his love of the Barrowland Ballroom. No suspects were ever identified following the call.

In 1969, at the time of the murders, Hannah Martin was raped by a man she met at the Ballroom. She would go on to give birth to the child of the rapist, who she believed was Peter Tobin. Though no DNA of the child was ever provided, if the story were true, then the child's DNA could prove who Bible John really was – or wasn't.

The World's End Murderer, Angus Sinclair, was also connected to the Bible John murders. Sinclair, who was linked to eight murders up until 1978, was already active in 1961 in Glasgow when he killed his eight-year-old neighbour. He was convicted of her murder but was out of prison six years later, at around the time of the Bible John murders.

Yet again, there was no solid evidence to connect Sinclair to Bible John. Many more suspects have been linked to the mysterious killer but Peter Tobin remains the prime candidate. Though his health is deteriorating, as he remains alive in 2022, there is still hope that a death-bed confession could be forthcoming.

If not, and Bible John was not Tobin, then an unidentified serial killer got away with murder for over half a century. Despite the huge ongoing interest in both Tobin and Bible John, the murders of three women in Glasgow from 1968 to 1969, remain unsolved to this day, and a footnote in a wider story of multiple serial killers.

THE FACTS

Born: August 27th 1946 | Active: 1991-2006

Arrested: October 3rd 2006 | Country: United Kingdom

Victims: 3-13+ | AKA: Bible John

Sentence: Life sentence plus 30 years | Status: Incarcerated

Trobec, Metod

Trobec was a Slovenian serial killer who claimed five victims. Slovenia was one of the surviving states of former Yugoslavia and Trobec was born a Yugoslavian. He began his crimes at an early age, mostly involving arson or theft. Then, over a two year period from 1976 to 1978, he raped, killed and cremated at least five women.

Trobec was born an illegitimate child and as such was prone to bouts of violence and antisocial behaviour. At the age of 14 he burned his neighbour's haystacks and acted cruelly around girls his age. At the age of 18 he stole a moped and was sent away for military service.

When he returned, he emigrated to Germany before going home to Slovenia in 1974 where he was arrested and sentenced to 13 months in prison for petty criminal behaviour. While there, his anger at the world grew. Upon his release, from 1976 to 1978, Trobec raped and killed five women before cremating their bodies on open fields.

IMAGE ATTRIB. A39

PETER TOBIN

METOD TROBEC

IMAGE ATTRIB. A90

GWENDOLYN GRAHAM

IMAGE ATTRIB. A18A/A18B

CATHERINE WOOD

His body count might have been higher but suggested victims have never been officially linked to him. He was the last person to be sentenced to death in Slovenia and spent the longest time in prison of any Slovenian criminal at 27 years inside. Trobec took his own life in 1996.

THE FACTS

Born: June 6th 1948 | Active: 1976-1978

Country: Yugoslavia/Slovenia | Victims: 5+

Sentence: Death penalty | Status: Died by suicide in 1996

Trudeau, Yves: The Mad Bumper

Yves 'Apache' Trudeau, known as the 'The Mad Bumper', killed 43 people from 1973 to 1985. He was a member of the Hells Angels North Chapter outlaw motorcycle gang in Quebec and was the gang's leading assassin, having taken part in multiple major biker conflicts throughout Canada.

He was labelled a psychopathic killer and killing machine by those who knew him and interviewed him afterwards. He became anxious through copious use of cocaine and soon suspected his fellow gang members were plotting to kill him. He uncovered a $50,000 contract on his head and decided to give himself up to police.

Trudeau became a government informant and received a lenient sentence in exchange for supplying information about the biker gangs. In 1985, he pleaded guilty to 43 counts of manslaughter, meaning he essentially got away with murder. 29 victims were shot dead, ten died from bombs, three from being beaten to death, and another one strangled.

Included in his plea package was a payment for $40,000 a year for four years, and $35 a week for cigarettes. He was given life in prison but was paroled in 1994 after only seven years and put into the witness protection program with a new identity. It was known he was arrested again in 2004 and sentenced to four years for sexually assaulting a young boy. In 2007 he was transferred to a medical centre where he died of cancer shortly after.

THE FACTS

Born: February 4th 1946 | Active: 1973-1985

Country: Canada | Victims: 43+ | AKA: The Mad Bumper/Apache

Sentence: Life sentence | Status: Died in 2007

Tuchlin, Pawel: Scorpion

Tuchlin was a Polish serial killer also known as the 'Scorpion' who was convicted of killing nine women and the attempted murders of another 11 people. Born in 1946 to a poor alcoholic father and mother, he was the eighth of 11 children and suffered abuse by both his parents.

He was a bed-wetter into his later childhood and his other siblings and parents would humiliate him for it. He joined the military when he was a teenager but was discharged for having bad hearing. From 1975 to 1983, Tuchlin attacked a total of 20 women across Poland and killed his victims with a bloody hammer.

The hammer was carefully wrapped up with a bandage because it made his stomach cold when he wore his pants looking for victims. Just four years into his killing campaign, authorities were already aware a serial killer was at large but had no suspect. In 1983, a special police group was put together to catch the killer, under codename: Scorpion.

Tuchlin was arrested in May 1983 on suspicion of theft and when police searched his farm they found a hammer covered in the blood of one of his victims. He was sent for psychiatric evaluation where he confessed to nine murders and 11 attempted murders. He was sentenced to death in 1985.

After his sentencing, Tuchlin believed the authorities would release him from prison in order to hunt down the real murderer. He believed the death sentence was a smokescreen to unveil the real killer. Despite his claims, the murderer of nine women was executed by hanging on May 25th 1987.

THE FACTS

Born: April 28th 1946 | Active: 1975-1983

Country: Poland | Victims: 9 | AKA: Scorpion

Sentence: Death penalty | Status: Executed in 1987

Ture, Joseph Donald Jr.

In Washington County, Minnesota on May 10th 1979, 18-year-old Marlys Wohlenhaus died of injuries sustained in a brutal axe attack two days earlier. She had been found by her mother on the floor of their basement. A $50,000 (USD) reward for information was offered which led to the arrest of a wanted serial killer.

Serial killer Joseph Donald Ture Jr. was later convicted of her murder. Born in 1951, Ture went on to kill at least six people by shooting or beating them with an axe. He was already serving time for the murder of waitress Diane Edwards when he was arrested and charged with the Wohlenhaus murder.

In 1981, he was sentenced to life in prison. But it was the tip of the iceberg as a more vicious crime was about to be attributed to him. Back in 1978, Alice Huling and three of her four children were shot dead with a shotgun at their home near Clearwater. The fourth child played dead to escape being shot.

Their murders remained unsolved until a 2000 trial found Ture guilty of their slayings. He was given an additional life sentence for each murder. As of 2022, he remains incarcerated at the Minnesota Correctional Facility in Stillwater.

THE FACTS

Born: 1951 | Active: 1978-1979

Arrested: 1979 | Country: USA

Victims: 6 | Status: Incarcerated

Turner, Chester Dewayne

Chester Dewayne Turner, sometimes known as The Southside Slayer was convicted of the murders of ten women in Los Angeles from 1987 to 1998 in addition to the murder of one of the victim's unborn child. On March 9th 1987, in Los Angeles, 21-year-old Diane Johnson was murdered by Turner.

On October 29th 1987, 26-year-old Annette Ernest was found dead along the hard shoulder near Grand Avenue and 106th Street in Vermont Vista. She had been raped and strangled to death by Turner. He got away with both murders until 2003, when DNA evidence provided by police confirmed that he was the killer of both women and he was finally arrested in September of the same year.

In 2007, he was first convicted of killing 10 women from 1987 to 1998, in addition to the death of an unborn child. By 2014 he was convicted of another four murders, bringing his total to 15 victims, and is suspected of many more. He is alleged to be one of the most prolific serial killers in the city of Los Angeles. He received death sentences in both trials, and as of 2022, remains on death row.

THE FACTS

Born: November 5th 1966 | Active: 1987-1998

Arrested: September 2003 | Country: USA

Victims: 15+ | AKA: The Southside Slayer

Sentence: Death penalty | Status: Death row

Unterweger, Jack

Unterweger was an Austrian serial killer who claimed between 10 and 13 victims from 1974 to 1992. He committed his crimes across many countries including Austria, West Germany, Czechoslovakia, and the United States. He was convicted first in Austria of a single murder in 1974 of a young woman who he strangled to death with her bra.

While in prison, he began to write voluminously, which somehow caught the attention of Austrian publishers who believed him to be rehabilitated because of it. He was released on parole in 1990 and became a popular playwright and journalist in Austria but was secretly killing women.

Due to his writing success in Austria, he was hired by an Austrian magazine to write about crime in Los Angeles. He travelled to the United States and met with local police, asking them to show him the red light districts. While there, he is suspected of killing three American sex workers, under the guise of writing about crime in the area.

He returned to Europe but was finally caught in Miami, Florida, in 1992, and extradited back to Austria. In 1994, he was convicted of nine murders but took his own life in prison by hanging in the same year. Unterweger would usually kill sex workers by beating them, raping them with tree branches, and strangling them with their own underwear.

THE FACTS

Born: August 16th 1951 | Active: 1974-1992

Arrested: February 27th 1992 | Country: Austria/USA

Victims: 10-13 | AKA: Vienna Woods Killer

Sentence: Life imprisonment | Status: Died by suicide in 1994

Urdiales, Andrew: The Monster in the Desert

EXTENDED CASE FILE

American serial killer Andrew Urdiales, sometimes referred to as The Monster in the Desert, was convicted on two counts of murder in 2002 and another five counts of murder in 2018. He is known to have killed eight women but may have killed at least two more.

He was said to have been raised in a happy home but when he was 11-years-old, he took a baseball bat and bludgeoned his family's dog to death. He told his parents that the dog had been injured after falling from a wall. After he completed school, he enrolled in the Marine Corps, served in Desert Storm in Iraq, and was stationed at Pendleton, California, until 1991.

He committed his first human murder in January of 1986. He chose his victim deliberately and followed her on numerous occasions, to know her routine. He then stabbed 23-year-old student, Robin Brandley, 41 times. Her body was discovered the next day in the spot where she had died. Urdiales was a serving Marine at the time, and while he was enlisted, he would kill five women.

He killed three more women, two of them sex workers, in 1988 and 1989. Most of the time, he didn't hide the bodies but left them where he had killed them. In 1992, a year after his discharge from the Marine Corp, he met 19-year-old Jennifer Asbenson, in California, while on holiday.

He lured her into his car, drove her out to the desert then raped her before dumping her in the trunk of his rental car. She managed to escape but her story wasn't believed by local police. It wouldn't be for many years until Jennifer's story finally rang true with police and with the public.

Out of fear he would be caught, Urdiales didn't kill again until 1995 when the urge became too strong to resist. Upon a brief return to California, he raped and murdered 32-year-old sex worker Denise Maney, before dumping her body in the desert. Urdiales would usually cross state lines in order to kill.

A forensic psychiatrist named Dr. Park Dietz, stated that Urdiales was motivated by a misplaced revenge on the world, he wanted to kill women who rejected him or didn't serve him as he wished. Another stated that he was a monster masquerading as a respectable member of the military.

On April 14th 1996, the body of 25-year-old Laura Ulyaki was discovered in Wolf Lake, on the border of Chicago and Indiana. She had been raped and murdered just days earlier. Three months later on July 14th 1996, the body of 21-year-old Cassandra Corum was discovered in the Vermilion River Mountains in Illinois. On August 2nd 1996, the body of 22-year-old Lynn Huber was discovered in Wolf Lake. She too had been raped and murdered and was his last confirmed victim.

He was arrested for a second time in April of 1997, after an attack on a sex worker. They checked his weapon against the outstanding murders, but before the results came back he confessed to eight murders. Because the murders were in multiple states, it wasn't until 2002, after a lengthy trial that he would be found guilty of two of the murders and sentenced to death.

His death sentence was commuted to life in 2011, when Illinois Governor, Pat Quinn, signed an order to abolish the death penalty in the state. But the trials didn't stop. In California, on May 23rd 2018, Urdiales was convicted of five more murders, and a few months later was also sentenced to death in California.

On November 2nd 2018, while on death row at San Quentin State Prison in California, Urdiales killed himself in his cell. Just one hour earlier, another death row inmate was found dead of a suspected suicide. 51-year-old Virendra Govin was sentenced to death in 2004 for the murders of four people. He and his brother had attacked four members of a family who owned the neighbouring motel. They strangled and beat them to death, before burning the bodies.

San Quentin State Prison confirmed that the two suicides were exactly one hour apart and by unknown causes, but some people didn't believe the official line. Some theorists at the time had claimed that something supernatural had stalked the death row cells of the prison and that the apparent suicides were not suicides at all. Still, the official line is that it was coincidence that they killed themselves on the same night.

In 2017, a year before Urdiales's death, Jennifer Asbenson, who escaped his clutches but was not believed, finally got to testify against her attacker.

"I just tried to go somewhere else in my mind. I wanted to die. He's nobody that will ever have a hold of my emotions again." – Jennifer Asbenson.

She took a documentary crew to the location where she had been kidnapped and where she had escaped. She said that as she ran away from the car, Urdiales was chasing after her with a machete. In October of 2018, Asbenson released a book about her life and ordeal and how she went from being a victim to an inspiration to victims all over the world. Her book: The Girl in the Treehouse: A Memoir, is available at most international bookstores.

THE FACTS

Born: June 4th 1964 | Active: 1986-1996

Arrested: April 23rd 1997 | Country: USA

Victims: 8 | AKA: The Monster in the Desert

Sentence: Death penalty | Status: Died by suicide in 2018

Vakrinos, Dimitris

On August 6th 1987, 43-year-old Panayiotis Gaglias was murdered by Greek serial killer Dimitris Vakrinos. Gaglias was a guest in Vakrino's house and had threatened to go to the police over a stolen shotgun. Vakrinos killed him as he slept in his bed by hitting him with an iron bar.

He moved the body and dumped it on the side of a highway not too far away from his home. The body was found eight days later. Between 1987 and 1996, Vakrinos was a taxi driver who murdered five people over minor instances of disagreement. He attempted to kill another seven, along with a raft of other crimes including arson and robbery.

Vakrinos was a serial killer who had a bad childhood caused by abusive parents which led to him associating with sexual oppression, low self-esteem and excessive anger. As he was shorter than the average man, he responded to challenges by using weapons in place of his smaller stature.

Vakrinos was caught and arrested in April of 1997. In May of the same year, he took his own life in the prison's shower rooms by tying shoelaces to the shower head. He never made it to trial and escaped justice but five victims were conclusively linked to him and he remains a rare Greek serial killer.

THE FACTS

Born: 1962 | Active: 1987-1996

Arrested: April 6th 1997 | Country: Greece

Victims: 5 | Status: Died by suicide in 1997

Vega, Jose Antonio Rodriguez

On August 6th 1987, in Santander, Spain, 82-year-old Margarita González was raped and suffocated by Spanish serial killer José Antonio Rodríguez Vega, AKA: The Old Lady Killer. He forced González to swallow her own false teeth, causing her to choke and suffocate to death.

Two more victims were named after being murdered in 1988 but their names were never publicly released. Vega was diagnosed as a psychopath who would ensure he knew his victim's routines inside out. He would then gain their trust until he was invited into their homes, where he would cold-heartedly kill them.

He also took souvenirs from each of his victims including a television from one of them. Most of the murders were thought to have been caused by natural causes due to the age of the victims. It was only after his capture that police released a video of the items that Vega had collected so that families of the victims could identify them.

Vega raped and killed at least 16 elderly women from the ages of 61 to 93 over a nine-month period from 1987 to 1988. He was arrested in May 1988, convicted, and sentenced to 440 years in prison. In October 2002, Vega was stabbed to death by two other prison inmates.

THE FACTS

Born: December 3rd 1957 | Active: 1987-1988

Arrested: May 19th 1988 | Country: Spain

Victims: 16+ | AKA: The Old Lady Killer

Sentence: 440 years in prison | Status: Killed in 2002

Watts, Carl Eugene: The Sunday Morning Slasher

Also known as 'The Sunday Morning Slasher', Watts's body count is suspected to be closer to 100 victims across an eight-year period. He was convicted of two murders but at least 80 more victims have been linked to him, with 14 being confirmed across the states of Michigan and Texas.

Ever since he was 12-years-old, Watts claimed that he began dreaming of torturing and killing girls and women. When he was a 15-year-old paperboy, he violently attacked a 24-year-old woman on his route. He was arrested and sent to a mental hospital in Detroit where he was diagnosed with delusional thought processes.

He was released the following year when he was 16 and attempted to hold his dark desires at bay. When he was 20, in 1974, Watts began kidnapping victims from their homes, torturing them and brutally murdering them. His crimes were not thought to be sexually related and it became difficult to link just one person with the murders.

He usually killed white women with various methods including strangulation, stabbing, drowning, and beating with blunt objects. The age of his victims ranged from between 14 to 44. It wasn't until 1982, when Watts was placed under surveillance, that his reign of terror came to an end.

He was arrested on May 23rd 1982 and convicted of two murders for which there was substantial evidence and sentenced to life without parole. He was confirmed to have killed 14 people but he claimed he killed over 40. Subsequent investigations have since linked him with closer to 100 murders across the United States and Canada. Many of the investigations into Watts's crimes ended when he died of cancer in prison in 2007.

THE FACTS

Born: November 7th 1953 | Active: 1974-1982

Arrested: May 23rd 1982 | Country: USA

Victims: 14-100+ | AKA: The Sunday Morning Slasher

Sentence: Life imprisonment | Status: Died in 2007

Waxin, Denis

Waxin is a French serial killer and child molester who killed three young girls between 1985 and 1999. During that time period he also raped another girl and two small boys. Waxin's father was strict while his mother was hard-working and it is claimed the parents never spoke to each other. He was neglected as a child and left alone in isolation, his only solace was his older brother who left the home when Denis was 17-years-old.

He became depressed and walked the streets alone for hours at a time. The same year, in 1985, Waxin lured seven-year-old Nathalie Hoareau to an area of wasteland. There, he raped and strangled her before stabbing her twice in the heart. Her partially nude body was discovered the same evening by police.

A few years later in 1990, he was confirmed to have killed nine-year-old Cathy Monchaux in Wazemmes. He lured her from her garden and took her to an abandoned football field where he raped her and then stabbed her fourteen times. Her body was found the next day by a dog-walker.

In 1992, four-year-old Nadjia Thebib from Moulins went missing. Waxin lifted her up in his arms as her Aunt ran after him. The Aunt fell to the ground as she pursued him and lost sight of the direction he went in. Waxin raped Nadjia, stabbed her in the neck and choked her with a plastic bag.

On January 6th 1999, a six-year-old girl named Wendy was lured to an abandoned factory. He threatened her by telling her that he killed little girls and so she allowed Waxin to undress and rape her. He let her go and followed her to let her know he was watching her. A passing driver saw her and carried her to the police station.

Wendy gave a facial description to police which subsequently led to Waxin's arrest. He was sentenced to life in prison for the murders of Hoareau, Monchaux, and Thebib, and the rapes of three other children. He was also linked to two additional murders in 1993 but was never charged with them. As of 2022, he remains incarcerated.

THE FACTS

Born: May 26th 1968 | Active: 1985-1999

Arrested: July 13th 1999 | Country: France | Victims: 3+

Sentence: Life imprisonment | Status: Incarcerated

West, Fred and Rose: House of Horrors

EXTENDED CASE FILE

On May 10th 1978, Shirley Robinson, a former lodger at 25 Cromwell Street, disappeared. She was murdered by serial killer Fred West. Mostly in league with his wife, Rosemary West, they would take the lives of at least 12 young women before being arrested in 1994. Their address of 25 Cromwell Street became synonymous with the murders and became known as the House of Horrors.

So much hate was subsequently directed towards the House of Horrors, that Gloucester City Council intervened. They purchased the property for £40,000 in 1996, in the knowledge that no one would live there. They then unceremoniously destroyed the property, and with it, any physical trace of the horrors that had haunted the building.

Fred West was born in 1941, raised during World War Two, and killed his first victim in 1967. In January 1972, he married Rosemary Letts, who was 18-years-old. By that point, during their blossoming relationship, Rose had already murdered Fred's daughter, Charmaine West.

It was unclear for a while who exactly had killed her but recent evidence showed that Fred West was serving a small sentence for unrelated crimes at the time of her death. Yet, he had already killed many years before Rose. Fred would later move the hidden body and bury it at their Midland Road address.

Throughout his life, Fred had displayed domineering control to all the women in his life. His violent sexual lust resulted in him abusing most of his children. He would sexually abuse them, beat them, and encourage them into prostitution. The crossing of dark souls with Fred and Rosemary West was a match made in hell.

At least eight of the victims had been raped, tortured, and mutilated. Before being murdered they were used in violent sexual fantasies where bondage played a heavy part of the household. They would then dismember the bodies and bury them in the cellar and garden of 25 Cromwell Street.

Fred killed two on his own and Rosemary killed one; Charmaine. The rest of their victims were killed as a pair. The level of control they asserted over others is as horrific as it is shocking. Rose worked as a sex worker and used an upstairs room in the house for her clients.

She would also engage in casual sex with both male and female lodgers. It was stated that when she had sex with other women, Rose would become more violent as the control slipped. She would partially suffocate them and insert exceptionally large sex objects inside them.

If they cried or showed fear or pain then Rose would become more excited. The room also had a spy-hole where Fred could watch his wife engage in violent encounters with clients and others.

Shockingly, when Rose's father found out about her prostitution, he would regularly visit her to have sex with his own daughter. By 1983, Rose had given birth to eight children, some of them black, but they raised them as their own. It was clear that both Fred and Rose took to extreme levels of sexual perversity. It was this that resulted in the deaths of so many.

Fred West also collected VHS videos that showed bestiality and child abuse. It has always remained unclear how he was sourcing these types of tapes but they were surely a catalyst to even more crimes. Since the marriage in 1972, the sexual violence would increase. It became shocking to many that these level of crimes were going mostly unseen in what was a busy residential street.

All of the West's children were abused in some form or another. They took 'great care' not to mark the children's faces or hands when they assaulted them. Any admittance to hospitals were explained away as accidents and never reported. All the children witnessed the abuse inflicted on each other and regular sexual abuse became the norm.

Eight-year-old Anna Marie, Fred's daughter from another relationship, was dragged to the cellar of 25 Cromwell Street and had her clothes torn off. She was tied naked to a mattress and gagged before Fred raped her as Rose egged him on.

"Everybody does it to every girl. It's a father's job. Don't say anything to anybody." - Rose West, to Anna Marie.

They would then sexually abuse Anna Marie at any time from then on, by tying her to various items of furniture and forcing her into degrading acts. Fred would rape her regularly and then force her to do her chores while wearing a mini-skirt adorned with adult sexual devices.

When Anna Marie was 13-years-old, she was forced to become a sex worker in 'Rose's Room' with Rose watching every encounter with clients in case Anna Marie revealed her true age. Anna Marie was only one of the children – others would suffer even worse fates at the hands of Fred and Rose.

"I made you, I can do what I like with you." – Fred West, to his daughters.

They killed 12 young women between them, mostly their daughters, or hitchhikers who ended up at the house. In 1987, they killed their daughter, Heather West, and buried her under the patio of their garden. Fred even put a wooden table over her makeshift grave, a table where he would have family dinners outside in the Summer. The other children didn't know their sister was beneath them as they dined.

It was the excavation of the patio after their arrest that led to multiple bodies and body parts being uncovered. The investigation found remains in the ground floor bathroom, multiple bodies in the cellar and a large number in the garden.

Each body had been heavily mutilated and had been subject to extremely violent sexual abuse before their deaths. They found severed limbs, a skull, knives and various bondage materials. Bizarrely, every one of the human remains were missing some of their bones, most notably; the phalange bones, which are generally considered to be the fingers.

Was this Fred's attempt at hiding their identity or was there something even more macabre at work? As he killed himself in prison on New Year's Day 1995, there is no way to know. Rose West remains alive to this day, incarcerated for the rest of her life. During his interviews, Fred West claimed to have killed 30 people. Since then, other crimes have been tentatively linked to him but have not been confirmed.

Rose West receives only one sole visitor; Anna Marie West. In 1999, Anna Marie attempted suicide but was saved by a friend. One of the West's sons; Stephen West, also attempted suicide in 2002. Later in 2004, Stephen was jailed for having sex with a 14-year-old girl. The West's horrific legacy continues to this day.

THE FACTS

Born: September 29th 1941 (Fred)/November 29th 1953 (Rose)

Active: 1967-1987 | Arrested: February 24th 1994 (Fred)/April 1994 (Rose)

Country: United Kingdom | Victims: 12+

AKA: House of Horrors | Sentence: Life imprisonment

Status: Fred (Died by suicide in 1995)/Rose (Incarcerated)

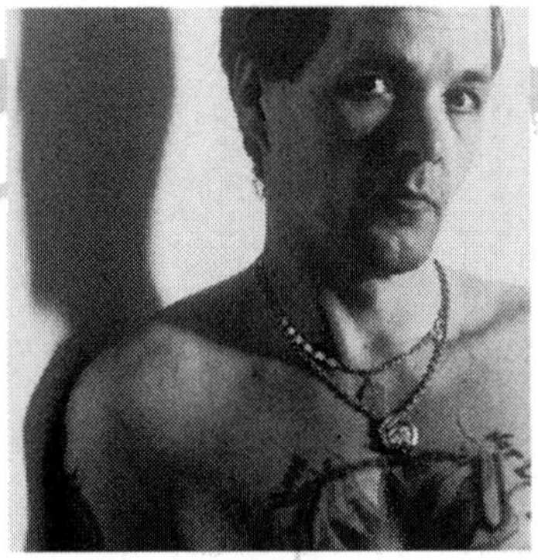

IMAGE ATTRIB. A31

JACK UNTERWEGER

IMAGE ATTRIBUTIONS
(ATTRIB A28) (ATTRIB A29A)
(ATTRIB A29B)

FRED AND ROSE WEST

Wilken, Stewart: The Boetie Boer

In Port Elizabeth, South Africa, serial killer Stewart Wilken AKA: The Boetie Boer, racked up a body count of at least 10 victims over a seven year period from 1990 until 1997. His victims ranged from female sex workers to young boys. He also engaged in necrophilia and cannibalism.

He murdered the son of his second wife and engaged in sexual acts with the corpse. Another victim had her nipples sliced off, and Wilken ate them. It is unclear whether he cooked them first. When he was six-months-old, in 1967, Wilken and his two-year-old sister were abandoned by their parents in a telephone booth. They were found by a house maid who took them to the home of her employer.

The man then abused Wilken in the most horrific of ways. He burned him with cigarettes, forced him to eat from a bowl on the floor, and then forced him to engage in sexual acts with his dogs. It is unclear what became of Wilken's sister. On September 29th 1995, Wilken killed his daughter from his first marriage. He claimed that his daughter had suffered sexual abuse from her stepdad, so Wilken had decided to save her soul by killing her, enabling her to go to Heaven.

On May 22nd 1996, the skeletal remains of a young girl were discovered beneath a blue tarpaulin, behind a Holiday Inn. At the time of the discovery, the girl couldn't be identified and it wouldn't be until Wilken showed police where he had hidden the bodies, that an identification could be made. The girl's identity has remained protected ever since.

Three days after the discovery, Wilken picked up 22-year-old sex worker, Katriena Claassen. He took her down to the shoreline where she provided him with her services. Afterwards, Wilken shoved a plastic bag down her throat and strangled her. He then raped her, before killing her and dumping her body on the beach.

Wilken was arrested in 1997 and convicted a year later on seven counts of murder. Three additional murders were not tried but he was confirmed to have killed them. He was handed down a life sentence for each of the convicted murders and remains incarcerated to this day.

THE FACTS

Born: November 11th 1966 | Active: 1990-1997

Arrested: January 31st 1997 | Country: South Africa

Victims: 10+ | AKA: The Boetie Boer

Sentence: Seven life sentences | Status: Incarcerated

Wood, Catherine & Graham, Gwendolyn

American medical serial killer couple Gwendolyn Gail Graham and Catherine May Wood killed five elderly patients in Michigan, in 1987. They worked at as nurse's aides at the Alpine Manor nursing home, where they killed all their victims. They fell in love in 1986 when they both met at the nursing home. Graham had recently moved from Texas.

Wood ended up testifying against Graham in order to gain a reduced plea but it has long been suspected that Wood was the mastermind and instigator of the murders. In January 1987, an elderly victim was killed when the couple smothered her with a small towel. Until their arrest in 1988, the five deaths later attributed as murders, were considered to have been the result of natural causes.

The first murder became a blood pact for the couple which in effect prevented the other partner from leaving due to their joint guilt. In 1987, a total of five elderly people were killed by the couple, most of the victims suffered from Alzheimer's. Wood portrayed Graham to be sexually and physically dominant and would turn the murders into a game. It was claimed that they took souvenirs from their victims but none were ever recovered.

They split up when Graham cheated on her with another nurse at the nursing home, before moving back to Texas. In 1988, Wood's ex-husband went to the police based on stories he'd heard Wood talking about. Both Graham and Wood were arrested and sent to trial.

Graham had secretly confessed to her new girlfriend, who testified against her. She was convicted of five murders and handed down five life sentences without the possibility of parole. As of 2022, Graham remains incarcerated in a Women's Correctional Facility in Michigan. Wood was charged with second-degree murder and conspiracy to commit murder. She was sentenced to 20 years but remained incarcerated until 2020.

She walked free from prison on January 16th 2020 after being granted parole. It has been claimed that Wood was the mastermind behind all the murders and was a pathological liar who could manipulate people to do her bidding. One suggested she had set up Graham in revenge for leaving her. Wood's whereabouts are currently known only to relevant law enforcement agencies.

THE FACTS

Born: March 7th 1962 (Wood), August 6th 1963 (Graham) | Active: 1987

Arrested: December 1988 | Country: USA | AKA: The Lethal Lovers

Victims: 5 | Sentence: Graham (life)/Wood (20 years)

Status: Graham (Incarcerated)/Wood (Released in 2020)

Woodcock, Peter

Peter Woodcock was a Canadian serial killer and paedophile who claimed the lives of three young children in Toronto in the 1950s. He claimed a fourth murder victim in 1991 when he was given a one-day release from a psychiatric hospital. It is claimed he abused and raped up to 50 children before he murdered the first three.

Born in 1939, he called himself David Michael Krueger but was born Peter Woodcock and lived in various children's homes as an infant before he was adopted at age three. Even by that age, it was clear that Woodcock was suffering from severe emotional trauma and was difficult throughout his childhood years.

When he was 17, on September 15th 1956, he lured seven-year-old Wayne Mallette to his death before leaving his body in the open. Woodcock had defecated beside the victim's body. Three weeks later, on October 6th, he abducted nine-year-old Gary Morris and killed him on Cherry Beach by strangling him to death and leaving bite marks on his throat.

The third child victim was on January 19th 1957 when Woodcock abducted four-year-old Carole Voyce. The cause of death was a tree branch inserted deep into her vagina. He was arrested and charged with Voyce's murder but was found not guilty by reason of insanity and committed to a maximum-security psychiatric hospital.

34 years later, in 1991, Woodcock was granted a one-day release from hospital, and within one hour of being outside the hospital walls, he beat to death another hospital inmate, Dennis Kerr, after meeting him in nearby woods. He mutilated the body, severed the head and had sex with the corpse, before turning himself into a police station. He was sent back to the maximum-security hospital and remained within its walls until his death in 2010. He was claimed to be the 'serial killer they couldn't cure'.

THE FACTS

Born: March 5th 1939 | Active: 1956-1991

Arrested: 1957 | Country: Canada

Victims: 4 | AKA: David Michael Krueger

Sentence: Institutionalised | Status: Died in 2010

Yapicioglu, Yavuz: The Screwdriver Killer

In Turkey, Yavuz Yapıcıoğlu, AKA: The Screwdriver Killer, was a serial killer said to hold the highest body count of any serial murderer in the country. Between 1994 and 2002, he killed at least 18 people, mostly by way of arson, but was suspected of killing up to 40 people.

After a troubled childhood, Yapıcıoğlu left home at a young age and dropped out of school shortly after due to an argument he had with his parents. By all accounts, he was an intelligent child who hit the highest grades in school. After many failed businesses, he joined a religious cult in Istanbul, searching for his place in the world. He began to lash out at people and quickly became aggressive towards others.

In 1994, he stabbed three people to death after one of them supposedly wished him a good morning. He was arrested shortly after and committed to a psychiatric hospital. While there, he attacked fellow patients and nurses, and then set his ward on fire. After a short while, he was discharged and then killed six more people in a manner of weeks, in the same year.

He then burned his brothers shop to the ground for not lending him money, then burned two of his relative's homes to the ground. He then attacked his father and killed his grandmother with an ashtray. His mother had a heart attack upon hearing that her son had killed her mother.

After being arrested again, he was committed to the same hospital, where he was discharged yet again after only a year. Upon his discharge, he killed three more people with a screwdriver and then drove to a neighbouring town to murder a night guard with the same screwdriver.

Finally, in 2002, he was arrested yet again, and this time was found criminally liable for the murders. This meant he was convicted and sentenced to life in prison. As of 2022, he remains in a Turkish prison without the possibility of parole and will likely stay there until his death.

THE FACTS

Born: 1967 | Active: 1994-2002

Arrested: 2002 | Country: Turkey

Victims: 18-40+ | AKA: The Screwdriver Killer

Sentence: Life imprisonment | Status: Incarcerated

Yates, Robert Lee: The Spokane Serial Killer

Yates, sometimes known as The Spokane Serial Killer, was a Washington-based serial killer who claimed the lives of at least 15 sex workers between 1975 and 1998. 13 were killed in Washington, and another two were murdered in Walla Walla and Skagit County.

Born in 1952, he was raised in a middle-class family and had a happy childhood. He joined the U.S. Army in 1977 and served in Somalia and Haiti. While on leave, he would murder sex workers who worked along Spokane's East Sprague Avenue. He would do drugs with some of them in his van then kill them and dump their bodies in rural locations.

He shot dead all of his victims with a bullet to the head, and eight were killed with the same gun, which later proved instrumental in his capture and conviction. He left the Army in 1997 and joined the Army National Guard just three years before his arrest in April 2000.

He was initially sentenced to death for two of the murders but his defence appealed a new plea bargain where Yates would receive an all-encompassing life sentence if he pleaded guilty to the other 13 murders. The death sentence was later commuted to life and Yates currently remains incarcerated for the murders of 15 women.

THE FACTS

Born: May 27th 1952 | Active: 1975-1998.

Arrested: April 18th 2000 | Country: USA

Victims: 15 | AKA: The Spokane Serial Killer

Sentence: Death penalty, commuted to life | Status: Incarcerated

Why Serial Killers Kill

This section contains a fascinating collection of exclusive research articles about the reasons why serial killers kill. It's a new study exploring the cultural, environmental, and societal reasons behind serial killings and violence. Always wanted to know WHY serial killers kill? Then you've found the right section for you.

What this section is not:

A detailed account of an individual serial killer, focusing on their childhood and formative years to ascertain why they killed another human being. There are many books and biographies out there regarding specific serial killers. Though this study mentions serial killers by name, it does not go in depth into just one serial killer.

What this section is:

A journey through 80 pages of cultural, societal, and environmental reasons that may lead a person to commit serial murders. There will never be just one reason why a serial killer kills. But a combination of some of the reasons listed here might play a major part in the creation of a serial killer.

Some of the reasons are psychological, such as the impact of war, child abuse, and cultural attitudes. Other reasons are environmental and societal, such as the introduction of highways, urbanisation, victim selection, and pornography. They contribute to the ever-increasing opportunities afforded to those of a violent mind-set and enable them to act out on desires that may have remained dormant.

The study covers facts and statistics from the United States and United Kingdom, with a focus on the 20th and 21st Century. Parts of the book are hypothetically related to time periods beyond 2022, using 20th Century studies to predict a rise in serial killing from 2030. These are added here for context and additional information. See the full bibliography at the end of this book for all studies cited.

Highways to Hell

In the United Kingdom, in 1958, the Preston Bypass opened, it would become part of the M6 motorway. In 1959, the first full-length motorway; the M1, opened for traffic. The United Kingdom could almost be seen a microcosm for the United States.

You can drive from the South of England to the North of Scotland in approximately 14 hours if the roads are clear. By comparison, the United States is huge. Construction on the United States highway systems began in 1956. In an act of congress known as the Federal Aid Highway Act of 1956. As of 2019, over 25% of all miles used by vehicles, use the interstates. Construction carried on through the 1950s, 1960s, 1970s and beyond.

American society reorganised its culture around the highway and led to the new wave of the commuting lifestyle. Before the introduction of the highways, the road to work would have been long and winding roads that slowed economic evolution.

Psychologically, the Interstates opened up huge areas of land connecting places that were only tentatively connected before.

The rise of the Drifter Killer

As construction passed through urban areas, they would isolate communities and create physical ghettos. Sound barriers protected them from the noise of the roads but hid them as well, becoming isolated communities to the millions of drivers passing them by. There is an even more unfortunate dark side that came out of the interstates; it opened up the country to the drifter.

It allowed potential serial killers to widen their geographical catchment area. They didn't have to stay in their hometowns or States anymore and could just as easily drive to the next State over. Or even across the entire country if they wished.

By the 1970s, the free-love generation had landed. Hippies were the in-thing and peace was the pledge of the decade. There was more trust amongst people than there was for governments. War and Watergate had seen people move from politics to pop culture.

Although hitchhiking was banned in almost all of the United States, many people were still using it as a form of travel.

Hitchhiking became a new way to select victims

The more people that thumbed for rides on the country's interstates, the more potential victims there were for drifter killers.

Randy Kraft, The Scorecard Killer, would mostly dump his victims on the side of highways. He killed between 16 and 67 people from 1971 to 1983.

William Bonin, The Freeway Killer, would also dump his victim's bodies on the side of freeways. He killed at least 21 people from 1979 to 1980.

Jeffrey Dahmer, The Milwaukee Cannibal, would count hitchhikers among his victims. He killed 17 young men and boys between 1978 and 1991.

Gerald Stano, The Boardwalk Serial Killer, would prey on sex workers and hitchhikers. He killed at least 22 women from 1969 to 1980.

The Highways of Tears list is made public in 2007 by the Royal Canadian Mounted Police's E-Pana investigation. It is a task force set up to investigate the disappearances and murders of at least 18 girls and women along Vancouver Highways in a 40 year period from 1977. The FBI officially launched their Highway Serial Killing database in 2009.

Their investigation showed over 500 cases where bodies had been dumped on highways in the decades before. Up until 2016, the FBI suggested there were approximately 300 'highway serial killers' active in the United States.

In 2004, an analyst from the Oklahoma Bureau of Investigation detected a pattern of crime whereby the bodies of murdered women were being dumped along the Interstate 40 corridor in Oklahoma, Texas, Arkansas, and Mississippi.

The analyst linked the cases to the national ViCAP system (Violent Criminal Apprehension Program) and found similar patterns across the United States. The pattern was so obvious that the FBI launched an extensive effort to investigate them, hence the Highway Serial Killing Database.

The victims had a pattern:

- Primarily women.
- High risk lifestyle.
- Drug abuse.
- Prostitution or transients.
- Picked up at service stations or truck stops.
- Were sexually assaulted then killed.
- Dumped on or near a highway.

Life is made difficult for law enforcement because of various state boundaries that exist.

Project E-Pana: Highway of Tears

Project E-PANA was created in 2005 to review and investigate numerous unsolved murders on Highway 16, which became known as the Highway of Tears. The investigators chose the name of PANA as it is an Inuit word describing the spirit goddess who looks after souls before they go to heaven.

The task force was set up by the Royal Canadian Mounted Police (RCMP) with the exclusive purpose of solving cases of missing and murdered people along the Highway. Highway 16 runs between Prince Rupert and Prince George, two cities in British Columbia that are 446 miles (718 km) apart. After just one year from the formation of the project, the investigation expanded to include Highways 5, 24 and 97.

In 2006, the task force had nine active investigations on the books. A year later in 2007 they had doubled to 18. The cases being investigated were cold cases from 1969 to 2006 and because more murders were diluting the investigation, they created a specific set of rules. These rules allowed them to focus on specific cases in the region and meant they could be added to the project E-PANA list.

- Victims had to be female.
- Involved in hitchhiking or prostitution, or other high-risk behaviours.
- Last known location to be within a mile of the three major British Columbia highways; 5, 16 and 97.

This could have been the last time she was seen alive or where her body had been found. Cases where evidence pointed to a stranger having committed the crime rather than a domestic attack or accident.

The E-Pana murder victim list

October 1969 – 26-year-old Gloria Moody – Last seen leaving a bar in Williams Lake. Her body was found in the woods at a cattle ranch six miles away.

July 1973 – 18-year-old Micheline Pare – Last seen beside the gates of Tompkins Ranch near Hudson's Hope. Two women had previously dropped her off there. Her body was found in the area in August 1973.

October 1973 – 19-year-old Gale Weys – She vanished while hitchhiking from Clearwater to Kamloops. Body was found in a ditch on Highway 5 just south of Clearwater. Suggested to have been a victim of serial killer Bobby Jack Fowler.

November 1973 – 19-year-old Pamela Darlington – Vanished from Kamloops while hitchhiking to a local bar. Her body was found the next day. Suggested to have been a victim of serial killer Bobby Jack Fowler.

December 1974 – 14-year-old Monica Ignas – last seen walking home alone from school. Her remains were found in April 1975, hidden in a dense forest. She had been strangled to death.

August 1974 – 16-year-old Colleen MacMillen – her body was discovered in September 1974. She was last seen leaving her home to hitchhike to a nearby friend's house. DNA evidence matched Bobby Jack Fowler to the murder who was also working in the area at the time.

May 1978 – 12-year-old Monica Jack – In one of the more well-known crimes in the area, Monica was last seen riding her bike near her home. Her disappearance remained a mystery until her skeletal remains were found by forestry workers in 1995. Serial murderer *Garry* Taylor Handlen was charged with her death along with another 11-year-old girl. On January 18th 2019, Handlen was finally convicted.

May 1981 – 33-year-old Maureen Mosie – She had been hitchhiking from Salmon Arm to Kamloops when she disappeared. Her body was found the next day by a woman walking her dog. She had been beaten to death.

August 1989 – 24-year-old Alberta Williams – Her body was discovered a month later, just over 20 miles east of Prince Rupert. She had been raped and strangled to death.

June 1994 – 16-year-old Ramona Wilson – She was hitchhiking from Smithers to stay with friends in Hazelton but she vanished. Her remains were discovered in April 1995 near the Smithers Airport. Several items were in a small, organized pile a few feet away from her, these included a section of rope, three interlocking ties and a small pink water pistol.

July 1994 – 15-year-old Roxanne Thiara – A sex worker who went missing in Prince George. She told her friend she was going off with a customer and she was never heard of again. Her body was found a month later in a bush along Highway 16. She was friends with the next victim on the list.

December 1994 – 15-year-old Alishia Germaine – Her body was found behind an elementary school outside of Prince George, just off Highway 16. She had been stabbed to death and was friends with Roxanne Thiara who had been killed a few months earlier. They had been seen working together multiple times before their deaths.

February 2006 – 14-year-old Aielah Saric Auger – Her body was discovered in a ditch on Highway 16, just a few days after she went missing.

The E-Pana missing persons list

1983 – 17-year-old Shelley-Anne Bascu – Vanished in 1983 and her body has never been discovered. However, personal items such as clothing and blood matching her blood type were found beside the Athabasca River. She is still officially a missing person's case.

June 1990 – 16-year-old Delphine Nikal – She had been hitchhiking from Smithers in an Easterly direction when she vanished. The teenager's body has never been discovered and she is a missing person's case to this day.

October 1995 – 19-year-old Lana Derrick – She was last spotted getting into a car with two unidentified men, at a service station in Thornhill. She has been missing ever since and no sign of a body has ever been found.

June 2002 – 24-year-old Nicole Hoar – in a similar fashion to the others, she was last seen hitchhiking to Smithers. She had been spotted at a service station just west of Prince George. An investigation suspected convicted murderer Leland Vincent Switzer. A search was carried out on his property but they found no sign of any human remains. Hoar has been missing ever since.

September 2005 – 22-year-old Tamara Chipman – She was last seen in Prince Rupert and had been hitchhiking east on Highway 16. As of 2022, no sign of her has ever been found and she remains a missing person.

As of 2022, only one murder has been solved and that was the infamous death of 12-year-old Monica Jack. Serial murderer, Garry Taylor Handlen was charged with her murder and the death of another 11-year-old girl.

American serial killer Bobby Jack Fowler was linked with DNA evidence to the murder of 16-year-old Colleen MacMillen. Fowler had also been working in the area at the time. He has also been linked with a number of other E-Pana investigations and is the prime suspect in the murders of Gale Weys and Pamela Darlington.

In 2012, they used the advancement in DNA technology to positively identify him in the murder of MacMillen. The Royal Canadian Mounted Police strongly believe that he was responsible for at least 10 of the other victims on the list. However, many more murders took place after his arrest in 1995, when he was picked up on a rape charge.

As Fowler died in prison in 2006, the investigation of his suspected murders has been made more difficult. Since 2010, the E-Pana investigation has lost 58 officers, dropping from 70 at its peak, to just 12. This has been due to budget cuts for the E-Pana caseloads. As of 2022, all cases are still active.

Cheap Travel and Open Borders

Back in the 1950s, the construction of the interstates and highways in the United States, and motorways in the United Kingdom, connected cities easily for the first time.

By the 1970s, the highways allowed the drifter killer to navigate easily between populous areas, finding possible victims along the way. In essence it created a surge in hitchhiking and a massive rise in cross-state serial killing.

Jump forward to the early 2020s and it's not just the cities in each country that are well connected, the entire world has opened up.

International travel is for everyone

As a foot passenger, you can travel from Portsmouth in the United Kingdom to Cherbourg-Octeville in France for around $40 (£30). From France you can catch buses or trains to every region of Europe and beyond.

If you book at the right time, you can pick up a flight from London to New York for $300 (£225). Travel has never been easier. Even in the 1990s, countries like

Cambodia, Vietnam and Laos were virtually off-limits, now you can get a package holiday from a high street shop.

You can go to Everest Base Camp for the price you used to pay for two weeks on the coast of Spain. Holidays used to be week-long torments in a caravan to Great Yarmouth or Blackpool. Now they're cheap flights and comparison sites.

If serial killers saw opportunity in the creation of the highway systems then they are more than likely seeing larger opportunities with the connection of the entire world. It wouldn't be difficult for someone to take a domestic or international flight, spend a few days indulging their fantasies, and then head back home as if nothing had happened.

Sex tourism and the new wave

Sex tourism has become a thing and since doing so it has increased exponentially. The Thai sex trade mostly makes its money from white westerners. Sex-tourism forums are some of the most popular adult forums out there.

Some of them include questions such as; why would a white man fight for a woman back home when he could have petite tanned girls on tap for the price of a DVD? There are even sites where men rate and review worldwide sex workers and escorts in the same way one might review a show.

The world in 2022 has afforded more opportunity than ever before for someone to act on their dark thoughts and fantasies through the internet or real-life access. Maybe there is a link between the supposed decline of the serial killer because of this easily accessible fantasy fulfilment.

> *'Sex tourism is, consequently, a complex concept and goes far beyond the immediate images of men travelling to the far east or the red light district of Amsterdam for sexual gratification from sex workers or children.' - Carol Jones from the 'center of crime and justice studies'*

Some have suggested that serial killers have not declined. The data shows this because they might have evolved with different methods and new ways of disposing of bodies. The more connected the world is, the easier it might be for a potential serial killer to plan their next victim.

Attitudes towards females in the 1970s

A 2015 study of serial killers showed that:

- 75% of male serial killers, kill because of sexual motives and gratification.
- 49% of male serial killers exclusively hunt women.

There is a branch of science known as evolutionary psychology. The argument is that humans have been evolving over such a huge amount of time that the human brain, genetics, and functions have become accustomed to a paternal ancestral society. It is said to be highly likely that these factors still genetically influence us in the modern era.

It is no surprise that male serial killers generally kill women. Females are generally weaker than men and make for an easier victim choice and men have the biological ability to reproduce in far greater quantities than women. Biologically, a female desires a mate for a lot longer time than a male desires a mate. It is in a male's nature to seek multiple mates to reproduce. This is scientific biology, caused by evolution.

Cultural and societal change from the middle of the 20th Century

Heading into the 1970s, it was all about to change, and rightfully so. The women's rights movement was a long overdue and needed societal evolutionary change. Yet it had varying effects on some men in the decade and the decades that followed. The women's rights movements of the 1970s moved forward at a frenetic pace. Overcoming sexism, free access to legal abortion, challenging oppression and seeking equality.

The 1970s marked the 50th anniversary of the women's right to vote in various Western countries including the United States and United Kingdom. So there was a large celebration of the movement and a push for greater rights for women. The country of Oman only passed a law that women could vote in 2003, so there's clearly still a long way to go to reach equality.

Feminism, as it would come to be known, had landed at the small end of the 1970s in a big way. This, combined with the flower power movement, put women in the limelight, more than they ever had been before. The movement led to many female-powered political organisations.

- National Organization for Women (NOW) (1966)
- National Women's Political Caucus (1971)
- Equal Rights Amendment Ratification Council (1973)
- Coalition of Labor Union Women (1973)

The above were just some of the more well-known ones in the United States alone.

Challenged men took offence to the notion that women should be equal

Some men, because of their upbringing or abuse traumas from childhood, began to take offence to the notion that women should be equal. More sexual attacks had begun to take place, more killings were occurring, and a hidden divide between men and women began to open.

One researcher claims that it was women's fault that more violent crime was recorded against women from the 1970s. I argue it was in the shallow-mindedness of some males that they were not able to accept that women should be equal to men.

Serial killers make up a ridiculously small percentage of murders in most countries. So to fear a serial killer is based on stories that have been spoken about them.

Generally in the UK, you're more likely to die by suicide or drug-related deaths. In the United States, you're more likely to die by gang-violence or firearms. Those deaths remain separate from the ones caused by serial killers.

Females were seen as possessions

Serial killers have been a loud epidemic since the 1970s. The fascination began to slow down in the 1990s but it's coming back in a bigger way than before.

A 2018 documentary entitled Conversations with a Killer, with Ted Bundy, offered up some telling quotes. He would say he loved women and indeed, loved his mother, which is an anomaly amongst serial murderers.

In one scene he appeared to be helping profile his own murders. Bundy tended to refer to himself in the third person, either as way of disassociating from the crimes or allaying responsibility.

'A person of this type chooses his victims for a reason. His victims are young, attractive women. Women are possessions. Beings which are subservient, more often than not, to males. Women are merchandise.'

In another section, he focused on the sexual aspect of his crimes which was something he rarely spoke of.

'Sex has significance, only in the context of a much broader scheme of things. That is possession, control, and violence.'

Subservient females, women as possessions, and control; the very factors that the feminist movement had been trying to change. It appeared that serial killers in the 1970s and even in modern times, still see women as objects to be controlled, rather than being equal to men.

Feminism was viewed by some as a threat to masculinity

Females suddenly had access to education and careers that were once exclusively for men. Suddenly these females had become rivals for someone like Bundy and others like him. It seemed that the one true threat to masculinity was a female of equal, or superior status. Ted Bundy's feelings of inferiority meant that he needed to have relationships with women and destroy others he was not in a relationship with.

His variable love and hate for women in equal measure, was reflected in a larger cultural misunderstanding that only certain females were worthy of a man's love. In

Bundy's case, he held his mother in high esteem and those who he was in a relationship with.

A certain level of misogyny tends to be present in serial killers. It also holds the notion that a worthy woman could just as easily become unworthy. Bundy handled the threat of a move to unworthiness by killing surrogate females, standing in for those who he deemed worthy.

Attitudes towards females in the 21st Century

From the start of the 21st Century, and especially now in 2022, there has been a growing perverse view of women from some men due to easily accessible porn and other factors. The feminist movements of the late 1960s and 1970s had their impact for many reasons already discussed. But it was nothing compared to the rise of girl-power and social media hashtag campaigns where men were constantly accused of saying the wrong thing.

Observing something like this from a psychological perspective is harder than one might imagine. It has to be reiterated that this is only an exceedingly small percentage of men but it is a growing percentage nonetheless and needs to be made known.

Women now make up more CEO positions than ever before and some state it's still not enough. The balance of power from men to women had been swaying ever since the mid-20th Century feminist movement kicked off. Female-focused pop groups such as the Spice Girls, kicked off the new wave of feminism and media-centric girl power.

The psychological damage of violent pornography

When combined with easy access to violent pornography and the proliferation of girl-power, some men focused their perverse attentions on their growing hate of women.

Misogyny returned ten-fold, if it hadn't entirely gone to begin with. Stories of presidents making degrading remarks and white men feeling like a minority hit the headlines.

Serial killers are mostly men and their victims are usually female, in around three-quarters of cases. It's no coincidence as to why; males are generally stronger than women and have the means with which to overpower their victims. From a study entitled 'Sexual violence as a sexual script in mainstream online pornography.'

> *'We found that one in eight titles shown to first-time users on the first page of mainstream porn sites describe sexual activity that constitutes sexual violence. Our findings raise serious questions about the extent of criminal material easily and freely available on mainstream pornography websites and the efficacy of current regulatory mechanisms.'*

Females are the most vulnerable of serial killer victims. Though it's not to say that men are not also killed, as is shown in the many serial killings of gay man throughout history.

Misogynistic attitudes towards women

Though it's not the only factor, it is something to be included when looking at the overall reasons as to why serial killers kill. Ted Bundy, himself, said that women were possessions to be controlled, and he wasn't the only one to think it.

Just as the rise of the feminist movement in the 1970s gave a reason for some men to kill, so might the recent rise of girl-power and hashtag campaigns do the same in the digital age. All of this is to do with anger at females who seem to be claiming power from men. In part, for serial killers, this might be due to some inadequacy they have received from a female in their life, either from their mothers or a partner.

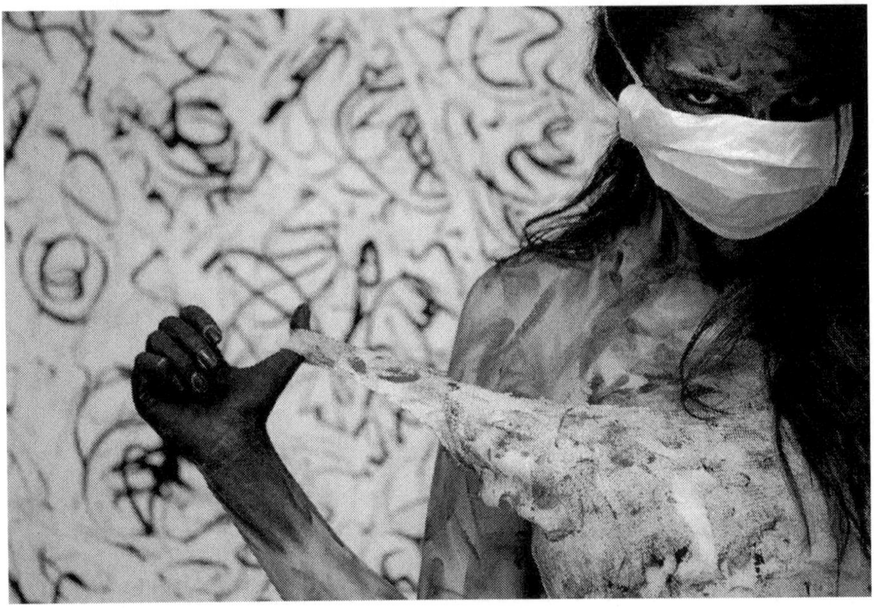

'One study found a positive association between men's pornography use and physical and sexual violence perpetration.'

The rise of female prominence in both eras then suggests that some serial killers will use this as a catalyst to bring their dark fantasies to life if they're not already.

Child Abuse from the 1940s-1960s

We look at this time period because the most active era of serial killers was in the 1970s and 1980s, when children born from the 1940s were becoming adults. One of the most difficult areas to research has been the data surrounding child abuse from the 1940s to 1960s. Generally this is considered during and after World War Two but pre-1970.

Most serial killers who were either active, caught, or started from 1970, were around the age of 30-years-old and were generally white males. As of 2022, an astonishing 90.8% of serial killers were white males.

Disconnected world of the mid-20th Century

Statistics show that most children are abused from the age of five-years-old and upwards for reasons including social, physical and cultural. In the disconnected world of the mid-20th Century, most child abuse cases never reached the attention of the authorities. It is reported that when they did, the response from welfare workers was mostly inadequate.

In the recent Northern Irish Historical Institutional Abuse Inquiry, a lot of information and data was sent out into the public domain. There seemed to be a lack of joined-up thinking and urgency up until the 1980s. This would have mostly been down to World War Two. Pre-1950, children who were abused were often depicted as unintelligent and slow in mind, as well as being sexually active themselves.

Children were placed into categories of sexual knowledge

Before World War Two, and for some time after, welfare workers tended to place children into categories of sexual knowledge. By doing so, most children then became culpable for eliciting abuse from adults. To think this was only recent history is astonishing enough, but that was only the tip of the iceberg.

In over 2,000 cases studied from 1927 to 1954, half the victims were under seven-years-old. Even then, they were not always portrayed as being the innocent party in the abuse. Less so if they were from a working class background.

In the British wartime evacuation of children from the cities, there had been a rise in young prostitution. This only served to move attention away from abuse. In another astonishing fact, during the evacuation of 827,000 children, only six psychiatric social workers were available during their removal.

Melinda J Waugh, from Plymouth University, wrote on the long-term impact of war experiences and evacuation on people who were children during World War Two:

> *'Significant numbers of the evacuees were found to have experienced abuse and neglect. Pre-evacuation abuse made continued abuse likely during evacuation, while abuse during evacuation led to children being more likely to continue to be abused on their return home.'*

It's obviously agreed that during wartime, there was a prevalence to have these kind of workers elsewhere. Yet, the chaos of World War Two on both sides of the Atlantic can never be underestimated. The following image shows evacuations from Brent Station in Devon, UK.

Social systems built around neglect

The Baby Boomer generation from 1946 to 1964 are also seen as being partially to blame for the rise and nonchalance regarding the abuse of children. Changes in social work and care saw a system that was open to neglect and abuse itself. Families were no longer being interviewed, especially foster parents and step-parents. Having young people in the workplace was still the way forward.

Those from impoverished backgrounds were even more at risk. Record keeping was few and far between and siblings were often separated in the years that followed the war. In the United States and across the Western world, there became a large focus on mother-child relationships. The main focus was the challenge of promoting marital bliss.

There was a commitment from governments to keep family members at home and families together in a projected harmony of circumstance. This meant that child abuse in all its forms was never seen as a good enough reason to remove that child from a family environment. In most cases there had deemed to be consent by the child.

Some did not understand the abuse was wrong, and others were indifferent to it happening. The downplay on post-war child abuse was obvious. They might as well have brushed any evidence of it under the carpet. Childhood abuse is one of the major factors when looking at why some people become serial killers.

The link between child abuse and serial killers

Childhood abuse throughout the 1950s and 1960s was generally being brushed aside. Disconnected authorities wrangled with families and the law, with most not knowing what needed to be done or even acknowledging it was taking place. There was more concern placed on the promiscuity of sexually active young people than there was for actual abuse. There was little interest in framing anyone as a victim of sexual abuse.

When child abuse was talked about in the 1950s and 1960s, it was generally regarded as delinquency or blamed on parents from foreign countries. The sexual abuse against young boys was even less talked about. There is a link between childhood abuse and those who go onto commit violent crimes. A 2005 report of 50 serial killers showed that 68% of serial killers suffered from childhood maltreatment of some kind.

It's important to understand what abuse is, as there are different ways of understanding it. The most common types are:

- **Physical abuse**: Violence and bullying towards another.
- **Sexual abuse**: Sexual violence and forced interaction with another.
- **Psychological abuse**: Emotional and controlling attitudes, along with neglect.

People make the obvious connection with sexual abuse in children as a precursor to later violence in adulthood and teen years. That's not always accurate but it has the evidence to back it up. In the same report, it was shown that 26% suffered sexual abuse and 35% suffered physical abuse. Half of everyone in the study suffered some type of psychological abuse from adults or older children.

Child abuse is generally common amongst serial killers but the results of the studies themselves are always brought into question. On one hand, an abused child may turn out violent, on the other hand, an abused child will grow up to be perfectly normal. How a child is raised, educated, and helped post-abuse, contributes to their adult behaviour.

A suspected 99% of child abuse went unreported before the 1980s

Most of the data is retrieved from third parties, who sometimes only have a tenuous connection to the serial killer in question. There is also the knowledge that a suspected 99% of child abuse went unreported before the 1980s. It still mostly goes unreported today.

Any study involving childhood abuse and serial killers draws only from substantiated reports from social workers. Thus the scale of child abuse throughout the 20th Century could potentially be monstrously high. Because child abuse from the post-war period was rarely recognised in the morally and lawful way we see it today, the information is not forthcoming.

Statistics on child abuse from the 1940s and all the way through the early 1970s are flawed. Data wasn't kept properly, victims were made to feel like victims, and any statistics that do come out of the period are mostly assumed to be the tip of an exceptionally large iceberg. More importantly, people kept getting away with it.

Control, betrayal, impulsion

Why were so many children abused during, after, and beyond World War Two? Most people ask why because they have a strong emotional connection to the question itself. The answer is not easy, the reasons are even harder.

It's especially important to note that these are common factors and should not be taken as overriding examples of those who might go on to abuse children. There are often more deeper factors involved.

- **Control**: A person who has control over a child might develop a sexual interest in them.
- **Betrayal**: They overcome the trust of the child and in doing so break down their own moral barriers in order to move to the next step.
- **Impulsion**: The abuser then acts on their sexual fantasies towards the child.

In understanding childhood sexual abuse, it is no way about forgiving the abusers. Every person that sexually, physically or psychologically abuses a child should rightfully be held accountable for their crimes.

Higher risk of developing violent tendencies as adults

We know that those abused in childhood have a higher risk of developing a tendency of violent acts in later life. This mostly happens when the person feels they have the required strength to overcome another human being.

We sometimes read that serial killers or violent people would hurt small animals as children, and there's psychological reasons for this. When a child is being abused, they suffer from many emotions, among them, and rarely talked about is anger. They feel as though they cannot fight back and become angry.

Due to their physical mass, they hurt animals or other children that are the same or smaller physical size than them. As they grow up, they are able to hurt older children. As adults, they have the strength to hurt other adults.

> *'Animal abuse does not always lead to violence toward humans, but points to an association between animal abuse and a host of antisocial behaviours, including violence.' - Arnold Arluke, North-eastern University*

Richard Trenton Chase, AKA: The Vampire of Sacramento was known to have hurt and killed small animals, even as an adult, which was a precursor to him killing people. Serial killers who were caught, active, or began killing in from 1970, would have been in the correct suggested age bracket for having suffered abuse in their childhood years from the 1940s.

It's important in the modern world of connectivity that we continue to collect and store data efficiently. NHS Digital is a prime example of where data collection is flawed and mostly incorrect. Collation and inter-agency correlation is utterly imperfect. The various Trusts in the NHS don't always share with other Trusts making the collation of data difficult and somewhat political. Without correct data, we will struggle for longer to understand the correlation between child abuse and violence in later life.

Serial killers who were abused as children

A small list of some of the serial killers who were abused as children.

Aileen Wuornos – abandoned, raped, and beaten – killed 7 people.

Albert DeSalvo – physical abuse – killed 13 people.

Albert Fish – tortured and beaten – killed 3 people, suggested over 100.

Andrei Chikatilo (previous page) – neglect and watched his four-year-old brother cannibalised – killed 53 people.

Anthony Sowell – beaten and abused – killed 11 people.

Carroll Cole – abused by mother – killed 16 people.

Donald Gaskins – neglected and raped – killed 9 people, claimed over 100.

Edmund Kemper – neglect and abuse – killed 10 people.

Gary Ridgway – neglect and abuse – killed 49 people.

Henry Lee Lucas – abused and beaten – killed 11 people, claimed over 600.

Jerome Henry Brudos – abused and beaten – killed 4 people.

John George Haigh – kept confined and abused – killed 9 people.

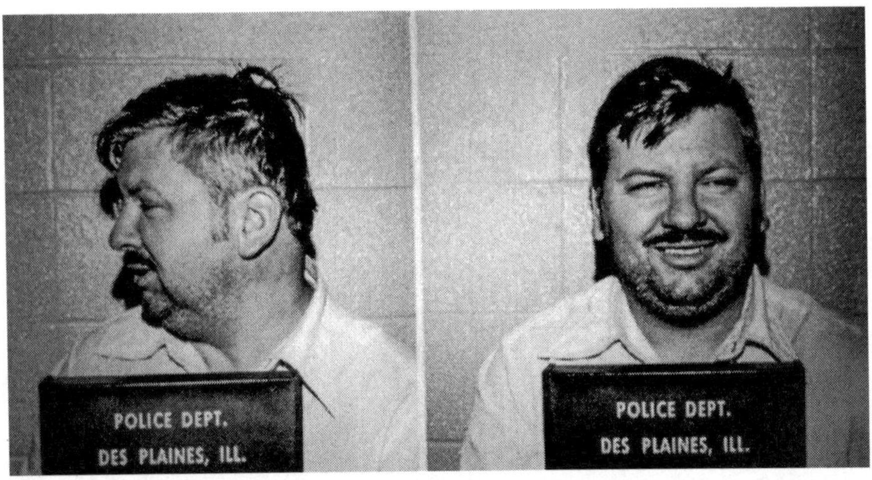

John Wayne Gacy (above) – abused by father – killed 33 people.

Mary Bell – put into sex work by her mother – killed 2 boys.

Pedro Filho – beaten by father – killed 71 people.

Pedro Lopez – raped and abused – killed 80 people, suggested over 300.

Richard Ramirez – beaten and neglected – killed 13 people.

Richard Trenton Chase – beaten by parents – killed 6 people and cannibalised some of their remains.

Child Abuse from the 1990s to 2000s

The decades that followed the 1980s had a lot to deal with. The satanic ritual claims of media and investigators led many to believe that evil cults were rampaging across the world. An astonishingly large number of people believed the cults were taking children and abusing them or even sacrificing them to the dark lord himself.

In an exceedingly small amount of cases, there had been elements of ritual abuse but generally they were considered rare.

> *'The number of children and adults tortured in the name of mainstream religious orthodoxy historically outweighs onslaught by Satanists.' - Valerie Sinason, Treating Survivors of Satanist Abuse*

Unfortunately, this led to some police forces and departments scaling back on claims of child abuse that cited ritual elements. Yet, unbelievably, child abuse has been on the increase ever since.

The internet created a haven for paedophiles

Some people look back at the 1950s to 1980s as having the largest number of cases of child abuse. Sadly, that's not true. There has been one ruling factor from the late 1990s that has led to the current increase; the internet.

Because of the media-led satanic revelations and charges of false memories amongst children, the child protection movement developed serious setbacks. Threats were sky-high and it was about the time that people began locking their doors a little more often. There was a constant and seeping doubt when accusations of parental abuse or abuse from strangers were reported. The threats were piling up but the authorities were struggling to play catch-up.

We can look back on this period with hindsight and discover paedophile rings that run to the highest levels of government (British), media (BBC), charity organisations

(Oxfam), and religion (Catholic Church). It was almost as if certain organisations were secretly blocking investigations into child abuse, and by all accounts they might well have been.

New laws were dropping in all over the world; Megan's Law in the USA, and Sarah's Law in the UK. They were both child sex-offender disclosure schemes brought about due to high-profile cases on both sides of the pond. Although it appeared that actually gaining information on offenders by concerned parents was not as easy as it seemed. The internet created a perfect haven for paedophiles.

The dark web and a 1,000% rise in child abuse cases

Hundreds of thousands of cases across the United States and United Kingdom were reported. Mostly involving children who had been groomed using internet forums and chat services. The subsequent public unveiling of the Tor network (which made the dark web accessible) saw images and videos of child pornography proliferate computers and hard drives with millions of images.

It has been suggested if the media had never run stories on the dark web then it would have remained more underground than it currently is. As soon as media outlets started talking about it, the masses discovered it when it could have remained hidden away. It led the curious to seek them out and the already disturbed to placate their own desires.

Large sting operations went into place but only a small fraction were ever caught. To this day, the UK-based CEOP (Child Exploitation and Online Protection Command) have warned of huge increases in paedophilia due to the proliferation and distribution of images online.

From the 1950s to the 1980s, the criminals and perverts used to have to physically seek out hard copies of images, thereby putting themselves at obvious risk of being caught. mToday, these offenders can access databases of images at the click of a button, on any device, anywhere in the world.

Even with all the laws and knowledge that was spreading through the new world, reports of abuse in developed countries was increasing exponentially from the 1990s onwards. In Japan, it was shown there was a 1000% increase in child abuse cases from 1990 to 2000.

Some priests claimed child abuse was acceptable

From the late 1990s and right up until 2022, the Roman Catholic church has been embroiled in a scandal involving the sexual abuse of children and young teens by priests.

'For decades, the Catholic church's failure to tackle child sexual abuse consigned many more children to the same fate. It is clear that the church's reputation was valued above the welfare of victims, with allegations ignored and perpetrators protected.' - Professor Alexis Jay, head of the catholic church abuse enquiry.

Tens of thousands of cases have been brought against the church across the world and still it carries on. The Pope astonishingly blamed it on 'Satan' and 'the 1960s'. One Australian priest claimed child abuse was acceptable as per the laws of the bible. This belief was held by a number of priests who came out in support of their brethren.

In the present day, there is the belief and knowledge that children are widely subject to physical and sexual abuse and it's not going away any time soon. As population increases and more people discover their dark desires online then the abuse will continue. The interest in child abuse is claimed to have been one of the most significant developments of the 1990s, leading in to the 2000s.

Child abuse is one of the reasons why someone might go on to kill

What we do know is that child abuse can sometimes lead their victims to violent crime in their teens or early adulthood. And some, as we've already learned from the data provided in the 1970s, go on to become serial killers.

We've looked at child abuse from the 1940s as one of the driving factors of the increase in serial killers in the 1970s and 1980s. If we use the same principle in today's world, then the huge increase in child abuse from 1990s to 2010s will also have an effect on violent crime from 2020.

That the abuse was rife and more common from the 1990s shows that there may be a rise of serial killing from around the 2030 mark. Though this is all conjecture, a rise in violent crime is a big possibility. Until child abuse and paedophilia can be eradicated from the world, we should look to psychological methods to help those affected by it.

Urban Strangers & Disconnected Living

In 1900, only 15% of the world's population lived in cities. According to the United Nations (UN), in 2018, 55% of the world's population lived in cities. As the cities grew in size it was suggested that crime was an unwanted side effect of urbanisation.

When more people live closer to each than before, meaning the cities instead of rural areas, there is a higher link with crime. In fact, urbanisation and crime go hand and hand and there are particularly good reasons for that. The higher the density of population, the higher the opportunity there is for crime.

Committing crime in cities is generally easier than it is in rural areas. Even covering a city with CCTV doesn't seem to make a difference because the population is much larger than before. An increase in population density is one of the reasons why serial killers kill because there are more victims to choose from.

The modernisation of urban areas has led to a rise in crime because more of the areas have become associated with income gap division. The working class are more likely to find themselves in highly urbanised areas than those of a middle or upper class.

Within these highly urbanised areas, we find that crime is more evident than in the richer areas. This is a consequence of urbanisation and serial killers became quite aware of that fact, taking advantage of urbanisation to their violent benefit.

Inequality, Population Density, Police Funding, and Unemployment

Urban centres have been around since the dawn of human civilisation. It's evidenced that people will always strive to be part of communities as our species are known as social animals. Except, the communities of 10,000 BC and the urban communities of the 1970s were vastly different in their structure and design. It's difficult to see any similarity beyond the point that both have humans in their societies.

Some of the reasons for more crime in urban areas are income inequality, population density per square mile, police fatigue, police funding and unemployment rates.

The talk of communities and neighbourhood groups within urban areas is honourable but are rarely cohesive or connected enough to prevent the rise of crime. The very presence of crime only serves to influence more crime. The image below is of Tokyo Skytree, in Sumida-ku, Japan. Metro population: 37.4 million.

This type of urbanisation is part of the modern area. There were cities thousands of years ago but population increases saw a wide-ranging change to the fundamental structure of their existence. The council estates and projects from the middle of the Twentieth Century were far more conducive to crime than those at the beginning of human history.

Projects, council estates and any area with a high population density allows for an unprecedented level of anonymity. Potential anonymity leads to more crime and might result in murders. A serial killer can take advantage of populous urban environments and exploit them to bring their own dark thoughts into reality.

The creation of the urban stranger

Before modern times, people tended to know one another by name. Communities were tighter and you would have known the family name of everyone in your settlement. People knew each other's routines, family history and personal details. Strangers, as rare as they were, were hardly ever encountered and when they were, they were met with fear and wariness.

A thousand years ago, one might have only seen a hundred or so strangers in their entire lives. In modern times, you could come across hundreds, if not thousands, on the streets of a city or on the journey to work. We live now amongst the urban stranger. We have no idea who is sitting opposite us on the train, we don't know who is in front or behind us in the queue of a supermarket.

Some people feign niceties so that they move on quicker with their own isolated existence. We don't always wish to know someone's name or routines, it puts us in the firing line for modern-day repercussions. We have to worry about saying the wrong thing to someone we don't know for fear of reprisal, unwarranted or not.

Urbanisation hasn't brought communities together, it has allowed strangers to live in their own worlds, sometimes right next door or in the flat above. We don't know anything about them and for the most part we don't wish too.

As population increases and people live longer, urban areas are becoming more packed than ever before and it will continue on an upward curve for as long as humans exist on the planet. There's no halting the bandwagon of evolution, we will continue to expand our numbers at the detriment of our own future and safety.

Serial killers usually prey on strangers, urban areas have provided them with a constant flow of what they need. It gives them with an ideal setting to act on their violent or perverse desires.

As the world changes and moves towards more privacy than ever before, some people are deliberately cutting themselves off from the world, not wishing to participate in social media or internet use. This in turn provides more victims for the potential serial killer. Just as in the 1970s when urbanisation was forcing the world into a new era.

Future of disconnected living

Loneliness or isolation are one of the biggest factors that lead to mental health disorder or suicidal ideation. It also allows some people to harvest their dark thoughts and subsequently see them in action. Some serial killers have spoken of isolation as one of their largest mitigating factors, and of course, most serial killers murder in isolation.

Skip back to the 1970s and video games were few and far between, sometimes only reserved for the better-off in society. Jump forward to 2021 and gaming is one of the biggest industries on Earth. Give it another decade and many will be using virtual reality as often as they use the internet, in fact both might be intertwined.

Skip forward a decade from now - the internet will have more control over our daily lives, and mobile devices will soon be able to access the internet wherever we go in the world. We will order anything we want from a phone and have it delivered to anywhere we need. High streets will be empty and bricks and mortar shops will be no more.

We will stream the latest films and music to any device in the home. There will be no need to even order physical media, no reason to go out and leave the house. We talk through microphones to people all over the planet who we meet in virtual worlds but we don't really know who they are.

'The internet brought the world together – and then allowed people to live in isolation without ever leaving their homes.' - Maika Elan, plight of hermits.

A decade from now, social media will have become more prevalent, taking over face to face interactions for the first time. We're interviewed online, befriended, loved or hated. We shop, download, stream and interact.

Disconnected living becomes the norm and we focus more on the inverted unreal world of The Net than we do with reality. Apply that thesis to one of an already disconnected mindset then the results can and will be devastating.

Hate is within easy reach with no real censorship

Porn, violence, extremism, occult activity, terrorism, brutal imagery, hate, all are within easy reach with no real censorship. The governments of the world might attempt to put a stop to it but it's not going to slow down people seeking it out.

The British Government implemented a soft ban on hardcore BDSM with the Audio-visual Media Services Regulations act of 2014. It included bans on spanking, face-sitting, humiliation, BDSM, and other acts deemed not fit by the Government.

But it didn't work. In 2019, pornography depicting the acts above and others, was again made legal after a review of obscenity laws.

'Even for people with no interest in pornography this is very important for consent and bodily autonomy.' - Myles Jackman, obscenity lawyer.

As we evolve into the digital age, the line between the real world and the virtual world are becoming blurred for some. There is a desperation at the heart of social media that holds validation over truth.

Those with dark desires can thrive in today's world

The danger in disconnected living is that it is too easy to float by in life and not contact anyone outside of online friends. Those with instincts to act on their dark thoughts have never found a bigger outlet and resource than there is in today's world. This level of disconnection and inward distraction is a boiling pot of mental health issues, violence and disassociation.

That line blurs fantasy with reality. The mind of a serial killer might already find it hard to associate with either. Disconnected living might give those thinking of acting on dark thoughts a more realistic opportunity of doing so. Throw urban strangers and disconnected living together and the risk of an increase in serial killers over the coming decades, is more likely than it has been in previous ones.

Though we might be out of the 1970s and 1980s, when serial killers were at their peak, the age of disconnected living is a breeding ground for the rise of the serial killer. Serial killers can kill mostly out of opportunity, whether created by them or through the mishaps of others.

Victim opportunities that came with urbanisation and now with disconnected living is one of the reasons, not just why serial killers kill, but how some can get away with it for so long.

The Lure of Celebrity Status

Becoming a celebrity can sometimes be an important motivation that gives impetus to a serial killer to carry on killing. Not all killers seek fame, or infamy to put it in a better context.

Randy Kraft, for example, hardly ever discussed his crimes, and definitely removed himself from them. Others like Alexander Pichushkin sought to better Andrei Chikatilo's body count, and in doing so, wanted to be known for his crimes.

It's not to say they don't all have their reasons for killing, they do, it's just that some killers seek fame and in some cases fortune. Charles Bronson would paint and then sell his art, Charles Manson wrote music, and Dennis Nilsen penned an autobiography.

Nilsen is not the first killer to write an autobiography and have it released. The book was subsequently banned by the British Government as they felt that some of the details were glorified and not in the public interest. At what point do you stop serial killers releasing detailed information and accounts of their crimes?

Hunger for fame or infamy

It's a bizarre paradox where both sides are hungry for more but then morality comes into play. Confessions and interviews are mostly readily available after conviction so the information is already there. Although they do tend to be only the facts of the crimes and not the reasons or intricate details.

On the one hand, people have a macabre fascination with all things relating to serial killers. On the other hand, the public don't really want to see them get rich off the back of their crimes. It's a bizarre paradox where both sides are hungry for more but then morality comes into play.

By allowing the written accounts of their crimes to come out into the public and the public consuming them, we are in a sense fuelling the fire. We want to know the gory details so much that we strive to see live interviews with the killers. We want to know how they were moved to kill and the processes by which they were caught.

It has been suggested those who claim to be serial killer fanatics may have even considered an act of evil themselves at one point in their lives. To follow serial killers and to consume their lives is akin to the love of horror movies.

True life horror

They are far removed from our own ideals but because serial killers live in the real world, the fear and danger are awfully close to home. They are true-life horror stories without the special effects. If we are to assume that most kill upon diminished responsibility, then the very act of reading their thoughts and memories is detrimental to the family members of the victims. Fame then, surely is inevitable, as we strive to know more about those who commit the worse type of crimes.

The Son of Sam Law, implemented after David Berkowitz came close to making money off his story, went some way to setting the standard for similar laws throughout the United States and some other countries. But it's not always financial gain that serial killers are generally after, it's fame. There would be no point in becoming financially rich whilst serving life or being remanded on death row.

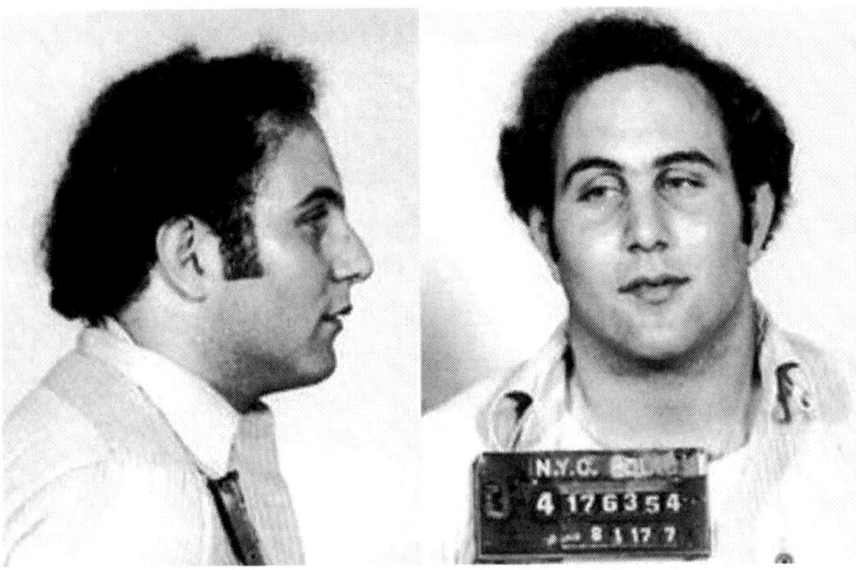

David Berkowitz (above) introduced the Son of Sam moniker to the world in 1977 when he communicated directly with the investigation for the first time. He left a handwritten letter addressed to the NYPD near the body of one of his victims. He had literally chosen the name by which he would become known.

The BTK Killer, Dennis Rader, sought to establish a brand name for himself and attract notoriety like the Son of Sam. He contacted the media in the Autumn of 1974 and left a letter for authorities at the local public library. It told them to call him; Bind. Torture. Kill. Thus the BTK Killer was born and he himself had chosen the name for which he would be remembered and spoken about in years to come.

During the late 1960s and most of the 1970s, the rise of the celebrity took hold. It was something witnessed during World War Two and slowly moved into the public eye to take hold of the flower power era. Never had so many people sought fame or celebrity status.

Fame then, surely is inevitable

Many children desired to be famous. The rise of popular culture was increasing at an astronomical rate. Gossip magazines, pulp fiction, celebrity in media and the increase in the output of movies would lead people to seek fame. Whilst some would seek it through legal and ethical avenues, others had already given up on all things moral.

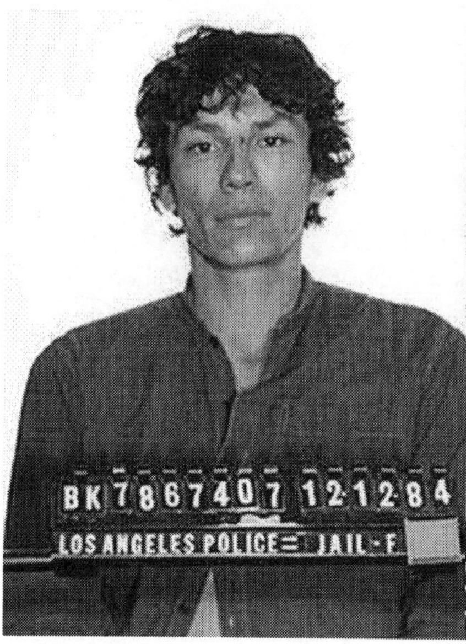

It is evidenced that once a celebrity status or moniker has been given to an active serial killer, then the murder rates tend to increase. The killers then seek to prove the media and public right, to prove they deserve the bizarre celebrity status that has been given to them. Almost all will follow investigations and news reports about their crimes.

'You know who I am, don't you? I'm the one they're writing about in the newspapers and on the TV.' - Richard Ramirez; The Night Stalker (previous page), to one of his victims who survived.

Then comes the danger of igniting the passions of those who might have held off acting on their dark thoughts. The celebrity status can motivate the killers to continue their crimes, but it can also inspire others. Many ignored and isolated potential serial killers become copycat killers, to achieve their own degree of celebrity status, or garner their own serial killer name.

Fan followings and sought-after art

The larger the body count, the greater the terror, the more chance they might make it to the front page of a newspaper or top-of-the-hour TV report. Certain magazines devoted to popular culture have promoted infamy to the point of making serial killer's grim legends in their own way. The villains to the heroes of the movie, music, and fashion world. Suddenly, true crime became entertainment for the masses.

People magazine once wrote huge swathes of information about the Unabomber, Ted Kaczynski, who began his campaign in 1978. Jeffrey Dahmer who began killing in 1978, shockingly made People's top 100 list of the most intriguing people of the Twentieth Century. Intriguing they may be, but they are subsequently given a platform far greater than they deserve.

And it doesn't stop there. The media and books were the tip of the iceberg. Images of serial killers are sometimes slapped on t-shirts, comic books, calendars, trading cards, baseball caps, mugs, pendants and jackets.

Their art is sold for thousands, they have their own fan followings, websites, member clubs, public funds and those who fall in love with them. The lure of celebrity means so much more than a newspaper clipping. It could make them world famous and see their crimes become internationally recognised for decades to come.

The lure of social media fame

Becoming known for their crimes could result in fame, or more correctly; infamy. The trappings of celebrity were often too much of a pull to refuse.

> *'Ignore the eternal display of social media, it is not real life. If people thinking you are living a happy life is more important than actually being happy then something needs to change.' – Harrison Lake, the Camden Killer.*

In the 1970s it was much harder to become famous. The entertainment industry was reserved only for the select few, if one had been lucky enough to get a foothold in the film, music, or art industry. In 2021, we have social media.

One could become famous for simply 'doing a funny dance' and posting it to YouTube with the right hashtags. You can film better quality movies on a $200 DSLR Camera than you could have done in the 1970s with camera equipment worth tens of thousands and sometimes more.

You can write a song, record yourself singing it and then publish it to the public for reactions, feedback, or even a career platform. The gateways to becoming famous have widened and more and more people are being lured into fame. Facebook, Twitter, Instagram, YouTube and many more, the platforms are eternal and perfectly suit either fame or infamy.

True stories have been written about murderers filming themselves killing someone and uploading it onto a social media platform. But they're not getting the infamy that was once afforded to those in 1978.

Desensitised society

Are people becoming desensitised to images of death, murder and killings? It's argued that as a society and as a civilisation, we have become emotionally dumbed down.

It's the same issue that links with the rise of pornography. You can find brutally violent images and videos online in just a matter of a few clicks. Mostly you can find those on social media platforms until they're taken down. There is moderation on some but only if its reported, meaning that some things that no human should ever see, are witnessed by millions.

Does this desensitisation pose an increasing problem as we move towards 2028 and the rise of the serial killer? As more people become desensitised to violent images and more people use social media to explore their individual tendencies then we could be walking into a hugely damaging second era of serial killing.

One has to wonder how much of an influence the supposed anonymity of social media will have as we move away from the carnage of the 1970s and into a new age of murder.

The Rise of True Crime Pornography

The influence of violent sexual images is still debated and argued over to this day. Although almost all men who see such images do not go on to sexually assault or even murder women, there are a small amount of men who do. Violent pornography is not a main cause of serial killing but it is attributed as one of the factors than can inspire someone to want to kill.

True crime pornography is vastly different from actual pornography as we perceive it to be in the 21st Century. In 1989, Ted Bundy claimed it was an overbearing exposure to the True Detective magazine that opened his eyes to what could be. Before his execution, he met with Dr. James Dobson, who was a campaigner against pornography and a religious psychologist.

He told Dobson when he was growing up, he had become addicted to True Detective magazine and other magazines similar to its type. The front covers of some of the magazines contain images that in this day and age would be considered exploitative and sexually explicit. They generally showed images of sexual violence against women.

In the next section we look at some of the true crime magazine covers that may have influenced some people to take part in violent crime. Due to their nature, the images are not included here. However, they can be found for free by heading over to https://www.benoakley.co.uk/monstrous-true-crime-magazine-covers or visiting the website and typing 'Monstrous True Crime Magazine Covers' into the search bar.

Murderous pulp fiction

True Police Cases, October 1971.

Front cover is of a woman in her bra showing cleavage and bare legs hidden only by small shorts. Her wrists are tied and her arms are hoisted above her head with rope. With the following headline; Before dying, the stabbed girl cried; "Please untie me, I've been raped."

Real Detective, April 1980.

Cover is of a scared woman, bound and gagged, her top has been ripped down the front and her cleavage is showing, barely protected by her bra. An unseen man behind her is leaning over her with a length of rope, ready to strangle her. Headline; "Now no one else can save her!"

True Detective, June 1959.

A man crouches behind a terrified women as she is on the floor. Her hands are tied behind her back and he is wrapping a cloth around her mouth to gag and silence her. Headline; "The frightened blonde who saw murder." At the bottom left corner is a smaller piece of text that says; "Girls for sale."

True Police Cases, October 1978.

A screaming woman is fighting with a man who has a gun in his hand, he has his arm around her neck. Her denim jacket is thrown open and she is not wearing a bra, her breasts are close to being exposed. Headline; "Playboy bunnies held as sex slaves! Drugged and defiled!"

Detective Cases, October 1976.

A naked women, barely covered by her bedsheets, tan-lines obvious, is sprawled out as if she has just been murdered. Headline; "It looks like a wild animal mauled her in bed." At the top line of the front cover; "Can you rape... a whore?"

Inside Detective, August 1976.

A topless man is holding a knife to a terrified woman's neck as she is laying on a bed. A mirror reflection shows her legs to be open, she is wearing a small pink top and her mouth is wide open. Headline; "An orgy of blood at the massage parlour."

Best True Fact Detective, September 1980.

A woman is laying on her front on the floor of a dark room, she has been tied with rope in a way associated with bondage and has duct tape over her mouth. She is looking at the supposed photographer with fear in her eyes. She appears to be topless and is wearing small pink panties that accentuate her rear. Headline; "Let's rape the girl next door."

That last one would be heavily censored, if not moved to the adult section of the shelves. The image is heavily comparable with BDSM and is just like those found in hardcore porn and fetish sites today.

Predilection towards sexual perversity

Images described in the previous examples with those types of headlines were all the rage in the middle to the end of the Twentieth Century. People couldn't get enough of it. Generally, the images didn't have much to do with the inner pages of the magazine but offer a tantalising entry into a world of true crime, murder and serial killers of the day. For the likes of Bundy and others, it had launched their addiction to violence

'Pornography can reach in and snatch the kid out of any house today. It snatched me out of my home.' - Ted Bundy to Dobson.

True crime magazines could be bought by incredibly young children with no age restrictions. Having reviewed a lot of the front covers of these types of magazines I would argue that some of them are borderline, if not clearly pornographic. Or at least they insinuate something else quite entirely.

It is in this insinuation that can lead one to use their own imagination and fill in the gaps. These types of teasing images can allow one to create their own story, their own fantasy around them. For those who already have a predilection towards violence or sexual perversity, it can give them opportunity to amplify their thoughts.

Hundreds of millions of people today view porn or sexual images, they might do so healthily and are not influenced to act upon any dark thoughts which may arise. But then most people have good moral boundaries and ethical ways in which they live their lives. Some do not and so porn or true crime exploitation fuels their already existing desires further.

Because so many serial killers have cited porn as one of their factors of killing, then it simply cannot be ignored. We can't blame true crime magazines, but we can look at the influence they might have had on allowing people to revel in their own fantasies. In some instances it might be the first stepping-stone to seeking out harsher and more sexually explicit images. A study put forward a four-step syndrome of how porn can affect a person viewing such images.

- Addiction to viewing images.
- Increased appetite to seek more images.
- Desensitisation to the images.
- Acting out the images.

True crime magazines for sex education

In the 1970s and earlier decades, sex education was not something that was generally taught in schools. Children would learn either through their family members, peers or exploratory methods. For some, true crime magazines had become their sex education. The publications put out a violent understanding of sexual encounters and were generally focused on domination and control.

There are other pop culture elements such as horror films, horror stories, thriller books, satanic music, and various other publications which might coerce one's view on violence and sex. Yet we cannot deny the availability of true crime magazines on the youth of the mid-Twentieth Century.

According to other killers like Dennis Rader, he claimed that the magazines inspired him to practice new ways of restraining his victims and got him in the mood to kill. Melvin Rees, Jr. killed seven people in the 1950s and blamed it on true crime magazines.

In the modern era, far more shocking images and videos are accessible from just a few clicks on the internet. Children can find a world of the most degrading sexual images at the click of a button. We could be headed for another violent crime epidemic if we're not already in the midst of one.

The Rise of Violent Pornography

That people like Ted Bundy claimed porn was an influence and motivation for their own desires is scary enough. That the type of porn available in today's world is more disturbing than ever – is even scarier.

In the 1970s, porn was a relatively new thing, at least to the mainstream masses. Amateur photography was on the increase and VHS was about to make its mark on history. It wouldn't have been easy to find porn back in the 1970s. The likes of Bundy and Dennis Rader said it had influenced their outlooks on women and was a contributing factor in both of their cases.

In 2020 and beyond, porn is at an unprecedented level of accessibility. It is one of the biggest industries in the world and one of the most searched for terms on the internet. Just a few clicks and every kind of porn is available to everyone.

It was relatively mild images that influenced the likes of Bundy and other serial killers. They used their own imagination to fuel their fantasies, using certain images only as a marker in their mind's eye. Today, there is no need for imagination.

Bizarre and degrading pornography

Every type of porn; bizarre or degrading, is instantly available to every age group on any device, anywhere in the world. Some countries have banned some elements of the internet but it doesn't stop people using proxy servers to navigate their way around a firewall to the entire World Wide Web.

Because of the type of images now readily available to everyone, the rise of the serial killer in 2028, fifty years after 1978, is inevitable. As is the rise in mental health issues amongst young people who are witness to such images and who use them as a basis for a normal relationship.

The days of soft-core true detective magazines are still with us. But they pale in comparison to the vast amount of violent pornography that fills over half of the known internet. Internet anonymity has afforded people with dark thoughts to talk to others about their fantasies or use social media to spark up dehumanising conversations.

Some comments underneath degrading images might leave one struggling to see any resemblance of the ethical and moral society we believed we lived in. This stuff is easily accessible by children, who's developing brains can and will be affected by what they see. It in essence changes their outlook on other people, sexual relations, and the way they perceive the world.

The Psychology of Serial Killers

The Macdonald Triad is a set of three factors that contribute to the psychology of serial killers and how people go on to commit multiple murders. It was first proposed by psychiatrist J.M. Macdonald and was written as a thesis in 1963 to be published in the American Journal of Psychiatry. The three factors of the Macdonald Triad are:

- Cruelty to animals.
- Obsession with starting fires.
- Bed-wetting past the age of five-years-old.

It is said if all three factors are present in a child's behaviour then there is a higher probability they will go onto commit violent crime as time progresses. Generally this is linked to murderous behaviour and sexual predation. Although subsequent research has not validated the thesis, it still remains one of the starting points in diagnosis and awareness of serial killers. What it did do was open up the research and debate among other psychiatrists and investigators.

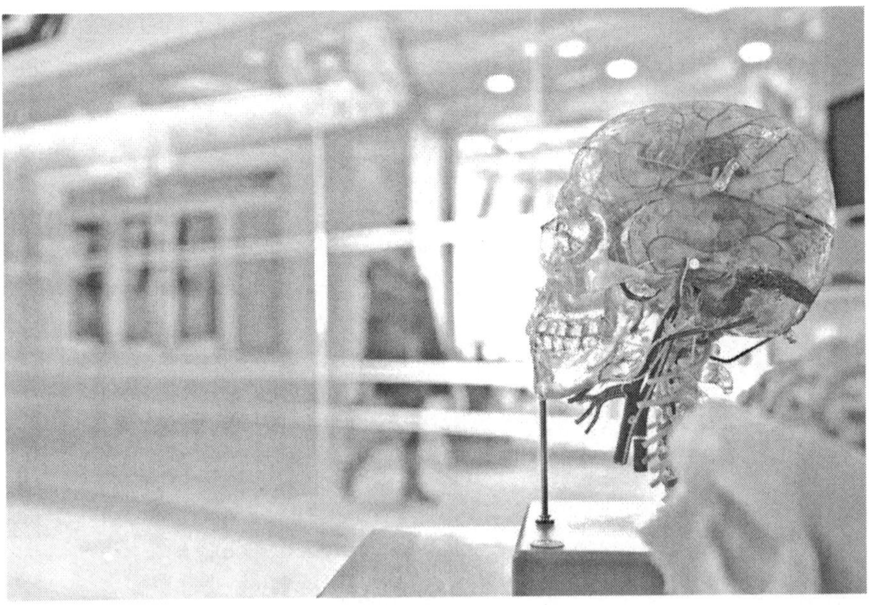

The Macdonald Triad connection to child abuse.

Since 1963, more reports have stated that the Macdonald Triad is linked more to childhood experiences of neglect and abuse. Setting fire to objects or property was seen as a way to release anger without resorting to dehumanising others or animal life. It has since been argued that the fire factor of the Triad can easily be replaced with other anti-social activities or behaviour. None of which are proof that a child will go on to become a serial killer.

Bed-wetting is seen as a humiliating factor for a child, especially when ridiculed by a parent or older sibling. There is evidence that abused children are more likely to feel or suffer humiliation than those raised in better households.

This humiliation is transferred in cruelty to animals. When a child is abused, they cannot retaliate to their abusers or captors. There is an obvious size differential should that child wish to fight back in any way. In one study of serial killers, it was noted that the same infliction of cruelty to an animal in their childhood years, was the same type of cruelty then inflicted on their human victims.

Cruelty against animals, generally small animals, is a route one might take because those animals are viewed as weak and vulnerable. In the same way that they themselves are seen as weak and vulnerable when an adult inflicts cruelty upon them.

In one study of serial killers, it was noted that the same infliction of cruelty to an animal in their childhood years, was the same type of cruelty then inflicted on their human victims. It is interesting to note that Richard Trenton Chase, AKA: The Vampire of Sacramento, exhibited all the factors of the Macdonald Triad. Chase fits into the Macdonald Triad thesis perfectly.

His fascination with torturing small animals and removing their organs was evident in what he would then do to his victims. He would drink the blood of small animals, just as he would with humans, when he was big enough to be able to attack humans.

In a study of violent inmates, over half admitted to having committed acts of violence against animals either in childhood, adolescence or their teenage years. The link was then made between animal abusers and childhood abuse, particular parental abuse.

It showed that those children who abused animals would have mostly suffered some kind of parental abuse in their formative years. In a 2004 study regarding patterns of violence, the authors found a link between repetitive animal cruelty and subsequent cruelty towards humans. They noted that although the links were more obvious than first thought, they offered a warning.

By focusing on just one aspect of possible rises to violent crime, it was detracting from other possible causes and reasons. It is clear now that most psychiatrists and investigators focus on more than three factors in relation to research and evidence of serial killer foundations. But it was the Macdonald Triad that paved the way.

The problem with the Dark Triad

Since the Macdonald Triad, there have been more attempts to create factors as to why someone might go on to commit serial murder. The Dark Triad is one of the more cited thesis in numerous research papers.

The Dark Triad is more of a psychological attempt at understanding why someone might go on to kill. It includes the following factors:

- **Narcissism**: Traits include; grand-standing, pride, egotism, lack of empathy.
- **Machiavellianism**: Traits include; manipulation, exploitation, cynicism, deception.
- **Psychopathy**: Traits include; antisocial behaviour, impulsiveness, selfishness, callousness, remorselessness.

The problem with the Dark Triad is that the three psychological aspects are virtually interchangeable to the point of cancelling each other out. Psychopathy and narcissism both can be mostly inherited by genetic components and then by how a child is raised. Machiavellianism is generally less found to be inherited than the others.

This has led many to argue that the Dark Triad is virtually baseless in its theory but it certainly does add more to the database of psychological understanding. Far beyond the psychological Triads, there are a greater number of factors present in what leads people to kill multiple times.

Victim Selection in the 1970s

The argument given for the decrease in serial killers from the 1990s onwards is that law enforcement simply got better. This might have meant that some potential serial killers were caught after just one kill or even with only the threat of murder on personal social media accounts.

The counter-argument is that there was simply a larger pool of victims in the 1970s than there is today. And that counter-argument is somewhat true. As we've already seen, the rise of the interstates and highways from the 1950s gave rise to the drifter killer. This meant that one could drive great distances, across States or Counties and open themselves up to larger opportunity.

Serial killers have a victim type in mind

The rise of urbanisation also played a major factor in the number of potential victims available. From 2000, urbanisation has increased even more but so has surveillance, both online and offline. Law enforcement has become more effective in the modern age than it was in the pre-DNA technology era of the 1970s.

We know that most serial killers are not opportunistic and have general plans in their heads or written down as to how they are going to kill. Mostly, they already have a victim in mind. The 1970s and 1980s offered more possibility than ever before and so serial killers were jumping at the opportunity.

The world was changing too quickly, less care was given to people's own personal safety. Hitchhiking became common as the highways expanded, and children played outdoors all the time. The rise of porn, true crime magazines, and an increase in prostitution, all led to people taking bigger risks than before.

Flower power was embedded into the minds of a generation, free love was theirs to share, and to lose. Population was increasing and the fallout of recent wars gave rise to a higher percentage of mental health problems.

When all is said and done, there was a larger pool of victims to choose from. This also goes hand in hand with the disconnected law enforcement of the period. Mostly due to a lack of internet and proper networking, it was more difficult to share information with other department's quick enough to catch the criminals.

Larger pool of victims

For gay men and women, the rise of the gay activist movements in the late 1960s and early 1970s gave rise to greater freedom than before. Although the 1970s were not as free as they are in the 21st Century, coming out was slowly becoming more acceptable.

There was an increase in gay magazines, celebrities and rallies. The rise of gay bars, bathhouses and gay saunas across the Western world, allowed men to live out their gay fantasies in somewhat anonymity. It also opened the door to a greater selection of victims.

The same could be said for the rise of prostitution. Sex workers were and still are at greater risk of becoming a victim of a serial killer than most other people. Ever since the stories of Jack The Ripper (below) in Victorian England, the lure of killing a sex worker has never been too far from the minds of serial killers.

According to FBI data it shows that female sex workers are 18 times more likely to be killed by a serial killer than someone who is not involved in the industry. Female victims are generally much higher in serial killer cases than in general murder cases.

Missing and murdered women represent an extreme cross-section of the consequences of a much larger, misogynistic culture that views women as sex objects who were "asking for it" or who "got themselves assaulted." Until society contends with these attitudes, there is little hope for stopping violent offenders of all stripes.

'FBI research shows us how serial killers have opened up about their crimes, revealing their various dark sexual fantasies that evolve into murder. This was more prevalent with the rise of true crime magazines depicting scantily-clad women tied up and about to murdered by a man.' - Jooyoung Lee, University of Toronto.

This along with the rise of porn, influenced some people to enact on their fantasies.

A greater chance of a successful kill

Most serial killers only choose a victim whereby the chances of success are extremely high. Of course, not all killers do this. Richard Trenton Chase, simply ripped through people without a thought on evidence and being tracked afterwards, but he still would have chosen his victims.

This is why the first murder victim might be a street sex worker or homeless person. Beyond that, once they've got that out the way, then the victim choice might be someone of a higher standing; a student, office worker, or nurse.

Combine this with the construction of new highways and a rise in unemployment leading to homelessness or prostitution then victims became easier. The Green River Killer, Gary Ridgeway, was a truck driver. He later claimed that picking up sex workers or hitchhikers was easy without anyone noticing or knowing any different.

He said he knew that no one would be looking for them straight away and a window of freedom would open up after the killing. At least for a short while after and in some cases much longer.

Sex workers as a victim of choice

The murder of a sex worker is especially difficult for police and other law enforcement. The very nature of the victim having had sex with multiple men and the interactions with hundreds, if not thousands of strangers, makes it even harder to investigate. They are also less likely than most rape or assault victims to report the crimes to police for exactly the same reason.

There was also the belief that law enforcement themselves wouldn't even worry too much about sex workers being murdered. It was the disconnection of various agencies and departments that slowed down the flow of information between them. There was also the possibility that some officers in the 1970s had used sex workers themselves and didn't want anything linking back to them.

Record-keeping and crime detection in the 1970s was far more difficult and disorganised than it is in today's digital world. Improvements in data collection and statistics is at a far greater level now.

The sharing of information was indifferent and sometimes frowned upon between different departments. The FBI was one of the solutions to this but then the discrepancies between their own investigations and the police ones were not always shared. Simply put, in the 1970s and 1980s, it was easier to get away with serial killing than in later decades, partly because victims were easier to find.

DNA Evidence Exploded in the 1980s

In England, on November 13th 1987, Robert Melias became the first person to be convicted of a crime using DNA evidence. He had been found guilty of rape and convicted by a British court. Scientists calculated that the chance of the sample from the crime scene not coming from Melias was 1 in 4 million of the male population.

Following Melias's conviction and in the same month, Tommy Lee Andrews became the first American to be convicted on DNA evidence. Andrews was also charged with rape, in Florida. DNA profiling was originally developed as a method of determining paternity that could link a child with a parent. But it was the Robert Melias case in England that changed it all. The investigation had sought the help of a molecular biologist named Alec Jeffreys, as he had begun to use DNA for forensic testing. The perpetrator was caught based on the DNA evidence and subsequently convicted because of it.

In Florida, Tommy Lee Andrews was convicted because DNA tests found a match from his blood and semen in a rape victim. In the years that followed, no one disputed or argued against DNA evidence in criminal trials. As soon as prosecutors began using DNA to convict then defence lawyers began questioning the admissibility of DNA.

During the late 1980s and early 1990s, there were a number of legal challenges against DNA evidence. The challenges against DNA evidence mostly arose because the validity of the techniques used were coming under scrutiny. Out of these cases came a national standard for collecting DNA evidence.

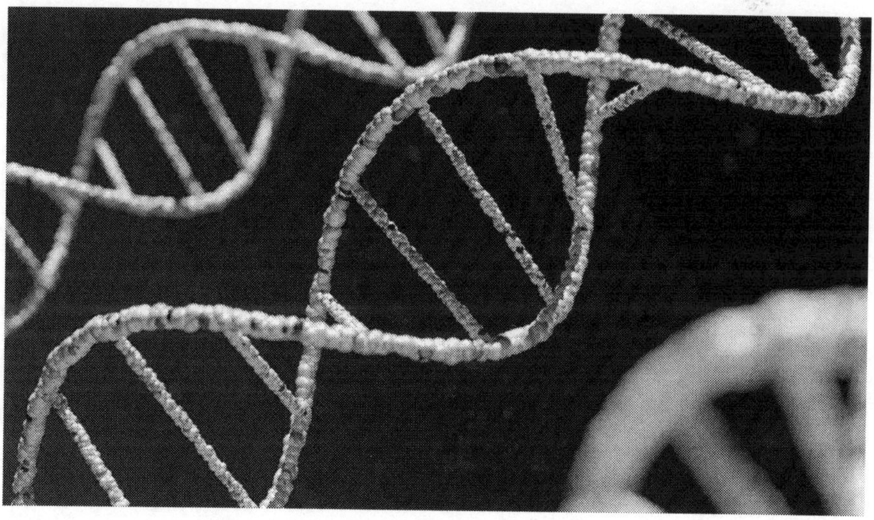

In many cases, a DNA testing laboratory protocols would be brought into question. Their validation processes were deemed insufficient, meaning evidence was denied. Once lawful protocols came into place then DNA testing would become common in criminal cases that required DNA as evidence.

The federal DNA Identification Act of 1994 meant that DNA profiles could be held on record for a set amount of time. It meant that laboratories had to adhere to a strict set of protocols for testing and uploading profiles to the database. In the same year, these protocols became uniform standards when the Violent Crime Control and Law Enforcement Act was implemented.

In the late 1990s and through the 2000s, the DNA databases helped solved a number of cold cases from the 1970s onwards. In 2002, Virginia became the first state to execute a criminal based on DNA evidence assisting in a cold case investigation. James Earl Patterson was already serving time for rape when he was linked to the murder.

The ability to use DNA testing to convict and to exonerate suspects changed the way that criminals were convicted, especially in rape and murder cases. It is now one of the most powerful tools that it used within the criminal justice system.

Victim Selection in the 2020s

Some say the decrease in the amount of serial killers in today's world is down to the fact that people are not getting away with it anymore. Victims are harder to find and investigations have become state of the art. Others aren't so sure.

In the Urban Strangers section we discussed the rise of urbanisation in the towns and cities. Jump forward to today's world and urbanisation has increased dramatically. In 1978, the population of the earth was estimated at 4.29 billion. In 2022, it is estimated at 7.9 billion. That's almost double in just over 40 years. By 2050, Earth's human population is expected to be in the region of 10 billion.

There are more potential victims than ever before and more people are going missing than ever before. This could be to do with population increase or it could be that more reports are being made for missing people. It could also be that the authorities are recording the data better than in the 1970s which is generally considered to be true. But people are still going missing.

Online stalking and missing people

In places like India and Africa, people are going missing on an astronomical scale. We long thought the slave trade to be a thing of the past. Yet, human trafficking has only increased, forced child prostitution is on the rise, and real life human beings are being traded for monetary value as a product or possession.

Serial killers choose their prey generally because they can overpower them. This is one of the reasons why male serial killer victims tend to be female. They also tend to be slim, young, and easy to overcome.

With social media on the increase, women are still being told to look a certain way. This leads to more people crafting themselves into the perfect victim of a serial killer. We tend to compare the worst parts of ourselves with the best parts of others.

Online forums, chatrooms, social media sites, private messaging and hidden chat services have led to an increase in private information sharing, hacking and stalking. One can find a lot about a person with just a few clicks.

Potential serial killers can stalk a victim online and find out everything about them. A lot of social media users share their home address, what they eat, where they shop, when they're out of their homes, relationships, thoughts, just damn near everything. The pool of victims is immeasurably immense.

The difficulty in the modern era is getting away with it. Some cite the belief that serial killers are stopped before they get to their second murder. And whilst in some instances this is true, it's certainly not for all cases.

In the United States in 2018, 239,847 females under 21-years-old were reported missing. Over half of these are found within a week, some runaway and return home, mistakes in reporting, or arguments with family. A lot more are found later but still thousands of young females simply never return home or are never found.

It is estimated that over 90,000 people are missing in the United States at any one time. In the United Kingdom, 180,000 are reported missing every year with London reporting a 72% increase in missing persons from 2008 to 2018.

The BBC called the rise of missing persons; unsustainable. The fact is that police are required to follow up each missing person. When crimes take precedent, sometimes they are never followed up and they wait for someone to book a flight or use their credit card.

With stories of people simply vanishing, there is a precedent for the rise of the serial killer. With access to a universe of information online, maybe serial killers have simply got better at not being caught.

Toxic Legacy of World War Two

Most readers might have heard of PTSD (Post-Traumatic Stress Disorder) but up until the time of World War Two, the term was not in use. Other terms including shell shock and battle fatigue were the sound-bites of the era. It wasn't until World War Two that Combat Stress Reaction (CSR) replaced the more poetic of the terms.

World War Two and indeed The Great War, left a toxic legacy of mental health issues and depression. It created a societal divide that remained difficult to return from. To put it simply, both wars led to a silent epidemic of mental disorders and isolation.

A study showed that adults who were around during World War Two, were 6% more likely to suffer from depression than those before the war. An astonishing 3% of the entire world's population was wiped out during World War Two alone. Even more humbling when it's noted that the United States currently makes up only 5% of the world's population. In Europe alone, 39 million people died and over half were civilians.

After the war, health problems and poverty increased and class divides were temporarily stalled as the affected countries struggled to pull through. The middle classes witnessed a higher loss of wealth as people rushed to rebuild their lives.

Destruction of family values

The true cost of such a war was far greater than the financial cost. Lives and families were destroyed, homes were bombed, poverty and hunger became the norm and education was few and far between. The world became a far different place than it was before. It was to be a long climb out of a deep dark hole.

A couple of decades later, one of the most prominent factors towards the rise of the serial killer was the destruction of family values. This also included the physical destruction and loss of family members. Many children lost their fathers and would witness the emotional fallout of war.

Some fathers who survived and returned home displayed poor mental and physical health and struggled to survive in the world they came home to. For the children, in all cases, a deterioration of family values would set in.

Gender ratios changed shortly after the war caused by the higher death of men during wartime. High stress and lower marriage rates caused more depression and the onset of mental disorders. These were then mostly put on the backburner of medical professionals. There was simply no time to focus on it when attention was needed and diverted to physical wounds and ailments. The current data of the fallout of World War Two is astonishingly hard to come by. Not enough has been done to measure the effects of war on families and children.

However, if we link what we know about mental illness after the war with child abuse data as previously spoken about in January 1978, then we do see a connection. It's no surprise that the abuse of children following World War Two increased more in that time period than any other. We see that more children were raised in broken families or without their biological fathers.

The government push with the Baby Boomer generation virtually punished families if they didn't seek a nuclear-family model. Those without husbands would mostly find new loves and expand their broken family.

The disregard of child abuse after the war in favour of the Baby Boomer's was something that would historically not go unnoticed. The link between broken families and abuse in childhood to violent criminals is well documented.

The post-war world was different in every way

There were also many children growing up without a family. Though some might have had a family of sorts, they were raised in a vastly different world than the one before the war. Just 40 years earlier, the world was only just coming out of the Victorian era and then suddenly the industrial revolution had provided mass weapons of war. That transition for some would have been harder than the transition from the pre-digital to the digital age of the present era.

During the war, many children would have seen dead bodies and some would have been adversely affected by the war. Point in case is Andrei Chikatilo, a Russian serial killer who was convicted of 52 murders and known as The Red Ripper. The seeds for his crimes, were developed during Joseph Stalin's rule of Russia. Chikatilo suffered hunger in his childhood and also in the years leading up to World War Two. His family was forced to eat grass and leaves to fight hunger in the Ukrainian SSR.

During the Nazi occupation of Ukraine, he witnessed the true horrors of war. Bombings, fires, shootings, raping, dead bodies, and a complete disruption to an already damaged childhood. His mother was raped by a German soldier, possibly in front of Chikatilo, who then gave birth to his sister. It was then claimed he watched his brother being eaten alive by cannibalistic soldiers. This later had a massive psychological effect that saw him enacting violence to relieve himself.

'When I used my knife, it brought psychological relief. I know I have to be destroyed. I was a mistake of nature.' - Andrei Chikatilo

Does war potentially create violent criminals? No, not to everyone. Most people, even in the face of utmost adversary, will maintain their moral stance. Yet, some people who lived through World War Two as a child or were born to a broken family during the war, might have gone on to commit violent crimes. For some of those people, the act of murder would become an outlet for their own suffering. Some might even go on to become serial killers, just like The Red Ripper.

Toxic Legacy of the Iraq War

The 2003 Iraq War was the first fully televised war. It was when 24-hour news was at its peak and they might as well have been live-streaming it, it was that detailed. Audiences remember watching the news as the first of the tanks rumbled over the border into Iraq. There has never been any war since that has been documented so vigorously by the media.

In the UK alone, the Ministry of Defence (MOD) and the NHS failed to meet the mental health needs of soldiers returning from the second Iraq War. This lack of support is evident in every conflict before and after.

Mentalhealth.org began a campaign to raise awareness of mental health and social problems in former military men and women, especially those involved in conflict. MOD figures from the 1991 Gulf War showed that 20% of returning servicemen and women were diagnosed with psychological problems.

These included depression, PTSD, suicidal ideation, anxiety and alcohol or substance abuse. With approx. 13% of those suffering from PTSD. Another study found that servicemen and women were being diagnosed with related mental health problems an entire decade after being in conflict.

If the very governmental body who send soldiers to war cannot deal with the mental health fallout then it is no wonder many will suffer as a result of serving in a conflict. The same argument that has been used regarding mental health services across the Western world 30 years ago is still being used today. They say that mental health services are over-stretched and under-funded and do not offer sufficient services to meet soldier's needs. Then the question remains; why not?

The onslaught of PTSD

We've already discussed in the section on World War Two, how damaging it can be on the returning military and the effect on the families of those coming home. If children are being raised by father's who are mentally ill, through no fault of their own, then that child might have to grow up witnessing the fallout of war and how it affects their parents. And indeed, their perception of the world around them.

If soldiers are returning home, suffering from PTSD, then they too will struggle to live in the world they are coming back to. Some might not re-integrate back into society as well as others and those that don't, might go back into the world with toxicity on their minds.

According to Shelter (UK homeless charity) and the Government's Social Exclusion Unit, 25% of homeless people in the United Kingdom are former members of the armed services. 41% of homeless people who attended homeless shelters had previously been in prison. It remains a melting pot of mental health disorders that are simply not being treated. They are virtually going unnoticed and somewhat ignored.

During the Falkland's War, 237 British deaths were recorded. Since then and up to 2013, an astonishing 95 ex-servicemen and women who returned from the Falkland's have taken their own lives. For the Gulf War, 107 suicides have been registered of returning servicemen or women. We know the Iraq war was bigger and more lives were lost. More soldiers were there than most other modern conflicts worldwide. The resulting fallout from it is deeply worrying.

The Vietnam War Divide

It is one of the longest campaigns by the United States, at over 17 years long, from 1955 to the American military withdrawing in 1973. There are said to be more than 35,000 books written about the Vietnam War, mostly from an American perspective.

Over 58,000 Americans were killed during the war but it pales in comparison to the estimated 3.8million Vietnamese. But what most of these books forget to mention beyond the action of the war, is the millions of lives affected by it.

We've already discussed the effects that World War Two had on families. Mostly, it was Europeans that had felt the brunt of the war but the Vietnam War was almost exclusively American. The displacement of families caused by the removal of young males was the first step to creating a generation of lost and damaged men. FBI reports show that murders in the United States increased amongst all age-groups during the Vietnam Conflict.

The war was unique within the United States as it split opinion and caused divide between the political parties and indeed most families across the country. The rise of violent crime after the country had pulled out of Vietnam, rose to a greater level than before. The link between the Vietnam Conflict and subsequent violent crime is well evidenced.

Sanctioned killings and the failure of war

Sanctioned killing during a war can have a subsequent effect on the level of violent crime and murder beyond the end of such a war. Although you won't find many books on the crimes committed by American military, more data is starting to come out from that lost time.

Because the killing of the enemy was sanctioned, the activities of some military personnel were brushed under the carpet. Many Vietnamese women were raped and murdered by serving American personnel. Many more Vietnamese civilians were murdered in cold blood.

Yet, mostly it was simply passed over as an act during war. Only a few cases ever reached military court and it didn't have the effect needed to stop the activities. The resulting failure of the Vietnam War infected the national psyche like a plague. Personal failure, wasted lives, national failure and a divide that reached the political parties. For some soldiers, the psychological aspect of surviving the Vietnam War was too much to bear and the country didn't seem to care. There was no soldier kissing a nurse like at the end of World War Two, there were no welcome home parades.

The following is taken from Kenrick Thompson's 'Photographic imagery and the Vietnam War: an unexamined perspective.' It describes the mood of the soldiers and the nation in its own painful way.

'Imagine if you had just graduated out of high school and were sent to a guerrilla warfare far away from your home. During the war, you were exposed to a lot of stress, confusion, anxiety, pain, and hatred. Then you were sent back home with no readjustment to the lifestyle in the states, no deprogramming of what you learned from the military, and no "welcome home" parades. You are portrayed to the public as a crazed psychopathic killer with no morals or control over your aggression.

'You find that there's nobody you can talk to or who can understand what you've been through, not even your family. As you re-emerge into civilization, you struggle to establish a personal identity or a place in society because you lack the proper education and job skills. In addition, there are no supportive groups to help you find your way, which makes you feel even more isolated, unappreciated, and exploited for serving your country.'

Most of those descriptors point towards causes and some consequences of mental illness. Isolation, feeling unwanted, lack of identity, lack of belonging, deteriorating social skills and being portrayed as a violent criminal. They are indeed as similar to the causes of mental illness as any other reasons.

These men were coming home to a nation that had failed. They were heading back to their families, withdrawn and depressed. There, they would struggle to raise their own children or cope with their own nightmares. A darkness that might have infected them from the experiences in the war.

Psychological effects of war

Most of the American military were drinking lots of alcohol or doing drugs. Some took part in violent rapes and senseless murders. Most were psychologically affected by their experiences. They all came back to the United States and brought their psychological disturbances with them.

The fact that PTSD was not really taken seriously until the early 1980s, meant that many suffered needlessly. Or they might have taken it out on their children or other people. The deadly combination of their own society rejecting them, the government ignoring their pleas, and their families not understanding them, caused Vietnam veterans to suffer both mentally and physically.

World War Two and the Vietnam Conflict gave rise to higher instances of violent crime in the years during and the years that followed. This was due to the returning soldiers themselves, the effects on them, and the effects on their families and children. Some of those who served in wars and went on to become serial killers are listed below.

David Berkowitz, The Son of Sam. Served with the US Army in South Korea.

Gary Ridgeway (next page) The Green River Killer. Served in the Navy and was sent for a tour in Vietnam.

Leonard Lake. Serial killer suspected of killing up to 25 people in the early 1980s served as a Marine in Vietnam.

Arthur Shawcross, The Monster of the Rivers. Killed 14 people between 1972 to 1989, including raping and killing a 10-year-old boy. He served in Vietnam.

Roy Norris, one half of The Toolbox Killers was deployed to Vietnam.

Howard Unruh, a spree killer who killed 13 people as he walked through his neighbourhood in 1949 was a US Army veteran of World War Two.

Rudy Bladel, The Railway Sniper. Killed up to seven people between 1963 to 1978. He served in the Korean War.

William Bonin, The Freeway Killer. Killed at least 21 young men and boys from 1979 to 1980. He served in the Vietnam War.

Only a tiny percentage of those who served in active wars go on to become serial killers. Most would go on to have happy lives but some would be psychologically affected from their experiences during wartime.

No conclusive studies have been completed on the effect of war within the countries where the wars have taken place. But it is suggested that millions more have been irreversibly affected by war.

The Afghanistan War Divide

Afghanistan divided people, not quite as much as the Vietnam Conflict, but divided, nonetheless. The West had just come out of the Iraq War and the people back home were tired of wars that seemingly served no real purpose.

The main issue with psychological effects of war is that they are never given as much attention as physical issues. Families experience loss and grief caused by the death of their loved one, people their loved ones knew, or those from the country of conflict itself. People learn to suppress war time anxiety and develop PTSD quicker than they may think.

If we link the Afghanistan War to the Vietnam War then the two are not quite as different as we might think. For starters both are on the border of China. This always raises the notion that China might be protecting their own borders by not allowing the United States to get a foothold in a neighbouring country.

Every war fought by the United States or NATO on the Chinese border has never ended well; The Vietnam War, Afghanistan War and Korean War. And for the British; the Opium War. Although the Opium War was seen as a victory where it really wasn't. It resulted in Britain maintaining control of Hong Kong for 100 years.

Drugs were rife in both wars and reports of drugs at Afghan bases were more telling than not. The public didn't want more war after Iraq and petitioned in their millions against the Afghanistan War but to no avail. This kind of belittling effect on the war itself and in turn on the soldiers was similar to the fallout of the Vietnam War. Soldiers suddenly didn't know what they were fighting for and many were coming back traumatised over what they had seen.

If the Iraq War was a swap-in for World War Two, then the Afghanistan War could be seen as a similar conflict to the Vietnam War. The public were divided on both and they came shortly after a larger war had been fought.

There is a psychological circle of depression, PTSD and violence that permeates through military families and circles of friends. Even now, some do not see their depression as a mental disorder and thus go under the radar, not even close to appearing on any data lists. The true number affected could be immense.

We talk about the children of war and the soldiers themselves but not about the women or partners that end up having to look after their children and their husbands or partners. The effect on all is dangerous, damaging and worthy of much more statistical gathering.

War shape's individual experience in ways that cannot be easily tabled or listed. Not everything should be labelled under PTSD or depression. The danger is that many are going undiagnosed and for those who end up homeless or removed from society then there's no telling what happens to them after that.

Exposure to Lead

When this particular factor was researched as a reason for the abundance of serial killers in the 20th Century, it was approached with dubious nonchalance. How could lead make someone want to kill? It turns out the evidence was overwhelming.

From the 1850s, many American cities built water systems using lead or iron piping. The water improved public health but was offset by the damaging effects of lead. Lead water pipes exposed entire city populations to much higher doses of lead than ever before and it was about to get much worse.

It was already suggested that lead service pipes increased the homicide levels of cities across the United States. Lead is a naturally occurring metal that is soft and pliable as well as being corrosion-resistant. It has been noted since the tenth century that exposure to lead may have health consequences.

Despite the hazards evident in all the centuries since, lead has been used more and more in glass, paints and then gasoline and it was this that led to an increase in crime. The use of lead in paint and gasoline has resulted in higher levels of lead in the air and earth around us.

Most cases of lead poisoning occur through inhaling or ingesting. As of the early 21st Century, there is no agreed-upon safe level of lead in the human bloodstream. However, any amount of lead in the blood can contribute to a huge number of health problems.

Studies have shown that lead can interfere with many neurotransmitters in the brain, most likely because lead can mimic calcium. It is said that exposure to lead can alter brain structure and function. Shockingly, exposure to lead can cause increases in impulsivity and aggression. It is considered to be one of the factors in the development of ADHD (Attention Deficit Hyperactivity Disorder).

Exposure to lead resulted in abnormal behavioural decisions

Being overly impulsive and aggressive, combined with mild mental disorders can result in abnormal behavioural decisions. The increase of the use of lead in gasoline up until the 1960s was never truly seen as being hazardous. The two world wars from the turn of the century had put the evidence on the back burner.

It wasn't until the 1970s that senate hearings would be held to talk about phasing out leaded gasoline and lead-based paint. It wasn't until later in the decade that blood-lead levels (BLL) would notably drop.

The various acts of the 1970s and the commissions that were set up to monitor lead in the industry were starting to have an effect. But it wouldn't be until the late Twentieth Century that lead was really starting to be phased out.

Lead poisoning can lead to anorexia, anaemia, tremors and stomach problems. In developing brains, lead exposure can be particularly damaging. Lead exposure in children can result in limited brain activity and stunted development of physical and mental faculties.

In males, the human brain reaches its peak at the age of around 22-years-old, in females it is much younger at 19-years-old. Exposure up until those ages are still likely to have further damaging effects.

In the United States, lead was finally phased out in 1996. Australia didn't phase it out until 2002. In a 2017 report, 120,000 children born between 1990 and 2004 were studied for the effects of lead poisoning and its relation to behaviour. Links were made between pre-school lead levels and later behavioural negativity in schools.

The researchers studied children who lived near busy roads because the soil near these roads was heavily contaminated with lead. They reported the effects of lead on those children and children who lived in quieter roads. Their conclusion was that the switch from leaded to unleaded gasoline played a big role in the reduction of crime witnessed in the 1990s and beyond.

No study has yet confirmed how much lead is needed in the bloodstream for someone to turn to crime but links have been made. Lead exposure can lead to reduced control of impulses and reaction times. It can also heighten aggression and disassociation. People who have these behavioural factors are more likely to commit a crime. Some are then likely to go on and kill.

Increased exposure to lead in childhood is linked to reduced brain activity in later years. It affects the prefrontal and anterior cortices of the brain. This is part of the brain that controls function, mood and most importantly; decision making.

The lead-crime hypothesis still to this day remains a theory but it is one that is still being researched as of 2020. No scientist or researcher has come forward to state matter-of-factly that lead is one of the main causes of crime and serial killing. It would be difficult to prove as the studies only consider the levels of lead and not the cultural differences, poverty division, family life, any trauma in an individual's life.

Bonus Content

Movies that Influenced Killers

The influence of movies inspiring crime is still debated and argued over to this day. Most people who watch violent movies do not go on to re-enact what they might have seen. But there are some people that do. Before we look at some examples, let's take a closer look at the truth of it.

> *'Pornography and violence poison our music and movies and TV and video games. The Virginia Tech shooter, like the Columbine shooters before him, had drunk from this cesspool.' - Mitt Romney, during his presidential campaign.*

Romney sat on the extreme side of the fence and was in effect blaming entertainment for the reasons behind violent crime. Is the death of Simba's father in 'The Lion King' any more violent than John McCLane taking out bad guys in 'Die Hard'?

Apparently it's only one's opinion on things that makes a difference. The assertions that violent movies cause people to become violent has been around for quite some time and a lot of research has been written on the subject. The fear has always been that watching a violent movie will make someone violent in real life. The same has always been said about gaming.

However, in an article in the Washington Post by Fareed Zakaria, he claims that people should look to Japan as a counter-argument for any claims of entertainment influencing violence. The Japanese are the biggest gaming-country in the world, when player and population ratio is looked at, yet the murder rate in Japan is close to zero. He put forward the argument that the main difference is the restrictions on firearms in Japan.

Many people want violent movies to be banned or at least restricted to a certain age group, which mostly they are. But some have claimed that it would mean censorship should reach all areas of entertainment, right down to fairy tales, which arguably have more written violence in them than most films.

On the flip-side, it has been proven that violent movies and games have more benefits than they do negatives. Researchers found that watching any type of movie, violent or not, can help people cope with their emotions. It can help people overcome challenging situations, expand their imagination, and relieve stress.

There is of course a bigger argument against the influence of movies on normal people. The people who go on to kill or commit crime after seeing a film were more likely to have been aggressive in the first instance.

Those who commit violent crime, including murder, already exhibited aggressive traits. Such attributes were predictive of criminal behaviour, and not the viewing of movies themselves. Movies might validate one's own beliefs, rather than changing them.

The Collector (1965)

This 1965 British film is said to have directly influenced a number of cases. Serial killer Robert Andrew Berdella Jr. AKA: The Kansas City Butcher remains one of the evilest killers in the modern era. His case was one of the first known instances of a movie directly impacting the thought processes of someone who had the potential to kill *and* would go on to kill.

The plot of The Collector is about a man who abducts women and holds them captive in his basement to add to his collection. It is a direct correlation to the exact process used by Berdella in his future murders. Except that he chose men instead of women. Berdella directly cited the film as an influence of how he could kill.

The Collector was also said to have influenced the serial killing duo Leonard Lake and Charles Ng. who together in the mid-1980s killed at least 11 people but was suspected to be 25. The pair built a bunker to imprison two of their female victims. They were planning on using them as sex slaves and housemaids. They documented some of their interactions on tapes but decided to murder them instead.

They had a self-built torture-chamber in a secluded area of forest which was home to a number of elaborate torture machines on the walls and all around. They had even built a dentist's chair used for restraining their victims.

Basketball Diaries (1995)

The film featured Leonardo DiCaprio as a basketball player who succumbs to heroin addiction. In a dream sequence he walks into his school wearing a black trench coat and carrying a shotgun. Then he massacres his classmates.

The 1996 school shooting carried out by Barry Loukaitis, was a virtual mirror to the scene in the film. He killed three people and injured more while walking through his school wearing a black trench coat. He was heard quoting lines from the film. In school shootings over the years that followed, many more would wear black trench coats.

It is suggested that these people would have done what they did anyhow, but they used certain entertainment mediums to provide the final inspiration.

Scream (1996)

In Belgium in 2001, Thierry Jaradin, a 24-year-old lorry driver lured and killed his 15-year-old neighbour, Alisson Cambier. She had visited Jaradin's house to swap some videotapes and have a chat. She then rejected his sexual advances and he excused himself shortly after.

He returned wearing a black robe and the 'ghostface' mask from the movie. He had two large kitchen knives in his hands as he lunged at Cambier. He stabbed her 30 times, and in doing so had ripped open the entire left side of her body. He then carried the mutilated corpse to his bed, slipped a rose into one of her hands, then called his father to confess.

In the 2006 murder of 16-year-old Cassie Jo Stoddart, Scream was cited yet again as a direct inspiration of the killing. After her boyfriend had left her home, two of her high school classmates went to her house and cut the power to the property. They then broke in and stabbed her at least 30 times. They had both planned the murder ahead of time and cited Scream and the Columbine Massacre as direct inspirations.

The Matrix (1999)

Unbelievably, the 'Matrix defence' has become a real thing. The premise of the film is that our reality is not real, instead we live in a giant computer program that we only perceive to be real. Several killers used the logic that people who were killed were not real people.

In Sweden, exchange student Vadim Mieseges killed and dismembered his landlady. Upon his arrest he told police that he had been sucked into the Matrix. In 2002, murderer Tonda Lynn Ansley of Ohio, also killed her landlady by shooting her in the head. She was found not guilty by reason of insanity as she had used the Matrix defence.

Robocop 2 (1990)

American serial killer Nathaniel White from New York killed six females from 1991 to 1992. He beat and stabbed them to death while on parole. White already had an aggressive personality but claimed it was Robocop 2 that inspired him to kill his first victim.

In the film, a victim's throat was cut and the knife slit down the chest to the stomach. White copied the exact same style of murder and then left the body in the same position as it had been left in the scene of the film. He was sentenced to 150 years in prison.

Interview with the Vampire (1994)

A day after Daniel Sterling had watched Interview with the Vampire at the cinema, he took on Vampiric tendencies. Lisa Stellwagen had seen the film with him and visited him again the next day at his home.

He told her that he was going to kill her and savour her blood. Then he stabbed her seven times and drank her blood for several minutes. Stellwagen survived and her testimony sent Sterling to prison. Sterling later claimed that he enjoyed the movie but wouldn't blame his attack on it.

The Renfield Syndrome

Renfield's Syndrome, also known as clinical vampirism, is a rare psychiatric disorder in which the sufferer feels a compulsion to consume blood by drinking or eating organs. The disorder is classified as some types of schizophrenia or paraphilia.

The condition is named after the infamous character of Renfield in Bram Stoker's novel Dracula. Renfield is a mental patient who consumes insects in the belief that he will absorb their life force. Eventually, he begins feeding flies to spiders and spiders to birds, then consuming the birds to obtain a greater concentration of life force.

People who suffer from this illness commonly believe they obtain some sort of power or strength through the consumption of another organism's blood or brain matter.

Sufferers of Renfield's Syndrome are usually male. The disorder is typically sparked by an event in childhood in which the sufferer associates the sight or taste of blood with excitement. During puberty, the feelings of attraction to blood become sexual in nature.

The condition typically follows three stages:

- **Auto vampirism or Autohemophagia**: The sufferer drinks his own blood, often cutting himself in order to do so.
- **Zoophagia**: This consists of eating live animals or drinking their blood. Obtaining animal blood from a butcher or slaughterhouse for consumption also falls into this stage.
- **Vampirism**: The sufferer's attention turns to other human beings. He may steal blood from hospitals or blood-banks, or drink blood directly from a living person.

After entering this stage, some individuals commit violent crimes, including murder. Richard Trenton Chase is one case of a known serial killer who clearly had this disorder. But even today, it is not fully recognised or understood by medical professions around the world and as such it is largely ignored. It will, however, be synonymous with the crimes carried out by the Vampire of Sacramento.

Active Serial Killers

Every decade, criminologists come out with some form of statistic that shows how many serial killers are currently active within the United States or other countries. Serial Killer and America have gone hand in hand for almost a century and it is the country with the most known convicted serial killers. We say known because in countries within Africa and some in Asia, it is difficult to get viable information out of their police records. The investigative systems are not as tight as they are in the West.

It is quite possible that in a countries like Laos or Cambodia there are serial killers who have been active for generations and probably many who have never been caught. Yet, we don't know about them, or information about them has never been made public.

It is a common piece of information that in the United States there are at least 80 serial killers who are currently active within the general population. It is said 20 in the United Kingdom and another 40 across the EU. The given figures are based on historical data.

How does anyone really know how many serial killers are currently at large? The truth is, no one does, but these types of statistics are drawn up by looking at previous convictions and any outstanding victims that have not been attributed to a known killer.

Of course, this does not just apply to the United States but many other countries where serial killers have been prevalent or in the least, known to have been active. Statistics are statistics and it all depends on how much of it has been tested or based on fact, and indeed how it is interpreted and presented to you.

If you read that 80,000 people go missing every year, you might just miss the part where it says that 79,000 either return home (runaways) or are found safe and well. Of course, that might mean 1,000 people have actually gone missing but it's not as bad as you might first think.

Simple logic and deduction tell us that there are serial killers out there who are actively killing victims in whatever vile way they please. So if we know there are serial killers out there who have never been caught then the next question would be; where are they?

The neighbours of Dennis Nilsen would have had no idea that the hard working civil servant employee was boiling heads in his broth pot at night or keeping bags of human organs in his wardrobe.

They only found out when their drains became blocked with human flesh on account of flushing the 'little bits' down the toilet. They would have spoken to him in the hallways and on the streets and claimed he was a genuinely nice man who wouldn't have hurt a fly.

In larger countries like the United States, Russia, and India, it can be easier for a serial killer to survive in the wild, longer than in smaller countries. Would Andrei Chikatilo of Russia have been able to commit as many murders as he did, in a country like Jamaica? Probably not. So he would have adapted and adaptation is the key. But then he might not have been led to commit the crimes in a country that wasn't torn to bits by the horrors of World War Two.

Serial killers tend to be moulded by their surroundings and their country of birth. If Chikatilo's parents had moved to Jamaica and given birth to him there, would he have grown up to kill? If you believe that serial killers are born to kill then you believe that it is nature that makes them evil. If you believe, as most criminologists do, that serial killers are moulded into killers by their experiences growing up, then you are on the nurture fence of the argument.

We do know there are more serial killers in larger countries. But an argument against larger countries making it easier for serial killers to kill is Harold Shipman, from the United Kingdom. Although it is one of the most 'populated per square mile' countries in the world, it can be famously difficult in the modern era to get away with severe acts of crime. The surveillance 'ring of steel' around London is an obvious deterrent.

Yet, the investigation into Shipman claimed he had managed to kill a suspected 250 victims during his time as a doctor, despite the United Kingdom's small size. He adapted to his environment and hid amongst his peers for decades whilst syphoning money from his elderly victims through their wills. Ironically, it was his greed in garnering their wills that got him caught and not the mistakes in which he killed people.

He was respected by his patients and his neighbours knew nothing untoward was happening in the shadows of his mind. So because we know that there must be serial killers out there, what's to say they don't live in your city? Or maybe your town?

Do you really know your neighbours that well?

Appendices

Bibliography

Selected bibliography, citations, data, and suggested reading.

A. Nortje, C. G. Tredoux, K. Kempen and A. Vredeveldt. (2013) "Applying Laboratory Techniques to a Real-Life Case: What Insight can we Provide about the Station Strangler Case?" American Psychology-Law Society.

Aamodt, M. G. (2016) Serial killer statistics. Retrieved (14/01/2019) from http://maamodt.asp.radford.edu/serial killer information center/projectdescription.htm Radford University.

Aamodt, M. G., & Moyse, C. (2003) Researching the multiple murderer: A comprehensive bibliography of books on specific serial, mass, and spree killers. Journal of Police and Criminal Psychology, 18(1).

Administration for Children and Families (2001) Victims. Child Maltreatment. http://www.acf.dhhs.gov/programs/cb/publications/cm01/chapterthree.htm. Childhelp USA.

Akbulut-Yuksel Mevlude. (2009) Children of the War: The Long-run Effects of Large-scale Physical Destruction and Warfare on Children. IZA Discussion Paper No. 4407.

Archer, Dane, and Rosemary Gartner. (1976) "Violent Acts and Violent Times: A Comparative Approach to Postwar Homicide Rates." American Sociological Review, 41(6).

Bale, A. Bolton, J. Gabriel, R. Jackson, M. Lee, H. (2002) Health Status and Clinical Diagnosis of 3000 UK Gulf War Veterans. Journal of the Royal Society of Medicine. 95.

Ballingtyne and Hanks. (2000) Lest We Forget: ExServicemen and Homelessness. Crisis.

Bartels, K. (1998). Serial Killers: Sublimity to Be Continued. Aesthetics and Criminal History. Amerikastudien / American Studies, 43(3), 497-516.

BBC News. (Jan 2004) "Shipman's 215 Victims." Retrieved from; http://news.bbc.co.uk/go/pr/fr/-/1/hi/uk/2138888.stm. BBC Article.

Bingham A, Delap L, Jackson L, & Settle L. (2016) "Historical child sexual abuse in England and Wales: The role of historians." History of Education, 45(4).

Branson, Allan. (2013). African American Serial Killers: Over-Represented Yet Under-acknowledged. The Howard Journal of Criminal Justice. 52.

Brunt, Martin. Sky News. (2008) "Ex-Detective Held Over Axe Murder".. https://news.sky.com/skynews/Home/Sky-News-Archive/Article/20080641313539 Sky.com News Archive.

Carlo, P. (2006) The Iceman: Confessions of a Mafia Contract Killer. New York. St. Martin's Press.

Carrabine, Eamonn. (2008) Crime, Culture, and Media. Cambridge, UK. Polity Publishers.

CBS Sacramento. (2016). "California Inmate On Death Row Since 1988 Dies In The Hospital" https://sacramento.cbslocal.com/2016/12/14/california-inmate-on-death-row-since-1988-dies-in-the-hospital/. CBS.

Central Intelligence Agency. (Retrieved 2019) Research papers and FOIA requests on Project MK-Ultra. https://www.cia.gov/library/readingroom/search/site/mk%20ultra. CIA.

Chang, S. (2005) The prodigal "son" returns: An assessment of current "Son of Sam" laws and the reality of the online murderabilia marketplace. Rutgers Computer and Technology Law Journal.

Chen, Edwin. Los Angeles Times. (April 27th 1989). "Man Convicted of 4 Murders; 2 Linked to Southside Slayer Case." https://www.latimes.com/archives/la-xpm-1989-04-27-me-1912-story.html. Latimes.com

Cohen, M. (1997). Inside the Murderer. Studies in Popular Culture, 19(3), 49-63.

Conrath, R. (1994). The Guys Who Shoot to Thrill: Serial Killers and the American Popular Unconscious. Revue Française D'études Américaines, (60), 143-152.

Dahl, G., & DellaVigna, S. (2009). Does Movie Violence Increase Violent Crime? The Quarterly Journal of Economics, 124(2), 677-734.

Danziger, Sheldon H, Robert Haveman, eds. (2001) Understanding Poverty. New York: Russell Sage Foundation. Cambridge: Harvard University Press.

Delap, L. (2018). "Disgusting Details Which Are Best Forgotten": Disclosures of Child Sexual Abuse in Twentieth-Century Britain. Journal of British Studies, 57(1).

Disaster Center Crime Data. (Retrieved 2019) http://www.disastercenter.com/crime. DCC.

Dodd, Vikram. Guardian, The. (2014). Cherry Groce inquest: officer takes full blame for shot that led to Brixton riots https://www.theguardian.com/uk-news/2014/jul/01/cherry-groce-inquest-officer-takes-blame-shooting-brixton-riots Guardian.com.

Donna Youngs, Maria Ioannou. (2013) A Model of Client-Related Violence Against Female Street Sex Workers. Journal of Forensic Social Work, 3(3).

Douglas, John E.; Allen G. Burgess, Robert K. Ressler, and Ann W. Burgess. (2006) Crime Classification Manual: A Standard System for Investigating and Classifying Violent Crimes. Second, Wiley.

Douglas, John. Mindhunter: Inside the FBI's Elite Serial Crime Unit. (1995) New York, Scribner.

Dresser, R. (2011). At law: Families and Forensic DNA Profiles. The Hastings Center Report, 41(3), 11-12.

E. G. L. (1919). The Statute of Limitations and the Conflict of Laws. The Yale Law Journal, 28(5), 492-498.

Egger, Steven A. (2000) Why Serial Murderers Kill: An Overview. Contemporary Issues Companion: Serial Killers.

Federal Bureau of Investigation. (2008) Serial Murder: Multi-disciplinary Perspectives for Investigators. Washington, DC. U.S. Department of Justice.

Federal Bureau of Investigation. (2009). Highway serial killing database release. https://archives.fbi.gov/archives/news/stories/2009/april/highwayserial_040609. U.S Department of Justice.

Feigenbaum, JJ, & Muller, C. (2016) Lead exposure and violent crime in the early twentieth century. Explorations in Economic History.

Forsyth, C. J. (2015) Posing: The sociological routine of the serial killer. American Journal of Criminal Justice, 40(4).

Fox, J. A., & Levin, J. (2015) Extreme killing. Understanding massive serial murder (3rd ed.). Los Angeles. Sage publications Inc.

Fox, J., & Levin, J. (1998). Multiple Homicide: Patterns of Serial and Mass Murder. Crime and Justice, 23, 407-455.

Foy, D. (1987). Disasters at Sea and their Prevention. RSA Journal, 136(5377), 13-24.

Friedrichsen, Gisela. (1995) Criminal Justice. https://www.spiegel.de/spiegel/print/d-9247676.html Der Spiegel 52/1995.

Gabriel, R. Neal, L. (2002) Post-Traumatic Stress Disorder following military combat or peace keeping. British Medical Journal. 324.

Gagnon, J. (1965) Female Child Victims of Sex Offenses. Social Problems, 13(2).

Ganesan, N., & Kim, S. (Eds.). (2013). State Violence in East Asia. University Press of Kentucky.

Godwin, M., (2008) (2nd Edition). Hunting Serial Predators. Jones & Bartlett Publishers, MA.

Gorman, Anna. (2004). "Ten Murder Charges Filed." Retrieved 2019. Los Angeles Times.

Guardian, The. (2012). Terry Waite returns to Lebanon 25 years after kidnapping https://www.theguardian.com/world/2012/dec/09/terry-waite-returns-lebanon-kidnapping?CMP=share_btn_tw. Theguardian.com

Gunner and Knott (1997) Homeless on Civvy Street: Survey of Homelessness amongst Ex-Servicemen. Ex-Service Action Group

Gurian, E. A. (2013) Explanations of mixed-sex partnered homicide: A review of sociological and psychological theory. Aggression and Violent Behaviour, 18(5).

Hacking, Ian. (1991) "The Making and Molding of Child Abuse." Critical Inquiry, 17(2).

Hans Gross, (1907, retrieved 2019) Criminal Investigation: A Practical Handbook for Magistrates, Police Officers and Lawyers.

Harrison, Marissa & M. Hughes, Susan & Jordan Gott, Adam. (2019) Sex Differences in Serial Killers. Evolutionary Behavioral Sciences.

Hart, Timothy C., Troshynski, Emily I. (2016) Perceptions of Stalking Victimization among Behaviorally Defined Victims. The Wiley Handbook on the Psychology of Violence.

Havill, Adrian. (2001). Born Evil: A True Story of Cannibalism and Serial Murder. New York, N.Y.: St. Martin's Press. Retrieved 2019.

Hickey, E. W. (2002) Serial murderers and their victims (3rd ed.). Belmont, Wadsworth.

Historical Institutional Abuse Inquiry. (2017) http://www.hiainquiry.org/index.htm Inquiry updated at https://www.nidirect.gov.uk/articles/historical-institutional-abuse

Holmes J, Fear N T, Harrison K, Sharpley J, Wessely S. (2013) Suicide among Falkland war veterans. BMJ 346.

Jacob Bucher, Michelle Manasse, Jeffrey Milton. (2015) Soliciting strain: examining both sides of street prostitution through General Strain Theory. Journal of Crime and Justice 38(4).

Jacquelyn Monroe PhD. (2005) Women in Street Prostitution: The Result of Poverty and the Brunt of Inequity. Journal of Poverty 9(3).

Jarvis, C., (March 20th, 1997). "Academic sleuth made startling predictions". News & Observer, Raleigh, NC.

Jones N, Fear NT, Jones M, Wessely S, Greenberg N. (2010) Long-term military work outcomes in soldiers who become mental health casualties when deployed on operations. Psychiatry. 73(4).

Jooyoung Lee, Sasha Reid. (2018) Serial Killers & Their Easy Prey. Contexts 17(2).

Joyce Prince and TCN Gibbens, (1963) Child Victims of Sex Offences. Institute for the Study and Treatment of Delinquency.

Kandel, Jason, (2011). "Police tie Grim Sleeper suspect to six more killings." https://www.reuters.com/article/us-crime-grimsleeper/police-tie-grim-sleeper-suspect-to-six-more-killings-idUSTRE7A20L120111103. Reuters.

Kathryn Ann Farr PhD. (2000) Defeminizing and Dehumanizing Female Murderers. Women & Criminal Justice 11(2).

Keenan, Thomas, 'Getting the Dead to Tell Me what Happened: Justice, Prosopopoeia, and Forensic Afterlives', in Forensic Architecture, ed., Forensic, 35-55.

Kesternich I, Siflinger B, Smith JP, Winter JK. (2013) The Effects of World War II on Economic and Health Outcomes across Europe. Rev Econ Stat.

LAPD Online. (Retrieved July 2019) Photos of Grim Sleeper Victims. http://www.lapdonline.org/grimsleeper. Lapdonline.com

Leskanic, T., (2004) "Inmate indicted in 1995 killing." Retrieved 2019. Fayetteville Observer.

Lewis, Jack. (May 1985) "Lead Poisoning: A Historical Perspective." EPA Journal article.

Lodinews. (2016) "Convicted killer Loren Herzog commits suicide." Lodinews.com. http://www.lodinews.com/news/article_64587e42-4122-11e1-b68e-001871e3ce6c.html

Louise A. Jackson. (2000) Child Sexual Abuse in Victorian England. London. Routledge.

Love, T., Laier, C., Brand, M., Hatch, L., & Hajela, R. (2015) Neuroscience of Internet Pornography Addiction: A Review and Update. Behavioral sciences.

McClellan, Janet. (2007) Animal Cruelty and Violent Behavior: Is There a Connection? Journal of Security Education.

McNichol, Dan. (2006) The Roads That Built America: The Incredible Story of the U.S. Interstate System. New York. Sterling.

Meija, Brittny. Los Angeles Times. (Nov 9th 2015). Grim Sleeper: Defense backtracks on expert witness https://www.latimes.com/local/lanow/la-me-ln-grim-sleeper-defense-backtracks-expert-witness-20151109-story.htm.l Retrieved 2019. latimes.com

Miller, G. (2010). Familial DNA Testing Scores A Win in Serial Killer Case. Science, 329(5989), new series, 262-262.

Montgomery, Ben. Zayas, Alexandra. (July 8th 2007). "Valley murder victims." Concord Monitor. Archived from the original in 2015. Concordmonitor.com.

Nathan W. Pino. (2005) Serial Offending and the Criminal Events Perspective. Homicide Studies 9(2).

Nelson, Harold E. (1987). NIST Interagency/Internal Report (NISTIR) – 87-3560. May 29th.

Nesta H Wells. (1958) "Sexual offences as seen by a woman police surgeon". British Medical Journal. Dec 6th article.

NSQCCA 327. (1999), Regina v Rose [1999]. New South Wales Criminal Court of Appeal. No. 60520 of 1998

Oakley, Ben. Luisa, Marina. (2019) Mentacracy: Living under the Rule of Mental Illness. United Kingdom. Twelvetrees Publishing.

Oakley, Ben. (2019) 1978: Year of the Serial Killer. 1987: Year of the Serial Killer Chapter 2. 1996: Year of the Serial Killer Chapter 3. United Kingdom. Twelvetrees Publishing.

Panayiotopoulos CP (1999) Typical absence seizures and their treatment. Archives of Disease in Childhood.

Parfitt CH, Alleyne E. (Jan 2018) Not the Sum of Its Parts: A Critical Review of the MacDonald Triad. Trauma Violence Abuse.

Pelisek, Christine (2007). "Death Penalty for Chester Turner". LA Weekly. Village Voice Media. Rtvd 2019. http://www.laweekly.com/2007-05-17/news/death-penalty-for-chester-turner/

Potterat JJ, Brewer DD, Muth SQ, Rothenberg RB, Woodhouse DE, Muth JB, Stites HK, Brody S. (2004) Mortality in a long-term open cohort of sex worker women. Am J Epidemiol.

Ram, N. (2011). Fortuity and Forensic Familial Identification. Stanford Law Review, 63(4), 751-812.

Randall and Brown (1994) Falling Out: A Research Study of Homeless Ex-Service People. Crisis.

Ressler, Robert K., Schachtman, Thomas. (1993) Whoever Fights Monsters: My Twenty Years Tracking Serial Killers for the FBI. New York. Macmillan/St. Martin's.

Rijt, Arnout & Song, Hyang-Gi & Shor, Eran & Burroway, Rebekah. (2018) Racial and gender differences in missing children's recovery chances. PLOS ONE. (13).

Robinson, Kathleen. (2012). "Puerto Rico fire is the second-deadliest hotel fire in U.S. history." NFPA Journal, November/December 2012.

Rosen, Fred (July 1, 2015). Body Dump: Kendall Francois, the Poughkeepsie Serial Killer. Open Road Media. ISBN 9781504022644.

S. Thompson, Kenrick & C. Clarke, Alfred. (1974) Photographic Imagery and the Vietnam War: An Unexamined Perspective. The Journal of Psychology.

Scheanette v. Office of Chief Disciplinary Counsel, Not Reported in F.Supp.2d, 2005 WL 3147874 (N.D.Tex. 2005) (Pro Se).

Schildcrout, J. (2014). Murder Most Queer: The Homicidal Homosexual in the American Theater. Ann Arbor: University of Michigan Press.

Schmid, David. (2005) Natural Born Celebrities: Serial Killers in American Culture. Chicago. University of Chicago Press.

Scottish Government. (Retrieved 2019) Public Inquiry into Child Abuse in Scotland, http://www.gov.scot/Topics/People/Young-People/protecting/child-protection/historical-child-abuse

Seltzer, M. (1995). Serial Killers (II): The Pathological Public Sphere. Critical Inquiry, 22(1), 122-149.

Smith, C., Lobban, G., O'Loughlin, M. (Eds.) (2013). Psychodynamic Psychotherapy in South Africa: Contexts, theories and applications. Johannesburg: Wits University Press.

Stevelink, Sharon & Malcolm, Estelle & Mason, C & Jenkins, Sarah & Sundin, Josefin & Fear, N.T. (2014) The prevalence of mental health disorders in (ex-)military personnel with a physical impairment: A systematic review. Occupational and environmental medicine. 72(10).

Susan L. Murray PhD, PE, Matthew S. Thimgan PhD, (2016). "Human Fatigue Risk Management."

Tallichet, Suzanne & Hensley, Christopher. (2004) Exploring the Link between Recurrent Acts of Childhood and Adolescent Animal Cruelty and Subsequent Violent Crime. Criminal Justice Review. 29.

Taylor MP, Forbes MK, Opeskin B, Parr N, Lanphear BP. (2018) Further analysis of the relationship between atmospheric lead emissions and aggressive crime: an ecological study. Environmental Health. 17(1).

Times, Los Angeles, (Retrieved 2019). "Guilty verdicts in Grim Sleeper serial killer case." https://www.latimes.com/local/lanow/la-me-ln-grim-sleeper-death-verdict-20160606-snap-story.html. latimes.com.

Trend, David. (2007) The Myth of Media Violence: A Critical Introduction. Malden, MA. Blackwell Publishing.

Trevor A. Kletz DSc, FEng, FIChemE, FRSC, (1990). Critical Aspects of Safety and Loss Prevention.

United Nations. (2014) World Urbanization Prospects: The 2014 Revision. Department of Economic and Social Affairs: Population Division

Walker, J., (1997). The Traumatic Paradox: Documentary Films, Historical Fictions, and Cataclysmic Past Events. Signs, 22(4), 803-825.

Weingroff, Richard F. (1996) “Federal-Aid Highway Act of 1956, Creating the Interstate System”. Public Roads. Article. 60(1).

Wright, Jeremy & Hensley, Christopher. (2003) From Animal Cruelty to Serial Murder: Applying the Graduation Hypothesis. International journal of offender therapy and comparative criminology. (47).

Image Attributions

Copyrighted photos used under license from relevant parties. Some photos used under licence from Unsplash and Pixabay.

Attrib 75.) Photo by: John Riojas. Description: Close up photography of white and brown pig photo.

Attrib 84.) Photo by Jonathan Korner. Description: Cityscape photo of Florence, Italy.

Attrib 157-158 + 200.) Twelvetrees Camden : Why Serial Killers Kill mock-ups. Serial killer montage.

Attrib 161.) Highway photo. Copyrighted to Patrick Hendry.

Attrib 162.) Hitchhiker photo. Copyrighted to Dmitry Shulga.

Attrib 164.) Condom photo. Copyrighted to Charles Deluvio.

Attrib 165.) Description: Paratrooper from the 101st Airborne Brigade applying mouth-to-mouth resuscitation to an injured soldier who was airlifted by helicopter to the medical clearing station near Kontum, Vietnam. Copyrighted to The New York Public Library.

Attrib 166-168.) Description: Female covered in paint. Female looking out window. Copyrighted to Engin Akyurt.

Attrib 170.) Brent Station evacuations, Devon. Copyrighted to The History Press.

Attrib 171-173/ 174-176/184-189/194-195/196-198) Photos used in why serial killers kill. Copyrighted to Gerd Altmann, Alexas Fotos, Looie Kang, José Martín, Ramírez Carrasco, Pawel Szvmanski, Vitaly Sacred, Warren Umoh, Jesse Orrico and Ehimetalor Akhere Unuabona.

Photos and images in public domain which qualify under fair use laws to illustrate the subjects.

Attrib 2) Photo of Baekuni. | Attrib 4.) Photo of Jeffrey Dahmer as a senior in high school. Date: 1978. Source: Reverie, yearbook of Revere Senior High School, Richfield, Ohio | Attrib 5.) Booking Photo of Gary Ridgway, the Green River Killer. Date: 30 November 2001. Source: Kings County Sheriff's Office | Attrib 6.) Prison Photo of Pedro Lopez. Date: 23 April 1987. Source: Fiscalía General de la Nación. | Attrib 7.) Ted Bundy in a courtroom. Date: 1979. Source: Florida Memory Project hosted at the State Archive of Florida. | Attrib 12-13.) Ted Bundy mug shot. Date: 13 February 1980. Source: Florida Memory Project hosted at the State Archive of Florida. | Attrib 14.) Suspect Theodore Bundy after his original arrest. Date: July 1978. Source: Florida Memory Project hosted at the State Archive of Florida. | Attrib 15.) Mug Shot of Steven David Catlin in 2007. Date: July 1978. Source: California Department of Corrections and Rehabilitation.

Attrib 17.) Photo by FBI. Description: Photo of Edward Wayne Edwards. Source: FBI database. | Attrib 19.) Chateau du Sautou, former home of Michel Fourniret. Date: January 2007. | Attrib 20.) Police search at Chateau du Sautou, former home of Michel Fourniret. Date: Released to public in January 2007. | Attrib 21.) Mugshots of Monique Olivier & Michel Fourniret. Date: Released to public in 2001. | Attrib 25.) White House photographer. Date: May 1978. Description: White House photograph of First Lady Rosalynn Carter with Democratic Party activist and serial killer John Wayne Gacy. | Attrib 23.) Mugshot of convicted serial killer Kendall Francois. | Attrib 24.) Photo of Lonnie David Franklin Jr. | Attrib 30.) Photo by: Wise County Police. Date: November 2018. Description: Samuel Little. | Attrib 32.) Photo of Stefano Baldi and Susanna Cambi, the victims of the fourth crime of the so-called Monster of Florence, killed October 23, 1981. | Attrib 33.) Photo of Horst Wilhelm Meyer and Jens-Uwe Rüsch, the victims of the sixth crime of the so-called Monster of Florence, killed on September 9th 1983 in Giogoli.

Attrib 34.) Photo of Jean-Michel Kraveichvili and Nadine Mauriot, the victims of the eighth crime of the so-called Monster of Florence, killed between 7th and 8th September 1985 at Scopeti. | Attrib 35.) Photo by Sutton Prison. Description: Dennis Nilsen mugshot. | Attrib 37.) Photo by California Department of Corrections and Rehabilitation, Sacramento, California, United States. Date: June 2007. Description: Inmate photo of American serial killer Gerald Parker. | Attrib 40.) Police photo of Joseph Swango | Attrib 42.) Police photo of Gerald Stano. | Attrib 43.) Photo of Anatoly Slivko. Date: 1986. | Attrib 45.) Police and court photo of Angus SInclair. | Attrib 47.) Photo of Loren Herzog and Wesley Shermantine. | Attrib 48 to Attrib 53.) Selection of photos from the personal collection of Rodney Alcala | Attrib 54-55.) Photos of the rear and front of Fox Hollow Farm. Description: Location where Herb Baumeister lived and killed some of his victims. | Attrib 56.) Photo of Herb Baumeister. Description: Mugshot of serial killer Baumeister.

Attrib 59.) Photo of David Berkowitz. Description: Mugshot of serial killer Berkowitz in 2003. | Attrib 61.) Photo of Richard Trenton Chase. Description: Mugshot of serial killer Chase. | Attrib 62-69.) Colonial Parkway Murder Victims. Source: High School yearbooks and police releases. | Attrib 79.) Photo of Pedro Rodriguez Filho. | Attrib 85.) Photo of Roger Kibbe. | Attrib 86.) Photo of Timothy Krajcir. | Attrib 92.) The Ford Econoline van used by William Bonin to abduct his victims. | Attrib 93.) Description: William Bonin, pictured in the North High School yearbook, c. 1963. | Attrib 100.) Richard Francis Cottingham, 1980, Bergen County Prosecutor's Office, New Jersey. | Attrib 101.) Image of American serial killer Louis Craine. | Attrib 103.) Somerset Medical Center, Somerville, NJ by Ekem, | Attrib 107.) Donald Leroy Evans mugshot. Mississippi Department of Corrections. | Attrib 109.) Luis Alfredo Garavito Cubillos on Apr. 23, 1999 after being detained for an attempted assault on a 12-year-old boy in the western Colombian region.

Attrib 110-111.) Gerald Gallego and Charlene Gallego mug shots. California Department of Corrections. | Attrib 112.) Michael Gargiulo. Los Angeles County Sheriff's Office. | Attrib 126.) Mugshot of Australian serial killer Paul Steven Haigh in 1977. | Attrib 130.) Mugshot of Francisco del Junco. | Attrib 131.) Mugshot of Finnish serial killer Junni, Ismo Kullervo | Attrib 133.) Mugshot of Finnish serial killer Michael Penttila, aka: Jukka Torsten Lindholm. | Attrib 135.) Photo of Robert Maudsley. | Attrib 138-140.) Police sketches of unidentified victims of the Long Island Serial Killer. | Attrib 142.) Photo of Gerald Parker. | Attrib 143.) Photo of Steven Brian Pennell. | Attrib 144.) Wanted poster of Vinko Pintaric. | Attrib 146.) Self-taken photo of Dennis Rader in women's clothes | Attrib 147.) Photo of James Michael Randall. | Attrib 148.) Photo of Terry Peder Rasmussen. | Attrib 154.) Photo of Robert Joseph Silveria Jr. in 1986. | Attrib 156.) Photo of Morris Solomon Jr. in 2007. | Attrib 159.) Ted Bundy in courtroom. | Attrib 179.) Andrei Chikatilo in cell. | Attrib 190-191.) Two photos of Richard Ramirez, side by side. | Attrib 192-193.) Two photos of David Berkowitz, side by side. | Attrib 199.) One of a series of images of Jack the Ripper from the Illustrated London News for October 13, 1888

Images and photos that qualify as fair use under United States and United Kingdom copyright law, where no free equivalent is available or could be created that would adequately give the same information to illustrate the subject in question. Used to illustrate an encyclopedic entry for educational and informational purposes only.

Attrib 9.) Photo by: Historica Canada. Description: Pickton at work. Accessed via the Canadian Encyclopedia in September 2021. | Attrib 10.) Photo by: Historica Canada. Description: Arial view of the Pickton Farm in Port Coquitlam, BC. Accessed via the Canadian Encyclopedia in September 2020. | Attrib 12.) Photo by: Mark T. Foley. Date: May 1979. Description: Tallahassee, Florida. Dr. Richard Souviron presents dental evidence at the trial of Ted Bundy for the Chi Omega Murders. | Attrib 16.) Source: Image was first published in Russian-language newspapers. Date: April 1992. Description: Andrey Chikatilo in court | Attrib 18.) Photo of Gwen Graham and Cathy Wood. Mugshots from source. | Attrib 27.) Photo by: San Quentin State Prison. Date: June 2007. Description: Mugshot of serial killer Randy Steven Kraft. | Attrib 28.) Description: Photo of Fred and Rose West.

Attrib 29.) Photos of Fred West and Rose West were released for criminal purposes in the British media. Images are at least 30 years old. | Attrib 31.) Photo of Jack Unterweger. Image is at least 30 years old | Attrib 38.) Photo of Alexander pichushkin. | Attrib 39.) Description: mugshot of Peter Tobin. | Attrib 41.) Photo of Peter Sutcliffe. | Attrib 46.) Photo by Wakefield Prison. Description: Harold Shipman mug shot. | Attrib 57.) Photo of Robert Andrew Berdella. | Attrib 58.) Photo of David Berkowitz. | Attrib 60.) Photo of Robert Black. | Attrib 61.) Mug shot of Jeffrey Dahmer. Source: Milwaukee Police Department. Date: July 23, 1991. | Attrib 71.) Description: Mugshot taken of John Wayne Gacy, taken following his arrest for murder. | Attrib 72.) Description: Mugshot taken of Danny Lee Barber, taken following his arrest for murder. | Attrib 73.) Description: Court photo of Velma Barfield. | Attrib 76.) Description: photo of Robert Pickton.

Attrib 77.) Description: Interior of Pickton's slaughterhouse. | Attrib 78.) Description: Photo of Peter Sutcliffe. | Attrib 80.) Photo of Charles Ray Hatcher. Mugshot from source. | Attrib 81.) Photo of Archibald Hall | Attrib 82.) Photo of Phillip Jablonski. | Attrib 83.) CP photo of Gilbert Paul Jordan. | Attrib 87.) Photo of David Parker Ray (mugshot). | Attrib 88.) Photo of David Parker Ray'S Toy Box | Attrib 90.) Police photo of Metod Trobec. | Attrib 91.) William George "Bill" Bonin's Feb. 4, 1980 mugshot taken just one day following the murders of Charles Miranda (aged 15) and James McCabe (aged 12) | Attrib 94.) Description: Robert Eugene Brashers. Sourced from the Missouri Highway Patrol. | Attrib 95.) Photo of Hadden Irving Clark. | Attrib 96.) Description: Mugshot photo of Hadden Irving Clark. Sourced from the Montgomery County Police Department.

Attrib 98.) Description: Headshot of Christiansen, Thor Nis. Notes: From Santa Barbara County Police. | Attrib 99.) Description: Photograph of serial killer couple, Ray and Faye Copeland. | Attrib 102.) Description: Photograph of serial killer Charles Cullen. | Attrib 104.) Description: Photograph of serial killer Marc Dutroux. | Attrib 106.) Description: Photo of Marc Dutroux's hidden cellar. | Attrib 108.) Description: Gary Charles Evans mugshot. New York State Police. | Attrib 113.) Description: Mug shot of American serial killer Carlton Gary by the Georgia Department of Corrections. | Attrib 124.) Description: Mug shot of American serial killer Sean Vincent Gillis by the East Baton Rouge Parish Sheriff's Department, Louisiana, United States, April 2004 | Attrib 125.) Description: Mugshot of American serial killer Vincent Groves. Denver District Attorney's Office.

Attrib 127.) Description: Photo of 19-year-old Lisa Brearley, victim of Paul Haigh. | Attrib 128.) Description: Mugshot of American serial killer Martha Ann Johnson. | Attrib 129.) Description: Mugshot of American serial killer Genene Jones. | Attrib 132.) Description: Mugshot of Derrick

Todd Lee in 2003. | Attrib 134.) Description: Mugshot taken of Henry Lee Lucas. | Attrib 141.) Description: Anatoly Onoprienko mugshot. Source: Zhytomyr Prison. | Attrib 145.) Description: Mugshot of Dennis Rader, aka the BTK killer, by the Kansas Department of Corrections. | Attrib 151.) Description: Mugshot of Altemio Sanchez. | Attrib 152.) Description: Photo of Tommy Lynn Sells via Val Verde County Sheriff's Department. | Attrib 153.) Description: Photo of Ershad Sikder. | Attrib 155.) Description: Photo of Samuel Smithers. | Attrib 183.) Description: Mugshot of John Wayne Gacy.

Creative commons licences. Images used under fair use laws with various licenses including CC BY-ND 2.0, CC BY-SA 4.0 and Attribution-Share Alike 3.0 Unported license.

Attrib 1.) Description: Prison photo of Rodney Alcala. Date September 2nd 1997. Author: San Quentin State Prison, California Department of Corrections and Rehabilitation. | Attrib 3.) Description: Painting by serial killer John Wayne Gacy. Date: January 1st 2007 release. Author: The Orchid Club. | Attrib 8.) Description: Pitkin County Courthouse in Aspen, that the American serial killer Ted Bundy escaped from. Date: circa 2005. Author: Matthew Trump. | Attrib 11.) Photo by: Stolbovsky. Date: July 2015. Description: Bitsevsky forest in Bitsa Park. | Attrib 22.) Photo by: Poughkeepsie Native. Date: December 25th 1998. Description: Kendall Francois' former home taken three months after police searched the house and removed the bodies. | Attrib 26.) Description: John Wayne Gacy in clown suit.

Attrib 36.) Photo by Chris Whippet. Date: December 2008. Description: Cranley Gardens, Muswell Hill. | Attrib 44.) Photo by Kim Traynor. Date: October 2011. Description: World's End pub, High Street Edinburgh. | Attrib 97.) Description: Captured image of lee choon jae from YouTube video by Ilsaef. | Attrib 105.) Description: Pencil sketch of Marc Dutroux made by Cart/Ann-Sophie Qvarnström. Original art. Sketch made and scanned directly afterwards. | Attrib 136.) Description: Map indicating the location of where the bodies were discovered. Author: Atiru. | Attrib 137.) Description: Sign for the Robert Moses Causeway along the Ocean Parkway. Author: Mitchazenia. | Attrib 149.) Description: Photo of John Edward Robinson. | Attrib 150.) Description: Photo of serial killer, Nikolai Aleksandrovich Sakharov, 1954-1979.

Bizarre True Crime Taster

Bizarre True Crime is a bestselling series from Ben Oakley and Twelvetrees Camden, exploring the wilder side of true crime. The books gives you the most varied collection of true crime related stories, from 16th Century witchcraft to cryptocurrency hacks, you name it, it's all in there!

From murder and serial killers, strange deaths, mysteries, the unexplained, cults, occult, gangs, gangsters, hackings, kidnappings, cons, prison breaks, and so much more. Here are two stories from the series to get you in the mood.

Ugly Tuna Saloona and The Smiley Face Killers

In one of the most baffling missing person's cases of all time, a man is seen on a security feed entering a bar but never leaving, in a rabbit-hole of a case leading to an unusual serial killer theory.

The Ugly Tuna Saloona

It seems illogical that someone could simply vanish into thin air but it's exactly what happened to 27-year-old Brian Shaffer in Columbus, Ohio, on 31st March 2006. Considered to be one of the most mysterious disappearances in recent history, no trace of him has ever been found, dead or alive.

Ohio-born Shaffer was a clean-shaven, well-dressed medical student in attendance at Ohio State University's College of Medicine. He had a good childhood, a good future ahead of him, and no known enemies to speak of.

On that fateful night, Shaffer hit the town with his friend, William 'Clint' Florence, in celebration of the beginning of spring break. After drinking at various establishments, they ended up at the unusually named Ugly Tuna Saloona bar, with Florence's friend Meredith Reed tagging along.

Sometime after midnight, they assumed Shaffer had gone home and were separated from him. At around 2am, Shaffer was seen on a security camera speaking to two women before re-entering the bar.

The door he had entered was the only public way in and out of the bar and the security camera never stopped recording. There was no sign of him leaving the bar on the camera's feed, and no-one had seen him inside after 2am. It was as if he had vanished into thin air.

Spring break

Shaffer wasn't reported missing until three days later, when on 3rd April he missed a flight to Miami that he was due to take with his girlfriend, Alexis Waggoner. He had only recently met Alexis in the New Year of 2006 but according to their friends and family, he was going to propose to her on their spring break trip to Miami.

He had long been drawn to what he called the tropical lifestyle. Though he was studying medicine, his true dream was to start a band and live in a warmer climate, like Miami, which he loved. He adored the band Pearl Jam so much that he had their logo tattooed on his arm and could only dream of one day being so big.

Just weeks before Shaffer disappeared, his mother died of bone cancer, leading to what would become a double tragedy for his father, Randy. Despite the death, Shaffer was said to be taking it well – as best as was expected.

His father later said that Shaffer was tired after having pulled all-nighters through the previous weeks and didn't think he would have the energy to go out. But the lure of spring break for a 27-year-old med student would always be too much.

Shaffer and William had started the night at the Ugly Tuna Saloona, drinking shots and beers, before leaving around 10pm and bar-hopping throughout the city. Shaffer phoned Alexis around the same time to tell her that he loved her and was looking forward to their Miami trip.

The pair, along with Meredith, ended the night back at the Ugly Tuna Saloona at around 1.15am. All three were spotted on the security camera going up the elevator to the upper floor drinking den. After losing sight of Shaffer in the bar, William and Meredith waited until the bar closed at 2am.

They exited with the other patrons and waited outside but Shaffer never turned up. When Shaffer was reported missing, the police investigation visited the bar and took hold of the security footage for the night of the disappearance. It was then that things started to get weird.

Disappeared into thin air

At 1.55am, Shaffer was seen on the security feed outside the bar talking to two younger women. Investigators watched him re-enter the bar followed by the women. A few minutes later, the bar closed and all the patrons began exiting.

As investigators watched the leaving crowd, there seemed to be no sign that Shaffer had left. Perplexed, they began the arduous process of identifying everyone who had been in the bar that night and finding them on the security feed.

The only explanation was that Shaffer was on the security feed and they had missed him. They assumed they would eventually pinpoint when Shaffer had left the bar and where he was on the feed. But the team managed to identify everyone on the feed, and intricately examined the footage.

It appeared that for some inexplicable reason, Shaffer was nowhere to be seen. He had gone back into the bar and never come out. The security feeds from the main entrance included a manual static camera and a panning camera, which made it impossible for someone to slip out undetected.

The bar closed just minutes after he had gone back inside. The only other exit was a closed service door that opened onto a construction site. There were no signs that the door had ever been opened at the time Shaffer was in the bar.

Police assumed he must have exited somehow, so they looked at the security footage of many other bars in the same street, and from retail buildings nearby. After splicing them together to form a timeline, not one of the security feeds showed signs of Shaffer.

Police dogs were used to search the nearby streets, alleyways, and dumpsters, but no scent was picked up. They also got permission to search the sewers but nothing useful was uncovered. Thousands of missing person's posters were put up around the city but nothing came of it.

His car was parked near his home and was exactly as he had left it. His apartment was clean and tidy, with no signs of anything untoward. It was simply the case that Shaffer had walked into the Ugly Tuna Saloona and disappeared into thin air.

No logical explanation

Without a logical explanation, the theories began, and some were no less strange. The obvious theory was that Shaffer had exited through the service door but the construction site was deemed too dangerous to have walked through, especially for someone as drunk as Shaffer would have been.

Had Shaffer been met with an unfortunate accident while exiting into the construction site then his body would have been found the next day by construction workers. There were no deep holes around, nor a place where a body would have been missed.

There was also no evidence he had exited through the door nor did dogs pick up a scent there. The lack of Shaffer on security footage from nearby establishments meant he had not walked from the bar via the service door exit.

An addendum to this theory suggests that Shaffer had jumped from the bar's outdoor balcony, but yet again, there was no security feed evidence to show he had exited that way, and he would have severely hurt himself if he had done.

The suspicion that he had taken his own life or run away due to his mother's death, went against everything Shaffer had believed in but there was one theory that supported it and his possible purposeful disappearance. Had Shaffer disguised himself on the way out?

The purposeful theory rests on the fact that Shaffer was deliberately attempting to disappear. He had gone back into the bar shortly before closing, changed his clothes, and exited in a disguise. Except, no abandoned clothes were found in the bar, and every single person exiting the bar on the security feed was identified.

His friends and family, though sometimes not the best witnesses in a case such as this, suggested he had no reason to run away and was not the type to take his own life. He was also as drunk as a skunk and planning a disguise and getaway would have been a tall order.

Leads that went nowhere

Since the disappearance, Shaffer's bank account and credit cards have never been used, and his friends and family concluded that he must be dead somewhere. Suspicions were aimed at the two friends with him that night, William and Meredith, and despite William refusing to take a polygraph, there was no evidence to suggest they were involved.

In 2008, Shaffer's father, Randy, died in an unfortunate accident, when a branch broke off a tree and hit him in the head. One of the online obituary entries was signed off as '*to dad, love Brian*', but was later discovered to be a hoax.

The two women who were on the feed talking to Shaffer were seen exiting the bar with the other patrons and were never linked to any disappearance or foul play. In 2009, a private investigator named Don Corbett claimed that Shaffer was still alive after speaking to the lead detective in the case.

His claim stemmed from the fact that William was starting to become a suspect and had instructed a lawyer to act on his behalf. Some family members believed William was somehow involved but Don Corbett claimed that it was Shaffer himself who was causing his family pain and should come forward.

In 2020, a photograph of a homeless man in Mexico who looked remarkably similar to Shaffer went viral but the FBI determined through facial analysis that it wasn't him. Despite many researchers believing he had disappeared purposefully, they were forgetting one major point; Shaffer had never left the bar.

Wild theories

Which leaves us still with a number of possibilities. One of the theories that stands out above the rest but still relies on extraordinary claims, is that Shaffer died of natural causes when he returned to the bar and was found by the staff who then covered up his death.

The theory goes that when William and Meredith were looking for him, Shaffer had already sat down in the bar and accidentally died of alcohol poisoning. Therefore, they couldn't see him as they scanned the crowd of people standing around the bar. But why would bar staff cover up a death?

If someone had died accidentally in a bar then there would be no reason to cover it up unless the staff were implicit in the death. Shaffer was seen five minutes before the bar closed and showed no signs of being ill, but death by a large volume of alcohol can be instant.

What if the bar staff murdered him? What would be their reason? Shaffer was not a violent person and stayed out of trouble and would not have given reason for the staff to murder him. Again, there was no evidence to suggest that a murder had taken place.

In the years since the disappearance, an unusual theory within a theory has emerged. Two New York City detectives Kevin Gannon and Anthony Duarte, and criminal justice professor Dr. Lee Gilbertson, developed a thesis that suggested a secret gang of serial killers were killing people unnoticed.

The Smiley Face Killers

The theory is that from the late 1990s to the 2010s, the remains of a number of young men were found in various bodies of water across some Midwestern states, including Ohio. Local police attached to each case concluded the men had drowned accidentally after being drunk.

Gannon, Duarte, and Gilbertson suggested the men didn't accidentally drown and were in fact victims of a serial killer or a gang of serial killers. As the theory gained traction, police released more information on each case, including graffiti of a smiley face near locations where the bodies were found.

The smiley face connection gave the possible serial killer murders a name; the Smiley Face Killers. The theory took off and has gained traction ever since. Astonishingly, the team working on the theory have connected 45 males of college age who have been found dead in water across 11 states.

All the men were last seen leaving parties or bars where they had been drinking. Most were successful students in their fields and almost all were white males. After discovering the Shaffer case, the team added his disappearance to the list, even though his name was the only one on the list whose body was never found.

This suggested that the Smiley Face Killers may have killed more people and their bodies had not yet been found. Local police involved in each case put forward by the theory believe the deaths were nothing more than unfortunate drinking accidents, with the smiley face graffiti being coincidence only.

Though the Smiley Face Killers theory is just that, to fit the case of Brian Shaffer would be an even larger step. It would suggest that one killer or a group of killers were in league with various bars across the United States, to pick off people at random, for unknown reasons.

Could the security footage have been doctored? Experts who looked at the footage confirmed there were no edits or manipulation. If the killer or killers were in league with various bars then it stands to reason that a body could be removed from the building in a refuse bin or in an empty barrel.

The Smiley Face Killers have become part of popular culture with various films and books, but the FBI and various local police forces believe it is nothing more than an unbased theory.

Glitches and appeals

Alexis Called Shaffer's phone every night after his disappearance in the hope that it was all a big mistake and he would answer but instead it just went to voicemail. Six months later, to her shock, the phone rang three times.

When police investigated, they were told by Shaffer's phone provider, Cingular, that it may have just been a computer glitch, and that a ping detected from the phone 15 miles away from the Ugly Tuna Saloona, may have been part of a standard quality check on their towers.

Of course, this led many to believe that Shaffer had turned on his phone briefly for an unknown purpose, which meant that he was alive somewhere or someone had his phone. The phone was never pinged or rang again.

In a 2006 concert in Cincinnati, Pearl Jam's lead singer Eddie Vedder, appealed to the audience for any information regarding Shaffer's disappearance, after reading that he had a Pearl Jam tattoo. Unfortunately, no new leads came in.

Over the years, various sightings have come in from as far afield as Sweden, but all have turned out to be hoaxes or dead ends.

What we don't see

The focus has long been on the security footage, deliberately forcing our attention towards it, but when it comes to cases like this, it's sometimes what we don't see that matters. We know that Shaffer was in the bar that night, twice, and we know he was seen entering the bar, twice.

The footage doesn't show him leaving but it doesn't mean he didn't. The footage is clear enough to make out everyone that leaves but the camera only has one point of view, even with the panning camera.

It is extremely possible that Shaffer is shown on the footage and that he is exiting with the other patrons in such a way that he is hidden in front of a small group or someone of similar size or build. Once on the street, there are a number of side alleys which would not have been picked up by the security cameras of other establishments.

What happened to Shaffer beyond the Ugly Tuna still remains a mystery, but as he was drunk, it might be plausible to assume he had walked home but ventured near to a body of water and fallen in, not as a murder victim but an unfortunate accident.

If Shaffer truly did disappear inside the Ugly Tuna Saloona, which curiously seems to be the case then it's no wonder many theories have abounded over the years.

What seems likely to be explained away with logic and common sense ends up becoming frustrating and unexplained. The disappearance of Brian Shaffer is one rabbit hole that the more we go down, the deeper we fall – and keep on falling.

The Strange Case of Two Men Who Died Over Dinner

When two Frenchmen enjoying a Summer dinner were found dead at their garden table, police assumed murder was afoot in the small town of Authon-du-Perche, but the truth was far stranger.

Scene trapped in time

On 3rd August 2017, in the small town of Authon-du-Perche, 90 miles (150km) south-west of Paris, a mystery was developing that had gripped the local community. A day later, the story was making headlines around the world.

At the home of 69-year-old Lucien Pérot, both he and his friend, 38-year-old Olivier Boudin, had been enjoying a lavish dinner at an outside terrace table and had seemingly passed out from the evening before. Lucien was slumped in his chair, and Olivier was on the floor next to the table.

In the early hours of the morning, a passing neighbour noticed them but thought they were drunk and sleeping it off. When she returned a few hours later, she saw the two men in exactly the same positions.

Concerned, she moved closer and called out to them but there was no response. She called the police who arrived within minutes and found a scene trapped in time.

Lucien was slumped beside a half-finished dish of roast beef, beans, camembert, a half-eaten baguette, and a glass of wine. Olivier was lying on the ground, his half-eaten dinner resting on the table where he had been sitting.

Mysterious murder

The police were baffled as there were no obvious signs of attack but the fact that two men had died at the same time over dinner led them to believe a double murder had taken place. As they searched the rural property, they found no signs of robbery or forced entry.

Looking into their lifestyles, the pair had no enemies and nothing that made them targets for a murder or a pre-meditated hit. It turned out they lived relatively simple lives and were well-known and liked around the village.

Due to the position of the bodies, Lucien on the chair and Olivier on the ground, and with both meals half-eaten, it was deduced they had died at exactly the same time. But with no clear signs of attack, police were becoming more baffled, until they suggested the pair could have been poisoned.

The food was taking away to the famous Pasteur Research Institute in Paris where they underwent intense examination. While the testing was being carried out, a poisoning theory was doing the rounds in France and beyond.

On social media, people pointed to the beans as a possible way of poisoning someone as they would have been canned beforehand and the diners would not have noticed a small entry point where poison could have been injected into it.

But the Pasteur institute released their findings along with a hammer blow that threw out the poisoning theory. They concluded none of the food contained poison or was dangerous in any way. This meant that a mysterious murder was now on the table.

No explanation

The bodies were sent off to be autopsied in the hopes of discovering the truth of what had happened. The logical explanation was that the two men had been poisoned but with the food coming back negative, police had to consider other possibilities.

As the mystery exploded in the press and went viral online, the police struggled to find a motive and method of the murders. One neighbour mentioned a connection to the Mafia, which was explored but went nowhere, as the lives of the two men were easy to sift through.

Online theories suggested they were killed by an assassin of high skill who had killed them in such a manner that the method of murder would be impossible to uncover. This stretched from injections behind the ears, tiny explosive devices that stopped their hearts, electrical attack, psychic attack, and – yep, you guessed it – aliens.

The glaring truth was that two men had died at the same time, at the same table, and no-one could come up with a theory that worked and seemed logical. The only other hypothesis that gained traction was the two men had taken their own lives.

Yet, the same question was posed – how did they do it? Lucien and Olivier were said to be like father and son and had no obvious reason to take their own lives. Even if there were reasons to do so, the method was a mystery. Until the autopsy results came back.

Strange deaths

After days of wild theories, the investigation held a press conference to explain what had really happened. It turned out that the pair were not murdered, nor had they taken their own lives.

Lucien had literally bitten off more than he could chew and had swallowed a large piece of the delectable beef rib he had cooked for them. The autopsy found the piece of beef lodged in his throat and concluded that he had choked to death.

Triggered by the sight of his friend choking to death, Olivier suffered a major heart attack and fell off his chair to the ground where he died. He was known to have had a genetic heart condition which caused the attack at such a young age.

Armed with the truth, the locals were in some part grateful that the Mafia hadn't visited the tiny village, or that the deaths were not the result of murder. Though the scene looked like the perfect murder, and something out of an Agatha Christie novel, the truth turned out to be far more tragic – and stranger.

Before the autopsies were carried out, many people claimed with absolute conviction that the pair had been murdered, even pointing fingers at possible suspects. The strange death of Lucien and Olivier is perhaps a lesson that sometimes, not all is what it seems.

For FREE BOOKS, true crime blog posts, more true crime books, and information on new releases for your collection, head on over to www.benoakley.co.uk

Printed in Great Britain
by Amazon

55625641R00309